D0935510

Policymaking
for Social Security

MARTHA DERTHICK

Policymaking for Social Security

THE BROOKINGS INSTITUTION
Washington, D.C.

Library of Congress Cataloging in Publication Data:

Derthick, Martha.
   Policymaking for social security.
   Includes bibliographical references and index.
   1. Social security—United States. I. Title.
HD7125.D48   368.4'00973   78-24811
ISBN 0-8157-1816-0
ISBN 0-8157-1815-2 pbk.

9 8 7 6 5 4 3 2 1

THE BROOKINGS INSTITUTION is an independent organization devoted to nonpartisan research, education, and publication in economics, government, foreign policy, and the social sciences generally. Its principal purposes are to aid in the development of sound public policies and to promote public understanding of issues of national importance.

The Institution was founded on December 8, 1927, to merge the activities of the Institute for Government Research, founded in 1916, the Institute of Economics, founded in 1922, and the Robert Brookings Graduate School of Economics and Government, founded in 1924.

The Board of Trustees is responsible for the general administration of the Institution, while the immediate direction of the policies, program, and staff is vested in the President, assisted by an advisory committee of the officers and staff. The by-laws of the Institution state: "It is the function of the Trustees to make possible the conduct of scientific research, and publication, under the most favorable conditions, and to safeguard the independence of the research staff in the pursuit of their studies and in the publication of the results of such studies. It is not a part of their function to determine, control, or influence the conduct of particular investigations or the conclusions reached."

The President bears final responsibility for the decision to publish a manuscript as a Brookings book. In reaching his judgment on the competence, accuracy, and objectivity of each study, the President is advised by the director of the appropriate research program and weighs the views of a panel of expert outside readers who report to him in confidence on the quality of the work. Publication of a work signifies that it is deemed a competent treatment worthy of public consideration but does not imply endorsement of conclusions or recommendations.

The Institution maintains its position of neutrality on issues of public policy in order to safeguard the intellectual freedom of the staff. Hence interpretations or conclusions in Brookings publications should be understood to be solely those of the authors and should not be attributed to the Institution, to its trustees, officers, or other staff members, or to the organizations that support its research.

Foreword

SOCIAL SECURITY, the foreword to an earlier Brookings book says, "is firmly established as a permanent American institution. . . . Administered with efficiency and integrity, the system has won widespread acceptance." This is as true today as it was when written eleven years ago in *Social Security: Perspectives for Reform,* by Joseph A. Pechman, Henry J. Aaron, and Michael K. Taussig. Nonetheless, it sounds faintly archaic. The social security system is even better established than in 1968, with more taxpayers, more beneficiaries, much bigger benefits, and a bigger bite out of the gross national product. But it is also more controversial. In the mid-1970s it developed a sizable deficit: Congress was forced to enact for the first time a social security bill that was primarily a revenue raiser, and presidents (first Ford, then Carter) began to propose benefit reductions in relatively obscure and questionable parts of the program. Once blessedly free of trouble and a favorite of politicians in both parties, social security is undergoing a change of political fortunes.

This book by Martha Derthick, director of Governmental Studies at Brookings, explains how social security was successfully institutionalized in the four decades after enactment in 1935 and why it is in trouble today. The author asks why a program of such obvious importance has stirred so little conflict and discussion in the past and finds answers both in the nature of policymaking (particularly its domination by an expert few) and in the nature of the program (which promised taxpayers a fair return for their taxes and in fact gave nearly all of the earliest taxpayers very much more than that). She argues that the debate now developing is healthy and long overdue. The book is the first full-length study of the politics of social security. As such, it complements previously published Brookings work on the economics of social security and fills a conspicuous gap in the academic literature on American public policy.

Miss Derthick drew heavily for source material on the Oral History Collection at Columbia University, and she thanks its staff—Kathryn A. Back, Janet L. Foley, Elizabeth B. Mason, and the director, Louis M. Starr—for help. She also thanks the staff librarians at Brookings, the Social Security Administration, the AFL-CIO, the American Life Insurance Association, the Lyndon Baines Johnson Library in Austin, Texas, and the John F. Kennedy Library in Waltham, Massachusetts.

Many persons gave the author permission to quote from interviews in the Oral History Collection or other locations: Robert M. Ball, J. Douglas Brown, Eveline M. Burns, Wilbur J. Cohen, Nelson H. Cruikshank, I. S. Falk, Arthur Hess, Reinhard A. Hohaus, Maurine Mulliner, Robert J. Myers, Roswell B. Perkins, Elliot L. Richardson, Lisbeth Bamberger Schorr, Sidney Saperstein, Charles I. Schottland, the late Alanson W. Willcox, Elizabeth Wickenden, and Irwin Wolkstein. Some of these persons also granted her additional interviews or commented on the manuscript. She acknowledges in particular the detailed comments of Mr. Ball and Mr. Myers. As men who devoted long and distinguished careers to constructing the social security program, they were extraordinarily valuable critics, but they are emphatically not responsible for the contents of the book, in which they necessarily appear as principal subjects.

Others who commented helpfully on all or part of the manuscript include Abe Bortz, Everest P. Derthick, Judith M. Feder, Clifford R. Gross, Peter Milius, William C. Mitchell, Rudolph Penner, Martin Rein, Charles A. Siegfried, Alair Townsend, and the following Brookings staff members: Henry J. Aaron, Lawrence D. Brown, Hugh Heclo, Richard P. Nathan, John L. Palmer, Joseph A. Pechman, Gilbert Y. Steiner, and James L. Sundquist. The critical comments of Mr. Brown and Mr. Heclo were exceptionally generous in length and useful.

Barbara P. Haskins edited the manuscript, Penelope S. Harpold checked its factual content, and Jack Gordon read the proofs. The index was prepared by Florence Robinson. David Morse, Radmila Nikolić, Celia Rich, and Donna Daniels Verdier shared the typing. Ms. Verdier also assisted with proofreading.

The research was in part supported by the Ford Foundation, and the Lyndon Baines Johnson Foundation awarded the author a Moody Grant that made use of the Johnson Library possible.

The views expressed are solely the author's and should not be attributed to the trustees, officers, or other staff members of the Brookings Institution.

BRUCE K. MACLAURY
President

March 1979
Washington, D.C.

Contents

PART THREE: THE POLITICS OF EXPANSION

PART FOUR: THE RISING CONFLICT

*Policymaking
for Social Security*

Social Security as a Political Puzzle

AMERICANS are becoming more aware of their social security program and less contented with it. As the 1970s advanced social security ran into financial trouble. A deficit appeared unexpectedly, and a change in official actuarial projections showed a serious long-term deficit too. Journalists proclaimed a crisis; officials denied it, but beneath their rhetoric of reassurance was a growing concern about the continued popularity of this biggest and most applauded of federal government programs. In 1977 Congress reluctantly took action to correct the deficit, and it had no sooner enacted new taxes than members began submitting bills to repeal or obscure them. A social security taxpayers' revolt seemed to be brewing, though the depth and seriousness of it were hard to estimate.

The benefits of social security are widely experienced and even more widely acknowledged. Sixteen percent of the population, slightly more than 34 million persons in a country of 218 million, were receiving cash payments under the program at the end of 1977, including nine of every ten persons over the age of sixty-five. Twenty-one million of the beneficiaries were retirees or their dependents, but large numbers qualified for disability benefits (4.8 million) or as survivors of covered workers (7.6 million). An elderly couple, in 1978, could have received as much as $8,280 a year, though the average was much less than that, around $4,800. There is not the slightest evidence that the American people would like to do away with the program, nor can there be any doubt that the aged people of this country are better off because of it.

On the other hand, the costs are high and rising at a rapid rate. The $83.8 billion in benefits in 1977, not counting $21.5 billion in medicare, amounted to one-fifth of the federal budget. Ninety percent of the work

3

force were paying for these benefits through taxes on their earnings, at
rates such that most workers paid more in social security taxes than in
federal income taxes. Since 1955 government spending for domestic
purposes has risen sharply as a proportion of the gross national product, and social security accounts for most of this increase.[1] Between
1970 and 1975 social security expenditures more than doubled, rising
from $32 billion to $67 billion, a pace that far exceeded the increase
in both the number of beneficiaries and the consumer price index.
The maximum tax payable by employees, which was $94.50 in 1957,
$290.40 in 1967, and $965.25 in 1978, is expected to be $3,045.90 in 1987.
This tax (when combined with the matching employer tax) consumes
more than 4.5 percent of the gross national product and puts a substantial burden on the private economy. The two taxes are thought to depress savings and the capital stock, and to be a burden on the wage
earner; they may also have a depressing effect on employment.[2] Confident that social security is a good thing, Americans are nonetheless
increasingly aware that it has a very high price. And it will continue to
grow, both in absolute expenditures and as a share of GNP.[3]

The great popularity of social security has been one of the axioms
of American public life. A decade ago in his *Newsweek* column, the
economist Paul Samuelson pronounced it the most successful program
of the modern welfare state. "It is a remarkable fact," he wrote, "that
both expert and layman will agree on this judgement."[4] Social security
had no serious political or administrative problems, in the opinion of
Samuelson's fellow economist, Otto Eckstein.[5] It had become a sacred

1. Charles L. Schultze, "Federal Spending: Past, Present, and Future," in Henry
Owen and Charles L. Schultze, eds., *Setting National Priorities: The Next Ten Years*
(Brookings Institution, 1976), pp. 323–69; Herbert Stein, "Spending and Getting,"
in William Fellner, ed., *Contemporary Economic Problems 1977* (Washington, D.C.:
American Enterprise Institute for Public Policy Research, 1977), pp. 53–81.
2. See, among numerous works by economists, Alicia H. Munnell, *The Future of
Social Security* (Brookings Institution, 1977), chap. 6; and Sherwin Rosen, "Social
Security and the Economy," in Michael J. Boskin, ed., *The Crisis in Social Security:
Problems and Prospects* (San Francisco: Institute for Contemporary Studies, 1977),
pp. 87–106.
3. *Staff Data and Materials Relating to Social Security Financing*, prepared by
the staff for the Senate Committee on Finance, 95 Cong. 1 sess. (Government
Printing Office, 1977), pp. 47, 87.
4. *Newsweek*, February 13, 1967, p. 88.
5. Otto Eckstein, "Financing the System of Social Insurance," in William G.
Bowen, Frederick H. Harbison, Richard A. Lester, and Herman Somers, eds.,
The Princeton Symposium on the American System of Social Insurance (McGraw-
Hill, 1968), p. 48.

cow that no politician dared to criticize, Milton Friedman wrote.[6] Like it or not (Samuelson and Eckstein did like it, whereas Friedman did not), social security in the late 1960s seemed beyond dispute or dissent.

Executive leaders of social security, who have been understandably proud of the overwhelming support for their program, have occasionally offered explanations for it. Robert M. Ball, a reflective man who headed the program for a long time, argued that it had proved highly acceptable and achieved revolutionary results for three reasons. First, it rests on old, accepted principles—the virtues of work, self-help, and individual saving. "This is not a program in which the Government or the well-to-do help people," Ball wrote. "On the contrary; it is primarily a program in which people help themselves, using Government as the instrument. The essence of our social security program is that people earn their security themselves out of the work they do." Second, it had been soundly financed on a "contributory" basis and had not had to draw on general revenues of the Treasury to pay for either benefits or administration. Third, it had returned nearly all of the "contributions" to the public in the form of benefits. Administration had consumed only 2.2 percent of revenues.[7]

This explanation is unconvincing. The first point—that social security is essentially a program of self-help rather than a government program—is one that spokesmen for the program habitually assert, and it is highly questionable. Only in the most general and abstract sense—the sense in which any government program in a democratic society may be said to be the work of the people themselves—is this true of social security. For the vast majority, participation is involuntary. People who do not pay taxes are punished.[8] Nor does the amount of taxes that people pay determine the benefits they receive. The relation between the two has been very weak. Second, Ball's explanation leaves some obviously important factors out of account. If the low rate of administrative expense has been important, far more so, surely, has been the high

6. *Newsweek*, April 3, 1967, p. 81.

7. Robert M. Ball, "The American System of Social Security," *Journal of Commerce*, June 15, 1964; encl. to SSA *Vista*, vol. 7 (October 2, 1964). SSA *Vista* was an in-house newsletter for Social Security Administration employees.

8. In 1961, for example, the Internal Revenue Service seized three horses belonging to Valentine Y. Byler, a farmer in New Wilmington, Pennsylvania, and sold them so that the government could collect $308.96 in unpaid social security taxes. A member of the Amish sect, which teaches that its members should care for one another, Mr. Byler had declined to participate in a system of social insurance. *Congressional Record* (June 26, 1961), pp. 11307–08.

rate of benefit return to individuals. Nearly all of the early participants have later received far more than they had paid in taxes. As of 1967, for example, Ball testified that beneficiaries and their employers had paid for about 10 percent of the actuarial value of their benefits.[9] Finally, this explanation leaves one wondering why, if the financial independence of the program has been so important to its popularity, its leaders in recent years have urged the introduction of general revenues. Is "contributory" (that is, payroll tax) financing at the root of its popularity, and, if so, should it be compromised?

The political foundations of social security deserve a thorough analysis, such as this book purports to provide.[10] Social security is a major public institution, affecting the present and future lives of nearly all Americans, and it is therefore important to understand the basis on which the program was advanced to the American people and accepted by them.[11] There are three steps to the analysis.

9. *Departments of Labor and Health, Education, and Welfare Appropriations for 1968,* Hearings before a Subcommittee of the House Committee on Appropriations, 90 Cong. 1 sess. (GPO, 1967), pt. 3, p. 869. An extreme individual example is Ida Fuller of Brattleboro, Vermont, who was in the program's first group of beneficiaries. She began getting social security checks on January 31, 1940. Miss Fuller had paid $22 in taxes before her retirement. When she died in a nursing home thirty-five years later at the age of one hundred, she had received more than $20,000 in benefits. If Miss Fuller had been a married man with a spouse's benefit equal to 50 percent of her own, this would have lifted the benefit-cost ratio to even more impressive heights. Miss Fuller and her relatives, and millions of other early beneficiaries and their relatives, had every reason to believe that social security was a wonderful thing. (*New York Times,* January 28, 1975.) For a recent academic analysis of the magnitude of "unearned" benefits in the program, see Donald O. Parsons and Douglas R. Munro, "Intergenerational Transfers in Social Security," in Boskin, ed., *The Crisis in Social Security,* pp. 65–86.

10. Two works of political analysis, both of them very brief, have appeared recently: Carl V. Patton, "The Politics of Social Security," in Boskin, ed., *The Crisis in Social Security,* pp. 147–71; and William C. Mitchell, *The Popularity of Social Security: A Paradox in Public Choice* (Washington, D.C.: American Enterprise Institute for Public Policy Research, 1977).

11. A note on terminology is called for. I use the terms "social insurance" or "social security" interchangeably in this book to denote a cluster of programs known officially as OASDHI, or Old Age, Survivors, Disability, and Hospital Insurance. This use of "social security" conforms to today's popular usage, except that the hospital insurance part of this program is more commonly known as "medicare." As medicare, it also encompasses what in official terminology is known as SMI, the Supplementary Medical Insurance system, which pays for doctors' fees and certain other medical services for persons sixty-five and over who have elected to participate in it and pay a monthly premium. In the Social Security Act of 1935, the term "social security" was used more broadly, to encompass government programs of

Part 1, the first step, rests on the assumption that there may be something about the system of policymaking—the formal structure, the participants, the process by which they have arrived at choices—that accounts for the low level of conflict and dissent in social security. It describes that system in detail, with chapters covering each of the major participants or leading sources of influence on policy choices. Each chapter assesses the role and policy perspectives of a leading actor or cluster of actors related by interest, ideology, or function (thus, for example, conservative interest groups are covered in one chapter, and various outlets of popular opinion—mass movements, political parties, and mass-based pressure groups—are treated together in another chapter).

The main argument is that policy has been made by a relatively constricted and autonomous set of actors with a strong sense of proprietorship in the program. Decisions about social security were generally made in isolation from decisions about other government activities, both structurally and financially. Within the proprietary group, there was a high level of consensus about guiding principles. Initiatives and choices generally followed paths well defined by programmatic doctrines and were treated as if they were technical matters. Major alternatives were hardly considered. The dominant mode was maintenance and enlargement of the program.

Even if it were possible to explain why the policymaking system took the form that it did, doing so would not necessarily explain why social security has been so free of conflict. It is possible—indeed, highly plausible—that the constricted, consensual policymaking I describe is the result of—not the reason for—this lack of conflict. Had disagreement over social security been wider, deeper, and more intense, that system presumably would have been very different.

---

public assistance (means-tested aid to the poor) and unemployment compensation as well as old age insurance, a program in which benefits were granted by right, regardless of need, in return for payment of payroll taxes.

This book is about policymaking for the OASDHI portion of the Social Security Act. It does not cover public assistance—which today is popularly known as "welfare"—except incidentally, as an alternative to social insurance, nor does it cover unemployment compensation, which is often classified as a form of social insurance. The analysis of disability insurance and medicare is limited to the policy decisions to add them to the basic program (see chapters 15 and 16). Both of these programs, medicare especially, are so important and complicated that policymaking for them would merit treatment as an independent subject altogether.

If this form of policymaking is indeed consequence, not cause, then it is necessary to look further for an explanation of the low level of conflict, and the logical place to look is the program itself. That is the purpose of part 2, which examines the major policy choices embodied in social security and the major features of the program that are potentially relevant to politics.[12] Here the central themes are ambiguity, inconsistency, obscurity, and paradox—qualities that I believe go far toward explaining the overwhelming, seemingly unqualified acceptance of social security. Ideological ambiguity and internal contradiction in the program meant that it could appeal simultaneously to liberals and conservatives and enable the individual decisionmaker to reconcile conflicting liberal and conservative impulses. Insofar as principles were seen to be at stake, everyone's principles could be satisfied. At the same time, the program had a powerful appeal to self-interest—the self-interest of the taxpayer-voter, who got back far more in benefits than he paid in taxes, and the self-interest of the politician, who could, all at once, provide the current taxpayer-voter with these excess benefits, defer high tax rates to a future generation, and proclaim with a straight face the "fiscal soundness" of the program.

By the end of part 2, after fourteen chapters of description and analysis, a puzzle remains. Two possible explanations for the low level of conflict regarding social security have been presented, one lying in the nature of the policymaking system, the other in the nature of the program. Part 3, carrying the inquiry a step further, tries to assess the validity and relative importance of the two. It is possible to do this because part 2 does not exhaust the set of major policy choices associated with social security. It covers only the basic program of cash benefits for the elderly and the surviving dependents of deceased workers—Old Age and Survivors Insurance (OASI), in official terminology—which was put in place between 1935 and 1950. Part 3 covers the major expansions of this program—the addition of coverage for the disabled in 1956; the addition of medicare, which pays health care costs for the elderly, in 1965; and a quantum increase in cash benefits between 1969 and 1972.

12. Some readers may wish to read part 2 before part 1. Part 2 is more meaningful if the reader has become acquainted first with the policymakers described in part 1, but part 1 is more meaningful to the reader who is cognizant of the issues and choices analyzed in part 2. I have tried to make each part comprehensible independently.

Those expansions proved contentious in a way that other decisions had not. The evidence on this point, along with pieces of evidence presented earlier, suggests that when major extensions of the public sector are proposed, there is no lack of dispute in social security. "Boundary" issues, as I call these questions over the public-private division of responsibility, have produced much more conflict and debate than "distributive" decisions, which involve the incidence of costs and benefits. The analytic conclusion of part 3 (chapter 18) considers why this is so and attempts to extract from the case of social security a plausible general description of the determinants of political controversy and the relation between politics and policymaking in the American system.

The case is useful for this general purpose because it deals with a sequence of policy decisions covering several decades and resulting in the institutionalization of a major government program. Much of the scholarly literature that analyzes policymaking focuses on "leading" or controversial cases—moments of crisis or innovation that are intrinsically interesting and undoubtedly important, but not in themselves typical. Policymaking is a compound of exciting, innovative events, in which political actors mobilize and contest with one another, and not-so-exciting routines that are performed without widespread mobilization, intense conflict, or much awareness of what is going on except among the involved few. I attempt to portray some of this variation and to consider the implications for the evolution of public policy. The absence of conflict, I suggest, does not signify the absence of change, and what is routine, though it may not be interesting to analysts at a given moment, is cumulatively very important.

In choosing to concentrate on how policy has been made for social insurance, I pay very little attention to the more fundamental question of why such a program exists. If this book had been addressed to that topic, it would have had to go extensively into comparisons with other countries and deeply into the history, economy, and social structure of the United States.

The modern welfare state is typical, not exceptional. Whether democratic or authoritarian, unitary or federal, "capitalist," "socialist," or "communist," virtually all nations of the world have laws providing income support for some parts of their populations. The scope of such support appears to be related to economic development; the wealthier, more developed nations in general spend a higher share of national income for social insurance than the poorer, less developed nations. Research has also shown that the longer a social insurance program has been in operation, the higher the spending for it tends to be, again as a proportion of national income. There is a tendency for such programs to expand incrementally. Coverage is extended to additional sections of the population and to additional hazards or causes of loss of income, and benefit standards are raised as time passes. But despite broad similarities in the evolution and purposes of income-support programs and a more-or-less common response to the forces of economic development, nations differ in the mix of programs they choose. They use wage-related benefits, flat grants to specified categories of the population, or means-tested programs in different proportions, and they give different emphasis to one or another category of beneficiaries or one or another type of revenue source.

The United States is distinguished from other industrial nations by the relative lateness of the development of its insurance programs, by the relatively heavy emphasis on wage-related benefits and the absence of flat grants, by commitment to the use of payroll tax financing, and by the persistence of the doctrine of "getting what you pay for" even as practice has deviated from the doctrine. The United States may also be unusual in the degree of influence exercised by the executive leadership, though it is hard to be sure about this. Comparative analyses consistently point to the importance of social insurance administrators in policymaking. Their influence is thought by some analysts to be a likely cause of the widespread pattern of incremental expansion. "With the passage of time administrative routines become established, consensus grows on what has already been accomplished, and administrators acquire an interest in further piecemeal expansion," according to Hugh Heclo's summary of this interpretation of events.[13] Heclo speculates that in the United States the limited development of a national administrative structure inhibited initiation of a social insurance program, but that "the very newness of the enterprise meant that framers of the policy could set up a new administrative apparatus that would be firmly committed to the new insurance doctrine and would insulate the basic policy approach against future interference from pluralistic politics."[14]

13. Arnold J. Heidenheimer, Hugh Heclo, and Carolyn Teich Adams, *Comparative Public Policy: The Politics of Social Choice in Europe and America* (St. Martin's Press, 1975), p. 192. Heclo's chapter on income maintenance in this volume is an excellent comparative analysis of the development of social security systems. See also the literature cited there.

14. Ibid., p. 197.

In the United States, the Social Security Act of 1935 marks the founding of the welfare state. An accomplishment of President Franklin D. Roosevelt's New Deal, the act was a response to the Great Depression yet was rooted in various social movements that had developed earlier in the century. When poverty and misery struck on a massive scale, the leaders of those movements were ready with ideas for national action. Besides old age insurance, the act provided for unemployment compensation, assistance payments to certain categories of needy persons (the aged, the blind, and children under sixteen who had been deprived of parental support), child welfare services, and maternal and child health services. Readers who wish to understand the origins of the act as a whole, or even alone the old age insurance portion of it, will do better to consult histories and memoirs than a political scientist's account of subsequent policymaking.[15] As history, this book begins in 1935, when the founding act became law and the executive leaders of the social insurance program, whom I believe to have been prime movers in the subsequent evolution of policy, were beginning to shape their organization and form a vision of the program that would be. As history, it can be said to end in 1972. With an extraordinary benefit increase in that year and adoption of a law that automatically tied future increases to the consumer price index, the program assumed its contemporary shape. On the eve of his retirement early in 1973, Commissioner Ball foresaw an era of considerable stability in the program of cash benefits. In contrast with the frequent tax increases of the recent past, the tax rates that were to go into effect in January 1973 would remain level or even drop slightly for the next forty years, according to a lengthy appraisal that he prepared as a valedictory.[16]

In retrospect, the transition year of 1972 appears to have led to an era of new turbulence rather than new tranquility. The short-run financial condition of the program soon took an unexpected turn for the worse as a result of dislocations in the economy, and long-run projections grew more pessimistic in response to changes in demographic and economic

15. For example, see Arthur J. Altmeyer, *The Formative Years of Social Security* (University of Wisconsin Press, 1966); Edwin E. Witte, *The Development of the Social Security Act* (University of Wisconsin Press, 1963); Frances Perkins, *The Roosevelt I Knew* (Viking, 1946), chap. 23; Merrill G. Murray, "Social Insurance Perspectives: Background Philosophy and Early Program Developments," *Journal of Insurance*, vol. 30 (June 1963).

16. Robert M. Ball, "Managing the Social Security Program," encl. to *SSA Vista*, vol. 16 (February 8, 1973).

assumptions. Meanwhile, changes in policymaking procedures had used up built-in margins for error. The government had to start a search for more funds for social security, opening up issues that were thought to be settled. The constricted, consensual policymaking system that I describe in part 2 may change under the new conditions. It has changed enough already that I deliberately write of it in the past tense, as if the system were a historical phenomenon that ended in 1972. Even so, it is a phenomenon of some significance, for it persisted through the program's founding decades and had important consequences for the early politics of social security.

Some readers will wish that more attention had been paid to the situation of the aged, disabled, and ill, who are the principal beneficiaries of social security. If the purpose had been to explain why a social insurance program exists, it would have been necessary to explore the economic and social conditions to which social insurance responded, but instead the focus is on policymakers and their choices. The study assumes that policymaking is worth understanding for its own sake, and that it is possible to appraise the making of public choices without detailed knowledge of the subjects of choice. The social problems in any case have varied considerably over time. They were surely much more severe during the 1930s, when the program was founded, than in 1965–75, when substantial enlargements of it took place. Expansion of the program appears to occur independently of change in social conditions, to which the analysis pays little attention, or of party regimes, to which it pays much attention. Policymaking and program expansion have a continuity, momentum, and political logic of their own. If social security is a representative case (and without question it is the leading case), aggrandizement is inherent in the modern welfare state, or at least inexorable. The closing chapter returns to this proposition, and considers how, if at all, options can be kept open. In a program where policymaking has long been characterized by constricted participation, doctrinal rigidity, and extreme inertia, the prime need is to enlarge the possibilities of choice.

It should be recognized at the outset that the range of choice in future policymaking is not likely to be wide. The chief actuary of the Social Security Administration was surely right when he wrote recently that "the program is so large and well-established and such an important and integral part of our national socioeconomic structure, that its momentum will not be halted. The only question is in what direction and by how much it will grow." The question, as he put it, is whether it will grow in "an uncontrolled and irrational manner, or in a logical way so that it will best match the economic needs of the beneficiaries and the financial ability of the taxpayers."[17] I agree with his assertion that the answer will depend "in large part upon the extent of the dialogue among an informed citizenry." I believe that this dialogue has been seriously deficient in the past, and I hope that this book, by showing this to have been so, will encourage improvement.

17. A. Haeworth Robertson, "OASDHI: Fiscal Basis and Long-Range Cost Projections," *Social Security Bulletin,* vol. 40 (January 1977), p. 48. But see also the article written by Robertson after he left office, in which he argued that failure to revise and contain social security—for example, by raising the age of eligibility—would result in destructive economic and social costs. "The nation must not be influenced unduly," he wrote, "by decisions made in the past by and for different generations of people living under different circumstances." Robertson was chief actuary of the Social Security Administration from 1975 to 1978. "Providing for Social Security," *Wall Street Journal,* September 6, 1978.

PART ONE

The Participants

CHAPTER ONE

Program Executives

"SOCIAL SECURITY will always be a goal, never a finished thing, because human aspirations are infinitely expandable . . . just as human nature is infinitely perfectible." This quotation from Arthur Altmeyer, who headed the social security program for most of the years between 1935 and 1953, is displayed in the museum at Social Security Administration headquarters in Baltimore. It says a great deal about the people who have run the program from inside the executive branch. It expresses their liberal faith in pure form, with its unabashed optimism about humankind. It also expresses in pure form their philosophy of public policymaking. Improvement in public undertakings, as in mankind itself, is the natural state of affairs, and the way of improvement is expansion.

The hagiography of the museum also tells something about the organization that Altmeyer shaped. His desk is there, with a telephone from the 1930s but not much else in the way of office clutter ("I was a clean-desk man," Altmeyer wrote to the SSA's historian, in a letter preserved under the glass desk top). There too—alive on film and sound track—are the great liberal presidents, Franklin Roosevelt signing the Social Security Act of 1935 and Lyndon Johnson signing medicare legislation thirty years later. Over 90,000 people work for the agency, 20,000 of them at its Baltimore headquarters, the central building of which is named for Altmeyer. The museum, if they pause to look at its collection of pictures, pamphlets, news clippings, and artifacts, reminds them of the SSA's heritage. It is one way in which this self-conscious organization tells its members what their past has been, what their purpose should be, and why they should be very proud of both.

Continuity and Commitment

The organization's leaders—or program executives as I call them—have been a small group with great staying power. Continuity and persistence are characteristic. Through most of the first forty years of social security, the shapers of executive action changed infrequently; a few personalities predominated.

The chief executive of the program was the chairman of the Social Security Board until 1946, when the three-man board was abolished; since then it has been the commissioner of social security.[1] Between 1936 and 1972, six men held these two offices:

John G. Winant	1935–37
Arthur J. Altmeyer	1937–53
John W. Tramburg	1953–54
Charles I. Schottland	1954–58
William L. Mitchell	1959–62
Robert M. Ball	1962–73

Even this small number, however, exaggerates the fluidity of leadership. Altmeyer and Ball between them held the chief executive's office more than two-thirds of the time. Furthermore, if one were to look beneath this formal list and try to identify the actual rather than the

1. Initially (1935–46), the Social Security Board was responsible for administering old age insurance and the other programs authorized by the Social Security Act. Within the SSB, a separate bureau, called at first the Bureau of Federal Old Age Benefits and then the Bureau of Old Age Insurance, was in charge of old age insurance. Following the 1939 amendments to the Social Security Act, it was renamed the Bureau of Old Age and Survivors Insurance, in recognition of the changed character of the program. In 1946 the board was abolished and replaced by the Social Security Administration. The BOASI survived, and the SSA continued to include other bureaus, responsible for other programs. Following a reorganization of the Department of Health, Education, and Welfare in 1963, the SSA finally became responsible for the insurance program alone, other programs having been moved elsewhere. Subunits multiplied within SSA to reflect the complexity of the maturing, expanding insurance program. As of 1972, SSA contained the following components: Office of the Commissioner, Office of the Actuary, Office of Administration, Office of Public Affairs, Office of Program Evaluation and Planning, Office of Research and Statistics, Bureau of Disability Insurance, Bureau of District Office Operations, Bureau of Data Processing, Bureau of Hearings and Appeals, Bureau of Health Insurance, Bureau of Retirement and Survivors Insurance, and Office of the General Counsel. In the text I use SSB, SSA, and BOASI. I have tried to use the designation that best fits the chronological and organizational context.

nominal chief executive, Ball's tenure would be seen to have been much longer than eleven years. It would reach back at least to 1953. Schottland, who was commissioner during most of the Eisenhower administration, made no claim in a subsequent interview to having run the social security program. Nor was it run by Victor Christgau, whom the Republicans appointed director of the Bureau of Old Age and Survivors Insurance. It was run by Ball, who was then the bureau's deputy director.[2]

Another way to illustrate the stability of executive leadership is to examine the career histories of holders of high offices in the Social Security Administration at a given time. In 1970, for instance, when the program was a generation old, Ball as commissioner, a deputy commissioner (Arthur E. Hess), and the four assistant commissioners (Jack S. Futterman for administration, Thomas C. Parrott for field operations, Alvin M. David for program evaluation and planning, and Ida C. Merriam for research and statistics) together had 191 years of service in SSA. All had entered in the 1930s and spent virtually their whole careers there. Although some of these leaders began in low-ranking field positions (Ball had started as a field representative in Newark), they had spent many years in positions of high rank in the central office. A semiofficial history of the Department of Health, Education, and Welfare describes the SSA as a "career-oriented organization." A very high proportion of the management structure has been composed of persons who have "grown up with the system."[3]

Building the program was a job—more, a mission—that some men and women devoted their lives to. The leadership was remarkably self-effacing. Altmeyer, who was the founding personality—"Mr. Social Security" to a whole generation of reverent employees—was a quiet man and never undertook "to put himself forward as an individual," according to his long-time deputy, William Mitchell, who was briefly commissioner himself. For Altmeyer, the program came first; he was "always thinking of plans, or policies, or programs."[4] Altmeyer's revealing assessment of self was not inconsistent with this:

I think the test of a good administrator is whether you are anonymous or whether you're a character, a public character. If you're a public character or

2. Interview with Charles I. Schottland, Oral History Collection, Columbia University (1965), pp. 42–44, 80–86, 123–25. (Hereafter Schottland, OHC.)
3. Rufus E. Miles, Jr., *The Department of Health, Education, and Welfare* (Praeger, 1974), p. 106.
4. Interview with William L. Mitchell, Oral History Collection, Columbia University (1965), p. 85. (Hereafter Mitchell, OHC.)

if you have any desire to be a public character, you're not likely to be interested in administration as such. I think anonymity is desirable so that you don't get the public involved in making decisions based on personality rather than on accomplishments. There's great need for a character standing out, like [Sargent] Shriver [head of the Peace Corps and then the Office of Economic Opportunity in the 1960s]. My goodness, you need a character like Shriver to sell a program and capture the imagination of the public. But that is as far from my capacities or interests as you can imagine. I would shrink from that kind of undertaking. So I have said many times that a successful administrator ought to be about as interesting as spinach—cold spinach at that. That ought to be the idea. . . . I don't think you'll find anything colorful in my whole career. I'd be surprised if you did.[5]

Robert Ball, as Altmeyer's heir (though not his immediate successor), thought of the job rather differently, as one that "required for success a lot of the capacities of a public figure." In Ball's view, the commissioner needed to be able to "make a stirring speech, negotiate with a union, do well on television, and inspire employees by direct human contact."[6] Those who knew Ball judged him to be very skillful in such tasks. One of his predecessors, Charles Schottland, described him as the social security program's "chief . . . philosopher, administrator, exponent. He is very glib, has a wonderful way of expressing ideas, [and is] very flexible intellectually so that he could figure out ways of handling situations where you needed compromise. He's smart and personable, extremely intelligent. He had a lot of courage. A very unusual person . . . and terribly able."[7]

Like Altmeyer, Ball subordinated self to the social task and inspired the strong loyalty of organizational subordinates. After he left office as commissioner in 1973 he lived in Washington and continued to devote himself to construction of the social insurance program. It is a sign of the missionary spirit of the social security leadership that officeholding has not been crucial. Some of the foremost leaders continued to perform many of the functions of leadership even when they were nominally private citizens.

5. Interview with Arthur J. Altmeyer, Oral History Collection, Columbia University (1967), p. 192. (Hereafter Altmeyer, OHC.)
6. From tape-recorded comments by Robert M. Ball addressed to the author, May 6, 1978. (Hereafter Ball transcript.)
7. Schottland, OHC, pp. 78–79. Schottland's phrasing has been slightly rearranged.

Clear Goals with Room for Compromise

The executive leaders knew what they wanted; they were very clear about first principles. Yet, dogmatic as they were about certain things, they were far from incapable of compromise. There were large areas of policy where the dogmas provided no definitive guides.

The dogmas pertained to operative features of the program. It should be contributory: people must qualify for benefits by making contributions (paying taxes). Having paid their contributions, they or their dependents should get benefits as a matter of right. There must be no means test, which is to say no need to prove need. Benefits should be related to wages. The program should be national in scope and should be run by the federal government. It should be universal and compulsory.

These are important matters, but they still leave a good deal to choice. Regarding their application, executives of the Social Security Administration could be quite flexible. People should make contributions, but they did not need to contribute very much for very long to qualify for benefits. Nor need the program be financed by contributions (and matching employer taxes) only. Very early, administrators proposed the use of general revenues and, in still another demonstration of tactical flexibility, dropped the proposal when Congress proved unreceptive. Though they insisted absolutely that benefits should be related to wages, they never stipulated what the precise relation should be. They also believed that social insurance benefits should be progressive, with a weighting in favor of low-wage earners. Thus they conceived of social insurance as a program that combined welfare purposes (the combating of poverty) with maintenance of customary standards of living; but just where this balance should be struck was a point on which they had no fixed views. Even in the matter of national administration, they were not inflexible. When it seemed that insurance against disability could be passed only if state governments were given an important role in administration, executive leaders of social security accepted this compromise with alacrity.

The points that these leaders were flexible about are not details, mere interpretations of how basic principles are to be applied; they determine how costs and benefits are to be distributed among different social classes, the "who gets what" of social insurance. Flexibility about tax sources, about benefit levels, and the relation between taxes paid and benefits received leaves open to accommodation and adjustment the most significant social choices embedded in the program.

In explaining and appraising the executive planners' success with social insurance, it is important to keep the scope of their goals in perspective. They defined their objectives largely in instrumental terms. They wanted to achieve a certain kind of program, designated by the name of social insurance, and to extend its coverage broadly over the population and over different types of risk, including retirement from work in old age, disability, and poor health. They were very successful in this. A big program exists today that conforms to the first principles laid down in the founding years. Had goals been defined in terms that stipulated ultimate social outcomes with some precision, success would surely have been much harder to achieve.

Had the executive founders been free to make the program conform to personal preferences, they would in all likelihood have made it more progressive than in fact it has been (though not, so I would judge, radically egalitarian). The program has been run by liberals, believers in using the power of government broadly and vigorously to achieve social welfare and to protect the poor in particular against misfortune. But if liberalism was the prevailing value among the executive leaders, pragmatism has always been at least as powerful a guide to conduct in office. Their overriding aim was to establish and extend the insurance program. For this they needed the acceptance of Congress and the public, and they were prepared to adjust program designs for that purpose.

Initially, the establishment of the program in and of itself could be regarded as a triumph for liberalism. Liberals and conservatives were divided—at least, say, until the 1960s—by issues over where the line between public and private activity should be drawn. That the program should exist was of much more concern to liberals, including its executive founders, than what it should do, and for whose benefit. That it failed to serve egalitarian ends to any great degree, and in fact often gave large benefits to relatively well-off persons who had paid small amounts of contributions, seems not to have required the founders to develop defenses or justifications either to themselves or to others. With apparent pride and serenity, Altmeyer once remarked that "nobody thinks they're being demeaned by getting that check, and I think they probably look forward to it. If they're very rich, they probably turn it over to their wife so she can go and do something with it that she wouldn't have done otherwise. And everybody's happy, happy as a lark."[8]

Expansion by Incremental Steps

Though the leadership of the program remained very much the same, the program changed constantly. It expanded. "More is better" could have been the motto of its leaders, who were never without a legislative agenda for the moment or ideas for an agenda for the long run.

According to one close and sympathetic observer, Eveline M. Burns of Columbia University, the explanation for this persistent drive is to be found in the liberal, humane values of the leadership. She once told an interviewer:

[It has been] an incredibly humane administration. Take old age and survivors insurance. They must now be reaching their 20-millionth beneficiary. Think how it could have been run. They could have started off with a suspicion of the claimant who comes in, and put it all on the claimant to prove that he is entitled to something. They could have seen their jobs as just not getting into policy at all. They'd been told to administer the act, and they could have done that, period, without asking themselves whether the act was as good as it could be. . . .

On the contrary, the emphasis in that program, right from the first and increasingly (and this is surprising with a big program), has been exactly the opposite. . . .

I think that, in considerable measure, this is Bob Ball's influence. He's permeated that agency with something of his own ideas. He's also been able to get some very good people working with him. . . . He is a remarkable person. He has those qualities which I think are so important—the idealism, the firm belief in the program, and the concept that the program exists to serve the people, and his idea of the job was to be constantly seeing whether it could be a better program.[9]

Robert J. Myers, who was the Social Security Administration's chief actuary for many years and who finally departed in dissent, found the

8. Altmeyer, OHC, p. 128.
9. Interview with Eveline M. Burns, Oral History Collection, Columbia University (1965), pp. 91–100.

explanation rather in the "natural" urge of public officials to enlarge their program. In a pamphlet for an English research organization, he wrote:

> Over the years, most of the American staff engaged in programme planning and policy development have had the philosophy—carried out with almost a religious zeal—that what counts above all else is the expansion of the programme. To some of them, to believe otherwise would amount virtually to being opposed to the programme. Thus, such persons have not necessarily tended to be partisan as between the political parties, but rather they have favoured and helped those who want to expand the programme the most.
>
> . . . it is only natural for people to advocate and work strongly for the growth of the activity in which they are engaged.[10]

To some extent, the expansionist drive was expressed in the use of administrative discretion. "Administration," Altmeyer wrote, "consists of more than organization, procedures, and personnel. . . . Administration also consists of interpreting social legislation in such a manner that it achieves its fundamental purpose most fully."[11] Even more important, however, was policy planning, through which proposals for legislative expansion were generated. Policy planning developed as a distinct function within the Social Security Board before it was generally established as such in organizations of the federal executive branch. The Social Security Act laid the foundation for this development by charging the board with the duty of studying and making recommendations regarding legislation and matters of administrative policy. Many of the founders of the social security program in 1934–35 were drawn from the academic world and believed in the value of research and formal analysis as elements of policy formulation.

Initially, the policy planning function was lodged in the Bureau of Research and Statistics. As officially described in 1949, the functions of this bureau (then a "division," later an "office") included developing "findings and recommendations on the most effective methods of providing social security through social insurance, with particular reference to unmet needs for protection during illness and disability."[12] Under I. S. Falk in the 1940s, this division was responsible most particularly for planning health insurance. It did not have exclusive jurisdic-

10. Robert J. Myers, *Expansionism in Social Insurance* (London: Institute of Economic Affairs, 1970), p. 29.

11. Arthur J. Altmeyer, *The Formative Years of Social Security* (University of Wisconsin Press, 1966), pp. 262–63.

12. *United States Government Organization Manual—1949*, p. 389.

tion over policy planning, however. A division of program analysis in the Bureau of Old Age and Survivors Insurance was also active. Significantly, subsequent leaders of the Social Security Administration (Ball, Hess, David) came from there, which suggests either that the most able members of the organization worked in that division or that work there was valued and rewarded more than work in other parts of the organization, such as field administration.

Policy planning in the Social Security Administration has always consisted of planning for changes within the framework of established programs. Social insurance has been assumed to be the preferred technique. The mission of the Office of Research and Statistics, quoted in the preceding paragraph, is indicative. It was charged with studying methods of providing social security "through social insurance." Relatively little attention was paid to the despised alternative, public assistance, for which the SSA was also responsible until 1963, nor were different ways to meet perceived social needs considered. The prevailing technique of policy analysis was to identify a social problem, such as lack of health care, and to develop the arguments and methods for dealing with it through social insurance. Consistent with this approach to policy analysis, the SSA's research was done internally, rather than being contracted out, in contrast to the practice of many other federal government agencies.[13]

This commitment to social insurance combined elements of dogmatism and pragmatism. The executive leaders of social insurance certainly believed that it was in principle the best kind of program for dealing with social dependency; they also believed that it was best because, having been established and accepted after 1935–36, it could with relative ease be enlarged upon. Incremental steps, in their view, were relatively acceptable to the public and Congress, and extensions of the social insurance principle, however novel their reach, could be presented as elaborations and emendations of a popular and accepted technique.

To the extent that executive leaders of the program have articulated a philosophy of policy formation, this philosophy stresses gradualism.

13. External advisory committees periodically urged the SSA to stimulate outside research and increase consultation with privately employed social scientists. See *The Research Program of the Social Security Administration*, Report of the 1967 SSA Advisory Committee on Research Development (Washington, D.C.: the Committee, 1968), pp. 1–5.

Wilbur J. Cohen, one of the most durable and influential of the group (although he did not actually hold office in the SSA after 1955), once summarized their outlook for an interviewer:

The men and women I worked with, while they were populists, while they were progressives, while they were strong believers in social legislation, they were also strongly of the belief of the inevitableness of gradualism. In other words, they felt it was more important to take one step at a time. Or perhaps I ought to put it this way—to digest one meal at a time rather than eating breakfast, lunch, and dinner all at once and getting indigestion. This was their philosophy. I think it's the right social philosophy.

. . . As a matter of fact, a recent magazine which was analyzing my conduct during the years had the heading, "Salami Slicer." It said that Secretary Cohen believed in the principle of salami slicing, which is to take a piece of salami and slice it very thin and then pile slice upon slice so that eventually you have a very good sandwich. And that is my concept of the evolution of social legislation; to take a bite at a time and digest it, and then to go on to the next phase in an orderly evolution that is acceptable by the body politic as being practical, realistic, and one that they're willing to build upon.[14]

Myers, after he left the SSA, described the gradualist tactics of his former colleagues unsympathetically:

The expansionists, as a matter of strategy, frequently use the "ratchet" approach. They do not unveil their ultimate goals in their entirety, but rather advocate only part. Then they are satisfied, for the time being, when they get only a fraction of that part. They believe that there is always another day to push further forward toward their goals, and they know that once a certain expansion has been achieved, a retreat from it is virtually impossible. . . . Usually, the ink is scarcely dry on a newly-enacted amendment before plans are being developed for the next legislative effort.[15]

In truth, the executives of the SSA were not always patient incrementalists. The Wagner-Murray-Dingell bill of 1943 was not the work of men who were content to settle for piecemeal change. A sweeping proposal, it called for a big increase in cash benefits, insurance against temporary and permanent disability, health insurance for the whole population, maternity benefits, and a fully federalized system of unemployment compensation. But it did not pass, or come close to being passed as a whole. Only by being broken up and considered piece by piece over many years, and with individual pieces tailored to fit political circumstances of the moment, did much of the Wagner-Murray-Dingell bill ultimately become law. A philosophy perhaps, incrementalism was also a lesson learned from experience.

14. Interview with Wilbur J. Cohen by David G. McComb for the Lyndon Baines Johnson Library (1968); copy in John F. Kennedy Library, Waltham, Mass.
15. Myers, *Expansionism in Social Insurance*, pp. 19–20.

Sensing that piecemeal steps were appropriate in the American political system, program executives nonetheless remained very much aware that other industrialized countries had created comprehensive social insurance programs, and they were confident that in time the United States would do so too. The movement for social insurance was international, and the leaders in various countries kept in touch through such organizations as the International Labor Organization and the International Social Security Association. Leaders in the United States tried to promote a version of social security that would be well adapted to American culture and values (hence the stress on wage-related benefits and individual work effort), yet they were also aware of being part of a worldwide movement and believed therefore that there was logic, even inevitability, in what they were trying to do.

Competence and Consensus

To a remarkable degree, the executive leaders of social security combined administrative with conceptual ability. Skillful as planners and expounders of policy, both Altmeyer and Ball were also skillful chief administrators, and they benefited from the exceptional ability of an early chief of the BOASI, John J. Corson, to whom insiders often give much credit for the SSA's outstanding administrative performance. The leaders assembled, trained, and motivated a staff of exceptional competence and esprit and maintained a high degree of internal discipline.

When the staff of the Social Security Board was formed after 1935, the members of the board controlled most high-level appointments themselves. They did not rely on the routine procedures of the Civil Service Commission. Although the board's staff was covered by the federal merit system, the Social Security Act provided exemptions for two classes of employee, lawyers and experts. Board members made liberal use of the expert clause to bring in people of their own choosing. The Bureau of Research and Statistics, expected to be the locus of policy planning, alone had fifty-four "experts" on its staff by February 1937, persons whose appointments had bypassed regular civil service procedures.[16]

The civil service exemption for experts was an old congressional custom usually reserved for patronage appointments. This was not so in the

16. Charles McKinley and Robert W. Frase, *Launching Social Security, 1935–1937* (University of Wisconsin Press, 1970), pp. 407–24, 435n.

case of the Social Security Board, in which a two-man majority of Winant and Altmeyer strenuously resisted patronage appeals in favor of merit appointments, although their own notions of merit were governing. An early administrative history of the Social Security Board concludes that the number of patronage appointments was remarkably small by comparison with other New Deal agencies or older agencies that had suddenly acquired new programs.[17]

If leaders of the Social Security Board did not pick party hacks, whom did they pick? McKinley and Frase say quite simply that they wanted the best people in the country. Altmeyer, in particular, who emerged as chairman after Winant's resignation early in 1937, had elevated notions of personnel policy. He viewed the board's job of recruitment as comparable to that of a university in selecting its faculty. He wanted creative minds. To get them, he and Winant relied on personal acquaintances, contacts with professional groups, and "friends of their friends."[18] The first appointees were inherited from the staff of the Committee on Economic Security, the cabinet-level committee that had planned the President's social welfare proposals in 1934 or came, as had that staff, from the universities, foundations, and other private philanthropic organizations. Backgrounds in the social sciences were preferred. By and large, the initial appointees did not come from other, more established federal agencies, although some transferred from New Deal agencies. They did not come, either, from the private insurance industry, and this became a point of contention between Altmeyer and the Civil Service Commission, which had to clear expert appointees. The commission had a hard time understanding why people with experience in private insurance were less expert than those who had backgrounds in academic social science. Altmeyer later recalled that he never was "able to get across the considerable distinction between private insurance and social insurance."[19] Those employees who did come to the board with a background in private insurance were subsequently judged by their superiors to be of inferior competence. They received lower efficiency ratings than the others.

At the lowest levels of the organization, consisting of assistants and clerks in the field offices, the board could not hire experts or the friends of friends of Winant and Altmeyer. It had to follow civil service pro-

17. Ibid., p. 424.
18. Ibid., p. 411.
19. Altmeyer, OHC, p. 45.

cedures, but it still stressed quality. The personnel director picked recruits from a civil service register that had been built on the requirement of a college education and the results of a written test of general knowledge. Like his superiors on the board, he believed that young persons trained in the social sciences and with high general intelligence would make the best employees, and such persons were of course more readily available for low-ranking civil service jobs during the Depression than they would be later, in more prosperous times. It was on this theory that the field offices of the Bureau of Old Age Benefits were staffed and a pool of future leaders of the organization was created.[20]

The career of Arthur Hess, who entered a field office in 1939 and ultimately became deputy commissioner, is illustrative. Hess studied political science as an undergraduate at Princeton. He had no particular interest in social security at the time he took a civil service examination, but, once in the organization, he found it rewarding for the opportunity to serve people. He told an interviewer:

I became very much interested in public affairs in high school and in college I majored in political science. Actually, my parents were both born in Switzerland and I had a good deal of travel and linguistic exposure, and I had hoped to get into the foreign service. . . . I took the foreign service examination. . . . So I was all ready to go with the State Department and I didn't pass the foreign service physicals.

In the meantime, I had taken the civil service examination, and one day in '39 I got a notice to come for an interview. Frankly, except for the fact that as any college student who's interested in public affairs would have paid some attention to the social security issue, I was really not oriented toward domestic affairs. . . . But I took the job with Social Security, started to work in the field, became very much interested in the public service aspect of this job. The field was one which had a good deal of job satisfaction to it. In dealing with

20. An anecdote from Wilbur J. Cohen shows the interest that Altmeyer and Winant took even in relatively low-ranking appointments. In a speech at the dedication of the Altmeyer building at SSA headquarters in 1973, Cohen recalled "opening the door between my office and Mr. Winant's office when Mr. Winant was Chairman of the Board. My little office adjoined both his and Mr. Altmeyer's. I opened the door—this was 1936—and I found Mr. Winant and Mr. Altmeyer down on the floor on their hands and knees with little 3 x 5 cards spread on the rug. On the cards were the names of all the people they were considering for appointment as the first field office managers of this great program. They had these cards down on the floor and were sorting them out. Ladies and gentlemen, nobody was appointed to a field office manager's job in 1936–37 but what Mr. Altmeyer and Mr. Winant had looked him over bit by bit. They knew every person." Social Security Administration, Office of Management and Administration, "Arthur J. Altmeyer: Mr. Social Security," OHR/DTCD Pub. No. 065-73 (7-75).

older people, you could help people get through this maze of bureaucratic red tape, help them to get signed up, help them to figure out how to get their proof and get their relationships straightened out, and I always found that there was a good deal of satisfaction at the end of the day.[21]

The emphasis on quality in recruitment helped to build an organization in which the members found satisfaction in associating with colleagues whose intelligence and ability they respected. Within the Washington community, the Social Security Administration developed an excellent reputation for administrative competence; it also developed a highly satisfying conception of self. Furthermore, because the organization's size and scope of activity steadily grew, members could be confident of promotion. The outstandingly able ones moved quickly from the field or from technical work to important jobs in the central office. Hess told his interviewer:

. . . I got pretty fed up with the field activity because it wasn't sufficiently intellectually challenging for the long run. And when I had the opportunity to come into the central office, first in management planning and then moving into program planning . . . I guess I just got deeper and deeper into social security program activity, got exposed to Ball and Cohen and David, and one thing led to another. I must say, frankly, I never have been tempted very seriously to cut loose from this agency.[22]

In a subtle way, recruitment procedures probably aided also the formation of shared beliefs and attitudes toward the program. Members of the Social Security Administration have been bound by a strong client-serving ethic: the organization exists to serve its beneficiaries. Recruitment procedures contributed to this by discriminating in favor of persons with a proven or presumed potential commitment to a public insurance program.

Bringing intelligence, education, and some measure of social awareness to the job, the typical new employee nonetheless had to be taught about the philosophy and administrative practice of social insurance. Begun at the outset of the program, training courses continued at a level of sophistication and concentration unusual among federal agencies. The training was not technical only. Rather than being confined to details of law and regulation, it was designed to instruct in the conceptual foundations of the program and to inculcate a commitment to serving the beneficiaries. Looking back, Altmeyer told an interviewer that this

21. Interview with Arthur E. Hess, Oral History Collection, Columbia University (1966), p. 13.
22. Ibid., p. 14.

training, with its insistence on the agency's social mission, accounted for the popularity of the program. In the local offices, the public met workers who had been trained to serve. "We kept clerks here, as well as the higher-ups, for months before they went out and set up local offices," he said. "So they just had religion. They had it complete."[23] So strong was the client-serving ethic that it precipitated a clash with the General Accounting Office, which charged that the Social Security Board was violating an old law that prohibited federal officials from encouraging a claim against the federal government. According to Altmeyer, "We had quite a time convincing them that this was a different kind of animal—that because of contributions there were certain rights, statutory rights, that had to be recognized and achieved, and we had an obligation."[24]

In a generally cohesive organization, only the Office of the Actuary, which is responsible for estimating costs, has been a locus of dissent. The first chief actuary, W. Rulon Williamson, concluded that the program was fundamentally in error and left office in the late 1940s. His successor, Robert Myers, concluded that continued expansion of it would be a threat to the nation's economy and left in 1970. But even in dissent, pride of organization persists. Though Myers did not hesitate to say that his colleagues at the top of the SSA were wrong in their policies and unethical in their alleged pursuit of these policies against the aims of Republican administrations, he never suggested that they were less than outstandingly able. In retrospect, he wrote that the SSA had been staffed from top to bottom by devoted and capable civil servants who had achieved efficient, impartial, and honest administration.[25] In the actuary's office as elsewhere, continuity and high competence were the rule. Myers was with the program for thirty-six years, having begun work with the Committee on Economic Security, and his own much-heralded professional skill adorned the organization.

This pride and cohesiveness, it should be made clear, characterized only the administration of social insurance. For many years the Social Security Board and its successor, the Social Security Administration, had responsibility for other programs too—public assistance until 1963 and unemployment compensation until 1949—but these were regarded by the executive leadership as inferior programs. Social insurance was the

23. Altmeyer, OHC, p. 199.
24. Ibid.
25. Myers, *Expansionism in Social Insurance*, pp. 15, 29.

shining star in the constellation of social programs. This situation created some tension and jealousy within the organization as a whole, but enhanced the esprit of the part that was in charge of social insurance.

From the perspective of 1978, it may seem that the SSA's long-standing reputation for administrative competence was not fully justified. When Supplemental Security Income (SSI) began in 1974 as a federal program of assistance to the poor, SSA's field administration broke down. Errors in determination of eligibility or in payments occurred in about a fourth of the cases; overpayments approached a billion dollars a year; applicants waited hours for service at area offices and then were served by employees who were poorly informed of the rules and hampered by computer breakdowns. Newspapers carried exposés and congressional committees rushed to investigate. The burdens of the new program and the revelation that the organization could not cope with the burdens badly undermined SSA's traditionally high morale.

It would be quite wrong, though, to conclude from the experience with SSI that SSA's reputation for administrative excellence was ill-founded. Recent history demonstrates, not that the organization was flawed, but that the tasks on which its reputation was built were relatively easy to perform. In the field, these tasks required a limited use of discretion because the law spelled out benefit rights under old age and survivors insurance in great detail. Because the applicant for payments was entitled by right if entitled at all, the field worker was not an adversary. And, because the administrative organization monopolized information about rules and about the individual applicant's relation to the system, the employee was typically in the position of helping the applicant to secure the benefits that were due him. He did not have to solicit or evaluate information from the applicant, a condition that makes the agency vulnerable to fraud and generates hostility between the employee and the beneficiary. It was the nature of the task (and not just technical competence or inculcated attitudes) that made errors few and the mutual satisfaction of client and agency employee high.

Expertise

The quality of expertise, which has been another distinguishing trait of SSA's leaders, follows to some extent from qualities already described: continuity in office, a high level of intellectual competence, and a heavy organizational investment in accumulation of knowledge through research. Executive leaders of the program brought a degree of skill and knowledge to policymaking that differentiated them from other participants, most of whom were far less expert.

The nature of the program also helps to account for this distinguishing expertise. To understand the operation of social security, including such basic matters as how eligibility and benefits are determined and how the program is financed, requires prodigious effort. Between the expert and the nonexpert lie a specialized vocabulary and a mountainous barrier of intricate fact, law, and regulation, much of which is imperfectly accessible to anyone who does not have training in law, economics, public finance, or actuarial science.

Nor is it simply present knowledge that distinguishes experts from nonexperts. It is a faculty for prediction as well, because formal methods of prediction are integral to policymaking. Following the model of private insurance, the SSA has based proposals on projections of revenues and expenditures prepared by an actuary, an expert in the calculation of insurance risks and premiums. Anyone who wishes to understand and participate in social security policymaking must understand the assumptions, methodology, and terminology of these projections. It is, or appears to be, an arcane business, with a distinctive technical language revolving around "level-premium costs," "percentages of taxable payroll," "covered earnings," "static earnings assumptions," and other such terms, the meaning of which is not immediately obvious to the layman and which are likely, on top of that, to be linked with numbers that are either incomprehensibly large or incongruously small. (Thus the cost of changes in the program is measured by fractions of percentages of taxable payroll—the total amount of income that is subject to social security taxation—and because the payroll is huge, the fractions are tiny.)

In policymaking to be incomprehensible is not necessarily an advantage. Experts cannot avoid dealing with the nonexperts who occupy elective office, and, while some nonexperts may be awed by what they do not understand, others are annoyed and frustrated. It is one more sign of the leadership's skill that, though expert themselves, they were able to conduct public dialogue in comprehensible terms. One of Robert Ball's great gifts as an executive was the art of clarifying inherently confusing subject matter; in testimony he was invariably articulate, patient, and lucid. Still, the fact remains that few outsiders could expect to compete with the insiders in mastery of the subject. The outsiders depended on the insiders for interpretation.

Executive Autonomy

The chief executives of federal government programs, meaning those officials who, as administrators or commissioners or bureau chiefs, have prime responsibility for major activities, must share executive authority with others. In programs that employ grants-in-aid to state or local governments, they share it with executives in the grant-receiving governments. Within the federal government, they share it with hierarchical superiors in the departments and with the president, who are accountable to Congress and the public for what their subordinates do. In the social insurance program, these other executives have not been a very important source of constraint or competition.

Executive leaders of social insurance do not have to worry very much about other governments in the federal system. Except for contracts with state agencies to certify hospitals and nursing homes for participation in medicare and an anomalous provision of the disability insurance program that gives state agencies responsibility for initial determination of disability, theirs is a federal program exclusively. Autonomy within the federal system gives them much more control over their program than federal administrators of grants-in-aid can expect to achieve.

For the first few years of its existence, the Social Security Board was an independent agency within the federal executive branch, free of any executive supervision except that of the president, who even then, with far less to do than he has today, did not ordinarily pay much attention to domestic administration. "He was not interested in administration," Altmeyer recalled of President Roosevelt. "He just assumed that Altmeyer knew his stuff, and he didn't want to be bothered."[26]

26. Altmeyer, OHC, p. 204. However, other evidence in the Oral History Project interviews indicates that the President did get interested in administrative matters if he sensed a potentially embarrassing situation. According to William Mitchell, who was director of the Bureau of Business Management in the early years of the Social Security Board, the President was concerned about newspaper reports that the board had a disproportionate number of Jewish employees. Within a week or two of her appointment to the board in 1937, Molly Dewson called Mitchell into her office and said that one of the things the President had instructed her to look into was the report that the staff was getting filled up with New York Jews. The

When the Federal Security Agency was created in 1939, the Social Security Board lost its independent status. With five other agencies (the Public Health Service, Office of Education, U.S. Employment Service, Civilian Conservation Corps, and National Youth Administration), which together constituted the new agency, it was made subordinate to the FSA administrator, a presidential appointee. The FSA's components retained a good deal of freedom, and the surviving ones continued to retain it after the FSA was reconstituted in 1953 as the Department of Health, Education, and Welfare.[27] The history of FSA and later of HEW is a history of slow, halting, hardly successful attempts of generalist administrators to assert control over the specialized bureaus that were nominally their subordinates.

In the case of the SSA, size and physical distance have presented special obstacles to generalist control. SSA accounts for nearly two-thirds of HEW's personnel. Its headquarters are located in Baltimore, Maryland, an hour's drive, more or less, from HEW headquarters in Washington. The separation began accidentally. There was not enough office space in Washington in the late 1930s to accommodate the rapidly growing Bureau of Old Age Insurance, so some of its activity was located in a manufacturing and warehouse building in Baltimore. This arrangement was supposed to be temporary, and the FSA headquarters building in Washington, finished in the early 1940s, contained special electrical ducts and reinforced floors, worth something like $1.5 million, for the data processing equipment that the social insurance program would require. But the BOASI never moved into the building, which was occupied initially by a war agency and then by other parts of the FSA.

Altmeyer decided to locate the BOASI outside of Washington precisely to protect its independence. William Mitchell, his deputy, later

---

President wanted to know if this was true, and, if it was, he wanted the situation cleaned up forthwith. Mitchell concluded, upon inquiry, that the staff was in fact heavily weighted "with New Yorkers and people of the Jewish faith," though he flatly disbelieved insinuations that this was the result of biased decisions by the board's personnel director, who was Jewish. Mitchell concluded that it was the result rather of the strict application of merit principles, combined with the superior performance of Jews on civil service tests. In response to the President's concern, the board began a "very confidential" and "very small" screening program, and the personnel director was moved to another job. Mitchell, OHC, pp. 17–19.

27. The Civilian Conservation Corps and National Youth Administration were abolished during World War II.

recalled Altmeyer's reasoning: "He told me confidentially . . . that he did that because . . . he wanted old age and survivors insurance to develop without extraneous, outside influences being brought to bear on it. If they were away from the center of government and from the overall organization of a Federal Security Agency, or later the Department of Health, Education, and Welfare, the bureau would have a much greater opportunity to develop objectively and soundly."[28] Mitchell argued with Altmeyer that while social insurance was important, it was not the only thing, and that the parts of the organization should be kept together for the sake of the overall program. According to Mitchell, Altmeyer eventually came to regard his decision as a mistake, but it proved to be irreversible. In the early 1950s an attempt to transfer the headquarters of the BOASI to Washington was defeated by the Maryland delegation in Congress.[29]

Two other obstacles to executive supervision have been the financial independence of the SSA and the reputation of its leaders for exceptional administrative competence. Virtually all of the SSA's operations, including even the construction and rental of office facilities, have been financed out of a payroll tax earmarked for social security purposes and credited to a trust fund. Until adoption in 1969 of the unified budget, which consolidated all trust funds with traditional budget items, the financial transactions of social security were recorded separately from those of the rest of the government, and this inhibited supervision by the Bureau of the Budget and the secretary of health, education, and welfare. Also, whether in the Budget Bureau or HEW, executive supervisors were invariably awed by the vaunted management skill of the social security leadership. "I had complete confidence in the rank and file," Charles Schottland told an interviewer, to explain why as commissioner of social security he had left the Bureau of Old Age and Survivors Insurance alone. In particular, he had confidence in Ball.[30]

CONSIDERED in isolation, the characteristics of the leadership are but a first step toward understanding the agency's role in policymaking. No matter how long they stayed in office, how certain they were of their goals, how much competence, commitment, and expertise they brought to their jobs, or how free from executive supervision they were,

28. Mitchell, OHC, pp. 84–85.
29. Schottland, OHC, pp. 103–07.
30. Schottland, OHC, pp. 42, 125.

the program's leaders could not make policy by themselves. The most authoritative expression of policy is law, and constitutionally it is Congress's function to enact the law. To create the program that the executive planners of social security envisioned, they needed the cooperation of Congress above all.

CHAPTER TWO

Congress

ON THE WHOLE, Congress has responded affirmatively to the executive's proposals. Had it not, the present program would not exist. Congress has responded slowly. There was usually a lag of some years between a major proposal such as disability coverage or health insurance and the adoption of it, and adoption was usually partial. Like the executive leadership—only more so—Congress worked incrementally. Its normal preference was to take small steps. However, what its action lacked in boldness and dispatch Congress compensated for with frequency. It was always legislating. For a decade beginning in 1950, it regularly enacted social security benefit increases or other liberalizations in election years. Between 1960 and 1972 it acted less regularly but on the average hardly less often.

Whereas program executives knew what they wanted, Congress and its committees were more or less continuously engaged in making up their minds. Purpose, expressed in a dominant goal or guiding vision, was very important, perhaps essential, to the functioning of the executive organization. Programmatic goals integrated the organization and provided motivation for the members. Defining purpose was a task intrinsic to executive leadership; hierarchy sustained unity. But for Congress and its committees—by nature representative and nonhierarchical—a clear conception of goals was neither functional nor feasible. Without diversity, they lacked legitimacy.

The very right of the legislature and its committees to make decisions depends on their representing differences of value, interest, and opinion, and on their reflecting the changes that are registered in an unending series of biennial elections. At times of decision a majority rules or diversity is reconciled through bargaining and compromise, but only for purposes of immediate decision. Each new decision requires a new exercise in reconciliation. What Congress is for, then, is what a constantly changing Congress has decided to be for in a continuing series of ad hoc choices. Accordingly, the following analysis of Congress as a policymaker for social security focuses on its internal structure, its role and attitudes, the general thrust or effect of its actions, and its relations with program executives, rather than on policy goals.

The Structure of Jurisdiction

Within Congress, responsibility for social security has been unusually concentrated. Jurisdiction over programs is ordinarily divided at least two ways—between the Senate and the House and, within each, between committees specialized by subject matter, which handle authorizing legislation, and appropriations committees, which act on the executive's requests for funds. In social security, however, jurisdiction has been located almost exclusively in two committees—the House Committee on Ways and Means and the Senate Committee on Finance. Appropriations committees have had a very limited role because funds for social security have not been appropriated out of the general funds of the U.S. Treasury. The program has been financed by a tax imposed on employer payrolls and employee earnings specifically for the purpose. These taxes are collected by the Treasury and then are automatically transferred to a trust fund from which the Treasury draws to meet social security expenditures. The usual process of appropriations is bypassed. Social Security Administration officials have appeared regularly before the appropriations committees, but the committees' questions have usually been confined to administrative matters such as salaries and construction. The appropriations statutes have set limits on these administrative items, which are financed in the first instance from general revenues but ultimately out of trust funds.

That jurisdiction has been so confined has had several important consequences for policymaking. It reduced the burden of persuasion borne by the executives. It limited opportunities for the two houses as a whole to get involved, since they had a chance to act only on authorizing legislation and not the second chance that normally comes when appropriations bills reach the floor. It limited the amount of congressional expertise, since the Ways and Means and Finance committees alone had a chance to master the subject. And, finally, it may have added impetus to program expansion by virtually removing the appropriations committees (which are normally more critical and constraining than the subject-matter committees) from the legislative process.

In the House, locating jurisdiction solely in Ways and Means had the further important effect of restricting the consideration of social security bills on the floor, for Ways and Means bills were customarily considered under a closed rule. Debate was limited to several hours and amendments were prohibited except for those approved by the committee. A motion to recommit the bill was permitted, but such motions always came from the minority party and almost always were defeated by a party-line vote. For tax bills, this practice began in the 1930s. For social security it began formally in 1949, but even before then Ways and Means had established its dominance on the floor, first through Democratic party discipline, then through bipartisan agreement within the committee. The original social security legislation in 1935 was considered under an open rule, but Democratic party leaders instructed their members to defeat amendments. Approximately fifty amendments were offered and none came close to passing. The amendments of 1939 were backed by a bipartisan committee majority, and thirty-nine floor amendments to them were easily defeated.[1]

One argument for the closed rule was that Ways and Means legislation was technically so complicated that it should not be open to amendment by the uninitiated. Another argument, understood even when it was not articulated, was that the committee's bills, which include taxation and tariffs as well as social security, are highly vulnerable to constituency pressures. The closed rule was a protection against expedient and irresponsible action. The House would not have submitted to this discipline, though, if it had not had confidence in the committee, and the committee kept the House's confidence by working hard and long to produce bills that were technically sound, by compromising rather than rejecting demands so that much legislation had bipartisan support within the committee, and by anticipating what members of the House wanted. After an exhaustive study of the committee in the 1960s John Manley concluded that its work was governed by a "norm of restrained partisanship." Though party differences dictated disagreements on many issues, internal deliberations were carried on in a nonpartisan

1. John F. Manley, *The Politics of Finance: The House Committee on Ways and Means* (Little, Brown, 1970), pp. 72, 173, 220–33; Edwin E. Witte, *The Development of the Social Security Act* (University of Wisconsin Press, 1963), pp. 98–99.

spirit, and the chairman, Wilbur Mills, conducted the committee so as to achieve the broadest possible agreement.[2]

The committee as a whole developed a reputation for expertise as a result of its practice of painstaking deliberation, but many members, although proud of this practice, were also bored by it. Mastery of social security was concentrated in a few at the top, especially Mills, who sat on the committee for thirty-four years (1942–76) and who was chairman for seventeen of them (1958–74). In tenure of leadership, he matched either Altmeyer or Ball on the executive side. Well before becoming chairman he sometimes managed social security bills on the floor; he was the Democrats' most skillful questioner in hearings and the most adept technician in executive sessions. When he spoke, everyone listened.

In the Senate, the Finance Committee was less dominant and debate was more open. There the closed rule that constricted the House's action on social security would have been unthinkable. Committee divisions were common; partisanship was less restrained; consensual decision was not the norm. Yet even the Senate, with its more individualistic tradition, ordinarily deferred to its subject-matter committee when making decisions on social security. Though there was no precise counterpart to Mills—no one who ruled the Finance Committee as long, with the same technical mastery of the subject matter or the same success in achieving agreement within the committee—the committee did have its strong men, such as Walter F. George and Robert S. Kerr, from whom other senators were prepared to take cues. And when, after George and Kerr were gone, the Senate did become less deferential and started loading social security bills with amendments against the committee's advice, Ways and Means often succeeded in removing them in conference. In the late 1960s, the example of the Senate confirmed Ways and Means members in their belief that a closed rule was essential if social security bills were not to be turned into Christmas-tree bills. As one Republican member of Ways and Means told Manley:

What the hell, you can't have both engaging in demagoguery or lord knows what you'd have. The Senators, Jesus Christ! They put this in, take that out, spend three days—and we've spent months on the bill. Someone has to be responsible, and it's up to us with the closed rule.[3]

The open procedures of the Senate fostered the political pathologies that the more restrictive House procedures were meant to prevent, but

2. Manley, *Politics of Finance*, pp. 44–53, 63–96.
3. Ibid., pp. 251–52.

by prevailing in conference, Ways and Means succeeded in maintaining the subject-matter specialists' control over social security policy.

Occasionally another committee would appear as an interloper, as when the Senate Special Committee to Investigate the Old-Age Pension System held hearings in 1941; or the Senate Committees on Education and Labor and then Labor and Public Welfare held hearings on national health insurance between 1946 and 1949; or the Senate Labor and Public Welfare Committee's Subcommittee on Problems of the Aged and Aging and subsequently the Senate Special Committee on Aging (the McNamara committee) held hearings and issued reports on health insurance for the aged in the late 1950s and early 1960s. Such committees might put social security issues on the public agenda— health insurance, notably—that the regular committees were not eager to have there, thus creating pressure to act, but until the regular committees did act, legislation had little or no chance of passage. As a general rule, Congress deferred to its program specialists.

Although the congressional environment of the program executives was relatively simple and stable, it was not always receptive, as the delay over disability insurance and even longer delay over health insurance show. Both measures encountered resistance from bipartisan conservative coalitions within the committee. But when committee majorities were unsympathetic, program executives need not give up. With patience to await new election results and persuasion to apply to the uncommitted, committee minorities could be turned into majorities. Meanwhile, legislative objectives could be pursued through the sympathetic minorities—a tactic far more feasible in the Senate than in the House, which would not act except on the recommendation of Ways and Means. When the Senate passed disability insurance in 1956 and again in 1964 when it passed an early version of medicare, it overruled a Finance Committee majority, cases that show how the greater openness of the Senate facilitated the program executives' pursuit of legislative objectives there.[4]

4. As a corollary, it is worth noting that the more restrictive procedures of the House sometimes helped program executives kill unwanted measures. Liberalizations of the retirement test, which limits the amount that a social security recipient may earn, were generally controlled in Ways and Means, which supported the SSA's view that money saved from applying the test could be better used for general benefit improvements. Mills took this position despite the fact that liberalization of the test was very popular in Congress; year in and year out, no issue connected with the program inspired so many members' bills.

When the interloping committees such as the McNamara committee supported their objectives, program executives might also work through them, but they were cautious about this, not wanting to upset working relations with their regular committees. As time passed, they developed a very close collaboration with those committees, which came to share the program executives' proprietary stance toward social security.

Attitudes and Role

Without showing much interest in the substance of the social security bill in 1935, the tax committees were concerned nonetheless to have jurisdiction over it. It was supposed to go to them because it rested on the government's power to tax. Fearing that they would be unsympathetic, the executive drafters of the legislation hoped that it might be handled by a special committee, and leaders of the Labor committees in the two houses—Robert F. Wagner in the Senate and David J. Lewis in the House—wanted to take charge themselves. When it appeared he might be bypassed, Ways and Means Chairman Robert L. Doughton of North Carolina went to see the President, whereupon the President told Frances Perkins, chairman of the Committee on Economic Security, that bypassing Ways and Means would "never do." Doughton's feelings and those of his Senate counterpart, Pat Harrison, would be hurt.[5] It was a shrewd judgment on the President's part. Without especially liking the old age insurance program, both committee chairmen stood loyally by it, perhaps in return for having been left in charge.

The committees' interest in the program deepened as they gained experience of it and the program gained beneficiaries. At least for the House Committee on Ways and Means, the amendments of 1950 appear to have been a formative experience. Though Chairman Doughton was still not intellectually engaged in the subject, he was a stern taskmaster, and he kept the committee in near-daily executive sessions from April to August 1949 during which the staff twice presented every section of the bill and a companion bill on public assistance, first for a tentative vote and discussion, later for the final vote. Many members shifted their votes as they became persuaded on particular points. When the com-

5. Frances Perkins, *The Roosevelt I Knew* (Viking Press, 1946), p. 296.

mittee was finished, Doughton introduced a clean bill with his own name on it, whereas at the start of the session he had introduced the administration's bill "by request," a change that signaled Congress's newfound stake in the subject.[6]

Executive sources testify to the sense of pride and proprietorship that came to characterize the handling of social security at least in the Ways and Means Committee. In an interview, one source stressed the committee's seriousness and striving for philosophic consistency:

I've watched the Ways and Means Committee operate for a long time, and I think that many of the key members—certainly one or two of the minority members like John Byrnes and certainly half a dozen of the majority members and the chairman himself—feel very strongly that the whole social security system . . . is the product of their own intellectual commitment. . . . And in many instances a point of view that a congressman may be propounding is not . . . consciously related to [constituent pressures]. . . . Very often it's his judgment as to the way in which the job ought to be done. He's thinking in terms of basic principles, in terms of what's right and what's wrong, and in terms of how the program can best be defended. . . . He has to have consistency [with] the philosophy and the objectives and the position he has taken in the past.[7]

Like the program executives, the congressional leaders came to resist the intervention of outsiders, such as those in the Executive Office of the President who would have bent the program to the purposes of macroeconomic policy. They thought of the program as a special trust, an activity apart from the rest of government, and of themselves as trustees.

The Ways and Means Committee's collective sense of pride and possessiveness regarding social security was sustained by the pragmatism of the membership and the consensual mode of decision. As Manley noted, committee members were rarely ideologues. They were "pragmatic in their outlook on politics, patient in their pursuit of objectives, unbending on few things, and inclined to compromise on all but the most basic issues."[8] As a creature of the New Deal, social insurance tested the pragmatism of the committee's Republican minority more than the Democratic majority. The Republican capacity to accommodate was best demonstrated individually by the post–1950 "conversion"

6. Interview with Fedele Fauri, Oral History Collection, Columbia University (1966), p. 8. (Hereafter Fauri, OHC.)

7. Interview with Arthur E. Hess, Oral History Collection, Columbia University (1966), pp. 30–31.

8. Manley, *Politics of Finance*, p. 47.

of the party's strong man, John W. Byrnes. Fundamentally opposed at first to social insurance, Byrnes was one of only fourteen House members to vote against the 1950 amendments, which were the last of the three founding pieces of legislation (after the 1935 act and the 1939 amendments). In the committee report, he concurred with Representative Carl Curtis's recommendation that flat payments financed out of general revenues be made to all elderly citizens. On the floor, he argued that it was neither sound policy nor honest politics to commit future generations of taxpayers to the rising rates that were inherent in social insurance. Social insurance, he said, would give something for nothing to the early participants, and that was wrong. In logic and morality, it was a powerful argument, but it lost. But, having lost, Byrnes did not join the minuscule group of right-wing Republicans within the committee, usually consisting of one or two members, who maintained a principled opposition to social insurance. These were men such as Noah Mason of Illinois, James B. Utt of California, and Bruce Alger of Texas. Instead he became a leader of the bipartisan majority that bore responsibility for evolution of the program. Mills, consistent with the consensual mode, worked amicably with him, granting him a share of the leadership.

In their proprietorship of social security (or "trusteeship" as they thought of it), the committee members found psychic as well as narrowly political rewards. Asked what he was most proud of as he neared the end of his career, Mills told an interviewer that "I like to think in terms of development of the social security program. . . . I like to think of that as my major achievement." He described its growth under his leadership, noting that it had made life "a little more pleasant for millions of beneficiaries."[9] Some observers of Ways and Means believed that the opportunity to dispense benefits through social security was the more attractive to the committee because its usual and predominant task, the imposition of taxes, was so unpopular and unrewarding. In social security, it had charge of a highly popular program—one that gave individual members of the committee frequent opportunities to sponsor and claim credit for liberalizations, and gave the committee as a whole opportunities to sponsor benefit increases and other liberalizations that were popular with Congress as a whole.

9. The interview was conducted by Paul Duke and shown on *Agronsky at Large,* WETA-TV, Washington, April 12, 1976. I am indebted to the station for arranging to play a tape for me.

Pride, possessiveness, and concern for doctrinal consistency were less characteristic of the Finance Committee than of Ways and Means, and this in time helped to establish Ways and Means as the more influential of the two. ("We sent over a henhouse filled with hens, and the House of Representatives conferees gave us back a bag of feathers," Louisiana's Russell B. Long complained in 1960, in frustration at the dominance of the House in conference.)[10] Ways and Means took a deeper and more consistent interest in the subject and had clearer guides to action, besides having the advantage of a constitutional right to initiate revenue bills, among which social security bills were included. The Finance Committee became a limited partner in the shared proprietorship, but it was not in general a dissonant one. There were no deep and enduring doctrinal disputes between Ways and Means and Finance, although there were often particular differences about priorities or the speed of the forward pace. The Finance Committee was more willing than Ways and Means to liberalize the retirement test; less ready to accept disability insurance in the 1950s; and more ready a decade later to enact a substantial increase in cash benefits. Its positions changed as its partisan and ideological composition changed, whereas in Ways and Means ideology was tempered by program doctrine, the consensual mode, and the enduring personal influence of Mills, so that positions on social security had greater stability.

The qualities that these "program legislators" brought to social security policymaking were very much like those of the program executives: expertise, continuity, autonomy, cohesion, and a commitment to programmatic doctrines, admixed with pragmatism. In combination, of course, with the legislature's formal right to decide the content of legislation, these qualities gave congressmen a substantial role in policymaking.

Policymaking came to resemble a prolonged symphony in which the movements were conceived by the executive "composers." There were no intermissions except that caused by World War II. A big increase in benefits and coverage having been achieved in 1950, the executive leadership concentrated on disability coverage. As soon as disability coverage was enacted, the drive for medicare began. Medicare was no sooner enacted than the next movement, meant to culminate in a big increase in benefit levels, opened. The congressional committees re-

10. Quoted by Senator Stephen M. Young in *Congressional Record* (June 26, 1961), p. 11306.

sponded in their own fashion, rejecting now, accepting later, and selecting to suit their collective preferences and the preferences of the whole legislature, pertinent interest groups, and the public as the committees perceived them. Policymaking, to pursue the metaphor, required harmonization (or the construction of consensus, in the language of political analysis). Composers themselves, congressmen often changed or added phrases in the executive composition, or reinterpreted a theme. After 1950 a theme mutually agreed upon brought benefits into line with price and wage changes every two years or so. The executive's grand movements, the congressional phrases, and the biennial theme had to be combined in a score that would stand as the definitive interpretation of social security policy, part of the continuing composition begun in 1935. The congressional committees did this, and did it in a way that would make the composition agreeable to the audience—the American voters. Congressmen recognized this to be their quintessential function. "There is one very important thing in this whole social-security program," Tennessee's Jere Cooper once remarked. (Briefly, between Doughton and Mills, Cooper was chairman of Ways and Means.) "It was recognized in the beginning and it has to be recognized all the time. You have to work it out on such a basis, and carry it forward in such a way, that you carry public sentiment along with you. . . . Once you lose public sentiment and the support of the public, you are in serious difficulty."[11]

Influence

Benefits were unambiguously popular, and the general thrust of congressional action was to deliver larger amounts of them, sooner, to more people. This was evident, for example, in the 1939 amendments, which both increased the size of benefits and advanced the date on which they were to begin; though designed by executive hands, these amendments were very much tailored to legislative tastes. It was evident again in the very important amendments of 1950, in which Congress made the eligibility standards for newly covered workers more liberal than the executive had proposed, facilitating the sudden addition of several million more beneficiaries. It was evident as well in the several hundred social

11. *Freezing the Social Security Tax Rate at 1 Percent,* Hearings before the House Committee on Ways and Means, 78 Cong. 2 sess. (GPO, 1944; revised), p. 103.

security bills introduced in each session of Congress in the 1950s and 1960s.

Benefit increases were distributed in a way that made it easy for Congress to claim credit. They were enacted often, according to a schedule that closely fitted the schedule of biennial elections, and they were dispersed widely. Representative Barber Conable, an astute veteran of the Ways and Means Committee, once described the way in which the committee resolved the choice between general benefit increases and liberalization of the retirement test. It was the nature of the political animal, Conable thought, to help as many people as possible.

We do have a tradeoff, and we have been through this time and time again on the Ways and Means Committee with respect to the earned income ceiling. You have a question of a $600 million windfall, . . . do you put that $600 million into a 5-percent benefit increase for everybody across the board, or do you give it to those few people who are still working and not drawing social security, because they are earning too much above the earned income ceiling?

. . . we generally opted for modest benefits for the large numbers of people affected rather than big benefits for a few. We are faced with that kind of a decision and the political reaction generally is to try to help as many people as possible if you can, rather than provide tremendous benefits for a few people.

Whether that is right or wrong, that is what the political animal normally does.[12]

General benefit increases such as Conable was describing enabled all congressmen to claim credit vis-à-vis a large number of constituents, but this was not the sole pattern of congressional action. Interwoven with the general increases were increases sponsored by individual congressmen for the benefit of particular groups. Congressmen specialized. Some concentrated on liberalizations of the retirement test; for North Dakota's William Langer, this was a "holy war," in a Senate colleague's phrase.[13] Others (John Byrnes in the House, Winston L. Prouty in the Senate) were interested in "blanketing in"—that is, covering elderly persons who did not meet established standards of eligibility. Senator Vance Hartke concentrated on liberalizing the disability insurance program for the benefit of the blind. Others (including Prouty) fought to raise the level of the minimum benefit. Within the Ways and Means Committee, the rule with pet proposals was to maximize the possibil-

12. *Economic Problems of Women*, Hearings before the Joint Economic Committee, 93 Cong. 1 sess. (GPO, 1973), pt. 2, p. 330.
13. *Congressional Record* (June 26, 1961), p. 11310.

ities for individual credit claiming by committee members rather than to maximize the number of constituent beneficiaries. Several cheap proposals had a better chance of adoption collectively than one equally expensive proposal because more members could be satisfied that way. "The way we have really handled it all of these years," a committee member, Martha W. Griffiths, once remarked, "is that each member figured out something he wanted corrected," and then an effort was made to satisfy as many members as possible.[14]

The difficult part, of course, was to manage the taxes. As much as it liked dispensing benefits, Congress disliked raising the revenue to pay for them. It showed this by repeatedly deferring scheduled tax increases and by resisting extension of the program to farmers, from whom it feared a taxpayers' revolt. J. Douglas Brown, one of the original planners of old age insurance and long a participant in policymaking through the advisory councils, saw tax avoidance as the dominant congressional impulse. He told an interviewer:

The senators and congressmen from farm states, thinking of the tax before ever realizing what the benefits would mean, were more likely to say, "We want to be excluded." So the political influence was more exclusive, whereas our interests were inclusive. We tried our best to get the nonprofits and various others in because we were continually thinking of the far end, of the benefit end, whereas the natural reaction of the congressmen having to sell it back home was the tax end. The time preference rate: you'll find in the development of all these things that the professional expert has to have a long time perspective. The typical politician has a short-term perspective. He's going to be reelected he hopes in two years. So there's always that conflict in planning.[15]

Perhaps the most important function of the legislative committees was to reconcile the legislature's conflicting impulses and strike a balance between benefits and revenues. For this purpose, the Ways and Means Committee enforced a norm of "fiscal soundness" that was absolutely central to policymaking for social security. At the heart of the concept was the notion of "self-support," which the committee affirmed in 1950. The program was to be financed entirely with its own tax, a payroll tax. It would not be allowed to run a deficit or to draw on the general revenues of the Treasury. When liberalizations were enacted, estimates of their future cost were calculated, and a schedule of future tax rates sufficient to meet the estimated costs was included. The com-

14. *Economic Problems of Women,* Hearings, pt. 2, p. 332.
15. Interview with J. Douglas Brown, Oral History Collection, Columbia University (1965), p. 65. (Hereafter Brown, OHC.)

mittees did not recommend legislation unless it was "actuarially sound" —that is, it included payroll tax provisions sufficient to cover benefit costs, as calculated by the SSA actuary. In this matter, Finance followed the example of Ways and Means. Here more than at any other point one sees the effect on program substance of the interests of the revenue committees. "They liked the program because it brought in its own money," a knowledgeable executive remarked. If they had had to finance it with general revenues, they would not have liked it as well. The payroll tax proved more acceptable to the public than the income tax, presumably because the taxpayers were promised specific benefits in return; the revenue-raising committees therefore liked the payroll tax, and liked the program of which it was part.

The Ways and Means Committee developed the practice of raising taxes whenever benefits were increased so as to remind the public that benefits had a cost. Mills once lectured a new secretary of HEW on this point:

I would like to call your attention to the way the committee has operated in the past and the way I would think it would almost be duty bound to operate in connection with [proposed] amendments, to get your reaction.

. . . the committee has followed a rule that I do not want us to deviate from if we can avoid it, of not [granting] these increases in payments to the recipients under the program . . . without at the same time imposing an increase in the tax to carry the cost of those increased expenditures, an increase in a tax that would go into effect fairly close to the time that the benefits themselves would go into effect. . . .

It is true that over the years . . . that has not always invariably been the case. We have adopted provisions since I have been a member of this committee, but not since I have been chairman of it, when we would put benefits into effect immediately and the tax would not go into effect until 1972.

However, that has been ten or fifteen years ago that we did some things like that.[16]

To be sure, the committee was not so meticulous as to impose the two increases at exactly the same time. Benefit increases were ordinarily effective immediately, typically within an election year, whereas the tax increase was not effective until the beginning of the next calendar year, but this discrepancy could be rationalized on administrative grounds even if it obviously implied a political advantage.[17]

The Ways and Means Committee took pride in its showing of fiscal

16. *Social Security Amendments of 1961*, Executive Hearings before the House Committee on Ways and Means, 87 Cong. 1 sess. (GPO, 1961), pp. 101–02.

17. *Congressional Record* (April 20, 1961), p. 6469. See also Edward R. Tufte, *Political Control of the Economy* (Princeton University Press, 1978), pp. 29–36.

responsibility. So did other participants in policymaking, such as members of the advisory councils, who followed the same rule of fiscal soundness in preparing their recommendations. The strict adherence of the Ways and Means Committee to its self-imposed standard of fiscal soundness put a brake on legislative generosity, as the history of relations between the houses shows. Whenever the Senate, in its indifference to the recommendations of the Finance Committee, enacted costly new benefits without providing taxes to cover them, the Ways and Means Committee reacted indignantly. "The House conferees have been firm almost to the point of being rude in telling us that if there was no tax to pay for . . . a benefit they were not even going to consider it," Finance Committee Chairman Russell Long told the Senate in 1969.[18]

But how strict was this standard? The fact is that the norm of fiscal soundness did not prevent steady expansion of the program. The actual norm of congressional action, as distinct from the proclaimed norm, was incrementalism—taking one small step at a time. John C. Watts, a Kentucky Democrat, once reminded his colleagues on Ways and Means that despite all the talk of fiscal discipline, both benefits and taxes seemed to rise inexorably:

> Mr. Chairman, I will go along with the report that in . . . the social security fund, we have been able to keep it more in balance . . . than we have our general fund. . . .
> But also, we have done this: I haven't seen that there has been a brake on increasing benefits, and increasing this, that, and the other, because every time this committee meets on social security, we increase the benefits to somebody, and we increase the taxes.
> . . . the social security tax has year by year, or every 2 years, gone up, whereas the general tax hasn't, and I am willing to concede that we have done a much better job of keeping income and outgo on a balance, but as to whether or not it has deterred us from spending any money is problematical.[19]

The practice was to let taxes rise by small, frequent steps. This is revealed both by an examination of the rates, which rose, on the average, by 0.4 of a percentage point every other year, and by a careful reading of Mills's speeches, such as one in which he told the House that the Ways and Means Committee was anxious not to let the social security tax rate "grow too rapidly."[20]

In application, then, the norm of fiscal soundness represented a

18. *Congressional Record* (December 5, 1969), p. 37233.
19. *Medical Care for the Aged,* Executive Hearings before the House Committee on Ways and Means, 89 Cong. 1 sess. (GPO, 1965), pt. 2, p. 804.
20. *Congressional Record* (April 20, 1961), p. 6466.

compromise between expansionary and restrictive impulses. Cast in conservative terms, it did impose short-run restraints. On any given occasion, the committees would decline to approve many expansionary proposals because they were too expensive; they would either violate the requirement of "actuarial balance" or they would require an unacceptably large increase in taxes. On the other hand, over the longer run, taxes did rise and much expansion did occur because the norm of actuarial balance did not imply a fixed tax rate or a program of fixed size. The actual practice was to test, step by small step, the public's tolerance of payroll taxes.

Executive-Legislative Relations

Program executives were quite conscious of the need to work intimately with Congress, and one among them, the ubiquitous, inexhaustible, irrepressible Wilbur Cohen, made a lifework of it. They learned the need to compromise their own positions, and to contribute to the patient search for legislative outcomes that would facilitate consensus within the congressional committees. Cohen was so much at the center of this process that it can best be described by describing him and his work.

As a student at the University of Wisconsin, Cohen came to Washington in 1934 to serve on the staff of the Committee on Economic Security. He stayed and became a special assistant to Arthur Altmeyer and then briefly director of the Division of Research and Statistics in the SSA. He left Washington during the Eisenhower administration for a professorship at the University of Michigan, but he did not really leave. He stayed in touch with friends and former colleagues in the Social Security Administration and in general functioned as a member of the leadership on political leave, in some ways the more effective by reason of being free of restraint. Following Kennedy's election he returned to office, first as assistant secretary for legislation in the Department of Health, Education, and Welfare, then as under secretary, and finally, in the closing days of the Johnson administration, as secretary. When the Republicans returned in 1969 he again "retired" to Ann Arbor but again did not completely retire. He continued to write, talk, keep in touch, come often to Washington, and be consulted by congressmen. It was a remarkable career, more varied as it progressed, and yet building the social insurance program remained always at the center of it, and at the center of Cohen's work of building was Congress. His lifework lay with knowing the legislative process and those legislators who were in charge of social security.

Altmeyer, explaining to an interviewer how he happened to choose Cohen as a special assistant, identified a number of the qualities that fitted him for his work on the Hill:

> I first became conscious of him when he was sitting just behind me when I was testifying on something or other, and I was stuck for an answer because I didn't have the facts and he reached over and handed me a sheet that gave me the information I needed to answer the question. I took a second look at the chap. . . . Then of course—I can't remember how I got to know him better and better—but I realized that here was a mind that turned over very rapidly. And he also had a personality that did not arouse antagonism or resentments. He could go to subordinates in the various bureaus and get information that was necessary, and the bureau chiefs wouldn't start howling that these requests should be channeled through them and they ought to know what was going on. He was that sort of person. He could assemble material regardless of bureaucratic lines. . . . Then he also had the knack of being able to talk with the assistants on the Hill, to these important political figures up there who really do the work. There was a two-way flow being established all the time without anybody's nose being out of joint, the senators and congressmen. Their prerogatives they didn't fear were being impaired because the staff people were consulting with each other. If I had gone to talk with their assistants and gotten them committed to something or other, there'd be hell to pay. They'd say, "Why didn't you talk with me?" You have to have that free flow.[21]

Altmeyer went on to explain that work on the Hill was not a formal assignment for Cohen—he gravitated to it naturally. He got to know and be known by people there. Nor did his acquaintance stop with fellow civil servants or the congressional staffs. He knew everyone who mattered, in the interest groups, the advisory councils, or wherever. It became his business to know them, and to understand the terms on which they could be satisfied.

Perhaps the best authority on Cohen is Cohen. He was fond of recalling that his father, who ran a variety store in Milwaukee, taught him to look at things from the viewpoint of the fellow who is buying the merchandise. The mercantile analogy recurs in his accounts of his approach to Congress, as in the following excerpt from an interview:

> The key to it is what I have sometimes called the principle of looking at the problem from the standpoint of the consumer. When you're in the executive branch . . . you're selling a certain product or service just like any businessman

21. Interview with Arthur J. Altmeyer, Oral History Collection, Columbia University (1967), pp. 228–30.

is. What you've got to do is turn the problem around and look at it from the standpoint of the legislator who is in that sense the consumer, and then try to see where he sees the price of the product is too high or the service is imperfect or how he wants it changed. . . . And if he can work out his problem, then you can get the legislation passed.[22]

That he knew people—that he knew and understood politicians in particular—does not fully explain Cohen's success. He also knew the program. He was no mere legislative liaison man, bringing messages to the Hill from executive planners. He was a planner too, knowledgeable and inventive, who happened to be very good at personal relations and political dealing. He did much of the staff work for the 1937–39 advisory council, in which the 1939 amendments were formulated. He worked with I. S. Falk in preparing the first proposals for national health insurance. He helped write the Social Security Administration's annual reports, in which its legislative program was outlined. The merchandise that he was selling on Capitol Hill was merchandise that he had helped to manufacture. Knowing the goods, he could more readily sell them as legislative liaison man; as program planner, he knew how to design the goods so as to improve the chance of sale. As he combined the functions of legislative liaison and program planning, he also combined the qualities of a technician with those of a political executive. A strong-willed legislator who knew what he wanted, a Kerr or a Mills, could ask Cohen for technical assistance and be confident that it would be given competently. A liberal Democrat who did not know what he was for and needed someone to tell him could equally turn to Cohen for policy and political guidance. As a man liberated after 1955 from the constraints of the civil service yet indubitably a technical expert, Cohen could offer a wide range of service to his congressional consumers.

Finally, he was pragmatic—his critics thought too much so. During the struggle over medicare in the 1960s, his close relations with congressional committee leaders made him suspect to militant elements of the pro-medicare coalition, and others, without sharing this suspicion, thought that he was a bit too fascinated with technique, a bit too excited by whatever artful coup could get a bill through, and a bit too eager to demonstrate that he was ever willing to make a deal. Interestingly, though, it took time and experience for Cohen to acquire his pragma-

22. Interview with Wilbur J. Cohen by David G. McComb for the Lyndon B. Johnson Library (1968); copy in John F. Kennedy Library, Waltham, Mass.

tism. Those who knew him as a young man thought of him as aggressive and inflexible. Perhaps this was because he was Altmeyer's agent then, and Altmeyer was a stubborn man. Perhaps, as the following recollection of Fedele Fauri, a close friend of his, suggests, the politicians in Congress taught him that pragmatism was the price of admission to their committee rooms. Fauri served as a staff member for the Ways and Means Committee in 1949, when it was considering major social security amendments, and thus was in a good position to watch Cohen at work:

Well, Wilbur at that time was a different man from today [1966]. Some of us talk about it. And he knows it too. At that time, it was quite difficult to get him to compromise on anything. He would take the White House line and push it and push it, and that was it . . . I recall very well about his being excluded from executive sessions, I've forgotten just what for, but he had pushed too hard, or some damned thing. And so by a vote of twelve to thirteen, he was told not to come back. Then, shortly thereafter, another vote was taken, and by a vote of thirteen to twelve, just by a jump—I think it was Wilbur Mills who jumped—he was brought back in.[23]

If facilitating consensus in Congress was Cohen's distinctive function, legitimating the legislative outcomes was the function of another leading figure among the program executives—Robert Myers, who was the chief actuary from 1947 until his resignation in 1970. He was connected with the program during his whole career. As a very young man, he prepared the actuarial estimates for the 1935 act. The original old age insurance proposals included a number of options, labeled M-1, M-2, M-3, up to M-9, that incorporated different combinations of benefit and tax schedules. "M" stood for Myers. "M-9" was Bob Myers's "ninth shot at it," J. Douglas Brown recalled.[24]

Myers's cost estimates removed the uncertainty that ordinarily inhibits action. In the social security program, uncertainty could have been especially crippling because the need to calculate future consequences is especially exigent. Policymakers in both the executive and legislative branches recognized that the full effects of the program would be long delayed. Participants would reach retirement age and qualify for benefits by stages. The full impact would not begin to be felt until virtually all elderly members of the society qualified for benefits (along with whatever other groups may have been "insured"), yet

23. Fauri, OHC, p. 19.
24. Brown, OHC, p. 18.

executive techniques enabled Congress to act as if uncertainty did not exist.

Myers presented cost estimates (typically in terms of percentages of taxable payroll) both for the program as a whole and for whatever specific proposals Congress was considering. The published estimates for the whole program routinely affirmed the need for caution—the estimates were only estimates and should be treated as such—yet Congress received all of the actuary's statements as if they were precise and completely reliable. No matter how often congressional committee members reminded themselves that the future was hard to foresee, there was something about the actuarial process itself that fostered an illusion of certainty: the fractions were so refined, the answers came so swiftly from the actuary when committee members asked what a particular change in the program would cost. Congress always felt safe in acting—safe and responsible—if the chief actuary assured it that the system remained "in actuarial balance"—that is, his estimates showed that revenues from scheduled taxes and income from the trust fund would meet obligations.

For Congress, the usefulness of the actuarial function was enhanced by its confidence in Myers. By all accounts, he was a highly competent man, respected by his peers in the private insurance industry for his professional skill and respected in Washington for the strict impartiality with which he applied it. For years he was regarded as the very model of the neutral, technically expert civil servant. Congressmen praised him extravagantly.[25]

The relation that developed between Myers and the congressional committees was a special relation that distinguished him from other civil servants in the SSA. He was perceived to be a servant of Congress

25. "I have always thought, Mr. Myers, that you are one of the great unsung public heroes, really," Senator Paul H. Douglas once remarked in hearings. Senator Harry F. Byrd of Virginia, whose political opinions were very different from those of Douglas, a few minutes later proposed to ask a question "of Mr. Myers, who is the best expert on figures I think I have ever come in contact with." Finance Committee Chairman Russell B. Long volunteered on the Senate floor that "most of us believe that Bob Myers is the most honest actuary and the most honest person to estimate the cost of something without fear or favor that we have in government. . . . I heard the Senator from Illinois [Mr. Douglas] . . . state that in his judgment the man I have named was the most honest actuary in the entire United States." *Social Security Benefits and Eligibility,* Hearings before the Senate Committee on Finance, 87 Cong. 1 sess. (GPO, 1961), pp. 73, 84; *Congressional Record* (July 8, 1965), p. 15909.

as well as the executive, neutral as between the branches besides being neutral conventionally as between the political parties. (Congressional documents sometimes identified him as "actuary to the committee" though he was on the executive's payroll.) On questions of policy and program expansion, he professed to be strictly agnostic. His own conception of his role is summarized in the following excerpt from an interview:

Although I may have views on the desirability or undesirability of the major proposals, I don't feel that it's my function to either express approval or disapproval. . . .

I feel very fortunate . . . that I'm not tied down by what some people refer to as "the heavy hand of bureaucracy" or the red tape of bureaucracy because I'm permitted to work freely with outside sources, with members of Congress, with congressional committees, to give actuarial cost estimates on their particular proposals, whether the department favors them or does not favor them, although of course there's always the confidentiality involved, that I can't and don't tell these people what the department thinks or what the department may be doing to defeat these other proposals that the committees or the members of Congress who are influential are working up for themselves. Likewise, I've been given the understanding on these matters that when the committee or the influential members of the committee are working on something that they need my help with, it's confidential and I don't repeat it back to the department. So I try to act in a purely professional and independent capacity.[26]

Still, it was not just Myers's own qualities or his special relation with Congress that induced Congress to rely so heavily on his estimates. Congressmen believed in them—*had* to believe in them if they were to reach agreement on and rationalize their own policy choices. In reducing the uncertainty that normally accompanies policymaking, Myers's estimates also very much reduced conflict. Congressional committee members conducted their deliberations with a single set of assumptions about cost, which were equally accepted by members of both parties. Without these estimates, it would have been far more difficult to arrive at the typical legislative outcome, which, on the one hand, expanded the program, to the gratification of constituents and of liberal interests, and, on the other, was always certified by an objective, universally respected expert as having met the fiscal test of actuarial balance. Furthermore, because the actuary estimated costs in quite specific

26. Interview with Robert J. Myers, Oral History Collection, Columbia University (1967), pp. 2–3. People who worked with Myers, however, judged him to be a man with definite views and doubted that those views were ever fully concealed from political figures.

numerical terms, as fractions of taxable payroll, compromise among policymakers was facilitated. Packages of program improvements, including benefit increases, could be assembled out of elements recommended by the administration or sponsored by individual committee members, and any differences in preference could be accommodated by exchanging elements of the package or adjusting their size. Since the cost of all proposed elements had been quantified, such adjustments and exchanges were relatively easy to arrange. The actuary's estimates supplied policymakers with a common currency, readily negotiable and divisible.

Social security specialists in organized labor, believing Myers's estimates to be too conservative, contemplated attacking them but then decided no—that such a critique could be self-defeating. They judged that the credibility of the estimates was indispensable to all legislation, and therefore was not worth jeopardizing in a calculated attempt to secure more liberal legislation.[27]

The Shared Proprietorship of Program Experts

Policymaking for social security culminated in sessions of the congressional committees at which the legislative experts sat down with the executive experts and worked out a bill. These were closed meetings, but even if outsiders had had access to the room they would hardly have understood much of what was said there, for the experts talked in a highly technical language. The following exchange between Mills and Myers in 1961 is illustrative. The Ways and Means Committee was considering a number of relatively minor changes in the program and deciding, with Myers's help, how to balance the costs:

The CHAIRMAN [Mills]: Since we met last, I began thinking in terms of how some of these proposals could be boiled down to fit within that amount [0.22 percent of payroll, a figure chosen because it could be financed with an increase in the wage base and would not necessitate an increase in the tax rate]. . . .

Now, what would be the cost of the program, Mr. Myers, that provided in place of the 85 percent of the worker's benefit, for the widow, what would it be for the widow if we said five-sixths?

27. Interview with Katherine Ellickson, Oral History Collection, Columbia University (1967), pp. 180–81.

Mr. MYERS. The level-premium cost for paying the widow a benefit equal to five-sixths of the primary benefit is 0.19 percent of payroll.

The CHAIRMAN. Have you worked it out on the basis that the actual deduction at 62 for men can avoid any cost to the funds?

Mr. MYERS. Yes, Mr. Chairman, that can be done.

The CHAIRMAN. What would be the cost if we raised the minimum in place of going 33 to 43 as we have in the bill, it would raise it just $5, say, to $38?

Mr. MYERS. The cost of that would be 0.04 percent of payroll.

The CHAIRMAN. What is the cost of that change from 1 out of 3 to 1 out of 4? [A reference to a proposal that would make it easier for a worker to achieve "insured status."]

Mr. MYERS. That is 0.02 percent of payroll.

The CHAIRMAN. What is the cost of the change in the disability program?

Mr. MYERS. 0.03 percent of payroll.

The CHAIRMAN. You have 0.08 as I go over it hurriedly.

Mr. ALGER [a representative from Texas]. What is payroll again?

The CHAIRMAN. When we say payroll, what is it in dollars?

Mr. MYERS. The current taxable payroll under the $4,800 earnings base is a little under $220 billion a year. If the base were increased to $5,400, it would be about $235 billion a year. . . .

The CHAIRMAN. Mr. Ball, let me ask you and Mr. Myers this question: If you kept this one out of four, increased [the] minimum to 38, and that is six one-hundredths, drop out this change in disability, not pass judgment on the 62 at the moment because that can be figured not to cost anything, how can we bring the widow's benefit down to 16?

.What would we have to provide for it to cost sixteen one-hundredths in place of nineteen one-hundredths?

Mr. BALL. You get a rather odd fraction, Mr. Chairman, of 82.5 percent. . . .

The CHAIRMAN. That would give you an unusual fraction. What would it be? If you take that case for purposes of simplification, and make it $80, which is a $5 increase at that point, that would be eight-tenths, or four-fifths, would it not, whereas, you have three-fourths at the moment.

What would that cost you?

Mr. MYERS. That would cost for the widows' benefit alone twelve one-hundredths of 1 percent of payroll.

The CHAIRMAN. Twelve one-hundredths?

Mr. MYERS. Yes, sir.[28]

Outside influences of course did reach into the committee room. Congressmen had constituents, often particular constituents, in mind as they acted. Fauri recalled the Ways and Means member from Georgia who was for disability insurance "primarily because of the charwoman that used to scrub his office and other offices, his law office in his home

28. *Social Security Amendments of 1961*, Hearings, pp. 109–10, 115.

town in Georgia, and became afflicted with cancer and couldn't work."[29]
In the extreme case of health insurance, the committee sessions followed years of public discussion and an extensive mobilization of interest groups. Always the committees were sensitive to what their respective houses expected of them. But in the end, it was a very small
official group—the program executives in collaboration with the program legislators—that settled on the substance of the bill and reconciled their decisions with program doctrines.

In acting often and acting always to expand the program, the committees responded to the great pressure from their houses to produce a
stream of benefits for which credit could be claimed, but they had
enough procedural defenses and other assets, including their special
relation with the executive technicians, to keep from being overwhelmed
and losing control of the contents of their bills. Ways and Means recommendations were presented to the House with assurances that the committee had considered them long and carefully, the House having first
agreed obediently to consider them under a closed rule. After a debate
that could have no effect on the outcome, the committee recommendations would pass. In the Senate, liberalizing amendments would be
offered from the floor. The Finance Committee's manager of the bill
would argue that in its deliberate wisdom and with the aid of the social
security technicians from HEW, the committee had considered and
rejected these proposals; that they would render the program actuarially
unsound; or that it was pointless to enact what the House conferees
would not agree to. It was not unusual for Myers to be admitted to the
floor to assist the committee's manager of the bill with his presentation.
In debates on other kinds of legislation, executive staff were almost
never admitted to the floor, but in social security there was an exceptional degree of symbiosis between the executive specialists and the
legislative specialists.

THIS DESCRIPTION of Congress begins to fill in the portrait of policymakers for social security. What starts to take shape is in the nature of
an intimate family portrait rather than a vast and complicated canvas.
Like the executive leaders of the program, policymakers for social security in Congress were few in number and expert in the subject matter.
Authority was less fragmented than usual, being lodged in two com-

29. Fauri, OHC, p. 15.

mittees only, and the authority of the House committee was reinforced by the procedural device of the closed rule, which limited intrusions by the House membership. The committees worked in close collaboration with program executives and shared their exclusive, proprietary attitude toward the program. They performed in a way that facilitated action without facilitating debate.

CHAPTER THREE

Political Executives

EVERY few years many of the founders, friends, and close followers of the social security program held a conference in Michigan, which served them as a midwestern outpost and refuge. Wilbur Cohen was based in Ann Arbor when he was not occupying federal office, and other specialists were drawn to the faculties of Wayne State and the University of Michigan. The conference was in the nature of a family gathering, and nothing made the family more nervous than the imminent prospect of a Republican administration in Washington.

"We are going to pray that the incoming administration will remember what the Bible says in Romans XII," Columbia's Eveline M. Burns remarked in 1968: " 'Hold fast to that which is good.' " She was praying that the Nixon administration would not replace Commissioner Robert M. Ball. Nelson Cruikshank, the AFL-CIO's expert on social security, who held a degree from Union Theological Seminary, was not to be outdone. He took his text from Matthew, where Jesus said: "Behold, I send you forth as sheep among wolves. Be ye as wise as serpents and harmless as doves." "Now," asked Cruikshank, "in modern terminology, just exactly what does that mean? He was saying in effect, 'Look boys, there's a Republican administration in the offing.' "[1]

Republican administrations were more worrisome than Republican congresses because they occurred more often: the Republicans held the presidency in twelve of the thirty-eight years from 1935 to 1972. And, in a program that owes much to executive leadership, the influence of political executives—those who represent the incumbent political party and are responsible for defining and implementing its policies

1. *Proceedings of the Sixth Social Security Conference* (Ann Arbor, Mich.: 1968), pp. 18, 40.

—would seem to be of great potential significance. The arrival of a Republican administration might be expected to halt hoped-for expansions in the program.

That did not happen. On the contrary, some of the big legislative gains that brought the program to its present highly developed state occurred while a Republican was president. Coverage of the population was much expanded and benefits were increased in 1954 under Eisenhower. Coverage of the disabled was enacted in 1956. Medicare, though not enacted under Eisenhower, gained considerable momentum at the end of his administration. Benefit increases greatly enlarging the protection offered by the program were enacted under Nixon. Development of the program was not interrupted by Republican presidencies or even, it would seem, much delayed.

The Development of Political Supervision

The layers of political supervision over program executives thickened with time. At first, Arthur Altmeyer as chairman of the Social Security Board reported directly to the president. Then, in 1939, the Federal Security Agency was created and the Social Security Board was placed under supervision of the FSA administrator, a presidential appointee. Seven years later the board was abolished and its functions were transferred to the administrator, who in turn delegated most of them to a commissioner for social security. The new commissioner was clearly a subordinate of the administrator, who appointed him and defined his functions. In 1953 a new Department of Health, Education, and Welfare replaced the FSA, with a secretary appointed by the president as its head. The commissioner under the new organization was appointed by the president with the advice and consent of the Senate and was to perform such functions as the secretary of HEW might prescribe. Besides the secretary himself, there were other political appointees in his immediate office—an under secretary and assistant secretaries whose number increased with the years. In particular, the assistant secretary for legislation, an office created soon after the department was set up, was a potentially significant source of political supervision. He was responsible for preparing the department's legislative program. For the Social Security Administration, which was largely free of budgetary supervision because of its independent financing and which was aggressive in promoting new legislation, legislative supervision could have been quite confining.

No matter what the form of organization, a precise "line" between political executives and program executives is impossible to discern. A political executive, I assume, is predominantly concerned with advancing the policies of his party and with securing its reelection to office, whereas a program executive is predominantly concerned with the management and evolution of the particular governmental functions for which his agency is responsible.[2] The president is indubitably a political executive, but he shares some responsibility for managing each of the programs that he nominally supervises, including social insurance. The chief of the Bureau of Old Age and Survivors Insurance, indubitably a program executive, became political too when the incoming Republican administration in 1953 removed the incumbent, who was a career civil servant, and replaced him with a party member. And when Wilbur Cohen, indubitably a program executive, moved into political offices in the 1960s—as assistant secretary, then under secretary, and finally secretary of HEW—those offices took on a strong programmatic bias.

There are, then, at least three reasons why the "line" is fuzzy: political and programmatic obligations are mixed in high offices; the presumed location of the line changes as different administrations decide that par-

2. The distinction is not equivalent to (and is only roughly parallel to) that between political appointees and civil servants. It is meant to apply to the dominant purposes or orientations of the individual in his job, not to a formal administrative status, source of official authority, or mode of qualification for the job. Most executives of the social security program were civil servants, and the leading program executives were all civil servants at some point in their careers. Arthur Altmeyer, Wilbur Cohen, and Robert Ball were variously civil servants, political appointees, and private citizens, and functioned as if they were program executives no matter which status they were in, although Altmeyer, in contrast to Cohen and Ball, was not highly active upon leaving office. I assume that to be a political appointee necessarily imparts to an incumbent some degree of political orientation, but that even "political" appointees may have a predominantly programmatic orientation. A safe generalization is that the higher the rank in the executive hierarchy, the greater the political content of the executive function. Particular programmatic responsibilities are progressively diluted, while responsibility for advancing party policies intensifies with the steps up the ladder from bureau chief to secretary, which successively increase distance from the career civil service and narrow distance from the presidency. For elaborate analyses of the relations between political officials and program specialists, see Hugh Heclo, "Political Executives and the Washington Bureaucracy," *Political Science Quarterly*, vol. 92 (Fall 1977), pp. 395–424, and Heclo, *A Government of Strangers: Executive Politics in Washington* (Brookings Institution, 1977).

ticular offices will or will not be "political" and manipulate civil service classifications and appointments accordingly; and particular individuals who fit the programmatic category cross the line into the political realm without, however, significantly changing their perspectives on the program. Which role predominates is an open question, to be resolved by observation of the particular office or incumbent.

In the office of the social security commissioner, the ambiguity has been extreme. Altmeyer as commissioner had civil service status, but it was widely recognized that his job was political. Tension developed between him and officials of the Eisenhower administration over the manner and timing of his departure in 1953—protocol became an issue and passions were aroused—but except for the AFL no one argued that it was wrong in principle for the Republican administration to make a partisan appointment to that job.[3] Soon, though, the commissionership became a job into which program executives with careers in the civil service were likely to be promoted. Both William Mitchell (1959–62) and Robert Ball (1962–73) reached it in this way, and both served administrations of both parties. One can think of the social security commissionership as being either predominantly political or predominantly programmatic, and of political supervision of program executives either as beginning there or as being lodged above the commissionership in the Office of the Secretary of HEW.

In theory, the political offices above the Social Security Administration and at the top of it (if one includes the commissionership) were a constraint on program executives. In theory, they were occupied by generalists who brought to bear on the program different values and perspectives from those of the program specialists. I argue here, however, that the program specialists dominated this relation and try to explain why, concentrating mainly on Republican political executives,

3. Nelson Cruikshank later remarked that "here was a civil servant in the best tradition and . . . we had hoped that social security . . . could be kept out of politics and that a good competent staff could be held intact and people could make a career of it. Now, we knew that a secretarial post had to be changed with the changing administrations. But people like Cohen and Altmeyer and Bob Ball and all those good, sound technical people should have been retained." (Interview with Nelson H. Cruikshank, Oral History Collection, Columbia University [1967], p. 108. [Hereafter, Cruikshank, OHC.]) Cohen and Ball were retained, though Cohen soon left of his own choice. The Republicans made Cohen director of research and statistics in place of I. S. Falk. He thereafter resented what he took to have been pressure to leave. The job as research director, though a better title than he had had, entailed a cut in grade and salary.

on the assumption that it was under the Republicans that the political executives' capacity for generalist supervision was most clearly tested. Democratic administrations generally supported the program executives' pursuit of expansionist goals.

Political Executives in HEW

Wilbur Cohen among the Democrats and Marion Folsom among the Republicans are conspicuous exceptions, but most political executives of both parties entered office in HEW as neophytes to social security and then stayed so briefly that expertise was hard to achieve and sustain. Between 1953 and 1973, there were nine secretaries of HEW, eight under secretaries, and seven assistant secretaries for legislation.

From the perspective of a veteran program executive, life with the political executives was a series of briefing sessions to prepare them for appearances before the highly knowledgeable committees on Capitol Hill. Robert Myers, the chief actuary, told an interviewer in 1967:

> Usually our secretaries have not been students of social security, so they'd need quite a lot of briefing. . . . Some secretaries realize that they can't learn everything in a day and that most of the questions are going to be handled by Wilbur Cohen or Bob Ball or myself; that they're just going to take the broad general ones. Other secretaries get, you might say, panicky and they think they ought to learn all about it, so that there are many more briefing sessions involved, of course, with the same result—that they can't answer the questions the committee asks them anyhow, because it's a very knowledgeable committee. . . . A secretary who's come in fresh can't match these fellows.[4]

Nor, to borrow Myers's phrase, could a secretary match the fellows in the SSA. Whether Democratic or Republican, incoming political executives had to learn their lessons on social security from the tutoring experts in the SSA and inevitably were influenced by them. They received from program executives a conceptual language—the assumptions and vocabulary by which social security was interpreted for purposes of politics and policymaking—even when the experts refrained from direct prescription and advice.

Political executives were much impressed by the executive leaders of social security, and not just by their expertise, but by the other qualities that distinguished the organization, including dedication to work,

4. Interview with Robert J. Myers, Oral History Collection, Columbia University (1967), pp. 23–26.

high morale, and internal discipline. "They were very good, and they thought they were even better than they were," one Republican who worked in HEW in the 1970s remarked. Another, a member of the secretary's office in the early 1970s, recalled with admiration how "artful" were the responses of the SSA under Ball to the stream of draft policy statements—presidential messages and the like—that routinely issued from the secretary's office for comment. Most subunits of HEW would reply that they had had insufficient time to comment and then would offer trivial corrections. A few would raise substantial objections without, however, offering a substitute. The SSA alone would send back a fully edited version with new language but written in a style perfectly suited to the consumer. As this source noted, it "minimized the chance of your inventing something on your own that would be other than what they wanted you to say about social security."[5]

In short, the SSA leaders were able, they were adroit, and they never left anything to chance. Political executives, mere transients who knew little of social security and had innumerable other matters to attend to, mostly in parts of HEW that seemed to be much less ably run than the SSA, could not escape heavy dependence on them.

Republican appointees in HEW, besides being dependent on program executives, often were liberal enough themselves to be sympathetically receptive to their advice. On the whole, Republican executives in HEW have been much more liberal than Republicans in Congress, when, indeed, they have been Republicans at all. They have not infrequently been Democrats. It is a remarkable fact that no active Republican has ever served as commissioner of social security. John W. Tramburg, who was the Eisenhower administration's first appointee, was "kind of a specious Republican," according to Mitchell, his deputy —"he was simply nonpolitical like a good many of us."[6] Charles Schottland, who succeeded him, was a Democrat who had served in the liberal Republican administration of Governor Earl Warren in California. Mitchell, who succeeded Schottland in 1959, was a career civil servant; following his retirement, he told an interviewer that although he had never registered, he was always a Democrat.[7] A Democratic administration replaced Mitchell with Robert Ball in 1962, and the Republican

5. Both sources requested anonymity.
6. Interview with William L. Mitchell, Oral History Collection, Columbia University (1965), pp. 124–26.
7. Ibid., p. 127.

administration that arrived with Richard Nixon in 1969 did not replace Ball until 1973. Then it chose a career civil servant who was comptroller of HEW. After retiring Ball headed a task force for the Democratic National Committee and advised the party's platform committee and candidate Jimmy Carter in 1976.

Above the level of social security commissioner, Republican appointees in HEW were more reliably Republican but still quite liberal by party standards. Oveta Culp Hobby, as a Texas Democrat turned Eisenhower supporter, is hard to classify, but her Republican successors—Marion B. Folsom (1955–58) and Arthur S. Flemming (1958–61)—were definitely from the party's liberal wing. So were Nelson A. Rockefeller as under secretary (1953–54) and Roswell B. Perkins (1954–57) and Elliot L. Richardson (1957–59) as assistant secretaries for legislation.[8] All were fundamentally sympathetic to the social security program, and Folsom was part of the program's founding family, having been on successive advisory councils and having stood for business support of social security. The Nixon administration of 1969–72 continued the practice of liberal appointees with Robert H. Finch (1969–70) and Richardson (1970–73) as secretaries, and John G. Veneman (1969–73) as under secretary. Republican presidents acted as if the department "belonged" to the party's liberal wing, perhaps because liberal party members sought the appointments, or because conservatives failed to seek them, or because presidents did not want to antagonize the career employees of HEW by appointing political superiors who were fundamentally unsympathetic.

Given the nature of Republican appointments to the department and the dependence of all political appointees on information from incumbent experts below them, it is plausible to suppose that the Republican political executives were much influenced by their putative subordinates in the SSA and that Republican administrations failed to halt or delay the program executives' planned developments because they were persuaded to support them. Yet this interpretation does not quite explain the events that need to be explained. Republican political executives in HEW did not in fact support the addition of disability coverage that occurred in 1956, nor did they support proposals developing in the late 1950s for the expansion of social insurance to cover hospital costs for the elderly, or a 20 percent increase in cash benefits in 1972. That they were more liberal than most other Republicans did

8. Technically, Perkins was assistant secretary for program analysis. The title of the office was later changed to assistant secretary for legislation.

not mean that they favored the kind or amount of program expansion nurtured by program executives. They typically occupied a policy position somewhere between the two.

More willing than conservative Republicans to acknowledge adverse social conditions and the need for government to act, Republican appointees were nevertheless unwilling to endorse the program executives' preference for comprehensive, compulsory measures. They were forever seeking solutions that would preserve a measure of individual choice, protect a sphere of action for private organizations, or involve the state governments. They would have done something about disability or health care, but they would have done less, and done it more slowly to allow time to judge the effectiveness of the lesser measures. They would have spent more money on enlarging social security in 1972 than conservative Republicans were willing to spend, but not as much as was spent. In following this middle path, they may well have been influenced by program executives, as they were influenced from the other side by more conservative members of their party; but they were not supine captives of the program executives. They had, or sought to have, a distinctive Republican position on issues relating to the social security system. Even with the advantages of office, though, Republican political executives could not secure precedence on the public agenda for their own proposals.

Obstacles to Partisan Control

Political executives in HEW could be no more powerful than the party they represented, and the party was a poor instrument for control of the government. The independent election of the executive and legislature in a government of constitutionally divided powers meant that party control could be divided, and when the Republicans held the presidency, it usually was. Democratic congresses sat on Capitol Hill, ready and often eager to receive the proposals of social security program executives for next moves.

Also, no matter what the range of the party's control of institutions, its effectiveness was compromised by internal differences over social welfare policy. Congressional Republicans were on the whole more conservative than executive Republicans, but there were ideological factions within both the congressional and executive portions of the party. Republicans in HEW, typically part of the liberal faction, could not count on receiving support from the President in internal contests, and even if he did support them, they could not be confident that congressional Republicans would support him.

Republican political executives in the Eisenhower administration, including the President, were unable to persuade the party's congressional leaders to back an alternative to the Forand bill for hospitalization insurance for the elderly, the program executives' favored measure (discussed in chapter 16). As one member of the secretary's office later analyzed it, the party divided four ways on the question. There were a large number of Republicans who thought nothing should be done about health care for the elderly. There were some who thought something ought to be done but hoped not to have to do it right away. There were some who thought it would be good politics to come up with a proposal that the party could point to. There were others who felt something had to be done and the party should have a program that would be accepted by Democrats too as a reasonable solution to a difficult problem. This last group, the participant-analyst concluded, was far outnumbered in the party as a whole.[9] Leading congressmen were opposed. So were political executives in the Bureau of the Budget and the Department of the Treasury. In the spring of 1960, HEW Secretary Flemming outlined a plan to a meeting of Republican congressional leaders at the White House. Although the plan was voluntary, called for participants to pay a share of the costs, and stipulated a significant role for state governments and private insurers, the congressional leaders rejected it. A week later the President publicly backed Flemming, but no Republican in the House was willing to introduce a bill incorporating his plan.[10]

Oddly, the Eisenhower administration could not rely on congressional Republicans even to oppose enlargements of social security to which the administration itself was firmly opposed. In 1956 the administration would have won its fight against disability coverage if it had had solid support from Republicans. The vote for the amendment was 49 to 47. Six Republicans voted with the majority, including one quite conservative member, George Malone of Nevada, who apparently wanted to settle a score with the administration or had been bought off by Majority Leader Lyndon Johnson with the promise of a special favor.

The Nixon administration learned the same lesson soon after taking

9. Interview with M. Allen Pond, Oral History Collection, Columbia University (1966), pp. 65–66.

10. James L. Sundquist, *Politics and Policy: The Eisenhower, Kennedy, and Johnson Years* (Brookings Institution, 1968), pp. 302–05.

office. The President supported a 10 percent increase in social security benefits in 1969, in proportion to the rise in the cost of living. Republicans in the Ways and Means Committee ignored their party leader and joined with Democratic committee members in support of a 15 percent increase.

The combination of divided party control of the government and factionalism within the Republican party opened up to program executives a fertile field for political maneuver. They rarely received explicit guidance from Republican executives in HEW, who, though putative representatives of the party, could not say what the party wanted to do. Program executives, who knew exactly what they wanted to do, could pick and choose targets of influence according to their strategic position and potential receptivity. They offered streams of proposals to Republican political executives, who were receptive to those that might be reconciled with the party's ideology and made to serve its interests. When Republicans resisted and official outlets were blocked, organized labor or program executives out of office (Wilbur Cohen after 1955) took up the work of promotion.

Unable to define policy for their own party, political executives were also unable to prevent program executives from nurturing programmatic changes quite contrary to a Republican administration's intent. Political executives might be expected to have more success in leading their executive subordinates than in leading their political party, for their powers within the executive are formal and hierarchical. Congressmen, elected independently of the President to membership in a constitutionally independent branch of government, are in no sense his formal subordinates, and it is not surprising that they often fail to follow the leadership of his administration. Within the executive branch, by contrast, the formal structure is arranged in the political executives' favor and is complemented by the civil servants' ethic of nonpartisanship, which commits them to serving the political executives of different parties impartially. Civil servants know that they are expected to serve and obey incumbent administrations, and while defining the proper range of obedience is bound to be a very difficult and subtle business, sometimes involving profound questions of law, ethics, and morality, the general expectation of loyalty gives some advantage to the administration.

The formal structure of HEW, however, was not as conducive to control by political executives as this simple hierarchical image suggests. The social security commissioner reported to the secretary of HEW and to him alone; the various assistant secretaries and other members of the secretary's staff had no authority over social security. A social security commissioner who disagreed with, say, the assistant secretary for legislation had no obligation to defer to him, and every right to carry his case directly to the secretary. This is significant because it was the secretary's staff much more than the secretary himself, a very busy man, who had the urge to supervise. "Once a secretary is in office," according to Robert Ball, "his main desire is to have things work well. He has no motivation to try to fix things that don't need fixing." For the first several decades of its operation, social security worked exceptionally well, and, again to cite Ball, "secretaries uniformly quite quickly developed the view that it was in their interest . . . to allow strong delegations to continue and not to encourage their staff assistants to interfere with the administration."[11]

Moreover, social security executives conceived of their role in a way that was not conducive to control by incumbent partisans. While they were quick to respond to the political executives' requests for advice and recommendations, their own program planning was not confined to such responses. They carried program planning ahead independently, and did not limit their plans to what they knew or could safely presume the incumbent administration would approve.[12] Even though the Eisenhower administration was known to oppose a government health insur-

11. From tape-recorded comments by Robert M. Ball addressed to the author, May 6, 1978. (Hereafter Ball transcript.)

12. Robert Ball, upon reading this passage, commented: "There is no way that an organization can fulfill its responsibility to be prepared for what may arise in the future if it waits each time for a new administration to lay out the areas in which it should do research and analyze alternative program developments. But a careful distinction needs to be made between this activity and promotion of programs contrary to the position of a president. When Marion Folsom was in office, we talked several times about the possibility of the administration backing a disability insurance program beginning at age fifty-five, and then later we discussed one beginning at age sixty. One couldn't even have discussed such a possibility without there having been work done prior to an administration taking a position. I was for it and so was Folsom, but in the end he had to testify against any kind of a disability insurance program because that was the President's decision. He gave the task of writing the testimony jointly to Rod [Roswell] Perkins and me, with a staff writer of his to actually put the words down. The reason was that Perkins was wholeheartedly and personally opposed to disability insurance and I was wholeheartedly and personally in favor of it. And what Folsom wanted was a statement against it, but still one that did not cut off all possibilities for the future and dig a big hole which he could have never climbed out of. Incidentally, we worked on that testimony all night long the night before he was to give it, and handed it to him as he went to the Hill. We fought over almost every word in it. I was, of course, not trying to develop a statement in favor of disability insurance, merely one that in opposing it didn't overdo the argument. At the time, of course, Perkins was a political appointee and I was a civil servant." Ibid.

ance program, the coverage and disability planning branch in the BOASI after 1956 had a unit assigned full time to the planning of health insurance. (But not called by that name. "Health insurance was not an official title for anything in the organization until the legislation passed," the head of health planning later told an interviewer.)[13] Neutrality, then, did not mean passivity; it did not mean waiting upon incumbent political executives for instructions. Political neutrality meant behaving the same way under Democratic and Republican administrations, and this behavior was dynamic and expansionist.

Nor did neutrality mean that advice, when it was asked for, should be given only to incumbent political executives. The Social Security Administration, Robert Ball explained to an interviewer, always took the position that it would give technical help to anyone who was trying to develop legislation. "That's the only way you can make the government work," Ball added. When Democrats in Congress passed the disability amendment in 1956 over the administration's opposition, Ball, with the approval of HEW Secretary Marion Folsom, worked with Democratic Senator Robert Kerr "on the technical matter of developing the best possible bill, which [Kerr] then got adopted on the floor of the Senate."[14] Nor was advice outside the department confined to members of Congress who were directly and immediately engaged, as was Senator Kerr, in passing legislation. It might be given to persons who did not hold public office at all, but were affiliated with private interest groups engaged in lobbying, as when SSA staff members worked at length with the AFL-CIO staff in preparing the Forand bill. Or the SSA staff might work with individual party activists functioning as assistants to congressmen or candidates. Thus in the early 1960s it gave assistance to Roswell Perkins, who had been an assistant secretary in the Republican administration of the 1950s but was then out of office and trying to prepare a liberal Republican alternative to the health insurance bills of the Kennedy administration. Neutrality, while it dictated serving political executives impartially, did not require serving them exclusively.

To give help to everyone who asks for it seems a fair enough rule. That is certainly one way for an expert bureaucracy to conceive of impartiality. Program executives in the career service can say to political figures: "You tell us what you want to do, and we will give you the

13. Interview with Irwin Wolkstein, Oral History Collection, Columbia University (1966), pp. 51–52. (Hereafter Wolkstein, OHC.)

14. Interview with Robert M. Ball, Oral History Collection, Columbia University (1967–68), pp. 11–12. (Hereafter Ball, OHC.)

information and advice that you need to do it in an effective, intelligent, and practical way." This practice did not, however, make the SSA neutral in the continuing struggle over public policy for social welfare.

The program executives' notions of neutral behavior were no help at all to the groups that wished to do nothing. Activist itself, with a heavy investment in program planning and development, the SSA received requests for assistance mostly from other activists—the party, faction, or interest group that wished to promote government action. Its advice and technical assistance were of only limited use to those political figures who wanted to do something but did not necessarily want to do it in the ways preferred by the SSA's own program planners. In the 1950s, this was the situation of Republican executives in HEW, who were looking for ways in which the federal government could help meet the costs of health care for the elderly without going as far as compulsory health coverage under social security. The SSA's technical assistance was of greatest value to those political figures—liberal Democrats in Congress, the staff of the AFL-CIO—who wanted to do what the SSA's own executives wanted to do—to meet perceived social needs by expanding the compulsory program of social insurance. To serve these consumers of assistance, the SSA staff could readily adapt the products of its own research and planning. The data and drafts were abundantly at hand. Assistance could be given relatively fast and with a fullness made possible by advance preparation, and it could be given with the energy, ingenuity, and resourcefulness that come with commitment. These consumers of technical assistance were well satisfied.

Regarding the program executives' collaboration with organized labor and other members of the liberal, pro-medicare coalition, it must be asked whether this was "technical assistance"at all. The distinction between the SSA as a technical assistant to others and as a political actor pursuing its own ends becomes very hard to draw. For example, was it technical assistance when the assistant chief of the coverage and disability planning branch, a member of the HEW general counsel's office assigned to SSA, and a secretary employed by the SSA prepared the McNamara bill in an office on Capitol Hill in 1959—the bill behind which backers of health insurance united in 1959–60? Was it technical assistance when the same assistant branch chief delivered a draft bill one night in 1960 to a Capitol Hill hotel room where Wilbur Cohen and members of organized labor were holding a strategy and drafting session?[15]

15. Wolkstein, OHC, pp. 9, 9a, 32a, 32b, 45–46.

The political consumers of the "technical assistance" so proffered did indeed have ideas of their own that might be said to constitute guidance. Always there were choices to be made over the breadth of health services covered, the classes of population to be covered, the size of deductibles, the relations between government and private providers of medical service, and the like. These were matters over which fundamentally allied parties could have a considerable difference of opinion. The SSA's technicians were not offering a fixed package, prepared in Baltimore and handed to political figures who were mere fronts for an aggressive bureaucracy. Neither can it be said, however, that the SSA staff were neutral parties in these encounters. The role of technical assistant merged indistinguishably with the role of political ally.

The delicacy and subtlety of the distinction between political activity and technical assistance made it hard for political appointees to pass judgment on the behavior of program executives. Besides, the highest ranking program executives, who were the most visible to political leaders and the most vulnerable to suspicion of political involvement, behaved with utmost sensitivity and circumspection. Ball, for example, took no part in the SSA's sessions on the Forand bill with officials of the AFL-CIO. When an interviewer asked him about his role, he cited the constraints he had been under as a civil servant. He had made it clear to political executives that he favored something like the Forand bill, but he had been unable to speak publicly about it because he was a civil servant in an administration that opposed the bill. "So a lot of these things that were going on to promote legislation I just wasn't in on," he said. "I knew about things because I had a relationship with a lot of the people that were working on it rather than being deeply involved in the political side." Ball referred the interviewer to a lower-ranking civil servant in SSA who had handled the discussions with the AFL-CIO.[16]

The political executives' influence over their programmatic subordinates appears to increase with proximity. The need to retain the confidence of political superiors and to maintain close working relations with them probably constrains program executives at the highest level, but has less effect lower down. There the norms of the civil servants' neutrality are more likely to be violated. On the other hand, it should also be said that those political executives with whom proximity was

16. Ball, OHC, pp. 10–12, 46. Accounts of the SSA's assistance to the AFL-CIO in regard to the Forand bill may be found in oral history interviews with Katherine Ellickson, Leonard Lesser and Lisbeth Bamberger Schorr, Irwin Wolkstein, and Nelson Cruikshank.

greatest—those located in HEW—were often believed to be privately sympathetic to the program executives' own ends. Program executives took satisfaction, for example, in noting that Marion Folsom endorsed the insurance approach to health care two years after leaving office.

The Republican Response

Republican appointees in HEW were not unaware of the collaboration among program executives, congressional Democrats, and organized labor.[17] To some extent they acquiesced in it. Secretary Folsom approved Ball's working with Senator Kerr on disability legislation in 1956, and in

17. The recollections of Roswell B. Perkins for an interviewer are particularly pertinent:

QUESTION: Do you know anything about the opposition [to the administration's position on disability coverage]—what they were doing in this?
PERKINS: Not a great deal. I'm reasonably sure that it was being masterminded by Wilbur Cohen from behind the scenes. It would have been virtually inconceivable, with the dedication that he had to it, that he could avoid being drawn into the discussions by those who favored the bill. It was nominally Nelson Cruikshank who headed operations but with Wilbur's extraordinarily keen strategy and advice. Also, Bob Ball I'm sure must have been operating behind the scenes to put this thing over.
QUESTION: Is this something that you suspect in retrospect or was this something that you probably knew at the time?
PERKINS: I think I probably knew it at the time.
QUESTION: But chose to overlook it.
PERKINS: I can't reconstruct my thinking on it at the time. Of course Bob and Wilbur were sufficiently astute in the way that they handled themselves so that certain of their conferences could be classified as the necessary response of government officials to requests from the Hill for information. It would be impossible to close off all telephone calls and contacts from the Hill to members of the staff of the department. They were public servants, and the fact that the administration, including the head of the department, disagrees with the positions being taken by elected representatives on the Hill doesn't give the heads of the department the right to foreclose the quest of congressmen and senators for technical and other information from the staff members in the department. Also, their personal lives and associations I never felt we could enter into. . . . It would have had to be a gestapo-like operation. . . .
QUESTION: So that you were fully aware of the fact that there were relationships continuing to exist between the AFL-CIO and people out at Social Security but had to overlook it.
PERKINS: I think that's a fair summary of it. I didn't try to know the precise nature of the relationship, but I was sufficiently sophisticated to know that probably a day wasn't going by that Wilbur Cohen and Nelson Cruikshank weren't putting their heads together—[even] before [Cohen] left the department—in one way or another over the progress of the disability benefits bill. (Interview with Roswell B. Perkins, Oral History Collection, Columbia University [1968], pp. 31, 33.)

1957 Commissioner Schottland signed a letter to the AFL-CIO legiti-
mizing exchanges between it and the SSA staff—a letter that was
arranged by SSA staff members when they began to get anxious about
the propriety of their active collaboration with labor. Some Republican
appointees may have given this sort of approval out of latent sympathy
with the program executives' goals (Schottland was unquestionably in
sympathy with them), or, in the case of collaboration with members of
Congress, they may simply have been bending to the constitutional and
political realities. The hierarchical forms of executive control over the
career program executives in the SSA were forms only. Congress, constituted and elected independently of the chief executive, was conceded
to have a right to make independent claims on the civil servants' stock of
expert advice and information. And, once this right was conceded, it
became impossible to control the character of the program executives'
communications with Congress. The political executives could never be
sure, one of them would later tell the author, whether when Ball gave
"technical assistance" to Congress he was pushing an objective of his
own or responding to a request for help in neutral fashion, but that he
had the right and the duty to give technical assistance to Congress under
the American constitutional system was not in question.[18]

   This did not mean that all Republican executives would equally have
approved the communications between career program executives and
their interest group allies, which were a different matter. It was hard to
cover aid to the AFL-CIO, along with aid to members of Congress,
under a cloak of constitutional obligation, or even a cloak of public-
serving pragmatism. While it was plausible to argue that the government would work better if Robert Ball were free to talk with Senator
Kerr about impending legislation, it was a good deal harder to argue that
the working of government depended on Ball's subordinates being free
to draft bills for the AFL-CIO. But here, in the zone where technical
assistance merged into political alliance, official relations merged in
a complex way with personal relations. The network of communication
about next steps in social security was bound by ties of personal acquaintance. Republican political executives, if they had tried harder,
might have made it harder for civil servants to communicate officially
with their interest group allies, but there is no way in a free society to
prevent people from talking to their friends.

   18. Author's interview with Elliot Richardson, December 2, 1977.

The people who decided what to do next with the social security program carried on a continuing conversation with one another. This conversation took place in different settings. It went on inside the SSA. It went on at the periodic advisory council meetings and in the conferences in Michigan. It went on whenever and wherever the family of insiders gathered, officially or unofficially. The arrival of a Republican administration did not put a stop to this conversation, but changed the pattern and locus. There were more exchanges outside the SSA and between the SSA and outsiders. The unofficial and social supports that sustained the network of communication among partisans of the program became more important when official supports weakened.

When Cohen, who had been a cue-giver and leader of the conversation from inside the SSA, moved outside, it changed the conversational pattern considerably without changing at all the actual participants. As both cue-giver and lobbyist, Cohen could function just as well outside as inside—better, in the Republican years. Roswell Perkins suspected him of leaving precisely to free himself from a civil servant's restraints. He could continue to get information—cost estimates and the like—by phone and letter from incumbent SSA officials. Republican executives could no more have put a stop to this kind of communication than they could have prevented the "commiseration party" that SSA civil servants and other members of the pro-medicare coalition held following a defeat on the Senate floor in 1960. (Commiseration was mixed with celebration, for the coalition was getting excitingly close to its objective.) A high-ranking member of the SSA was host, and the leading members of the coalition were there except for Cohen, who was having dinner with Senator Kerr and working out a substitute, the Kerr-Mills bill.[19]

If proposed initiatives in social security had bypassed them altogether, Republicans in HEW would have been more aroused, but SSA proposals came to them routinely. Ball worked closely with Republican executives in preparing the Eisenhower administration's legislative program. Richardson, who was assistant secretary for legislation at that time, spoke very favorably of relations with him to an interviewer:

I had a lot of dealings with Bob Ball. Whenever he came up with what he considered to be needed amendments to the Social Security Act, they would come through the commissioner of social security, then Schottland, to me; and we would always have a meeting in my office to discuss them in general form before they were developed more fully and before any drafting was

19. Cruikshank, OHC, p. 269.

done, and then we might have later meetings to discuss the more specific questions presented by the draft and so on.

I found him to be an extremely intelligent, completely dedicated, able man, balanced in judgment, scrupulously fair, honest in his dealings with people. He seemed to me a fine administrator and with a very intelligent awareness of the system he was administering.[20]

Nor did Richardson change this assessment after working with Ball again in 1970–71, while Richardson was secretary of HEW and Ball was commissioner of social security. Richardson took office as secretary determined that Ball should remain as commissioner despite the interest of the Nixon White House in being rid of him. "He was the greatest bureaucrat I ever worked with," Richardson said in 1977, no small tribute from a man who had by then spent several decades in public service and had served at or near the head of five of the federal government's executive departments. Richardson added that he "liked people who were resourceful infighters on behalf of their programs," and Ball was certainly one of them. "He had all the moves," Richardson remarked, and "was extremely well plugged in on the Hill," but "he was always perfectly straight in anything you called him on. If you were smart enough to ask the right questions, he would give you honest answers." Was Richardson, then, confident that as secretary of HEW he had been fully informed of Ball's actions? "Within some limits," he replied, adding that he could not be sure exactly what those limits were. If he had had more time to spend with Ball, he could have achieved more understanding of Ball's actions, given their relation of mutual confidence; but so great and varied were the demands on a department head that there could seldom be time for that kind of effort at understanding in depth.[21]

Lack of time was always a critical constraint on political executives— even for one like Richardson, who was more than ordinarily willing to master the substance of policy, to work at developing a party position, and to solicit the program executives' cooperation. As assistant secretary in the Eisenhower administration, Richardson had set out to prepare a health bill that would use the social insurance approach but be stamped with Republican principles. He gave the career experts guidance that called for providing benefits as a right rather than on the basis of need, introducing guarantees of individual choice, and providing for the great-

20. Interview with Elliot Richardson, Oral History Collection, Columbia University (1967), p. 53. (Hereafter Richardson, OHC.)

21. Interview with the author, December 2, 1977.

est practical degree of participation by commercial insurance carriers. They raised objections on administrative grounds, and Richardson left the department before he could bring the effort to a satisfactory conclusion. He could not decide how to appraise the merit of their objections:

I've often wondered whether if I'd stuck it out, fought it through and ironed out some of the problems, a plan along these lines might not have been presented by the administration in 1960. . . .

I've never had an opportunity to go back to this and spend enough time on it to make up my own mind whether the administrative difficulties that were presented by the departmental personnel were really insuperable. I don't think it would be fair to say that they raised difficulties because they were psychologically committed to a wholly government program. I think it's sufficient to say that I wasn't satisfied when I broke off my involvement with the problem that they were indeed insuperable.[22]

The President

Presidents have so many other responsibilities (the conduct of foreign relations, command of the armed forces, party leadership, promulgation of a program of domestic legislation, symbolic leadership of the country) and are so busy that they do not have much time to spend supervising all of the executive agencies that they nominally head. Some departments receive more attention from the president than others (State, Defense, Treasury) because they support him in the exercise of responsibilities that are especially exigent; others, including most of the domestic departments, are likely to command the president's attention only when trouble occurs—an administrative blunder that threatens to embarrass him, or an issue that requires his intervention to settle. Historically, social security has not raised this sort of trouble. "You get very few complaints," a former social security commissioner recalled of the administrative operations of the program. "The result is that the Social Security Administration is kind of the fair-haired boy of the

22. Richardson, OHC, pp. 37–40. Robert Ball, upon reading this passage, commented: "I still think that Richardson's idea was unworkable. Essentially the problem was that he would have had people pay over their lifetime toward paid-up health insurance in old age, just as the final medicare program did. The problem, though, was that he wanted people to be able to elect into and out of the system so that some would reach age sixty-five having paid in for a few years and others having paid in for all their years of coverage. I still see no way to work this out, and not just because I'm a Democrat." Ball transcript.

department and certainly of the party in power because you're passing out 19,000,000 checks a month. That's always very nice."[23]

If social security was not a probable source of trouble for the president, was it not on his mind as a potential source of political gain? It offered a way to supply benefits to a large and generally appealing constituency, the aged. As the number of beneficiaries rose with time, presidents of both parties began to find it very attractive as such and sponsored liberalizations, but they also had to balance the political attractions of bigger benefits against the political costs of higher taxes and weigh the macroeconomic effects of program enlargements. In making these choices, some Democrats were much more committed to liberalizations than others (Lyndon Johnson, for example, compared with John Kennedy), and Democrats in general were of course more committed than Republicans. Republicans might, indeed, have been expected to use the special resources of presidential power to contain unwanted expansion, such as the enactment of disability coverage in 1956 and a 20 percent increase in benefits in 1972.

As chief executive, the president possesses unique assets. He has the constitutional power to veto the acts of Congress. Whereas Republican political executives in HEW might not be able to prevent Wilbur Cohen

23. Interview with Charles I. Schottland, Oral History Collection, Columbia University (1965), p. 76. Social security also offered frequent opportunities for thoroughly benign symbolic gestures by the president, including the recognition of such milestones as the birthdays of extremely aged recipients or the mailing of a check to the x-millionth beneficiary. In 1965, for example, President Johnson sent greetings on her ninety-first birthday to Ida Fuller of Brattleboro, Vermont, whom the SSA had long honored as the "first" social security beneficiary, and explained to her that she would soon get an extra social security check as a result of his having signed a benefit increase into law. Milestone beneficiaries, to be honored if possible in White House ceremonies, were picked by the SSA with great care. In 1968, the SSA's acting commissioner recommended as a 24-millionth beneficiary "a dignified and respectable citizen" who was about to retire as superintendent of buildings and grounds at Johns Hopkins Hospital in Baltimore. His race, age, marital status, and job history were given, and he was described as "personable and photogenic." (Letter, Lyndon Johnson to Ida Fuller, September 3, 1965, Gen WE 6 WHCF, Lyndon Baines Johnson Library, Austin, Texas; Memo, Arthur Hess to Wilbur Cohen, May 24, 1968, Gen WE 4 WHCF, LBJ Library; and Memo, Wilbur Cohen to Douglass Cater, May 27, 1968, Gen. WE 4 WHCF, LBJ Library.) Documents in the Johnson Library also show that the President was concerned with such administrative matters as the amount of employment in the SSA's district office in Austin, Texas, and the choice of a manager for that office, but that degree of involvement in SSA operations was unusual among presidents. In the Johnson administration, relations between the White House and the SSA sometimes dealt with matters as minor as the assignment of a social security number to the newborn child of a White House aide.

from leaving office to pursue a disability bill, a president could refuse to sign the result. Also, the president is assisted by a sizable staff of career civil servants—generalists, yet knowledgeable and experienced— who are strongly imbued with the norm of institutional loyalty. Founded in 1921, the Bureau of the Budget was older than the FSA or HEW and unencumbered by particular programmatic commitments. The Budget Bureau existed to serve the president, whoever he might be, and to perform central staff functions on his behalf. Among those functions was legislative clearance, the review of departmental proposals to assure that they were "in accord with the program of the President." Here was, at the least, an additional check on the actions of program executives, possibly more effective than departmental checks precisely because more detached. In fact, neither the president's veto nor the president's staff had much effect on the development of social security.

No Republican president ever vetoed a measure expanding the program. Democratic congresses, which were the congresses that Republican presidents almost always faced, enjoyed sending Republican presidents expensive social security bills that they either had to sign, contrary to the party's principles, or had to veto, contrary to the party's interests. Republican presidents signed the bills. Possibly the hint of vetoes sometimes had a restraining effect. In 1958, for example, Democratic Senator Robert Kerr defended the Finance Committee's benefit proposals against liberal Democratic amendments on the floor by citing the prospect of a veto. "I do not propose to kid the old people in Oklahoma," Kerr said. "They would not receive any benefit from a veto. They could not eat a veto. They could not clothe themselves in a veto."[24] But there is not much evidence that the threat of a veto has consistently been a restraining force, or that Republican presidents have bargained with it successfully to reduce the impact of unwanted measures. On the contrary, it is likely that competition between Democratic congresses and Republican presidents for political credit caused the program to grow faster in periods of divided government than it would have if both the executive and legislative branches had been controlled by the same party, even if that party were the Democrats. During Republican administrations, Democratic congresses have outbid presidential offers of benefit increases and either dared him to cast a veto at great political risk or denied him the use of the veto by attaching the increase to a veto-proof

24. *Congressional Record* (August 16, 1958), p. 17959.

bill such as a last-minute increase in the debt limit. The only president ever to use the veto in regard to social security used it to protect the program. Democrat Harry Truman three times vetoed acts of the Republican Eightieth Congress that narrowed coverage by narrowing the definition of "employee" under the Social Security Act and excluding certain newspaper and magazine vendors. (The vetoed acts were inspired partly by a belief that administrative interpretations of the term "employee" had exceeded congressional intentions, and Democrats joined Republicans to override two of Truman's three vetoes.)

Vetoes are always hard to use because they are the very last step in the legislative process. In their nature, they thwart a legislative majority already formed and made formal by the public act of voting. Presidents seek to use their power more effectively by using it sooner and making the administration's position known in the early stages of legislation. Legislative clearance procedures are meant to assure that communications to Congress correctly state the president's views. As a technique of political supervision over social security, however, legislative clearance by the Bureau of the Budget added little or nothing to what was done in the department. Budget Bureau reviews depended heavily on formal submissions and focused on gross amounts of expenditure and on interagency coordination. The bureau's clearances resolved themselves largely into clearance with other executive agencies—Labor, Treasury, or whatever—to which the bureau routinely submitted bills for comment. Its supervision did not reach deeply into the SSA's own legislative planning or widely into negotiations with congressional committees. Congressional committees did not invite representatives of the president's staff to attend the executive sessions at which the content of legislation was normally settled on.

The remoteness of the Bureau of the Budget from social security legislation may be illustrated by an incident in 1960. Congress finished action on omnibus amendments in the late summer, following a partisan preelection debate over how to provide health care for the aged. HEW sent President Eisenhower a draft of a statement to be issued when he signed the bill, but the Budget Bureau's staff argued that he should not use it. As an example of what they objected to, they cited HEW's proposed statement that a change in the retirement test was "a significant improvement" that followed an approach developed by the department. "The fact is," the bureau staff wrote, "that the administration opposed a liberalization in the retirement test and that on White

House instruction the Bureau of the Budget did not give the Department clearance for any recommendations on this subject." The department had nonetheless submitted a report to the Ways and Means Committee "without Budget Bureau clearance or knowledge."[25]

This kind of tension between the SSA and the Budget Bureau has not been confined to Republican presidencies. The Bureau's staff under President Truman was similarly piqued by the SSA's failure to keep in touch about the 1950 amendments to the Social Security Act at a time when there was no doubt of the President's general support of what the SSA was doing.[26] The earliest initiatives for health insurance, what became the Wagner-Murray-Dingell bill in 1943, went to the Hill without being cleared formally with the President's staff. Arthur Altmeyer told an interviewer:

We had to function in the role of providing technical assistance to members of Congress who were prepared to take the responsibility. I as chairman discussed the matter with the other members of the board, and they were all agreeable to having the Division of Research and Statistics provide the data and draft the bill. And I testified in favor of the subject matter and the program, but I never, as I recall, specifically endorsed the bill itself in all of its details. . . . I think that my public speeches endorse all of the things included in the Wagner-Murray-Dingell bill. But I didn't say that I was supporting or that the administration was advocating the passage of the Wagner-Murray-Dingell bill because I wasn't officially in a position to do so. You see, you have to get clearance from the Bureau of the Budget and we never got clearance from the Bureau of the Budget. We never pressed for clearance, as I recall.[27]

25. "Enrolled Bill H. R. 12580, Social Security Act Amendments of 1960," memo, Michael S. March, Labor and Welfare Division to P. S. Hughes, September 8, 1960 (File HR 12580-86 PL 778 R8-2/60.1 vol. III, National Archives).

26. "FSA Report on H. R. 6000," memo, I. M. Labovitz to the Director via J. W. Jones, FSA Report, January 16, 1950 (File Social Security Act Amendments of 1948 and 1949—Public Welfare Act of 1949, R8-4/48.4 vol. II, National Archives).

27. Interview with Arthur J. Altmeyer, Oral History Collection, Columbia University (1967) pp. 36–37. (Hereafter Altmeyer, OHC.) I. S. Falk, director of research and statistics for the SSB, who, with Wilbur Cohen, was the principal author of the Wagner-Murray-Dingell bill, recalled nevertheless that the Bureau of the Budget and the White House staff had been consulted informally. "We were in each other's offices and in each other's hair, too," he told an interviewer. "We were working with global omnibus programs, and with fractional programs. We had scores of explorations of that kind going on. And very gingerly the board would decide what it would put out in its annual report or in a speech that Altmeyer would make or someone else would make and try them out. And the White House and the Budget Bureau were watching the reactions to see what they would endorse and what they wouldn't. This wasn't any solo performance." Interview with I. S. Falk, Oral History Collection, Columbia University (1965–68), pp. 241–42.

To have gone through the clearance process would have given SSA officials the right to speak as the President's agents. However, Altmeyer had reason to believe that clearance could not be obtained. He had asked the President what kind of health legislation he would support, and Roosevelt had said a limited hospital construction program financed with grants-in-aid to the states—that was all. As Altmeyer recalled it, Roosevelt did not oppose introduction of the Wagner-Murray-Dingell bill as a trial balloon, a way of testing sentiment, but was not prepared to back it. Lack of clearance did not compel program executives to keep silent. Under the strategically convenient cloak of technical assistance, program executives could proceed independently of the President's office, and in a Democratic administration, in contrast to a Republican one, this could be done with the confident presumption that political executives tacitly approved of what was being done.

The Democrats in Office

If having Republicans in control of the executive branch was not as big a disadvantage to program executives as it might seem, neither was the incumbency of Democrats an unalloyed advantage. It was advantageous, of course, to have the backing of political administrators for big initiatives. There was some limit to what could be done through pressure group allies. Medicare could be kept alive and on the agenda in the Republican years, but so momentous a change, involving so complicated a law, could best be achieved—perhaps could only be achieved—through the full mobilization of the career bureaucracy, including the general counsel's office, and that required the administration's support. With the Democrats back in HEW after 1960, the official base of activity expanded rapidly but not always harmoniously. In a way, there was more tension and conflict in the program executives' relations with Democratic administrators than with Republicans, for it was harder to maintain distance from the Democrats. When Democrats were in office great things could be undertaken, but they had to be undertaken in collaboration with political officials. As the burden of cooperation increased, so did the incidence of conflict. Tension developed over strategy, tactics, and the division of labor. Recrimination followed defeats.

Such had been the case after defeat of the Wagner-Murray-Dingell bill during the Truman administration. Each side, the political and the programmatic, concluded that the other did not understand politics. Oscar R. Ewing, who was FSA administrator under Truman, told an interviewer:

[I. S.] Falk [with Cohen the drafter of the bill] was an excellent technician on this subject. . . . My one criticism of him was that, in a way, he had little feeling for the politics of the situation. The Wagner-Murray-Dingell bill as introduced in Congress seemed to me to have unnecessarily stirred up certain oppositions that didn't need to be stirred up. For instance, it provided that the government could set the price of drugs. Well, that got the whole pharmaceutical industry against the bill, whereas it was not necessary at all. . . . Falk very honestly thought that it was wise to get all the opposition out at once and take care of it. I would have preferred the gradual approach. But the pattern for that was set before I ever got into office.[28]

According to Ewing, following defeat of the Wagner-Murray-Dingell bill it was his idea to adopt the less inclusive approach that ultimately succeeded.

Altmeyer's recollection was the reverse of Ewing's. He recalled that he and Cohen decided they ought to suggest a reduced proposal to Ewing as something that might be rescued from the wreckage. According to him, it was Ewing who had pushed too hard for too much on health insurance:

When it came to legislation, his feeling was that he had authority and responsibility—and he did; there's no question about it; he was right. This meant that instead of the surgeon general and the chairman of the Social Security Board developing a program and going up on the Hill to explain it and push it, he was going to be the one who would develop a program, depending— I'm sure he would say—[on] his subordinates to give him technical advice. But he would make all the decisions as to what went into the legislation, and he would be the one to interpret it and he would be the one to push it. He felt that in that regard he was far superior to any of his subordinates because he was a politician that knew how to talk with politicians, and whether he knew anything about administration, he did know everything there was to be known about political action. . . .

So he really got going great guns and we shivered as regards health insurance because we felt that there were many shoals there and that the ship of state had to be steered pretty carefully to avoid them.[29]

Similar tensions recurred in the successful yet halting drive for medicare between 1961 and 1965 (discussed in chapter 16). The political protagonist in this case was Ivan A. Nestingen, a former mayor of Madison, Wisconsin, whom Kennedy had appointed under secretary of HEW to

28. Interview with Oscar R. Ewing, Oral History Collection, Columbia University (1966), pp. 41–42.
29. Altmeyer, OHC, pp. 131–32.

pay off a political debt. Nestingen set out to take charge of the administration's campaign for medicare although in doing so he was certain to conflict with Cohen, who was then assistant secretary for legislation. At one point, the White House put Nestingen rather than Cohen in charge of the administration's presentation in congressional hearings. Pro-medicare activists in Washington divided into a Nestingen camp whose orientation was political and a Cohen camp which was programmatic. At one point, following a defeat in 1962, things were so bad that the President was persuaded to give the two groups a pep talk and to appeal to them to cooperate. Ill-feeling was so strong that some at the White House meeting would not shake Cohen's hand. For his part, Cohen looked on Nestingen and his followers as a bunch of blundering interlopers.

The differing goals of Republican political executives and program executives precluded cooperation on leading issues of program expansion, medicare above all, but when the Democrats were in office, the sharing of goals created a presumption that cooperation was possible, and in the effort to cooperate the differences between politically oriented and programmatically oriented officials were revealed. In the course of building their program, program executives had also built a network of relationships with other policymakers—the congressional committees, most importantly—who had some continuing share of responsibility for the program and some proprietary interest in it. Political executives, transients in the department, were not particularly sensitive to the existence of this network, were not integrated into it, did not understand its rules for making policy, and did not attach much importance to observing the rules. (In the eyes of the Cohen group, the indifference of the Nestingen group to costs showed how naive they were about social security policy. One said: "The Nestingen people wanted to throw this in and that in. . . . And people who had worked in Social Security always knew that you had to meet the costs; and if you didn't do that and Bob Myers said it wasn't actuarially sound, you were never going to get any place.")[30] As administrators, program executives also had to be sensitive to prospective working relations with hospitals, physicians, and insurers, whereas political executives did not. Program executives, in short, were accommodationist, nonideological, and quite attentive to the working relations needed to sustain their program. Political officials, more willing to accept conflict, were looking for partisan

30. Interview with Leonard Lesser and Lisbeth Bamberger Schorr, Oral History Collection, Columbia University (1967), pp. 57–58.

and presidential victories that could be advertised to a mass constituency.[31] Their approach to legislation was to arrange mass rallies, whereas the approach of the Cohen group was to calculate votes in the Ways and Means Committee and to ask themselves what changes in their bill could win over another vote, the ultimate prize, of course, being the vote of Chairman Mills.

When the law was finally written in 1965, it was Cohen, the epitome of the inside strategist, who sat down with Mills and his Ways and Means Committee to work it all out. Cohen replaced Nestingen as under secretary after the election and, as a program executive turned political executive, brought a highly accommodationist approach to the congressional negotiations. With a program executive completely in charge for the administration, the conflict with political executives evaporated. Significantly, even in Democratic administrations, when the larger, more activist, talent-laden party was in power, a distinctively partisan leadership did not take charge of executive policymaking for social security. It was the other way around: the leading program executives moved into partisan positions. The Democrats appointed Robert Ball as social security commissioner and came to rely on Cohen to manage the passage of health insurance legislation.

POLITICAL EXECUTIVES do not figure prominently in the portrait of social security policymakers being constructed in this part of the book. They depended for influence on their position as party leaders, but the parties barely existed as sources or instruments of guidance regarding social security. Transients in the government, pressed for time while there, and typically inexpert, they came to depend very much on career program executives for advice, interpretation, and proposals. Nor did they constitute a powerful constraining presence, for they accommodated to norms that gave career program executives great latitude in communicating with congressmen, pressure groups, party activists, and others outside the executive branch. Such communication was acceptable if confined to "technical assistance," and technical assistance was acceptable on the theory that it was politically neutral. But in the practice of policymaking, it was not neutral. It aided most of all those participants who shared the program executives' programmatic ends.

31. Altmeyer speculated that Oscar Ewing in 1947–48 saw national health insurance as a political vehicle that would carry him to high office, perhaps even the presidency itself. Altmeyer, OHC, p. 133.

CHAPTER FOUR

Advisory Councils

IN VIEW of what is said in preceding chapters about policymaking for social security, it would be surprising to find that a group of outsiders—citizens serving part time in advisory councils—have carried much weight. The pattern that is emerging is one of constricted participation. At the core of policymaking were a small number of highly expert program executives and a small number of congressional committee members some of whom in time became expert themselves. If political executives, holders of high office inside the government, could not find places in this proprietary network, it would be surprising to find that appointees to advisory councils could.

And yet they have. The student of social security policymaking soon learns that he is expected by program executives and close observers of social security affairs to take citizen advisory councils seriously, as places where important decisions are made.

Citizen advisory councils have been created for social security intermittently since the start of the program, and in 1956 were prescribed by statute. Here as elsewhere in the federal executive branch, which contained over 1,200 such committees and councils in 1973, they are a familiar form.[1] Probably more in social security than in other programs, they are also regarded as significant. The most important of them in the past have been integral to policymaking, and their deliberations constituted a useful, possibly vital, stage in achieving consensus on major measures. Before both the 1939 and 1950 amendments, they functioned much like precongressional legislatures, representative bodies in which the major affected interests reached agreement about significant policy

1. *Federal Advisory Committees: Second Annual Report of the President Covering Calendar Year 1973* (GPO, 1974), pp. 1–3.

proposals. Nonetheless, it would not be accurate to see the councils as consisting of outsiders who successfully staked out a policymaking role independent of other policymakers. More accurately, the advisory council became for the SSA's executives a convenient mechanism of "cooptation"—in Selznick's classic definition, "the process of absorbing new elements into the leadership or policy-determining structure of an organization as a means of averting threats to its stability or existence."[2] Though the councils were discontinuous—each one was created anew— their leadership was continuous. A few individuals served time after time, developed their own strong sense of proprietorship in the program, and were absorbed into the structure of policymaking. Through them, and through the SSA leadership's influence on the councils' deliberations, the councils as a whole were absorbed too.

Origin and Structure

Program executives did not initially conceive of the advisory council as an instrument of cooptation. Arthur Altmeyer, as chairman of the Social Security Board, did not want to create the first council. It was thrust upon him in 1937 by the chief Republican critic of the program on Capitol Hill, Senator Arthur H. Vandenberg.

Perhaps it was the recollection of experience in 1934 that made Altmeyer wary. There had been an advisory council to the Committee on Economic Security then, and it had not worked well. It was quite large. Some of the members were highly opinionated. The CES staff was so engrossed in its own work that it did not know what to do with a group of advisors, and the council was assembled so late—just two weeks before the deadline for the committee's report to the President— that even the pretense of meaningful advisory participation was impossible to sustain. The members concluded that they were being used, and they rebelled. In all, it was not an experience that Altmeyer would have cared to repeat, but when Vandenberg insisted in a Finance Committee hearing that an outside group be formed, Altmeyer could not get out of it.

If nothing else, the partisan and critical context of Vandenberg's proposal would have made Altmeyer reluctant. Urged on by leaders of

2. Philip Selznick, *TVA and the Grass Roots: A Study in the Sociology of Formal Organization* (University of California Press, 1949), p. 13.

the insurance industry, Vandenberg was conducting a fervent campaign against the accumulation of a large reserve fund, which conservatives feared would encourage government profligacy and undermine private investment opportunities. He had introduced a concurrent resolution calling on the Social Security Board to prepare a plan to abandon the huge reserve, and the Finance Committee was holding hearings on this resolution. Altmeyer agreed that the board would make a study, but Vandenberg was not satisfied with this. "With great respect to the Social Security Board," he said, "I am not willing to leave the investigation solely with them, because I think it is prejudiced in favor of the existing system."[3] He proposed that Congress make its own study. Thus trapped, Altmeyer agreed to the creation of an advisory committee that would be responsible jointly to the Finance Committee and to the Social Security Board. The appointment of the council was announced in May by Senator Pat Harrison, Finance Committee chairman, and Altmeyer, but Altmeyer was still reluctant to proceed. By September the council still had not met and Altmeyer was unsure whether it should. He solicited President Roosevelt's advice on the point and was told to go ahead.

Altmeyer need not have been so anxious. Before very long the twenty-five-member council was agreeing to nearly all of the SSB's proposals for change in the 1935 law, including the very significant recommendation that monthly benefits be paid to surviving dependents of deceased workers. Marion B. Folsom, who was one of the representatives of business on the council, recalled the experience:

Now, if you had taken a vote on this council when we started in, I bet you would have found about two to one against survivors' benefits. Before we got through, we were all for it. You see, we met with the social security people. They sat in on all our discussions, so everybody came out all together on the thing. When we got through, we were pretty well unanimous on it. . . . That really was an educational process—that committee.[4]

This second and far more favorable experience with an advisory council showed the leaders of the Social Security Administration that the form need not be feared—could, in fact, be quite useful—and in 1947 they urged the Senate Committee on Finance to create a council again. The social security payroll tax was scheduled to rise from 1 percent to 2.5 percent (for both employers and employees) in 1948, but

3. *Reserves under Federal Old-Age Benefit Plan—Social Security Act*, Hearing before the Senate Committee on Finance, 75 Cong. 1 sess. (GPO, 1937), p. 22.
4. Interview with Marion B. Folsom, Oral History Collection, Columbia University (1965–68), pp. 116–17, 205. (Hereafter Folsom, OHC.)

the SSA leaders were sure that Congress would postpone the increase as it had always done before. Rather than try to prevent the freeze on the rate, SSA executives and their allies in organized labor elected to accept it but simultaneously to ask the Finance Committee for a new advisory council. They approached Senator Vandenberg with the idea, and Senators Eugene Millikin and Walter F. George, the ranking members of the committee, introduced the necessary resolution, which authorized the committee to create an advisory council to study coverage, benefits, taxes, and all other aspects of social security. Congress was Republican at the time, and Senator Millikin, as the committee's Republican leader, took charge of constituting the council in consultation with Senator George.

That the council of 1947–48 was created under Republican auspices increased the frustration of partisan critics of social security when this council too endorsed the social insurance program and called for enlargement along traditional lines. In the House in 1949, Representative Carl T. Curtis filed a minority report in the Ways and Means Committee that criticized social insurance comprehensively and concluded with a critique of the advisory council in particular. Because they were important people, Curtis said, the members had been too busy to make an independent study and almost inevitably accepted the proposals of the Social Security Administration. Curtis called for a study by persons who could work full time for several months and be wholly independent of the administration.[5]

The third in this series of advisory groups alarmed the SSA leadership, for it was created by a Republican administration at a time when the political environment in general was more threatening than ever before. For a brief time, the advisory group itself seemed a threat.

In the fall of 1952, soon after the election of President Eisenhower, the U.S. Chamber of Commerce issued a policy declaration that the SSA leaders took to be a fundamental attack on their program. It called for covering all of the aged and for pay-as-you-go financing.[6] The SSA interpreted this as a repudiation of contributory, wage-related social insurance. Program executives feared that an incoming Republican administration, in combination with a Republican Congress, might be receptive to this proposal from a conservative source, and this fear intensi-

5. *Social Security Act Amendments of 1949*, H. Rept. 1300, 81 Cong. 1 sess. (GPO, 1949), p. 184.
6. The Chamber of Commerce statement is discussed in chapter 6.

fied momentarily when the new FSA administrator, Oveta Culp Hobby, began meeting informally with a five-member advisory group of whom three had been members of the Chamber of Commerce committee on social security policy. Partisans of social security labeled it "the Hobby lobby."

In response to criticism from organized labor, Mrs. Hobby promptly enlarged her "lobby" into a conventionally representative group. Seven members were added, including two members each from organized labor and organized agriculture, and this enlarged committee, meeting in the spring of 1953, followed its predecessors down the path of uncritical support for the established program. It declined to consider the chamber's plan, which was tantamount to opposing it. Its own report consisted of a series of recommendations for increased coverage, steps on which Republicans and Democrats, business and labor, could agree. That was the one kind of expansion that conservatives wished to push farther and faster than liberals. It was an easy thing to get agreement on, even in a time of political turbulence.

Once again, the staff work was done by SSA. Roswell B. Perkins, a young Republican lawyer who entered the Hobby administration with an assignment to work on social security, later recalled that the consultants' advisory report was "a straight SSA report . . . just churned up right out of Ball's boys."[7]

Mrs. Hobby's consultants were the last advisory group to be assembled ad hoc. The Social Security Act amendments of 1956 formalized the councils by providing that they should be created periodically. The first statutory council was to be appointed in 1957, and succeeding ones were to be set up in advance of each scheduled tax increase. This provision was added, it appears, at the request of the AFL-CIO, which may well have concluded after the experience of 1953 that it was risky to leave too much to chance and the discretion of the secretary of health, education, and welfare. The law provided that the commissioner of social security should serve as chairman of the advisory council, and that twelve other persons should represent employers and employees in equal numbers and self-employed persons and the public, a composition that of itself gave partisans of the program an influential if not dominant position.

At first the AFL-CIO was not wholly satisfied with the consequences

7. Interview with Roswell B. Perkins, Oral History Collection, Columbia University (1968), pp. 139–41. (Hereafter Perkins, OHC.)

of the change. The law of 1956 provided that the council should study financing only, contrary to the AFL-CIO's initial request that it consider the adequacy of benefits too. In 1958 the Republican administration took the position that benefit increases should await an advisory council report in 1959, a tactic that the AFL-CIO's Nelson Cruikshank said perverted the purpose of the councils. "The Secretary's suggestion that we hold back and do nothing for a while until this council can report seems to me to be against the trend," he said, "because advisory councils have recommended broadening and improving the programs, how to broaden them, how to improve them, how to extend coverage, and this seems to me to be putting the council to the use of how to hold back the program, which is certainly against what the experience of the advisory councils has been."[8] In fact, Congress increased benefits as well as taxes in 1958 without having heard from the advisory council, and in 1960 it amended the law to provide that the next (1963–65) council should consider extensions of coverage, the adequacy of benefits, and all other aspects of the program besides its financial condition.

The statutory councils, like their less formal predecessors, applauded the program and attested to its financial soundness. "[The] almost universal acceptance of this program of social insurance is well deserved," the 1957–59 council said. "The Council finds that the present method of financing . . . is sound, practical, and appropriate for this program."[9] The council of 1963–65 endorsed the extension of social insurance to cover medical costs of the elderly and disabled. The council of 1969–71 helped lay the basis for a 20 percent benefit increase in 1972 by endorsing a change in actuarial techniques.

This brief history poses an obvious puzzle. The six advisory groups between 1937 and 1971 were strikingly different in their origins and strikingly similar in their results. The first one was inspired by Congress, even if it was technically a joint executive-legislative creature. The second was created by Congress though inspired by executives behind the scenes. The third was created by the administration acting alone. The last three were appointed by the executive (the secretary of HEW) according to statutory prescription. The second, third, fourth, and sixth

8. *Social Security Legislation*, Hearings before the House Committee on Ways and Means, 85 Cong. 2 sess. (GPO, 1958), p. 768.

9. *Financing Old-Age, Survivors, and Disability Insurance: A Report of the Advisory Council on Social Security Financing* (Washington, D.C.: the Council, 1959), pp. 2–3.

councils began under Republican auspices. So did the first, if Vandenberg is regarded as its originator. Only one—the council of 1963–65—was unequivocally the creature of a Democratic administration. Yet they all approved the program fundamentally. None ever produced a substantial, significant critique of it. Most called for major expansion.

Relations with the SSA

Robert Myers, as chief actuary of the SSA, stood always a bit apart from the other program executives, privately not altogether of the faith, and one sign of Myers's detachment was his assessment of the advisory councils. "They were biased," he told an interviewer in 1967. The membership was "always selected so that you include a majority of the people who are going to think the way you want them to think." In Myers's opinion, the councils ought to contain "people on all sides of the fence," including the side that favored a need-based, means-tested form of assistance to the aged.[10]

Opinion in the councils was of course not completely uniform, but differences were confined within a spectrum defined by acceptance of social insurance as a general approach to aiding dependent persons. "I have long been a strong supporter of the principles that have been incorporated in our social security program," Reinhard Hohaus, an insurance company executive, wrote in 1965, in a separate statement that questioned the arguments for medicare. This was typical of advisory council dissents; it was a dissent at the margins. Hohaus questioned only the proposed expansion to include health insurance and not the basic principles.[11]

The councils were ordinarily composed of three groups—representatives of labor, of business, and of "the public." For various reasons (analyzed in chapter 5), organized labor generally supported the social security program uncritically. Businessmen were a more likely source of dissent, except that the businessmen who served on advisory councils were in general distinguished by their relative liberalism. They were the

10. Interview with Robert J. Meyers, Oral History Collection, Columbia University (1963), pp. 67–68. (Hereafter Myers, OHC.)

11. *The Status of the Social Security Program and Recommendations for Its Improvement: Report of the Advisory Council on Social Security* (Washington, D.C.: the Council, 1965), pp. 93–94.

statesmen of the corporate world, businessmen with a social conscience, whose own corporations (for example, General Electric, Eastman Kodak) had been leaders in the development of pension plans. The public members were typically university professors with an interest in social insurance. In 1963–65, when the subject of health insurance was to be considered, the medical profession was represented by the president of the National Medical Association, an organization of black physicians, and not by the American Medical Association, which was implacably hostile to government health insurance.

Even when SSA executives did not, as in 1937, directly participate in constituting the councils, they suggested names informally to the appointing authorities in Congress or the HEW secretary's office. They knew who their friends were, and their friends identified potential friends. Thus, for example, in finding businessmen to serve on the councils, Altmeyer consulted Folsom, a reliably sympathetic business executive whose identification with the social security program dated from service on the advisory council of 1935. Without any prompting from SSA executives, organized labor could be counted on to insist on membership in advisory groups. Nelson Cruikshank of the AFL-CIO recalled for an interviewer how Senator Millikin had been importuned privately to include labor representatives in the council of 1947–48, through a plumbers' union official who had belonged to the legislature in Colorado, Millikin's home state.[12] In 1953 labor pressured Mrs. Hobby publicly to expand her consultants' group. After 1956, of course, labor was guaranteed representation by statute, and labor representation of itself guaranteed a solid bloc of support for the program within the advisory councils.

With the exception of the council of 1947–48, the advisory councils were always staffed by the SSA. Altmeyer, Cohen, and others attended the meetings of the council of 1937–39, and the headquarters organization prepared proposals, supporting technical data, and legislative drafts. "It is essential," Cohen later wrote, "that such a council be given adequate technical assistance, not only so that it can do a good job but in order that it will not set up a separate staff by itself."[13] The SSA served the councils with its customary energy and competence. (The technique,

12. Interview with Nelson H. Cruikshank, Oral History Collection, Columbia University (1967), p. 39. (Hereafter Cruikshank, OHC.)

13. Wilbur J. Cohen to M. S. Pitzele, August 28, 1941 (File 025 Federal Security Agency, R. G. 47, SSA Central Files 1935–1947, Box 15, National Archives).

so it seemed to the heretical Myers, was to "flood them with material that they can't possibly read, and then they're so embarrassed that they haven't read it all that they don't dare speak too much because somebody is going to say, 'Oh, didn't you read this?' ")[14] Being amply served by the SSA, advisory councils had no motive to look elsewhere for staff assistance unless for independent expertise.[15]

Senator Millikin appears to have sought independent expertise in 1947. The charter of the 1947–48 council authorized it to appoint its own staff, as well as to request assistance from the executive branch. The result of Millikin's interest in being served by "outsiders" was the hiring of Robert Ball as staff director. Ball by then had had seven years of experience in the SSA, but had left it in 1946 to give training in social welfare and public administration to state and federal officials under the auspices of the American Council on Education. Several other members of his small staff in 1947–48 had had experience in the SSA, and his executive assistant was on detail from the agency. When Representative Carl Curtis charged that the advisory council had lacked independent expertise, Millikin replied that it was impossible to obtain. "The cold fact of the matter is that the basic information is alone in the possession of the Social Security Administration," he told Curtis. "There is no private actuary for any insurance company, including the biggest, that can give you the complete picture on this subject. . . . I spent a whole summer working on that problem, sweating here in Washington when I did not have sense enough to stay in the Senate Office Building, trying to find those kinds of people, and I finally—by the admission of the people in private business—had to give up the job because those people were not available. They did not have them."[16] Through the ubiquitous Cohen, the SSA kept informed of the council's work, and it performed staff assistance for the labor members. When one business member prepared a statement in favor of holding the line on the wage base, Cohen drafted a statement for the labor members in support of a big increase. When the same business member prepared a statement opposing a disability insurance program, Cohen supplied the labor

14. Myers, OHC, p. 62.

15. See the comments of the chairman of the 1974–75 advisory council, W. Allen Wallis, in *Financing the Social Security System,* Hearings before the Subcommittee on Social Security of the House Committee on Ways and Means, 94 Cong. 1 sess. (GPO, 1975), p. 104.

16. *Social Security Revision,* Hearings before the Senate Committee on Finance, 81 Cong. 2 sess. (GPO, 1950), pt. 3, pp. 1953–54.

members with a statement in support of one.[17] Thus, even when the SSA was not actually in charge of staff work for the councils, it was very influential indirectly.

As Cohen was the central figure in the SSA's relations with Congress, Ball was for some years central to relations with the advisory councils. Ball, Charles Schottland once remarked in admiration, was a "terrific teacher."[18] On the subject of social insurance, he was also a very experienced one by 1947. He had entered the SSB in 1939 as a field representative, moved two years later to the central office to do research, and soon after that to the training office, where he taught the principles of social insurance to new employees. It fitted him well for his later work of teaching social insurance to secretaries of HEW, congressmen, and advisory councils. He was always clear, patient, knowledgeable, and very good at laying out the alternatives and explaining their implications. He was also self-restrained rather than opinionated and aggressive—in other words, the kind of teacher who helps his students reach their own conclusions, or at least to leave the classroom believing that they have. Marion Folsom, who observed him in 1947–48 and in later councils after he became deputy director of the Bureau of Old Age and Social Insurance and then commissioner of social security, told an interviewer, "He's very impartial. He'd generally say, 'It's up to you.' He'd have all the facts and everything, but he wouldn't try to impose his own views on us."[19] Eveline Burns, an astute observer who thoroughly admired Ball, had this to say of his handling of Mrs. Hobby's consultants' group in 1953:

The evidence of what he can do [was] most clear to me, at the time of what we used to call "the Hobby Lobby" in 1953, that committee that laid the groundwork for the 1954 amendments. Bob was, at that time, the staff secretary to the committee.

He was absolutely remarkable. It was perfectly clear that he thought the committee recommendations should move in certain directions, but he never intruded himself. This is a very difficult role for a staff person who is known personally to everybody, and we're all on first-name terms, to remain in the

17. A. J. Altmeyer to Nelson H. Cruikshank, February 19, 1948, and enclosure (File 025 Social Security, acc. no. 62A-82, R. G. 47, Box 26, Washington National Records Center, Suitland, Md.); and route slip, Wilbur J. Cohen to AJA [Arthur J. Altmeyer], no date [1948], and enclosure (File 025 Advisory Council 1948, acc. no. 56-A533, R. G. 47, Box 6, Washington National Records Center, Suitland, Md.).

18. Interview with Charles I. Schottland, Oral History Collection, Columbia University (1965), p. 82.

19. Folsom, OHC, p. 120.

background, to hear some member say something that you know is just not true, and not jump in. Where Bob is so skillful is that, quietly and gently, and in connection with something else, he will bring out, without in any way involving a confrontation, what the true facts are—gently, sweetly, with his great depth of knowledge. By knowledge I mean not just about the program but about the implications of various alternatives. Bob was the one who really had all the knowledge. You could always turn to Bob and he could answer all your questions. He would skillfully push things into that committee.

That pleased me very much, because I also wanted some of those things. But never, at any point, did the committee resent what he did. . . . At the end of the meeting, the committee agreed to a most flowery and affectionately appreciative statement of Bob's contribution. . . . And then we had a great discussion within the committee, as to whether this should appear in our printed report that would be published by the secretary, or whether, if we left it in, it would be picked up . . . as an argument that we had been tools in the hands of the administration. So, in the end, we had it printed on a very special piece of paper and took it to the secretary so that Bob Ball should get credit. . . .

The impression he made on the committee was astounding, and it was a quite mixed committee. . . . Everyone was impressed by Ball's integrity, his knowledge of the act, his helpfulness, and his self-restraint.[20]

In the advisory councils, as in the congressional committees, there was also "the other Bob," as Eveline Burns called him—Myers, the chief actuary, who provided cost estimates. Myers would tell the councils, as he would tell congressmen, what various proposals for changing the program would cost, and the councils, like Congress, would make choices secure and self-satisfied in the knowledge that they had taken costs into account after hearing from a competent technician.

Because they served as staff to the councils, SSA officials were in a position to influence their agendas. Sometimes they had an interest in keeping the agenda narrow, as in 1953, when they wished to discourage consideration of the fundamental criticism raised by the Chamber of Commerce and Representative Carl Curtis, and sometimes they wished to broaden it, as in 1937, when Vandenberg wanted to talk about keeping taxes low and reducing the reserve fund, whereas Altmeyer wanted to talk about adding new types of protection. The 1937–39 council had its agenda laid out in the original announcement of the council's formation. What the advisory council was to study, such as the advisability of commencing monthly benefit payments sooner than 1942 and extending benefits to survivors of deceased workers, turned out to be a fairly

20. Interview with Eveline M. Burns, Oral History Collection, Columbia University (1965), pp. 99–100.

good guide to what the group would recommend. And what it was to study was outlined by the Social Security Board.

If the membership of the councils could be limited to persons who were in general supporters of the program, and if staff assistance could be limited to persons drawn directly or indirectly from the SSA, and if the councils' agenda could be limited to topics the SSA's leaders judged to be timely, there was not much danger that these groups of outsiders would get out of control and produce unwanted recommendations. The SSA's techniques of influence minimized the risks associated with admitting such a group to a role in policymaking. Furthermore, whatever risks there were diminished with time. It was unlikely that a part-time group of citizens, however distinguished or independent, would question what was firmly established and widely accepted. Social security executives, watching one after another of these groups assemble, were never entirely sure that they would not do something quixotic. "I must say I never worked with any council without feeling that it might go off the deep end with inconsistent and peculiar recommendations," Robert Ball recalled.[21] But they never did.

The Councils' Functions

From the perspective of a thoroughly experienced insider, the advisory councils served two main functions. Princeton's J. Douglas Brown, who served on all of them between 1935 and 1972 but the informal Hobby lobby, came to see them as an instrument of executive-legislative relations and independent legitimators of major policy decisions. For so important a program, he argued, the ordinary processes of executive presentation and congressional hearings were insufficient. Something more was needed to supplement the deliberations of congressional committees that were overburdened and an administration in which outsiders, including Congress, were bound to suspect bias.[22] He also believed that the councils improved the depth and objectivity of deliberation and that this reassured the public, especially in regard to the fiscal

21. From tape-recorded comments addressed to the author by Robert M. Ball, May 6, 1978. (Hereafter Ball transcript.)
22. J. Douglas Brown, *An American Philosophy of Social Security: Evolution and Issues* (Princeton University Press, 1972), p. 44. Interview with J. Douglas Brown, Oral History Collection, Columbia University (1965), p. 73. (Hereafter Brown, OHC.)

soundness of the program. "I would say . . . it is the strength and prestige of the general conclusions that have influence," he told an interviewer. "A group, including people from industry, public, labor, and all the rest, has come to these conclusions after months of discussion and having every possible source of information . . . so that the ordinary industrialist, or ordinary labor leader, the ordinary member of the public could say, 'Well, those fellows have put a hell of a lot of time into it, and I guess they can't be too far wrong.' "[23]

Leaders of the SSA, from their different but hardly more detached perspective, came to view the councils as important for rather different reasons. Asked to evaluate the councils, Altmeyer stressed their representative role. "They do give you the opportunity to understand what the reaction is of interested groups."[24] Robert Ball's interpretation was similar. He suggested that policy for social security historically had emerged from areas of agreement between business and labor. The advisory councils discovered and defined these areas.[25] From the perspective of program executives, then, the usefulness of the councils lay primarily in their serving as a channel of communication with salient interests and a medium through which differing interests could be reconciled.

These differing interpretations express different emphases only. The three roles—link between the executive and legislative branches, independent legitimator of policy choices, reconciler of competing interests —were not mutually exclusive. I suggest, however, an interpretation of the councils somewhat different from any of them, though compounded of their elements.

In my view the councils evolved into a distinctive form well suited to the practice of program-oriented policymaking. Constituted in representative fashion, so that various interests could be spoken for, they nonetheless functioned so as to foster program-serving attitudes and choices. The councils did serve to legitimate social security policy, but they were not strictly independent legitimators, for they developed their own corporate pride and sense of proprietorship. That they were influenced by the SSA is only part of the explanation for their lack of detachment. Beyond that, a group dynamic was at work. Having a

23. Ibid., p. 147.
24. Interview with Arthur J. Altmeyer, Oral History Collection, Columbia University (1967), p. 80. (Hereafter Altmeyer, OHC.)
25. Interview with the author, February 2, 1976.

life of their own, the councils acquired their own particular stake in maintaining and enlarging the social security program.

"We're trustees, you see," Brown once remarked of the councils, whose function was to prevent anyone, including the federal government, from "fooling with the system."[26] This choice of language, like that of Ways and Means Committee members, who also thought of themselves as "trustees," suggests something of how the advisory councils conceived of their task. In the councils, the "we" consisted of a core of leading members who returned to service again and again—Brown, of course, who served five times; Nelson Cruikshank, from organized labor, who served four times of the six; and Marion Folsom, representing business, who served on three councils, participated informally in the Hobby lobby, and could not serve in 1957 only because he was then secretary of HEW. Reinhard A. Hohaus, an actuary of the Metropolitan Life Insurance Company, was another veteran—he chaired Mrs. Hobby's group, served twice thereafter, and before that had served as an adviser to the actuary's office and to the council of 1937–39—but as a member of the insurance industry he was always a bit suspect to program executives and did not become an insider in quite the same sense. The triumvirate of Brown, Cruikshank, and Folsom reflected the tripartite composition of the councils—"public," labor, and business—and each informally led his respective subgroup, tutoring those newcomers who needed initiation into the principles of the social security program.[27] This relieved SSA executives of much of the burden of guiding the councils in acceptable directions. With reliable leaders present in the councils, SSA officials could confine themselves to staff

26. Brown, OHC, p. 89.
27. Brown told an interviewer:

> May I just say this? It sounds awfully smug, but there were three of us who have sort of followed through: Marion Folsom, as an industrial member, . . . Nelson Cruikshank on the labor side, and myself. The three of us have appeared repeatedly on advisory councils. So in a way it was fortunate that we were on three sides, so to speak. We'd each help educate our own side. Nelson time and again would have to explain to [Emil] Rieve of the textile workers why this would have to work the way it did or some other trade unionist. Marion would quietly in a very calm way explain to some industrial member why this wouldn't work. Now, with the public members, since I was the old hand, they'd often listen to me. I had one public member this time who said, "Doug, whenever you are in favor of something, I'll go along with you."
> I said, "Don't do it unless you really think it out." "Oh, no. That's all right. You've been at it longer." (Brown, OHC, pp. 81–82.)

functions and minimize the risks of intrusion. Brown, who was certainly no cynic about such matters, perceived the SSA's interest in having familiar hands at the helm. "I think Bob Ball and the secretary . . . purposely did that," he remarked, to explain the presence of himself and the other old hands in the council of 1963–65.[28]

Of the veteran leaders, Brown was the most important to the councils' functioning. As a "public" member, tied neither to business nor labor, he was perceived to be neutral politically. Everyone trusted him. But if he was neutral in respect to competing interests, he was certainly not neutral about the program. He had a better claim to have been its founder than any of the SSA executives. As a staff member of the Committee on Economic Security in 1934, he had been one of the small and inconspicuous subgroup that planned old age insurance. The other members—Barbara N. Armstrong, a law professor at the University of California, and Murray W. Latimer, an economist who later became chairman of the Railroad Retirement Board—did not remain for long in the inner family of social security, whereas Brown did. No full-time executives of the SSA could have had a deeper commitment to the program than he, and none could have had a more powerful conviction of its uniqueness and of the need when making policy to treat it as a distinct entity.

Within the councils, Brown functioned in the manner of a legislative statesman who urges others to be guided by the common good, and the content of the common good was defined for him by the principles of the social security program. He resisted the notion that interest representation was at the heart of the councils' function. A committee leader's customary desire to achieve consensus was powerfully reinforced in his case by the perception that consensus within the advisory council would be good for the social security program. He believed that solidarity was essential if the councils' purpose of reassuring the public was to be achieved, and he worked hard to achieve unanimity and to discourage or tone down dissents. For its part, the SSA contributed to the formation of consensus by declining for many years to put before any advisory council what was certain to be the most divisive agenda item of all—health insurance. There would have been "a donnybrook fair" if an advisory council had considered that subject, Altmeyer once

28. Ibid., p. 84.

said.[29] No council did so until 1963–65, when congressional consideration of legislation was far advanced and the council, except for a much-
moderated dissent by Hohaus, endorsed the administration's bill.

Under Brown's leadership, and with SSA officials as staff, the advisory
councils became a means of drawing interest group representatives into
program-oriented policymaking. Through the councils, interest group
leaders learned the rationale for the principal features of the social
security program, participated in the decisions concerning it (albeit
advisory, not authoritative, decisions), and in some measure became
program leaders too. If, for example, one were to characterize Cruikshank's career in a phrase, it would be hard to know whether to call
him a leader in social security or a leader of organized labor; the identification with the program rivaled identification with an organization.
Insofar as interest group representatives developed allegiance to the
program, they moderated group claims that were in conflict with program principles. Pressures from their constituencies were countered
with pressures from fellow program leaders, and, in the actual deliberations of the councils, the latter became more compelling.

Having "learned" program principles through the medium of the
councils, business and labor leaders could in turn be expected to convey
them to their constituencies; and some, as prominent and influential
individuals in their own right, could also be expected to enter positions
of social or political leadership, where their acquired expertise in social
security would be an asset to the program. Such expertise could of
itself constitute a qualification for office, as it did for Folsom, the most
prominent council member and program partisan to turn into a holder
of high office. Secretary of HEW between 1955 and 1958, Folsom before that was under secretary of the treasury in the Eisenhower administration. Mrs. Hobby, who was a complete novice in social security,
called on him for advice, and SSA leaders, who had no confidence in
the incoming Republicans generally but much confidence in Folsom,
turned to him for support. On his last day in office as social security
commissioner, Altmeyer saw Folsom to say goodbye and urge him to
take part in the Eisenhower administration's discussions of social secu-

29. Altmeyer, OHC, p. 83. According to Robert Ball, the 1947–48 council decided
on its own, after considerable discussion by the executive committee, not to take up
health insurance. Ball transcript.

rity.[30] Folsom's marginal position—as a high-ranking executive in a Republican administration, trusted by other political executives, yet a partisan of the social security program and trusted by program executives—was good for the program at a potentially troublesome time, though it proved to be hard on Folsom. Roswell Perkins, in his recollections for an interviewer, remembered that Folsom as secretary had "tortured himself for weeks" over the administration's position on covering disability, and only "with considerable emotional difficulty" decided that he must oppose cash disability benefits.[31]

That the councils helped to indoctrinate outsiders does not gainsay their usefulness also in bringing outside reactions to bear on the proposed next moves of the Social Security Administration. Communication did run in both directions. Within the limits of the agenda, which took the basic program as given, the SSA's solicitation of advice and opinion was often genuine enough. The dialogue among interests that normally develops when Congress considers legislation was anticipated and in some measure preempted by deliberations of the advisory councils. However, to the extent that consensus was reached within the councils, their effect was to constrict rather than expand the policymaking arena. The interplay of interests took place within a narrow, relatively controlled forum, to which program executives had ready access.

That the advisory councils were dominated by supporters of the program in combination with the SSA staff meant that service on them could be frustrating for someone who stood outside the consensus. Charles A. Siegfried, who was vice chairman of the board of the Metropolitan Life Insurance Company, found the 1969–71 advisory council a "dismal experience" and filed a dissenting statement.[32] He sensed that the chairman,

30. Arthur J. Altmeyer, *The Formative Years of Social Security* (University of Wisconsin Press, 1966), pp. 214–15.

31. Perkins, OHC, p. 28. Ball commented as follows: "My belief is that Folsom was directed to oppose cash disability benefits. All during this period he was talking to me about possible entering-wedge type proposals, age sixty for the disabled and so on." Ball transcript.

32. Both the business members and the labor members filed dissents to this report. The 1969–71 council was more than usually divided, perhaps because it was the first in which the business and labor representatives were nominated by business and labor organizations. Representative Thomas B. Curtis, an outspoken conservative Republican, had charged in 1963 that the newly named council was stacked by the administration and was just " 'window dressing' for things some of the Social Security staff want put into law." Two years later the law was changed to provide that mem-

who was a former secretary of HEW, was leading the group toward predetermined results with the support of Commissioner Ball. From this and other experience, he concluded that policymaking for social security was concentrated heavily in the hands of an expert few within the government, and that the councils reinforced the domination of the inner group rather than dispersing power.[33]

Cooptation of outsiders is likely to have a price even under conditions favorable to the coopting organization, and SSA officials did not always get exactly what they wanted from the advisory councils. In 1937–39 they had hoped that the council would endorse a disability program, but it did no more than agree in principle that disability benefits were socially desirable. In 1947–48 a clear majority favored disability benefits, but only after so compromising the recommendation that Cohen was very upset by the outcome. Cruikshank later said that he learned from this experience the danger of premature compromise.[34] The proponents had given in and given in until the recommendation was very narrow, and then the two dissenters proceeded to dissent anyway. One of the most important recommendations of the 1947–48 advisory council— that an "increment" for each year of work under social security be dropped from the benefit schedule—had been opposed by Altmeyer and Cohen. It is hard to judge how costly such defeats were to the SSA. Administrators were not bound by the advisory councils' recommendations. From the SSA's point of view, advisory council support for its own proposals was highly desirable but not essential. "We would have

---

bers of the councils should represent *organizations* of employers and employees as well as the self-employed and the general public; in response, the secretary of HEW solicited nominations from leading business and labor organizations and made his selections from among them. Another change in the law eliminated the provision that the social security commissioner serve as council chairman. Close observers of the councils believe that these changes have increased their independence somewhat. They may also produce tension between the organizations that nominate council members and the secretaries of HEW who name them. For example, when the 1974–75 council was named, the Nixon administration's secretary of HEW, Caspar W. Weinberger, rejected some of the AFL-CIO's nominees, whereupon the AFL-CIO leadership boycotted the council. The only labor members whom the Nixon administration could induce to serve on the council were relatively obscure members of the building trades and teamsters unions. Curtis's criticisms appear in the *Congressional Record* (May 23, 1963), p. 9246, and *Congressional Record* (September 17, 1963), pp. 17309–11.

33. Interview with the author, November 3, 1976; Society of Actuaries, *Transactions*, vol. 22, pt. 2 (1970), p. D508.

34. Cruikshank, OHC, p. 104.

made exactly the same proposals even if . . . there'd been no advisory council," Altmeyer said, recalling the legislation of 1939.[35] And when an advisory council did diverge from the SSA leadership (as did that of 1948 in proposing to eliminate the increment), it was not necessarily to the political detriment of the program. Because dropping the increment meant lower costs in the long run, it made possible a major increase of benefits in the short run, a trade that enabled the advisory council to present a nearly unanimous report and that also proved highly popular in Congress. Robert Ball's service as director of this council, far from putting him seriously at odds with the leadership of the program, marked his emergence as a member of it.

Congress, of course, was no more bound by the recommendations of the advisory councils than was the administration. The council's recommendation for a disability insurance program in 1948, though much too weak to satisfy Cohen, was too strong to get through the Senate Finance Committee, which rejected it in favor of grants-in-aid to the states for relief of the disabled. Congress did not uncritically accept advice even from the early councils that were its own creatures, and much of the advice that it did accept was obviously congenial. This was advice that called for paying benefits sooner and more broadly in the short run.

Nevertheless, leaders of the SSA believed that the councils were quite helpful in producing legislation, particularly the crucial amendments of 1939 and 1950. By arriving at a consensus among representatives of disparate groups, the councils performed a useful service for a Congress that was still groping its way with an unfamiliar program.[36] Thus when a dissident council member, Walter D. Fuller, suggested to the Ways and Means Committee that the 1937–39 council had compromised to such an extent that its report could not be of much use, committee member Jere Cooper received this observation with skepticism. In a congressman's eyes, it was precisely the compromises that gave the report its value:

Mr. FULLER. . . . Based on a year and a half experience with the Social Security Advisory Council . . . my own personal belief is you gentlemen would get greater help if you had one committee of employers, let us say, one committee of representative labor and perhaps a third committee of the so-called public, and let each of them make their own report. I think in that way you

35. Altmeyer, OHC, p. 78.
36. See chapter 11 for the council's discussion of financial issues in 1937–39.

might get a more complete statement and you could judge. . . . The difficulty with a [council] like this is you are bound to compromise your position.

Mr. COOPER. Just on that point, from a practical standpoint, . . . suppose we follow up the suggestion just made. . . . Then instead of the whole council being under the necessity of making a compromise and reaching some common level, they would just pass the responsibility to us to do the same thing, would they not?

Mr. FULLER. That is true, and I think that is where it ought to be.[37]

Also, the working of the councils created a supply of highly credible individual witnesses, the council leaders, on whom Congress could rely for well-informed, presumably expert, advice. In 1939 both Brown and Folsom testified at length. As individual witnesses, members did not necessarily support everything that was in the council reports, but in general the weight of their testimony supported both the reports and the administration's bills, with which the reports closely corresponded.

As congressmen improved their understanding of the new program, they became less dependent on outside opinion. The diffidence of 1939 eventually gave way to the mastery of Wilbur Mills. Probably no subsequent council was more important than that of 1937–39, which offered solicited advice to a Congress puzzled and divided over the issue of financing and unable as yet to get any guidance from the most comforting and credible witness of all: experience. Besides developing its own expertise in the person of Mills, the Ways and Means Committee in time developed intimate working relations with SSA officials, and after these routines were worked out, advisory councils receded to the periphery of policymaking. Once a link between executive and legislature, by the early 1960s they were more of an appendage.

Still, the councils remained potentially useful to program executives as a channel for putting items on the legislative agenda in a legitimized form that congressmen could not readily ignore and might, at their discretion, make use of. By endorsing significant changes in actuarial and financing techniques, the 1969–71 advisory council laid the basis for the 20 percent benefit increase of 1972, which was one of the foundations of the modern program. Mills, who took the initiative in proposing the big increase, was responding to the political situation created by the appearance of the council's report, which defined political opportunities in a new way. In justifying his response to this new situation,

37. *Social Security,* Hearings before the House Committee on Ways and Means, 76 Cong. 1 sess. (GPO, 1939), vol. 3, pp. 2083–84.

Mills made a point of citing the expert authority of the advisory council.[38]

ADVISORY COUNCILS composed of "outsiders" reinforced rather than compromised the program-oriented character of policymaking. The outsiders tended to become insiders as they were drawn into the councils' deliberations; a few who served time and again became in effect members of the proprietary inner family. Leadership, membership, staffing, and the definition of the agenda all combined to preclude consideration of alternatives that were in conflict with program maintenance, and to assure recommendations falling within a range that program executives would find acceptable. Typically, advisory council reports paved the way for the program executives' own current recommendations.

38. *Congressional Record* (February 23, 1972), p. 5270.

CHAPTER FIVE

Organized Labor as Collaborator

IN BUILDING the social security program, organized labor was by far the most important ally of the Social Security Administration. It supported the SSA inside the advisory councils and lobbied and testified for the agency's legislative proposals. It largely conducted and financed the public campaigns for medicare, including an effort in the 1960s to organize pro-medicare propaganda in key congressional districts. It founded and helped finance the National Council of Senior Citizens, a nationwide organization of the elderly that lobbied for medicare and subsequent enlargements of the program. Perhaps most important of all, labor was an unofficial outlet for proposals that SSA officials were not free to promote themselves because they lacked approval from political superiors.

Despite these many and presumably quite valuable services, organized labor has left no distinguishing marks on the program. If the SSA paid a price for labor's support, it is hard for the analyst to detect. On the whole, labor has been an acquiescent partner of the SSA in program-oriented policymaking, supporting both the basic principles of the program and particular legislative initiatives. The program executives' agenda was labor's agenda too, with no concessions sought or granted to serve the distinctive goals or interests of the pressure group ally. "Alliance" is perhaps the wrong term for this relation, for it suggests a negotiated agreement between independent parties. Organized labor and the SSA were, instead, intimate collaborators. There was little bargaining between them, little give-and-take over social insurance. Rather there was a bond of sympathy, of shared commitment to social insurance as the chosen instrument of social welfare, and a shared antipathy to the program's real and putative enemies on the right.

The Beginning of Collaboration

The collaboration of the SSA with organized labor took the better part of the decade after 1935 to develop. Not until the middle of the 1940s, when the Wagner-Murray-Dingell bill first appeared on the public agenda, was this collaboration made secure. The necessary preconditions were politicization of the traditionally apolitical American Federation of Labor and deradicalization of the militant, highly political Congress of Industrial Organizations, the young dissident of the American labor movement. The precipitating event was the bill itself. Initiated by the Social Security Board and prepared in cooperation with Senator Wagner and his staff, this was a piece of social legislation that a politically conscious but essentially accommodationist labor movement could support with enthusiasm.

"Voluntarism"—the belief of AFL leaders that terms of employment should be settled by collective bargaining, free from government interference—did not disappear instantly with the coming of the New Deal. It took time for the AFL to adjust to the dramatically changed social and political agenda while an internecine war was going on. The late 1930s, when the split with the industrial unions occurred, were a turbulent time for the AFL, and, while fighting, the AFL was also growing. With vigorous organizing efforts of its own, the AFL more than made up its losses to the CIO. In 1939 its membership was at or near an all-time high and was more varied than ever, extending beyond the traditional craft unions to include large organizations of teamsters and machinists as well as industrial rivals to the CIO such as textile workers and rubber workers.[1]

During this period the AFL had no very clear or fixed position on social insurance. Though it supported old age insurance in 1935, it took very little part in preparing the Social Security Act, and such interest as it showed was mainly in unemployment insurance.[2] Three

1. Milton Derber, "Growth and Expansion," in Milton Derber and Edwin Young, eds., *Labor and the New Deal* (University of Wisconsin Press, 1961), pp. 1–44, especially pp. 12–18.
2. Frances Perkins, *The Roosevelt I Knew* (Viking, 1946), p. 288; Edwin E. Witte, *The Development of the Social Security Act* (University of Wisconsin Press, 1963), pp. 87–88; Arthur J. Altmeyer, *The Formative Years of Social Security* (University of Wisconsin Press, 1966), pp. 32–33; Edwin E. Witte, "Organized Labor and Social Security," in Derber and Young, eds. *Labor and the New Deal*, pp. 241–55.

members of the AFL were appointed to the advisory council on social security in 1937 but rarely attended the meetings. Disappointed, Wilbur Cohen wrote to a friend that "on the whole, members of labor have usually so much to do, so little time to do it and so few assistants in technical capacities that they are usually absent or incapable of contributing anything."[3]

The change came in the early 1940s. In 1941 an article in the *American Federationist* by a leading AFL official argued the need for health and disability insurance.[4] The following year, the AFL became the sponsor of the Eliot bill (H.R. 7534, Seventy-seventh Congress), a little-known forerunner of the Wagner-Murray-Dingell bill. The Eliot bill was a comprehensive piece of social security legislation drafted within the Social Security Board but was without official standing because it lacked the President's endorsement. The congressional sponsor, Democratic Representative Thomas H. Eliot of Massachusetts, had been general counsel of the Committee on Economic Security in 1934 and then general counsel of the Social Security Board. When President William Green announced to the AFL convention that the organization was sponsoring this bill, he anticipated criticism. It might seem, he conceded, "a bit revolutionary," and some AFL affiliates did object to it.[5] Voluntarism died hard, but by 1943, when the Wagner-Murray-Dingell bill succeeded the Eliot bill (SSB officials having in the meantime added health insurance and attracted more renowned sponsors in Congress), internal opposition was no longer evident. President Green directed all central labor unions and state federations to call upon their representatives in Congress and to argue labor's need for adequate social insurance after the war. The immediate objective was to get the House Committee on Ways and Means to hold hearings. The AFL, which only four years before had been ill prepared to testify on the 1939 amendments to the Social Security Act, was now mustering its members to lobby for legislation far bolder and more controversial. As

3. Wilbur J. Cohen to M. S. Pitzele, August 28, 1941 (File 025 Federal Security Agency, R. G. 47, SSA Central Files 1935–1947, Box 15, National Archives).

4. Robert J. Watt, "The Next Frontier," *American Federationist*, vol. 48 (March 1941), pp. 16–17, 32. The author, a native of Scotland, was the AFL's representative to the International Labor Organization between 1936 and 1947 and a member of a commission appointed by President Roosevelt to study labor conditions in Britain and Sweden; this gave him considerable exposure to foreign examples, made him the AFL headquarters expert on social legislation, and put him in touch with officials of the Social Security Board.

5. *Report of Proceedings of the Sixty-second Annual Convention of the American Federation of Labor* (Washington, D.C.: AFL, 1942), pp. 414, 608–09.

far as social insurance was concerned, the transition from voluntarism to government action had been completed.

Meanwhile, the CIO was moderating its radical politics. Unlike the AFL, the CIO had a very definite position on social insurance in the late 1930s, a position well to the left of the Social Security Board. It opposed the dual system of contributory federal old age insurance and state public assistance payments to the needy aged because it "does not take care of our needs in any satisfactory way and does not exhaust the limit of our resources." It called for a single program that would pay $60 a month to everyone aged sixty or over (or $90 to a married couple), to be paid for by "taxes upon aggregates of wealth and income." Tantamount to endorsing the Townsend plan (discussed in chapter 8), this was a complete repudiation of the administration. To the goal of economic security, the CIO joined the goal of economic equality: the program should correct "the present mal-distribution of income," a radical objective that had no place in official rhetoric.[6] In 1940 the CIO opposed increases in the social security payroll tax, partly on the ground that the funds "are used to subsidize government expenditures that now go largely into armaments."[7]

The CIO's transition on social insurance, like the very different transition of the AFL, dates from the early 1940s, but whereas the AFL's leftward move responded to changes in mass membership, the CIO's rightward move responded to changes in leadership. The volatile, combative John L. Lewis was deposed as president after Roosevelt's reelection in 1940 and was replaced by Philip Murray, who was more sympathetic to Roosevelt and the New Deal. Within the CIO, which contained myriad leftist elements, international events were also important. Hitler's invasion of the Soviet Union in the summer of 1941 brought an end to the isolationism and pacifism of American communists, and communist and noncommunist factions inside the CIO promptly united behind their new president in support of the war and the Roosevelt administration.[8] CIO conventions thereupon ceased to

6. *Daily Proceedings of the Second Constitutional Convention of the Congress of Industrial Organizations* (Washington, D.C.: CIO, 1939), p. 138.

7. *Daily Proceedings of the Third Constitutional Convention of the Congress of Industrial Organizations* (Washington, D.C.: CIO, 1940), p. 98.

8. Len De Caux, *Labor Radical: From the Wobblies to the CIO* (Beacon Press, 1970), chaps. 13–14. The deradicalization of the CIO was not completed until the expulsion of communist members in the late 1940s. See also Juanita Diffay Tate, "Philip Murray as a Labor Leader," Ph.D. dissertation, New York University (1962), p. 75.

pass dissenting resolutions on social insurance. Instead the convention of 1941 noted that President Roosevelt would soon recommend a number of changes in the social security system and promised to give them full consideration. In 1942 the convention was silent on the subject of social insurance: Roosevelt had in fact not acted, and the administration bill had appeared instead under the sponsorship of Representative Eliot and the AFL. Then, in 1943, the CIO endorsed the Wagner-Murray-Dingell bill. The two wings of the labor movement had finally converged regarding the social insurance program. They had converged with each other and also with the Social Security Board.

For their part, SSB executives had tried to woo labor support ever since the program had started. Arthur Altmeyer addressed the AFL conventions every year, though not the CIO, and frequently visited AFL headquarters. A "labor information division" was set up within the board to maintain liaison, for example, by supplying material to the *American Federationist;* it was headed by an official of the electrical workers union who worked for the government part time. In the presidential election of 1936, when the program came under attack from the Republican candidate and from some industrial employers, the SSB turned to the AFL for help in repelling the attack. Shortly before the election, 125 employees of the board stuffed 33,000 envelopes with 100 copies each of a pamphlet, "Security in Your Old Age," for mailing to local AFL unions throughout the country.[9] The pamphlet assured taxpayers that they would always get back more from the government than they paid in social security taxes. But while the AFL was receptive to this sort of effort, it remained a passive partner, a channel for propaganda of official origin rather than being independently active.

As labor became more inclined to collaborate, the SSB became more in need of a collaborator. It needed political support and sponsorship for the initiatives it was planning, and when the President declined to be the sponsor, liberal congressmen and organized labor took his place. Program enlargement could proceed independently of presidential politics, though presidential support, of course, was always a help.

Officials of the Social Security Board and of the Public Health Service, which shared authorship of the Wagner-Murray-Dingell bill, urged their newfound ally to make a substantial investment in the legislative campaign. Wagner himself, among other official backers, pleaded with

9. Charles McKinley and Robert W. Frase, *Launching Social Security* (University of Wisconsin Press, 1970), p. 358.

labor leaders to set up a committee for that purpose.[10] For a time the AFL and CIO considered creating a joint staff; the convergence on policy nearly took an organizational form.[11] When that failed, the AFL went ahead on its own in the fall of 1944 to create a social security department. The vacuum of which Cohen had complained in 1939 had been filled. Henceforth, when the SSB turned to organized labor for cooperation, it could be sure of finding someone to cooperate with.

The Collaborators in Action: The Effects of Party

Although it did not pass—or, more correctly, because it did not pass —the Wagner-Murray-Dingell bill set the agenda for social security legislation for years to come. Organized labor and SSA executives would pursue the various parts of it for two more decades as partners in the great task of building a comprehensive social insurance program. They collaborated in managing relations with Congress and in planning strategy within the advisory councils. Each protected the other's place in social security policymaking, and labor always stood ready to do those things that only a private pressure group was free to do. When the Eisenhower administration removed several leading program officials from their offices, the officials could not protest—but labor did. When the Eisenhower administration opposed disability insurance and health insurance, program officials could not openly campaign for them —but labor could. Always, labor had a useful role as surrogate sponsor of what in reality were proposals initiated by the SSA.

Nelson Cruikshank, organized labor's long-time specialist on social security (he headed the AFL's office and then the office of the merged AFL-CIO for some twenty years), once acknowledged labor's surrogate function within the semiprivacy of the social security "family." At a social security conference in Ann Arbor, Cruikshank introduced Alvin David, who was assistant commissioner for program evaluation and planning of the Social Security Administration. "I know that he has had very much to do with the planning and development programming

10. Robert F. Wagner to William Green, March 3, 1944 (File 011.1, Social Security Board 1941–48, R. G. 47, Washington National Records Center, Suitland, Md.).

11. Interview with Nelson H. Cruikshank, Oral History Collection, Columbia University (1967), p. 29. (Hereafter Cruikshank, OHC.)

of our social security system," Cruikshank said. "I also know something that is not written on this slip which is before me, that he's so full of ideas that they every now and then run over, and when he has more than his administration can handle, he calls his friends from the labor movement and says 'Why don't you get somebody to propose this?' And we never heard of it but we think it's a great idea."[12] This remark was made in 1968, after two terms of a Democratic administration. The 1960s were not exactly years of political repression for the SSA, but the need for a private outlet persisted no matter which party was in power.

The need was much greater during Republican years than when Democrats were in office, however, and the depth of labor's involvement in social security affairs therefore varied with the partisan composition of the executive branch. Much of the staff work in support of medicare in 1957–60 was done at AFL-CIO headquarters. Drafts of bills were typed, arguments were marshaled, speeches were written for congressional sympathizers. Especially in the campaign year of 1960, when the Senate voted on a medicare proposal for the first time, it was an exciting time for Cruikshank's staff, one of whom, Lisbeth B. Schorr, later recalled the moment:

> The AFL-CIO became a sort of headquarters offering at least logistical support—desks and mimeograph machines—for people who were trying to get something done about health insurance for the aged. I can remember the library in the IUD [Industrial Union Department] when we were assembling, cutting and pasting a bill . . . we were in a terrible rush for some reason, and I think it was Wilbur Cohen and Leonard Lesser [of the IUD staff] and Nelson Cruikshank and myself, and somebody had the stapler and somebody had the scotch tape.[13]

But when the Democrats returned to power with Kennedy's election, action abruptly shifted back to the executive branch, and life at the AFL-CIO ceased to be so exciting. Lisbeth Schorr described the change:

> Some of the work of making estimates and so on [before 1960] was actually done by people who were at HEW at the time, who again could sort of do it maybe half on their own time and on office time but they couldn't reproduce it and they would send it over to the AFL-CIO to get it typed up or whatever it was. And all of this of course was no longer necessary after there was an administration which was committed at least to the principle. But I think it's interesting that an organization like AFL-CIO can play that kind of

---

12. "Income Maintenance and the Social Security System: Proceedings of the Sixth Social Security Conference" (University of Michigan, 1968), p. 55.

13. Interview with Leonard Lesser and Lisbeth Bamberger Schorr, Oral History Collection, Columbia University (1967), pp. 3–5. (Hereafter Lesser-Schorr, OHC.)

a role, which of course completely changes when you have the executive branch of the government committed to doing something.[14]

The relation with labor was therefore least valuable to program executives when the Democrats were in office, and it was at just such times that important action was most likely to occur. Ironically for labor, it was most able to influence the social insurance agenda when the stakes were lowest. Between 1957 and 1960, when labor was the sponsor of health insurance bills, it had more to say about what went into them than it did after 1961, when the President became the sponsor. Social security executives continued to consult with labor but the consultations were less likely to result in concessions to labor's views. Lisbeth Schorr, who was for seven years a shrewd participant-observer, judged them to be largely formal: "Much of the consultation which occurred—let's say in the last two years before the passage of the bill, and there was indeed much consultation that occurred—was a ritual, was ceremonial, was sort of keeping the labor boys happy without anything of real substance happening as a result."[15]

The program executives' independence during Democratic administrations helps to explain labor's compliant relation with the SSA. Freedom from official constraint, which was labor's distinctive asset, ceased then to be of great value, and there was not much to put in its place. Influence with Congress might have enabled labor to bargain with the executive for concessions or to stake out an independent position except that labor's access to the Ways and Means and Finance committees was inferior to that of program executives. Leonard Lesser of the Industrial Union Department, who collaborated with Cruikshank on much of labor's staff work in support of medicare, recalled in an interview: "If it had been another committee, we could have talked to the members of the committee really and said, 'Look, this is terrible. You ought to push for this, this, this, and this.' And we might have lined up enough of the committee to influence it. You really couldn't do this in the Ways and Means Committee."[16] It could not be done because committee members deferred to the technical and political mastery of their chairman, Wilbur Mills. Even those who were sympathetic in general to appeals from labor did not have the command of subject matter that would have been necessary to pursue independent positions. Members

14. Ibid., pp. 4–5.
15. Ibid., p. 75.
16. Ibid., p. 80.

left matters of the program's substance to Mills, and labor, on its side, left them to Cohen, whom Kennedy had named assistant secretary for legislation in HEW.

Democratic incumbency constrained labor in another way too. Bound to the SSA in a programmatic alliance, organized labor belonged as well to a partisan alliance with the Democrats' liberal wing, the "presidential" portion of the party. Like the programmatic alliance, the partisan one dated from the mid-1940s. It was the election of 1944, according to Greenstone, that marked organized labor's emergence as a national campaign organization for the Democratic party.[17] When labor's party controlled the presidency, labor was reluctant to criticize its policies and programs, knowing that in the next election it would be mobilizing the party's vote.

The conditions of Democratic incumbency were not, in fact, conducive to an independent role for organized labor in social security policymaking, but neither were the conditions of Republican incumbency, for different reasons. When Republicans were in executive office, the collaboration between program supporters in the SSA and in organized labor had a partly defensive character. The two were driven to close collaboration by the belief that unity was essential in the face of threats (at worst) or limited opportunities for progress (at best). This defensiveness increased their mutual dependence rather than encouraging labor to assert independence. Thus, whether the Democrats were in or out of office, organized labor was reluctant to differ from program executives. When the Democrats were in, it would have been tantamount to breaking with labor's party at the very time that progress seemed possible. When they were out, it would have risked giving a dangerous advantage to political enemies at the program's expense. These enemies were perceived to be menacing and powerful. When locked in struggle with the American Medical Association, Carl Curtis, the U.S. Chamber of Commerce, or other enemies along the path of social progress, a solid front seemed imperative.

Labor's Stake in Social Security

Labor's attitude toward the social security program depended on labor's stake in it. Two points are pertinent to the politics and policy-

17. J. David Greenstone, *Labor in American Politics* (Vintage Books, 1969), p. 51.

making of social security. First, of the two major national federations, paradoxically it was the CIO—historically the more political, more activist, and more oppositional—that took the lesser interest in social security legislation. The greater interest was found in the AFL, politically the more conservative and the more inclined, by reason of its voluntarist tradition, to approve uncritically a government program of which it was claimed that workers paid their own way. Second, in neither the AFL nor the CIO were elected leaders intensely concerned about the subject. This meant that staff specialists in social insurance had a great deal of discretion, and these specialists, precisely because they were specialists, developed a strongly programmatic orientation.

Labor unions exist to engage in collective bargaining, and in politics the first priority of their national federations is given to measures that affect the unions' capacity to maintain themselves and to bargain with employers. Unions as a class, James Q. Wilson has pointed out, are even more preoccupied than most organizations with organizational maintenance, for they have to enroll most or all of the work force in a given plant or industry to make collective bargaining succeed.[18]

Labor leaders were more concerned, then, with legislation such as the Taft-Hartley Act, which affected organizing conditions, than with Social Security Act amendments, and it could be argued that for them to be interested at all in social security legislation was perverse. Retirement, health, and disability benefits can be provided publicly or privately. For unions to provide them through private action—either directly through union-sponsored plans or indirectly through collective bargaining with employers—would provide an inducement to workers to join unions. But if these benefits were supplied by the government, even though under political pressure from labor, there would be no such inducement. This perception, as well as a deep distrust of government, underlay the historic voluntarism of AFL leaders.[19]

In time, the choice between public and private action became more of a dilemma for the CIO than for the AFL. With a favorable ruling from the National Labor Relations Board, which in turn was upheld in federal courts, industrial unions began negotiating successfully for pensions and other fringe benefits in the late 1940s. There were break-

18. James Q. Wilson, *Political Organizations* (Basic Books, 1973), chap. 7.

19. Historically, the AFL opposed industrial pensions and employer welfare programs as well as government programs, believing that they were designed to discourage the formation of unions. Witte, "Organized Labor and Social Security," p. 270.

throughs in the steel, auto, aluminum, and coal industries. CIO convention resolutions insisted that there was no conflict between social security and collective bargaining for pensions, and when social security was enlarged and liberalized in 1950, the CIO was quick to claim that its own collective bargaining victories had roused Congress to act. Yet the ambiguity of CIO's position was inescapable. Convention resolutions on the subject of social security were quite inconsistent. "We again emphasize that the collective bargaining contract is and must remain the worker's primary bulwark against insecurity and exploitation," the 1948 convention said.[20] The next year the benefits of collective bargaining were described as a "necessary supplement" to government programs, but when the time came for the CIO to testify on pending social security legislation, President Murray did not bother to appear and instead inserted in the record a newspaper story describing gains from collective bargaining. There can be little doubt that the CIO would have been more active in Washington had it not been so successful in Detroit, Chicago, and Gary.

Once converted to social security, the AFL showed none of the same ambivalence, presumably because its constituent unions were less able to win pension benefits through collective bargaining than the industrial unions were. Cruikshank analyzed the reasons for this in a speech to an academic audience. For union bargaining to succeed, he said, three conditions must be met: there must be a stable employee-employer relationship; the union must be in a strong bargaining position; and the industry must be able to pay the costs. He argued that building tradesmen, for instance (an example that was, of course, the backbone of the AFL), failed to meet the first condition. Plumbers, electricians, painters, and carpenters were likely to move from one city to another and one contractor to another. Cruikshank went on to criticize union-negotiated security plans on the grounds that they immobilized the labor force, threatened to depress wages for current workers, and were inequitable: "Some consumers should not be called upon to pay for security which other workers, by the chance nature of their employment, cannot secure for themselves."[21] The 1950 amendments, for which the CIO was so ready to take credit, did not put the AFL al-

20. *1948 Proceedings of the Tenth Constitutional Convention of the Congress of Industrial Organizations* (Washington, D.C.: CIO, 1948), p. 333.

21. Nelson H. Cruikshank, "Labor's Stake in Social Security," University of Illinois, Institute of Labor and Industrial Relations (1949–50).

together at ease in these matters. The 1951 AFL convention said: "It is important to emphasize the fact that the widespread adoption of individual company pension plans achieved by unions through collective bargaining does not eliminate the need for an improved and extended federal Old Age and Survivors' Insurance system. The industrial pension plans are a method for increasing the security and living standards of *some groups* of workers, but it will still be necessary to have a comprehensive social insurance program with broad coverage to assure adequate income in their old age to all groups in the population."[22]

Whereas the CIO claimed to have won the 1950 amendments at the collective bargaining tables in industrial centers, the AFL claimed credit for its effort in Washington. President William Green, in contrast to Murray, did appear before the Ways and Means Committee and was accompanied by twenty-one representatives of AFL unions and departments. There was, too, a continuing disparity in the status of AFL and CIO staffs on social security. Whereas the AFL had set up a separate social security department, in the CIO social security matters were handled by a member of the research department. When the merger occurred at the end of 1955, the AFL social security director became head of the merged staff more or less automatically, and through him AFL influence over social insurance persisted in the consolidated organization.

Within the national federations, the social security staff had a great deal of influence. Though Cruikshank reported to a social security committee and through it to the AFL or AFL-CIO president, determining the organization's position on social security affairs was largely up to him. Cruikshank's personal qualities contributed to this. Because he was competent, prudent, and trustworthy, he had the confidence of federation presidents; to a critic who accused him in the early 1960s of selling labor out, he confidently replied that the accuser should take his case to President George Meany.[23] But if Meany was prepared to trust in Cruikshank, this was not only because Cruikshank had demonstrated trustworthiness; it was also because social security was not at the top of an AFL-CIO president's concerns. "Social security issues really were peripheral," Lisbeth Schorr recalled. "This meant that as a staff depart-

22. *Report of Proceedings of the Seventieth Annual Convention of the American Federation of Labor* (Washington, D.C.: AFL, 1951), pp. 174–75. Emphasis added.
23. Cruikshank, OHC, p. 92.

ment we had a great deal of freedom. . . . Nelson really didn't have to check with his committee, . . . which was no restraint on him at all."[24] From his very different vantage point, Arthur Altmeyer similarly recalled that "on the whole it was the bureaucrats—Nelson Cruikshank, Leonard Lesser, Kitty Ellickson—that had to carry the ball and were always moaning and groaning that they couldn't get their principals really steamed up."[25]

Even when committee members did have strong opinions of their own, Cruikshank had room to exercise his own judgment. Thus, for example, some of the more progressive members of the committee— those representing the United Auto Workers and the United Steelworkers of America—wanted in 1957 to sponsor a bill that would provide comprehensive health services to the elderly. Cruikshank favored including hospitalization only. The result was a compromise proposal that included surgical services but not all doctors' services. Subsequently the surgical services were dropped. Against what committee members wanted, Cruikshank balanced his judgment of what it was most feasible to add to the program at the time. To go beyond benefits for hospitalization would make the bill far more difficult to pass. This was the kind of tactical calculation that program executives made, and Cruikshank, as their close collaborator, joined in.

He became virtually one of them. The purposes and rewards of Cruikshank's career were hardly distinguishable from those of Cohen or other official founders of social insurance. A socialist in the 1930s, with views so advanced that they were hard for the Methodist Church to tolerate in one of its ministers, Cruikshank was committed to the work of promoting social legislation, social insurance particularly. The program became the mission and the labor movement a vehicle for pursuing it. To Schorr, working with Cruikshank after 1958, it seemed that medicare was the ultimate prize:

[Medicare] dominated the interests and the work of the department so much that most other things became very much secondary. And I think that was in part because . . . other things weren't as significant, and secondly because of the very personal identification that Nelson Cruikshank felt with this issue. I think the fact that it came at a period when he knew it was probably going to be the last big fight that he was going to be involved in before he retired was quite crucial, and it grew in his own thinking to where—at least I had

24. Lesser-Schorr, OHC, p. 20.
25. Interview with Arthur J. Altmeyer, Oral History Collection, Columbia University (1967), p. 170.

this impression—he saw this as a test of the significance and success of his entire career; that if legislation to provide health insurance for the aged through social security was passed, it would all have been worthwhile.[26]

Cruikshank himself, when asked to evaluate the satisfactions of his career, declined to single out medicare. He was also proud of the 1950 amendments and of disability insurance, he said. But what he was most proud of was having kept labor's sights always on the legislative objectives—on what needed to. be done and could be done—rather than taking part in the petty organizational quarrels to which the splintered American labor movement was prey. Others concurred in his assessment, invariably remarking that Cruikshank had put the social mission, as expressed in the program, above self or organizational interests. In this he was like the official program executives, Altmeyer, Cohen, and Ball, all of whom he greatly admired.

Personally and on behalf of organized labor, for which he could speak, Cruikshank came to hold a piece of the proprietorship. So compelling was this claim to a proprietary share in social insurance that it was acknowledged even by Republicans. Nelson Rockefeller, when he was under secretary of HEW in the Eisenhower administration, virtually promised that top-ranking appointments to the SSA would be acceptable to labor, and the appointments of the first two social security commissioners thereafter were cleared with Cruikshank.[27] When the Democrats returned in 1961, Cruikshank himself was sounded out about being commissioner. Members of the Kennedy administration wanted to know if he would be interested, but he said he would not. Labor had objected to treating the job as a partisan appointment when the Republicans had removed Altmeyer, and Cruikshank thought it would be unwise to reverse that position. Labor preferred the practice of nonpartisanship, which was tantamount to putting a career program executive in charge. In this case it would be Robert Ball, who had actually been in charge for years anyway, and was, in Cruikshank's view, as deserving of the commissionership as he was well qualified. During a Democratic administration, there was nothing to gain by labor's claiming the appointment since the program would be safely in the hands of close friends and collaborators anyway, and there could be much to lose in Republican years if the practice of partisan appointments was established.

26. Lesser-Schorr, OHC, p. 18.
27. Cruikshank, OHC, pp. 128–33.

Staff Relations with the SSA

Policymaking for social security was structured in a way that attracted sympathetic outsiders and converted them into insiders; that was the function of the advisory councils, to which Cruikshank was regularly appointed. Assimilation was easier in Cruikshank's case than for some other outsiders because the general disposition of the organization he represented was highly favorable to the program and its expansion. He was not pulled this way and that as were representatives of manufacturing industry like Marion Folsom or the insurance industry like Reinhard Hohaus. In the specific case of organized labor, the formal method of cooptation embodied in the advisory councils was powerfully reinforced by personal and informal working relations. The labor-SSA collaboration was rooted in communications between labor's social security staff and the staff of the SSA, particularly Wilbur Cohen, who was the leading cue-giver regarding legislative strategies. The personal relations so formed furthered the collaboration of organizations.

In this network of personal relations there was also one important member, Elizabeth Wickenden, who had no formal connection with either organized labor or the Social Security Administration yet helped to make their alliance effective. Wickenden worked for various New Deal agencies (the Emergency Relief Administration, the Works Progress Administration, the National Youth Administration) after graduating from Vassar. From 1941 to 1951, she was Washington representative of the American Public Welfare Association, an organization of public assistance administrators, and during the 1950s and 1960s a consultant and adviser to a congeries of public and private welfare organizations and lobbyist on behalf of welfare causes, including medicare. A friend of both Lyndon Johnson and Wilbur Cohen, she helped bring the two of them together at a time when Johnson's power in the Senate was rising, and she was instrumental in formulating the APWA's position in support of social insurance. Public assistance administrators might have been expected to oppose the growth of social security as a rival program; that their organization supported it and urged the governors to support it too, on the ground that social security would relieve the state governments of assistance costs, owed something to Elizabeth Wickenden's organizing skill and argumentative power. She was also on close terms with labor's representatives on social security, and this helped the social security coalition when the labor movement was badly split. She told an interviewer: "I became nominal, I'd say, leader of the social security lobby in that period [during the years as Washington representative of the APWA] because, at least in the beginning, the AFL and the CIO were separate organizations. Green would not permit the AFL men to sit down with the CIO woman on social security unless a third party brought them together. So I became that third party. We had a very closely knit group of people who worked on social security during that period."[28]

Organized labor's social security staff was employed by the national federations—the AFL, the CIO, and after 1955 the merged federation —and was based in Washington. Only a few of the national and international unions, the federation units, had social security staff specialists, and when they did, as in the leading case of the United Auto Workers, it was primarily to handle the pension agreements that were the subject of collective bargaining. Within the CIO, these staff specialists occasionally met in Washington, but the meetings were discontinued after the merger and, in any case, had considered social insurance only as one subject among many. As program specialists, then, the Washington staff had virtually exclusive jurisdiction. They were responsible to social security committees made up of elected union officials, and they had to share staff functions with legislative representatives—specialists in lobbying—but as staff specialists in social insurance they were practically unrivaled.

In the CIO the staff specialist after 1942 was Katherine Ellickson, a Vassar graduate who began work in the mid-1930s when the CIO was still a fledgling dissident within the AFL. Laid off in 1937, she got a job at the National Labor Relations Board and then in the Social Security Board's Division of Research and Statistics before returning to the CIO.

28. Interview with Elizabeth Wickenden Goldschmidt, 1974, p. 23, Lyndon Baines Johnson Library, Austin, Texas. The inner core of the working coalition for social security, as Elizabeth Wickenden thought of it, consisted of Wilbur Cohen, Nelson Cruikshank, Fedele Fauri of the Library of Congress staff, Katherine Ellickson of the CIO (see below), and herself. They had no formal place or schedule for meetings, but had almost daily phone conversations while the 1950 amendments were under consideration. Others who were more loosely attached to this working coalition, in Wickenden's view, were Ball, Altmeyer, and I. S. Falk within the SSA; several congressmen and their legislative assistants; and other labor representatives, particularly those connected with the autoworkers and steelworkers. Interview with Elizabeth Wickenden, Oral History Collection of Columbia University (1967), pp. 24–26.

At the Social Security Board she went through the agency's usual course of intensive training and then helped edit the *Social Security Bulletin* and prepare the annual reports. She did not then know Cohen personally, but stood in awe of him as a junior staff member would. When she went back to the CIO, its radicalism had been subdued by both internal changes and the wartime antifascist alliance of the United States with the Soviet Union. Lee Pressman, the radical lawyer at CIO headquarters who had written the resolutions on social security, was no longer writing them, though he remained on the CIO staff until a purge of communist members took place in 1947–49. Katherine Ellickson would henceforth write them.

As a former employee of the agency, Ellickson fitted comfortably into the developing pattern of cooperation with the SSA. One of her first tasks at the CIO was to prepare a pamphlet in support of the Wagner-Murray-Dingell bill. In this she worked closely with the SSA staff, which supplied detailed editorial advice.[29] Less in awe of Cohen when the professional distance between them diminished, Ellickson nonetheless deferred to his leadership in the handling of legislation. "Wilbur would tell us [labor's social security staff] what ought to be done," she later recalled, "and we would be the link with the lobbying people."[30] When the merger occurred she remained on the staff as an assistant to Cruikshank, her AFL counterpart who became director of the merged department, but she left after 1960 because, she told an interviewer, the job ceased to be exhilarating when the Democrats returned to power and labor lost leadership of the medicare campaign.[31]

On the AFL side, Cruikshank came to his job in 1944 innocent of experience with social insurance or acquaintance with the SSA's staff, "but I guess if there was one, there were fifty people who told me that the first thing I should do was get acquainted with Wilbur Cohen," he later said.[32] After ten years in social security planning and administration, Cohen was the epitome of expertise. Cruikshank was a novice. Though trained to be a minister, he had become a union organizer in-

29. *Investigation of the Participation of Federal Officials in the Formation and Operation of Health Workshops,* Hearings before the Subcommittee on Publicity and Propaganda of the House Committee on Expenditures in the Executive Departments, 80 Cong. 1 sess. (GPO, 1947), pp. 99–100.

30. Interview with the author, May 7, 1976.

31. Interview with Katherine Ellickson, Oral History Collection, Columbia University (1967).

32. Cruikshank, OHC, p. 31.

stead and then worked for the War Manpower Commission. There was no one at AFL headquarters who could help him much with social security. Having been hired to work for passage of the Wagner-Murray-Dingell bill, in an office created partly at the SSA's urging, he turned naturally to the SSA for guidance—and the principal source of guidance was Cohen. This would be true for years to come.

Intelligent and well educated, Cruikshank of course gained understanding with experience, but his staff was very small (he worked alone at first) and had to handle a wide range of issues in addition to old age insurance, including unemployment compensation, workmen's compensation, and public assistance. In these circumstances, it was not unusual for Cohen or other SSA officials to prepare the AFL's public statements on social security, as well as, of course, the complex bills that labor formally sponsored. "We would talk back and forth a bit, and then I would say, 'Write it up,' " Cruikshank later recalled. He lacked time, he explained, and the necessary familiarity with technical terminology to do that sort of thing himself.[33]

The intimate collaboration with the SSA continued as long as Cruikshank was in office. SSA officials learned that they could count on him for support, and, having built this bond of confidence, he did nothing to jeopardize it. "Nelson went quite far to avoid any break or seeming break with the administration," Lisbeth Schorr concluded of the medicare campaign. "The fact that the administration people could count on Nelson to support them helped them to trust Nelson a great deal in a way that they would not have trusted somebody who was willing to risk more."[34]

That Cruikshank was acquainted with the Washington milieu of policymaking provides one final explanation for organized labor's agreeing closely so much of the time with the program leadership in the SSA. Members of the governing community in the nation's capital learn to accommodate to one another as well as to speak for their constituencies. Initiatives depend on some assessment of how others in the community, Congress in particular, will react. Thus Cruikshank learned to balance what labor wanted against what had the best chance of being passed. Program executives performed comparable calculations from their own organizational perspective, and if the two arrived at similar conclusions, it was not only because organized labor's staff was sensitive to official

33. Interview with the author, May 14, 1976.
34. Lesser-Schorr, OHC, pp. 24–25.

cues. It was also because both were sensitive to opinions and relations of power in the same governing community. Always, they shared a concern about their common enemies on the right, especially the AMA.

Within organized labor, Cruikshank's close relations with SSA officials were on the whole an advantage. Labor sought and was gratified by official recognition. When the AFL finally became interested in old age insurance in the 1940s, it was largely because it wanted a share in policymaking. Cruikshank's membership on advisory councils and intimate personal collaboration with SSA officials provided the kind of recognition and entrée that labor sought and enhanced Cruikshank's own standing and influence within the AFL and AFL-CIO. Labor peers and superiors accepted him as an expert on social security on the showing that he had been awarded recognition by the ultimate experts in the SSA. Not until 1965, when Cruikshank retired, did the more militant elements of the AFL-CIO, always potential dissidents, move to assert themselves regarding social security.

Defection of the UAW

After 1965 labor divided and the dissenting portion, the United Auto Workers under Walter P. Reuther, adopted a position on social insurance more advanced and more liberal than that of the programmatic mainstream. To analyze why the alliance with the SSA fragmented in this way will make it easier to understand how and why the alliance had functioned so smoothly in the two preceding decades.

In a way, the late 1960s were a reprise of the 1930s. In withdrawing from the AFL-CIO, the UAW reasserted its historic radicalism. According to Reuther, the split was over whether the labor movement would commit itself to social struggle and change. (The AFL-CIO, minimizing policy differences, accused the UAW of a campaign of vilification and cited a series of purely organizational differences.) However, in the changed conditions of the 1960s, without the catalyzing influences of the Communist party and a violently hostile auto industry, the genuine militance of the founding generation could not be recaptured. Nor did Reuther's UAW propose to sweep away the legacy of the New Deal, the large pieces of the welfare state already in place. Its critique of social insurance was less fundamental than what had come from Lee Pressman's pen thirty years before. Then the CIO had opposed contributory social insurance and called for universal pensions for the elderly paid for out of general revenues. In 1966–67 the UAW accepted social insurance but wanted to enlarge it and make it more egalitarian. "A comprehensive system of social insurance should be the basic mechanism for providing a guaranteed income for workers and their dependents," it said.[35] And it wanted this change to occur right away. "We need to raise our sights and stop this endless patchwork approach to social security where we tinker over here, we tinker over here, we use a little baling wire over here, and then we say, 'Well, we fixed it up until it catches up with us the next time,' " Reuther testified.[36] The UAW rejected the incrementalism that had become the settled way of policymaking for social security.

With the enactment of medicare in 1965, the agenda defined by the Wagner-Murray-Dingell bill had been exhausted. Not every item had been achieved in its entirety (health insurance in particular was incomplete), but the basic structure was now established, and the agenda was open. For the proprietors of the program, it was a time for defining new directions. Things were in flux, and, as always, it was Wilbur Cohen who pointed the way. The medicare act became law on July 30, and in October 1965 the *American Federationist* carried an article in which he signaled a campaign for bigger benefits. Social insurance, he said, should have a larger part in combating poverty. Raising benefits for the aged and disabled could reduce the poverty rolls by one-fourth to one-third.[37]

The AFL-CIO responded with a fervor that probably surprised its long-time friends in the SSA. The convention of December 1965 called for a benefit increase of 50 percent, a big rise in the wage base, the introduction of general revenues, a lower retirement age, and liberalization of the medicare and disability programs. Except that he had not mentioned using general revenues, this was consistent with what Cohen had laid out, but it went further than officials were accustomed to going in one step. Cruikshank had retired in the fall of 1965, and the UAW, which had earlier been restrained by his presence, had moved into the vacuum.

35. *President's Proposals for Revision in the Social Security System*, Hearings before the House Committee on Ways and Means, 90 Cong. 1 sess. (GPO, 1967), pt. 3, p. 1450.

36. Ibid., p. 1422.

37. Wilbur J. Cohen, "The Role of Social Insurance," *American Federationist*, vol. 71 (October 1965), pp. 2–6.

Matters did not come to rest with the convention resolution of December 1965. The UAW would not settle merely for having influenced the position of the federation, and it soon set forth an independent position on social security in a bill that Senator Robert F. Kennedy introduced in the summer of 1966, shortly after President Johnson announced that he would make social security proposals in 1967. Kennedy's proposal was announced first, and it was bigger; the rival bidding that sometimes took place between parties over social security benefits was taking place within the Democratic party. Kennedy, who was elected to the Senate in 1964 following his brother's assassination, was taking independent positions on a wide range of issues, laying the ground for his own claim to party leadership. In collaborating with Kennedy, the UAW was not breaking with the party, but was aligning itself with the President's rival for party leadership. The existence of so prominent and aggressive a rival was one condition of the division between labor's left wing and the SSA. The usual partisan constraints on division had weakened.

The Kennedy-UAW bill never came to a vote, although Kennedy reintroduced it in 1967. SSA officials meanwhile had presented to Congress President Johnson's proposals for a 20 percent benefit increase and other measures to improve the effectiveness of social insurance as an antipoverty program—proposals that had perhaps been enlarged in response to the Kennedy-UAW pressure. The AFL-CIO supported the administration's proposals while the UAW carried on its dissent to the left of both. The National Council of Senior Citizens, labor's organized adjunct of the elderly, followed the position of the federation rather than the UAW, which caused the UAW to withdraw funds from the council.

In 1967, with the UAW in open dissent and approaching departure from the federation, Meany retreated somewhat from the expansive resolution of 1965 for which the UAW had been responsible. Whatever strain the AFL-CIO's advanced position had caused the alliance was eased. The alliance, it was clear, was still functioning but had suffered a relatively minor crack parallel to organized labor's own schism.

THE CONSTRAINTS on official conduct meant that program executives needed a private collaborator, an unconstrained ally outside the government. They found one in organized labor—the AFL principally, as represented for years by Nelson Cruikshank. This outside ally could freely do things that they could not: sponsor bills that an incumbent administration opposed, openly lobby and engage in propaganda contests, enter into campaign activity against program critics in Congress. However, the constraints on official conduct were never so rigid or so binding as to prevent program executives from collaborating very closely with this private ally, to whom they provided a steady stream of policy cues and usable information. Without this stream of official support and stimulation, the private ally would have been less active and less complaisant. With it, a close, mutually supportive relation was formed. The program proprietorship of the official executives merged harmoniously with the unofficial proprietorship of organized labor, to the advantage of their shared positions on policy.

CHAPTER SIX

The Conservative Resistance

IT WOULD be misleading to write of opposition to social insurance. Not since 1936, when Republican presidential candidate Alf Landon called for repeal of old age insurance and was beaten badly in the election, has any important public official or private organization urged that the program be ended. On the other hand, there has been a great deal of resistance to its steady expansion from the major national business organizations (the National Association of Manufacturers and more particularly the Chamber of Commerce), the insurance industry, and with greatest intensity, the American Medical Association.

In general, conservative interests have neither sought to repeal enacted legislation and restore the status quo ante, nor to put forth alternative public measures as rivals to social insurance. Instead, there has been a reflexive effort to hold the line wherever the line might be at the moment. The effect of this conservative resistance has generally been to delay or to restrict officially sponsored expansion but not to defeat it—not for very long, anyway—in favor of a fundamentally different alternative.

If the pattern of inertial development of the social insurance program was to be challenged, alternatives to the official proposals for expansion had to come from somewhere, and conservative interest groups are one place from which, logically, they might have come. I explain below why in general this did not happen, and why conservative activity fell rather into a pattern of piecemeal resistance to piecemeal advances within a framework that most participants in policymaking came to accept as fixed.

After considering why this pattern of conservative resistance developed, my analysis considers two significant exceptions. One is the lack of conservative resistance to the addition of dependents and survivors benefits in 1939. It is an anomalous and intriguing fact that much of the impetus for this crucial act came from conservative sources, and that some of the conceptual work in support of it was performed inside the Metropolitan Life Insurance Company. A second significant exception is a proposal sponsored by the Chamber of Commerce in 1953 that would have extended social insurance immediately to all of the aged, without regard to their payroll tax contributions, and ended federal grants-in-aid to state governments for the indigent elderly. Here was a well-considered initiative from a conservative source that would have made an important change in the social insurance program, and it failed completely. Far from being adopted by Congress, it was not even seriously considered.[1]

The Logic of Resistance

If one may put it so, resistance was the course of least resistance for the conservative interest groups. To actively oppose, rather than to merely resist change, would have required internal consensus and considerable organizational effort, which could only have been achieved if conservative interests felt fundamentally threatened by social insurance. This was true whether opposition took the negative form of arguing for reversal of policies or the more positive form of offering conservative alternatives for public action—alternatives that would presumably have safeguarded a larger sphere for voluntary action or would have been designed with more concern for containing long-run costs.

Following Landon's defeat in 1936 and a Supreme Court decision in 1937 upholding the constitutionality of social insurance legislation, negative opposition would have been feckless, an utter waste of effort. Business opponents thereafter had to wait for the arrival of a Republican regime—and they waited a long time. While they were waiting, they got used to the idea and the institutional reality of social insurance and ceased to be strident in opposition. (None would have said in 1953, as

1. Though it fits the pattern of resistance to be described here, the activity of the American Medical Association in opposition to health insurance was so much more intense than other conservative activity as to constitute a special case. For that reason, and because it was special also in being largely confined to health insurance, it is analyzed separately in chapter 16 on the adoption of medicare.

Silas Strawn, a past president of the American Bar Association and U.S. Chamber of Commerce, said in 1935, that the Social Security Act was "economically preposterous and legally indefensible.")[2] Indeed, some became converts through a changed perception of corporate interests. As the big CIO unions began to demand pension plans through collective bargaining, big businessmen such as Charles E. Wilson of General Motors developed a positive enthusiasm for social insurance.[3] After steel and auto strikes over pensions, the National Association of Manufacturers formally revised its historic opposition to the program.[4]

While a large majority of businessmen initially opposed social insurance, fearing its costs and the effects on work attitudes and the economic system, there was also from the start a small number of prominent business executives who were prepared to argue the social necessity of it. Having a strong sense of social responsibility, such men were readily available for public service, and, having a need for business support, the Roosevelt administration and the Social Security Board were eager to engage them. Several such men, including Gerard Swope, president of the General Electric Company, Morris E. Leeds, president of Leeds and Northrup, Walter S. Teagle, president of the Standard Oil Company of New Jersey, and Marion B. Folsom, treasurer of Eastman Kodak, served on the advisory council of 1934 and subsequently constituted the Social Security Committee of the Business Advisory Council, an organization of corporate statesmen relatively sympathetic to the New Deal that was attached to the Department of Commerce. As coopted supporters of the program these executives helped to counteract business opposition in the early days of strident opposition to the New Deal and eventually to win a measure of business acceptance for social insurance. Folsom in particular was active as an emissary to business. Having been drawn into official circles, he became an expert on the government program. Then, as an expert, he held offices in the business associations. He chaired the social security committees of both the Chamber of Commerce and the National Association of Manufacturers and was instrumental in bringing them around to a "constructive" position.

2. *Proceedings of the Thirtieth Annual Meeting of the American Life Convention* (Chicago: ALC, 1935), p. 130.

3. See the excerpt from Wilson's speech of January 6, 1950, "Economic Factors of Collective Bargaining," before the Chicago Executives Club, in Neil W. Chamberlain, *Sourcebook on Labor* (McGraw-Hill, 1958), pp. 999–1002.

4. Interview witth Marion B. Folsom, Oral History Collection, Columbia University (1965–68), pp. 60–61, 76.

As ambivalence and internal division inhibited negative opposition, they also inhibited the formation of conservative alternatives to social insurance. Basically suspicious of government action in support of social welfare, conservative interest groups lacked an independent agenda, and they could not consolidate support for the occasional legislative idea that happened to spring from their side. This was particularly evident in the course of the long contest over health care legislation. Republican officeholders in Congress and in the Eisenhower administration inter-mittently cast about for alternatives with which they might deflect the campaign for government insurance while winning electoral credits of their own. They got no support from the insurance industry or the AMA, which viewed any government action as a fatal entering wedge. The insurance industry, the AMA, and the Chamber of Commerce all declined, for instance, to support an Eisenhower administration pro-posal under which the government would have shared the risk of private insurers who experimented with wider health care coverage.[5] Govern-ment "reinsurance" would have reimbursed insurance companies for up to 75 percent of their losses. Many conservatives joined a solid bloc of liberals in opposing the bill. Similarly, representatives of the conserva-tive interest groups declined in the early years of the Nixon administra-tion to support the automatic adjustment of social security benefits to cost of living increases, which Republican officeholders hoped would slow expansion and deprive Democrats of political credit for benefit increases.

Equally unable to advocate retreat or advance, the conservative in-terest groups were united in favor of holding still, unless for the purpose of reaching additional classes of workers. Universal coverage, but with low benefits, became the conservatives' objective. They accepted old age insurance once it was enacted, but opposed increases in the wage base or in benefits unless they were strictly tied to increases in the cost of living. They opposed the addition of disability and health care coverage.

The public assistance alternative (which would have confined federal support to the needy, linked it to a means test, and left administration to state and local governments) was always more acceptable to the con-servatives than a federally administered program that gave benefits independently of need. Public assistance was the approach conserva-

5. *Proceedings of the Forty-ninth Annual Meeting of the American Life Con-vention* (Chicago: ALC, 1954), pp. 27–28.

tives advocated whenever an extension of insurance was proposed. But not even this alternative was a conservative invention. As a mode of federal action for social welfare, it was a creation of the New Deal, which incorporated federal grants for support of the indigent aged and dependent children in the Social Security Act along with the more controversial measures for old age insurance and unemployment insurance.

The Limited Response of the Insurance Industry

The insurance industry is the group from which the most vigorous reaction to social insurance might have been expected to come. It had a more consistent stake in social insurance legislation than did the AMA, which felt profoundly threatened by health legislation but cared nothing about cash support of the aged, and it was more directly affected by social insurance than the general run of business organizations that made up the Chamber of Commerce and the NAM. As employers, businesses in general were compelled to pay a 50 percent share of the social security payroll tax, but the actual cost fell elsewhere (in the form of lowered wages for employees or higher prices for consumers), so that their concern about social insurance was mainly the diffuse concern that profit-making entrepreneurs always felt about government incursions into the economy. They might worry about the effects on the capitalist system and on work attitudes, but not specifically about next year's profits. The insurance industry alone was directly threatened by government competition. Yet the industry was never aroused enough about social insurance to engage in much political activity. In February 1935, when the Social Security Act was pending, the Association of Life Insurance Presidents, a leading trade association, decided against taking a position on it.[6] Eventually, the industry fell into the common conservative pattern of reflexive resistance to expansion.

It was not clear to insurance company executives in 1935 how their business would be affected. Few demonstrated much knowledge or concern about the impending bill. Of those who did, some were apprehensive while others argued that a government program would make the public more conscious of the need for insurance and hence more suscep-

6. *Social Security Legislation*, Hearings before the House Committee on Ways and Means, 85 Cong. 2 sess. (GPO, 1958), pp. 604–05.

tible to commercial sales.[7] A proposal in the social security bill that the government sell insurance, with a program of voluntary individual annuities to supplement the compulsory program, understandably appears to have caused some concern, and on the initiative of a Democratic senator from Connecticut, Augustine Lonergan, that provision was dropped from the bill. Presumably he was acting in defense of the industry, which then as now contained a heavy concentration of companies in Connecticut. But even on this seemingly sensitive point, industry opinion was divided. The vice president and general counsel of the industry's giant, the Metropolitan Life Insurance Company, told a convention of the company's managers in 1935 that the "Met" would not object if the government sold individual annuities.

Even in retrospect it is not easy to assess the effect of the government program on the private industry. On the one hand, the industry remains a giant; on the other, private investment in life insurance has nowhere near kept pace with increases in national income. An industry survey prepared by Standard & Poor's in the mid-1970s noted that the life insurance industry had enjoyed a good level of growth in the previous two decades, but cited as a negative factor the recent expansion of old age security provided through social security, company pension and profit-sharing plans, and medicare.[8]

Because the effects of the government program on the private industry were always difficult to assess, they could be interpreted differently by different subgroups within the industry, and life insurance was a divided industry. Agents were divided from management, and management was divided between the giant companies of the eastern seaboard, most of which were mutuals, and the smaller companies of the South, Midwest, and West, which were mainly stock companies.[9]

Agents have been organized in the National Association of Life

7. R. Carlyle Buley, *The American Life Convention, 1906–1952: A Study in the History of Life Insurance* (Appleton-Century-Crofts, 1953), vol. 2, p. 794; Leroy A. Lincoln, "The Economic Security Legislation as Viewed by a Life Insurance Company," an address before the Annual Convention of the Managers of the Metropolitan Life Insurance Company, February 2, 1935; M. Albert Linton, "The Federal Old Age Security Program," in *Proceedings of the Thirtieth Annual Meeting of the American Life Convention* (Chicago: ALC, 1935), pp. 109–27.

8. *Standard & Poor's Industry Surveys: Insurance Basic Analysis* (January 17, 1974), sec. 2.

9. Stock companies are owned by shareholders who elect a board to direct the company's management and have an equity in the company's earnings, some portion of which may be distributed to them in the form of dividends. Managements of mutual companies are elected by their policyholders. Mutual companies typically

Underwriters. Until a merger that created the American Life Insurance Association in 1973, management was divided between the Life Insurance Association of America (LIAA), a New York–based organization of the Eastern giants, and the American Life Convention (ALC), Chicago-based, which brought the smaller, outlying companies together. Both were formed in 1906, soon after an investigation of the big New York companies by a committee of the New York State legislature (the Armstrong investigation). The two groups of companies fought over shares of the market, over regulatory actions that affected their competitive positions, and over the differing impact of federal income tax laws on stock and mutual companies. Merger of the two trade associations proved very hard to achieve even though, as time passed, most of the Eastern companies joined the ALC. Fear of the giants persisted in the ALC, and contempt for the smaller companies in the LIAA.[10]

Management worried that their agents, along with the politicians and social security administrators, were responsible for fueling the public's appetite for social insurance benefits. The more enterprising agents organized sales strategies around a showing that social insurance was inadequate and needed supplementing. The fact that the public program was incrementally revised, far from putting them out of business, constantly refreshed the opportunity to review a client's coverage: a new law on the books meant a foot in the door. However, if agents were more receptive to the program than management, this difference was not revealed in positions of their trade association, which social security executives judged to be relatively antagonistic.[11]

---

issue only participating policies on which the holder is entitled to receive dividends. There are about nine times as many stock companies as mutuals, but the mutuals accounted in 1972 for about two-thirds of the industry's $240 billion in assets and slightly more than half of its insurance in force. The giant companies are overwhelmingly concentrated in the Northeast (New York, New Jersey, Connecticut, Massachusetts). (Ibid., p. 16.) For an analysis from the 1930s, see David Lynch, *The Concentration of Economic Power* (Columbia University Press, 1946), pp. 118–25, which is based on hearings of the Temporary National Economic Committee between 1938 and 1941.

10. Interview with Albert Pike, retired official of the American Life Insurance Association, October 4, 1976; Buley, *The American Life Convention*, vol. 1, intro., chaps. 4 and 5.

11. Charles W. Campbell, "The Field Man Looks Ahead," *Proceedings of the Forty-fifth Annual Meeting of the American Life Convention* (Chicago: ALC, 1950), pp. 189–90, and W. T. Grant, "Why Are YOU Here?" *Proceedings of the Forty-ninth Annual Meeting of the American Life Convention* (Chicago: ALC, 1954), p. 228; author's interview with Robert M. Ball, February 2, 1976.

Within management, the leaders of the Eastern giants were less resistant to social insurance than executives of the smaller companies in the hinterlands. The difference paralleled the difference between the Republican party's Eastern progressive wing and its conservative Midwestern core. Neither part of the industry welcomed the government's entry into insurance, but the Easterners, according to a veteran industry source, fell into the "roll-with-the-punch school," whereas the Midwesterners suffered from what some of the Easterners called "foot-and-nose disease"—they invariably deplored the foot-in-the-door and the camel's-nose-under-the-tent. Their instinct was for absolute opposition.[12]

It was significant for the development of social insurance politics and policymaking that the more progressive Easterners generally spoke for the industry and had greater influence in defining its position. Beginning in 1945 the industry intermittently issued policy statements regarding social security, typically through joint action of the ALC and LIAA. In the first of these, the industry endorsed social insurance as a means of replacing charity and public relief "because it is more orderly, dignified, and reliable," but declared that it should provide basic, minimal protection only. Above the publicly provided minimum, security should continue to come from "the exercise of personal industry and thrift."[13] A few leading Easterners plotted this path of constructive yet qualified acceptance, neutralizing the negativism that was latent in much of the rest of the industry. Two men in particular were influential: M. Albert Linton, president of the Provident Mutual Life Insurance Company of Philadelphia, and Reinhard A. Hohaus, an assistant actuary with the Metropolitan Life Insurance Company in the 1930s who eventually became chief actuary and senior vice president of the company. Linton chaired the industry's first social security committee and Hohaus followed him.

The more progressive and socially conscious members of the industry prevailed because they overwhelmingly surpassed the executives of the smaller companies in expertise and staff resources, because they believed in social action, and, not least, because it was they who received official invitations to participate in social security policymaking. They were

12. Interview with Albert Pike, October 4, 1976.
13. "Social Security," a statement by the Social Security Committee of the American Life Convention, Life Insurance Association of America, and the National Association of Life Underwriters, February 1945, as quoted in E. J. Faulkner, "Social Security and Insurance—Some Relationships in Perspective," *Journal of Insurance,* vol. 30 (June 1963), p. 200.

the logical targets of cooptation. Linton was an actuarial adviser to the Committee on Economic Security in 1934 and a member of the first two advisory councils. Hohaus testified before the 1937–39 council, served on two later councils, and chaired the "Hobby lobby" of 1953. But though they were on the outer progressive edge of the insurance industry, they did not quite belong to the inner family who shared proprietorship of the social insurance program. Differences of interest and opinion were too deep to be bridged by forms or even by personal friendship, such as bound the good-natured and pragmatic Hohaus to the similarly good-natured and pragmatic Wilbur Cohen. Hohaus dissented from the advisory council recommendation on medicare in 1965, even though under the gentle coaxing of J. Douglas Brown he repeatedly moderated the language of dissent. Linton before him, along with Marion Folsom, had dissented from the advisory council recommendation on disability coverage. Linton was greatly preoccupied with the program's long-run costs, and Hohaus, though less a fiscal conservative and less a representative of the industry than Linton, was similarly concerned. The private-industry connection, the fiscal consciousness, and the dissents on major measures of expansion inescapably differentiated them from the official and quasi-official family, despite the proven depth of their interest and their long participation. Within their sphere of activity, the official establishment and the private industry overlapped, but the mutual adjustment remained imperfect. Vis-à-vis the insurance industry, the advisory councils could be only partly successful as a medium of cooptation.

Whether in regard to social security or any other subject, the industry was reluctant to take a conspicuous part in national politics. This was true especially of the dominant Eastern wing. The industry's great size and wealth made it an inviting target of government inquiry, as the Armstrong investigation in New York State in 1906 and the investigations of the Temporary National Economic Committee in Congress in the late 1930s showed. Measured by its assets, the Metropolitan Life Insurance Company was the biggest business in the country in 1937, though it subsequently gave way to another insurance company, the Prudential Insurance Company of America. In 1972 both exceeded the assets of Standard Oil of New Jersey and General Motors, their nearest rivals, by more than $10 billion. For such behemoths to pursue an aggressively self-interested course was a considerable risk to public relations, and it has been a point of pride with insurance company executives that they did not spend big money in national politics in contrast, say, to the petroleum or dairy industries.[14]

To solicit or to accept federal favors risked inviting intrusion; hence the industry's resistance to the Eisenhower administration's proposal for health "reinsurance," which would have subsidized portions of the health insurance business. On the other hand, to attack federal policy could invite regulatory counterattack. In response to the industry's opposition to medicare proposals, Wilbur Cohen warned that it was in danger of winning the battle in Washington but losing the war. The consequence of industry opposition to medicare, he said, would be federal controls to ensure that private insurers acted in the public interest.[15] Given these risks, the industry generally preferred to keep a low profile in national government affairs. It is noteworthy that although they maintained small Washington offices, neither of the two big trade associations had a Washington headquarters until their merger in 1973. Much of the lobbying was done by company executives who traveled to Washington to appear with trade association officers at public hearings and then remained to talk informally and privately with committee members. The industry never mounted mass campaigns such as the AMA undertook in opposition to health insurance.

Finally, to the extent that the industry did become involved in social security politics and policymaking, some of its leaders consciously chose a pragmatic, accommodationist course in the belief that this would preserve access to important decisions. This was notably true of the executives of the Metropolitan, principally Hohaus. To secure access to decisions it was necessary to win acceptance and esteem from the official family of program proprietors in Congress and the executive. Without such acceptance, there could be no access, and without access there could be no influence—influence valued for its own sake, since insurance executives are no more immune than anyone else to the excitement of being part of important events, and influence considered essential, even by the most sympathetic industry executives, to restrain this ever-expanding program. One sign of the accommodationist attitude was

14. For a historical explanation of the insurance companies' political reticence, see Morton Keller, *The Life Insurance Enterprise, 1885–1910: A Study in the Limits of Corporate Power* (Harvard University Press, 1963), part 6 of which deals explicitly with the companies' "disengagement from power."

15. Wilbur J. Cohen, "The Challenge of Aging to Insurance," *Journal of Insurance*, vol. 27 (December 1960), pp. 16–17.

Hohaus's angry reaction in the early 1960s when Ray Peterson, vice president and associate actuary of another New York giant, the Equitable Life Assurance Society of the United States, began writing contentious articles about social security. Executives at the Met believed that Peterson's combativeness would jeopardize the industry's credibility in Congress. Significantly, when visiting Capitol Hill the Met's executives usually carried their case to Wilbur Mills, the Democratic chairman of Ways and Means, rather than to the committee's Republican members— again, a sign of the executives' accommodation to the political realities, and a source of constraint on their behavior.[16]

A combination of uncertain stakes, internal differences, aversion to political involvement on the national plane, and sheer pragmatism inhibited the insurance industry. Creation of a public rival for the provision of insurance produced much apprehension and some active resistance, but not the kind of organized and aggressive political response that would have engaged the industry deeply in social security policymaking.

Conservatives as Activists: The 1939 Amendments

Conservative passivity interwoven with official zeal formed the basic pattern of social security policymaking, but interesting irregularities appear in this pattern, of which the 1939 amendments to the Social Security Act were first. Otherwise critical of the insurance industry's negative role, Wilbur Cohen conceded in 1960 that industry representatives had been instrumental over twenty years earlier in preparing the amendments that extended benefits to aged dependents and to survivors.[17] Industry resistance to expansion, though eventually sustained over decades, was initially delayed. Whence came the anomalous activism of 1939, so welcome in retrospect to social security officials? The answers are to be found in the nature of the issues in 1939 and the nature of the industry's involvement.

The critical issue in 1939 was not an issue over expansion, or, if so, it was so thoroughly ambiguous, confused, and complicated by other questions that to separate the opponents of expansion from proponents is

16. Interview with Charles A. Siegfried, November 3, 1976.
17. Wilbur J. Cohen, "The Challenge of Aging to Insurance," p. 16.

impossible. Insurance industry executives attacked one feature of social insurance—the planned accumulation of a huge reserve—largely on the ground that it would induce unwarranted expansion. In doing this, they laid the basis for an immediate, expansive reconstruction of the original program. Program executives, who had never favored so big a reserve anyway—that was the Treasury Department's doing in 1935, not theirs— conceded much of the criticism in regard to financing and responded with a program revised to spend more money sooner. A conservative critique had paved the way for a liberal outcome, one of many illustrations of the ambiguity and adaptability of social insurance policy, in which it is often hard to tell the sides apart or who won.

Still, the 1939 amendments were not just the perverse outcome of a conservative criticism designed with other ends in view. One of the strongest arguments for the program extensions of 1939 came from Hohaus. In testimony before the advisory council in 1937, and later in a journal article, he made a powerful case for emphasizing adequacy in a social insurance program. The article became a classic of the literature on American social insurance and was used by the Social Security Board to instruct its employees. Hohaus wrote of the need to found a social insurance program "on broad social concepts rather than on reasoning centered around the individual" and laid out the next steps in that direction. It was a remarkable contribution to public policymaking from a private source.[18]

But this was distinctively an individual contribution or at most the contribution of one very large leading company. For some years the Met had taken an interest in social policy, and it had sent study teams, Hohaus included, to England and the European continent. This pioneering research had been published in a series of monographs by the company's actuaries, whose accumulated expertise was now applied to the planned revision of the American program.[19] Hohaus, who was Catholic, recalled in later years that the inspiration for his work came from papal encyclicals, a source far removed in space and spirit from, say, the proceedings of the American Life Convention. He did not, in retrospect, think of himself as a representative of the industry.

18. Reinhard A. Hohaus, "Equity, Adequacy, and Related Factors in Old Age Security," *The Record,* American Institute of Actuaries, vol. 27, pt. 1 (June 1938), pp. 76–114.

19. On the social consciousness of the Met, see Marquis James, *The Metropolitan Life: A Study in Business Growth* (Viking, 1947).

Linton, who was a member of the advisory council that received Hohaus's testimony, indubitably sat there as an industry representative. As a company president, active in the LIAA, he could not credibly have disclaimed that role. Yet he combined it indistinguishably with other roles—that of a citizen deeply concerned with public good, and of a professional actuary applying his expertise to important issues of public policy. (Even Arthur Altmeyer, who was not notably generous toward political adversaries or the representatives of private interests, emphasized Linton's moral character to an interviewer.[20] A Quaker, Linton, like Hohaus, was a religious man.) More than anyone else, Linton was responsible for making the conservatives' powerfully reasoned case against full reserve financing. While insurance company executives endorsed his argument and Republican politicians infused it with partisan emotion, the intelligent conception and formulation were his.

Their personal characteristics and activities aside, the most convincing evidence that Hohaus and Linton did not represent an industry position in 1939 is that as yet there was no such position. It was not until the 1940s that the trade associations formed social security committees and began work on a policy statement under Linton's direction. Hence the activity of the two men in 1939 has to be interpreted as highly individual. It was not inconsistent, presumably, with industry interests as they may have conceived them, but it was not determined by those interests either.

Conservatives as Activists: The Chamber's 1953 Proposal

The second case of conservative activism, a proposal put forth by the Chamber of Commerce in 1953 and introduced in Congress the following year by Representative Carl T. Curtis, is of much greater analytic interest both because it cannot so readily be dismissed as the work of individuals and because it came at a time when an initiative from a conservative source should have had a good chance to succeed. It was issued by the chamber's Economic Research Department, approved by its Committee on Social Legislation, and endorsed overwhelmingly by the local membership in a referendum. The published version—a long, well-informed, and well-reasoned piece of work—was widely circulated and

20. Interview with Arthur J. Altmeyer, Oral History Collection, Columbia University (1967), p. 64.

strategically timed to address a Republican government—the first in nearly two decades since the Social Security Act was passed.[21]

The timing of the chamber's proposal suggests that the earlier passivity of conservative interest groups was in part the response to a hostile political environment. It cannot be explained by sheer negativism, internal ambivalence, or official cooptation. As long as the Democrats controlled the national government, conservative critics of the program were afflicted with an understandable defeatism. It seemed hopeless to propose alternatives when partisans of the established program monopolized public office. Thus, when an individual critic—the former actuary of the Social Security Administration, W. Rulon Williamson—offered a very different alternative to the Ways and Means Committee in 1949, including universal coverage of the aged, a uniform benefit independent of need, and pay-as-you-go financing, he received a sympathetic but skeptical response from Representative Curtis:

Mr. Curtis. How long have you lived in Washington?
Mr. Williamson. Since 1936.
Mr. Curtis. Were you a member of the Social Security Board?
Mr. Williamson. I was not a member of the Social Security Board; I was their actuary.
Mr. Curtis. I take judicial notice, then, that you know something about politics. Could a change as sweeping as you have proposed be enacted into law unless the administration, through its Treasury Department, its Bureau of the Budget, and its Federal Security Administration, joined in and headed up the job of selling it to the American people and pointing out the fallacies in our present set-up?
Mr. Williamson. I think the point you make is a very important one.[22]

Given this view, it would take the installation of a Republican government to galvanize a conservative reaction to the sequence of official action begun in 1934–35.

Part of a Republican government arrived after the mid-term election of 1946, in which the Democrats lost control of Congress. The politics and policymaking of social security did change at that time. In Republican hands, legislative powers were opposed to the expansionist drive of the executive; Congress briefly became the center of the conservative resistance. A House subcommittee on publicity and propaganda in the

21. Chamber of Commerce of the United States, *Improving Social Security* (Washington, D.C.: the Chamber, 1953).
22. *Social Security Act Amendments of 1949*, Hearings before the House Committee on Ways and Means, 81 Cong. 1 sess. (GPO, 1949), pt. 2, p. 1502.

executive branch conducted a hostile investigation of the SSA's Bureau of Research and Statistics, after which the House reduced the bureau's appropriations by more than half.[23] (The bureau at that time was the nerve center of the campaign for national health insurance.) The House Committee on Appropriations, in a rare display of its power over administration of the program, drastically reduced the budget for Commissioner Altmeyer's office and instructed that many of the functions located there be transferred either up to the FSA administrator's office or down to the bureaus.[24] Finally, Congress passed two separate resolutions that narrowed social security coverage. One of these, which President Truman had successfully vetoed in 1947, exempted certain newspaper and magazine vendors from coverage. Another, which affected many more persons, reversed a Bureau of Internal Revenue ruling (based on a 1947 Supreme Court decision) that broadened the Social Security Act's definition of an "employee" and thereby extended coverage to some 625,000 life insurance agents, door-to-door salesmen, and persons employed in their own homes. Both measures were passed over Truman's veto with support from a majority of Democrats as well as Republicans.[25] With control of the government divided between a Democratic president and a Republican Congress, social security policy was stalemated. There were no important changes in the program in those years.

The Republican administration that came to Washington in 1953 had no fixed or very well informed views about social security. If one took the Democrats' campaign rhetoric seriously, the program was in mortal danger from Dwight Eisenhower, but if one credited Eisenhower's replies, it would be improved and extended. As is usual with campaign statements, the concrete meaning of all this was obscure. The Republican candidate had never had occasion to study the subject, and neither had the Texas Democrat, a former wartime head of the Women's Army Corps, whom he named to head the Federal Security Agency, shortly to become the new Department of Health, Education, and Welfare. Oveta Culp Hobby felt lonely in the job. Underneath a seemingly dis-

23. *Investigation of the Participation of Federal Officials in the Formation and Operation of Health Workshops,* Hearings before the Subcommittee on Publicity and Propaganda of the House Committee on Expenditures in the Executive Departments, 80 Cong. 1 sess. (GPO, 1947).

24. *The Supplemental Federal Security Agency Appropriation Bill, Fiscal Year 1949,* H. Rept. 1821, 80 Cong. 2 sess. (GPO, 1948).

25. *Congressional Quarterly Almanac,* vol. 3 (1947), pp. 439, 588, and ibid., vol. 4 (1948), pp. 143–45; H. Rept. 1821, 80 Cong. 2 sess.

tant, sometimes curt, manner, subordinates thought that she was unsure of herself. In an early press conference, she declined to comment on social security. It was the most complicated subject she faced, she said.[26]

Conservative critics of social security outside the government were well prepared by contrast. Whatever the reason for their ultimate failure, it was certainly not ignorance of the subject, in which some of them had been deeply engaged for years. Leonard J. Calhoun, the Washington lawyer who wrote the Chamber of Commerce report, had done much of the Senate staff work on the original Social Security Act, had served as an assistant general counsel of the Social Security Board, and had headed a technical study of social security for the Ways and Means Committee in 1945–46. Besides Calhoun, the Chamber's committee on social legislation included Linton and Hohaus.

Conservative dissatisfaction with the program had sharpened as the 1950 amendments evolved, but had been poorly expressed. Though many critiques had been forthcoming from individual sources, there was no organizational sponsorship to give form and effect to the criticism. Conservatives felt that they had abandoned the field to the protagonists in officialdom.[27] Therefore, no sooner had the act of 1950 been passed than proposals for a new series of studies issued from conservative sources. The next round of proposals, they seemed to be saying, should not go by default, and it was a forgone conclusion that a next

26. *New York Times*, April 28, 1953.
27. In 1950, in an endorsement of a proposal to create a study commission, Calhoun wrote despairingly of the dominance of the "official philosophy":

Perhaps the most important single function of the Commission . . . would be the formulation and publication of a social security philosophy. . . . Quite probably, the actual end result of such an effort would be the formulation, by factions of the Commission, of two or more social security philosophies. I cannot believe it likely that any clear-cut philosophy could be developed to which all members would subscribe. However, if opposing philosophies are announced and spelled out by factions of the Commission, this would be a striking advance over the present situation. . . .

Today we have only a kind of an unacknowledged official philosophy concerning individual and state obligations. This official philosophy is evidenced by official viewpoints of the Federal Security Agency, . . . and these viewpoints coincide, for most practical purposes, with the viewpoints officially expressed by labor leaders. Both have issued an enormous amount of propaganda to support their conclusions.

While a strong protest has been voiced to some specific recommendations that have been predicated on this unadmitted official philosophy, those disapproving, by and large, have not presented arguments derived from any clear-cut common philosophy. (*American Economic Security*, vol. 3 [June–July 1950], p. 24. *American Economic Security* was a periodical published by the Chamber of Commerce for twelve years beginning in 1944.)

round would occur soon, for the program was not fully formed: disability and health coverage had yet to be added, and large parts of the working population were still not covered.

The chamber's plan was in every respect designed to reveal the actual costs of supporting the aged. The social insurance program would have been extended to cover ("blanket in") all of the aged immediately, whether or not they had paid payroll taxes, and federal grants-in-aid to the states for old age assistance would have been ended. Social insurance payments would have been financed out of payroll taxes on all current workers, set high enough to meet current need but not to create a reserve. All current workers would have been covered. Social insurance would have clearly been revealed as a program through which current workers supported the currently retired. To demonstrate the costs of doing this, the chamber believed, would tend to contain them. The "dangerous and swelling stream of social security," stated the proposal, would be rechanneled "to reduce the hazard of its bursting out of control."

President Eisenhower's first State of the Union message gave no encouragement to the critics of social security. It contained no fundamental criticism of the program and no call for a fundamental review of it. On the other hand, what the new President did propose—a major extension of coverage—was perfectly consistent with the conservative agenda. The issues that the chamber was trying to raise could still be considered open after the President's speech in early February. In the event, the Department of Health, Education, and Welfare studied social security policy through most of 1953, in two different phases using quite different deliberative procedures, but in neither phase did the department prove receptive to a new approach to policy.

The ad hoc group of outside advisers that Mrs. Hobby assembled soon after taking office was supposed to consider the chamber's plan— she told a press conference that it would, and she told the advisory group itself that it should—but in the end it did not. Instead it very quickly issued a short, heavily technical, noncontroversial report on extension of coverage and then disappeared.[28] This was the group that social security insiders pejoratively called "the Hobby lobby" because it contained three members of the Chamber of Commerce committee

28. *New York Times*, April 28, 1953, p. 30; *American Economic Security*, vol. 10 (March–April 1953), p. 4; Consultants on Social Security, "A Report to the Secretary of Health, Education, and Welfare on Extension of Old-Age and Survivors Insurance to Additional Groups of Current Workers" (HEW, 1953).

on social security; but it also contained nine others, including representatives of the AFL, CIO, and the organized social work profession. Arthur
Altmeyer believed that Mrs. Hobby initially intended to have a smaller,
less formal, business-dominated group and that other members were
added only because organized labor complained.[29] The broadening of
representation narrowed the potential range of discussion and inhibited
conservative innovation. Extending coverage was the one measure on
which the forces contending over social security policy could agree. Perhaps for that reason, it was the only measure that the representatives
of these forces, organized in a small consulting group, talked about.
Primed to insist on a thoroughgoing review of the program, their case
ably prepared by Calhoun over the course of a year, the conservatives
did not press that case in an official forum ostensibly created to solicit
advice. To do so would only have provoked a fight, and this would have
embarrassed the administration—"their" administration, the first since
1932. Just as organized labor was constrained during Democratic administrations by a reluctance to make trouble for its friends, conservatives were constrained at this seemingly opportune yet fleeting moment.[30]

Though the Hobby lobby disbanded in default on the fundamental

29. Arthur J. Altmeyer, *The Formative Years of Social Security* (University of
Wisconsin Press, 1966), pp. 213–15.

30. The general point is well illustrated by the recollections of a Metropolitan
Life Insurance Company executive, Charles A. Siegfried, albeit he was referring to
tax policy rather than social insurance:

My first experience with advisory groups dates back to 1954 in the early days
of the Eisenhower administration. Tax reform on a broad front seemed to be
under consideration. The field of pensions and employee benefits and group insurance presented some apparent tax anomalies, and it was thought by some that
it would be desirable to bring together a group of people who had a broad exposure to these questions to see what could be done to bring about an improved
situation.

. . . We had a number of sessions which were informative although I believe
the possibilities for change diminished the more we talked. . . .

Prior to 1954, wage continuation payments made by an employer to an employee were being subjected to federal income tax. . . . On the other hand, accident and health insurance benefits provided by an employer under a group policy
were specifically tax-exempt. This seemed like an appropriate state of affairs to
me, and I was deeply concerned when I realized that I was a member of a group
that might be influential in changing this situation adversely to insurance. Some
of my company colleagues shared my concern, and we undertook to report to our
chief executive, LeRoy A. Lincoln. Mr. Lincoln listened to my story, and after
I finished he remained quiet and thoughtful for what seemed a long time. Then
he said, "Charlie, we've waited for a Republican administration for sixteen [sic]
years. If giving up this advantage we have had is a price we must pay, I think we
should not resist it." (*Transactions*, Society of Actuaries, vol. 22 [1970], pt. 2,
p. D503.)

issues of the day, upon transmitting its recommendations to the President in late summer Mrs. Hobby promised that the program would remain under study. At least formally, the issues raised by the chamber's report could still be regarded as open.

In lieu of a committee composed of interest group representatives, the second phase of the Eisenhower administration's deliberations on social security policy was managed by an individual distinguished by analytical skills. Roswell B. Perkins, a young lawyer from New York, joined HEW in the fall of 1953. As he recalled his role: "It was to come in and really do an analysis of this thing so that [department officials] could prepare their position and be ready . . . and, as a part of that, develop a positive program—not just to develop a negative posture but after having done the studies, to have a positive program."[31]

Perkins proceeded in a lawyer-like way. He crammed his head with the facts, prepared two notebooks that outlined the choices and arguments, and asked the tutoring experts, Robert Ball and Wilbur Cohen, what he hoped were hard, skeptical questions. He had a generalist's innocence of social security, unlike most of the consulting group, whose positions were fixed by a combination of long experience and organizational obligation. Perkins could perform with the freedom of a detached analyst freshly meeting the subject matter. Here, it would seem, was an approach to policymaking that would produce objective appraisal of a wide range of alternatives.

Perkins's notebooks did canvass a wide range of choices, but with explicit recognition that some of these choices were included merely for the sake of completing the analytic exercise. Universal payment of flat pensions out of general revenues and payments confined to the needy fell into the category of proscribed policies. They could not be omitted from a formal list of choices, but simply because they were fundamentally different from old age insurance, they were dismissed as unrealistic.

Because it was less outré and because it had the political appeal inherent in any expansion of benefits, the Chamber of Commerce proposal for blanketing in all of the aged received careful consideration. The chamber's plan could be interpreted as a fulfillment of the old age insurance program rather than as a fundamentally different alternative. It would have preserved the payroll tax and wage-related benefits (those

31. Interview with Roswell B. Perkins, Oral History Collection, Columbia University (1968), p. 143. (Hereafter Perkins, OHC.)

newly covered who did not have wage records would have received a minimum benefit). To blanket in all the aged would achieve prompt maturation of the program yet leave essential principles intact.

Or would it? That became the issue. The effects of blanketing in were hard to foresee. The contributory principle, which was already being badly strained by the 1950 legislation that made it very easy to qualify for benefits, would have been further strained—and strained so visibly that the public might have ceased to credit the contributory concept altogether. If benefits were not to be based on contributions, there would no longer be an argument for relying on the payroll tax. If a demand arose (presumably from liberal sources) for introducing general revenues, it would be hard to resist. And, if general revenues were introduced, a further demand (presumably from conservative sources) might arise for limiting benefits to needy persons. By such a chain of logic and legislative change, blanketing in might destroy the program.

Republicans in the Eisenhower administration were unwilling to take that risk, for reasons that were politically and ideologically ambiguous. "Liberal," "conservative," and pragmatic motives mingled in the Republicans' choice in a way that highlights the political ambiguity of the program itself.

As *liberal* Republicans, officials in HEW shared the belief of liberals in general that the contributory principle protected the recipients' pride and self-respect. Perkins recalled Nelson Rockefeller's attitude toward social security as follows (it was Rockefeller who, as under secretary, was dominant in preparing the department's legislative programs):

> Governor Rockefeller by his general outlook and orientation . . . had what I might call a generally sympathetic social outlook and approach to the problems of people. . . . Accordingly, he was looking for ways in which government could promote the well-being of people, and he had a basically favorable orientation to the social security system. . . . He believed strongly in the notion of people contributing to their own future retirement security, and he felt that the philosophy of the system was soundly based in giving everyone the feeling of setting aside a certain amount of money for his own future, whether or not the tax flow worked out so that the money was actually in fact being banked for him. He liked the fundamental philosophy of the system.[32]

Perkins also recalled in later years having been influenced in 1953 by Arthur Larson, a leading liberal member of the Eisenhower administration and a student of social security policy who became under secretary of labor in 1954. (As a law school professor, he had specialized in work-

32. Ibid., p. 6.

men's compensation.) At about the time Perkins was conducting his analysis, Larson prepared a paper on social security for a conference at Arden House in New York. It might have been written by Wilbur Cohen or Arthur Altmeyer, so powerful and eloquent was its defense of the contributory principle. Perkins found it persuasive.[33]

As *Republicans,* with a commitment to individual self-reliance and to limited, economical government, Eisenhower administration officials also found conservative grounds for supporting the contributory principle. Larson, who wrote that a contributory program protected individual pride and dignity, also wrote that it avoided teaching the false, corrupting lesson that something can be had in this world for nothing. Moreover, it prevented the public from being transformed into a "single, gigantic, monolithic lobby with a cash claim upon the government." "All that stands between us now and such a fate," Larson wrote, "is the well-understood proposition that, if benefits are to be raised, premiums also will have to be raised. With that gone, it is hard to see what would hold back the tide."[34] Particularly if general revenues were introduced, discipline would be sure to break down. Costs would become invisible to the individual, and the public's appetite for increased benefits would be insatiable.[35] The prospect of general revenue financing counted heavily against blanketing in among Republican officials.

The conservative argument in favor of blanketing in—that it could inhibit growth by revealing the program's true costs—seemed less important to Republican officials than preserving the contributory principle, upon which they judged public support of the payroll tax to depend. Besides, even with blanketing in, the ultimate cost of the program could not be predicted because increases in the proportion of elderly persons in the population would continue to drive the cost inexorably upward.

Finally, as *officeholders,* Republicans had pragmatic grounds for

33. Interview with the author, November 2, 1976.

34. Arthur Larson, "Social Insurance Legislation: The American Pattern," in American Assembly, *Economic Security for Americans* (the Assembly, 1954), p. 56.

35. HEW's internal analysis took the view that if the contributory principle were abandoned, the public would divide politically into a pressure group of the aged against a pressure group of taxpayers, and it questioned whether this was "as healthy to our democratic system as restraints on the individual (i.e., am I willing to pay now for higher benefits for myself in the future?)." (Memo, "Blanketing in Present Aged," November 30, 1953.) I am indebted to Roswell Perkins for a copy of this memorandum. Perkins judged that the Republican position owed something to the "coaching of Messrs. Ball and Cohen." Perkins, OHC, p. 13.

adhering to the contributory principle. They would have had to bear the political and administrative costs of any change. The AFL bitterly opposed blanketing in, and though labor opposition could probably have been bought off if blanketing in had been financed by general revenues, that was not a price that a Republican administration wanted to pay. The AFL was prepared to portray any Republican departure from the established evolutionary path, real or imagined, as an attack on social security. President Eisenhower's State of the Union message, which was really quite innocuous on the subject of social security, had seemed to the AFL to be "loaded with potential danger."[36]

Whereas pursuing the chamber's plan would have provoked a noisy fight with organized labor, not pursuing it would provoke a fight with no one. Conservative interests were not in general agitating for the plan's adoption. Its ambiguity, which reflected the underlying complexity and ambiguity of the program, probably accounts for this. It was very hard for the nonexpert to grasp why blanketing in was a conservative measure. Officials in local chambers of commerce wondered why they should rally in support of a bigger, more costly program. The reason that the chamber's staff had submitted the proposal to a referendum of the membership was that they were not confident of winning support for it from the organization's board.[37] Conservatives inside the Eisenhower administration had no interest in it; Perkins could not recall that Secretary of the Treasury George M. Humphrey, the cabinet's most influential conservative, had had a word to say on the subject, and he would surely have been alarmed at the suggestion that blanketing in could lead to general revenue financing. Nor did the insurance industry rally to the chamber's support. It was left to one quite conservative and politically conscious executive—E. J. Faulkner, president of a Nebraska-based insurance company—to write to insurance executives urging them to support the chamber's proposals. The industry trade associations did nothing. Nobody, it turned out, was much in favor of the chamber's plan except a few expert critics who had prepared it and found in the Chamber of Commerce a suitable outlet for their criticism.

Under very little pressure to adopt the chamber's plan, threatened with an attack from organized labor for "destroying social security" if it did so, and doubtful about the long-run merits, the Eisenhower ad-

36. *New York Times,* February 4, 1953.
37. Interview with President William J. Baroody, American Enterprise Institute for Public Policy Research, November 8, 1976.

ministration ended by choosing a few steps forward within the established framework. It recommended wider coverage and bigger benefits. The elaborate survey of alternatives by a new administration of the conservative party ended in recommendations for more of the same.

Without support from Republican executives, conservative critics of social security had to depend on support from the Republican majority in Congress, but here the events of 1953–54 confirmed the lesson of 1947–48: Congress was not good at independent initiative.

Under Republican control, the Ways and Means Committee early in 1953 formed a subcommittee to conduct a critical inquiry into social security. In creating this subcommittee, Chairman Daniel Reed, a conservative from upstate New York, eschewed "patchwork" and seemed to call for fundamental change. The subcommittee chairman was Carl T. Curtis of Nebraska, who had thoroughly condemned the evolving program in a cutting minority report in 1949, and the staff director was Karl T. Schlotterbeck, coauthor of a 1950 Brookings book that had fueled conservative criticism with a critical analysis of social insurance financing.[38]

Curtis's hearings failed to galvanize conservatives inside or outside of Congress. Oddly enough, they were not designed to do so. Schlotterbeck conceived of the hearings as an exercise in pure fact-finding. Hence there was no legislation before the committee, and there were no witnesses from the Chamber of Commerce or any other interest group. The hearings were designed to expose the mythic quality of the analogy to private insurance—this on the optimistic assumption that the public, if given the pure truth instead of official propaganda, would support fundamental change in the program. Much time was spent exploring the semantics of insurance, showing that individual benefits would greatly exceed contributions for many years, and proving that the long-run costs of the program were very hard to predict, contrary to the impression usually given by official statements.[39]

The public did not in fact get much aroused by the news that it would get far more in benefits than it had paid for, nor did Republican politicians in Congress. Curtis lacked partisan support even within his own subcommittee; one member, Howard Baker, Sr., of Tennessee, was

38. Lewis Meriam and Karl Schlotterbeck, *The Cost and Financing of Social Security* (Brookings Institution, 1950).

39. *Analysis of the Social Security System,* Hearings before a Subcommittee of the House Committee on Ways and Means, 83 Cong. 1 sess. (GPO, 1954), pts. 1–6.

surreptitiously cooperating with organized labor in defense of the established program. In the end the Curtis subcommittee failed even to issue a report. A staff report and a response from the Democratic members were the only products.[40] Curtis sponsored a reform bill in 1954 based on the chamber's recommendations, but it did not receive a hearing. Attention focused instead on the administration bill.

Whereas conservative interests were hesitant, divided, and uncertain about their objectives, the system's defenders in the SSA and the AFL were aroused in their brief moment of peril and secure in their doctrinal certitude: the "contributory" program must be preserved. They did not receive the conservative proposal as a rational and debatable alternative to an imperfect, debatable program. They received it as an assault upon their faith and a threat to their proprietorship. There was in particular something about the Curtis inquiry that stirred their emotions. Even before it started, they identified Curtis and Schlotterbeck as enemies, Curtis because of his minority report in 1949 and Schlotterbeck because of the Brookings book. Because it challenged official pronouncements, the inquiry was received as an attack on their integrity, and it must have seemed dissembling, self-righteous, and hypocritical with its puritanical devotion to "the facts" when the subject was so controversial and value-laden that it could hardly be approached in a disinterested way. It did not help that Curtis and Schlotterbeck offered to employ Arthur Altmeyer, the revered outgoing commissioner of social security, as a "consultant" with the explanation that they wanted "all the facts" and that he must have a better command of them than anyone. That this enemy attack on their program should present itself to the public as objective and disinterested was intolerable, and the program's proprietors responded with denunciations and exposures fed to the Washington press by the AFL. What should have been a serious debate about social security policy instead degenerated into a battle over propaganda symbols— both symbolic personalities (Altmeyer on one side, Curtis and Schlotterbeck on the other) and words (was it "insurance" or wasn't it?).

Once this war started, and once the struggle was perceived as an adversary encounter in which "enemies" of social security were engaged, the defenders of the established system had virtually won the real and

40. *Social Security after 18 Years*, A Staff Report to Hon. Carl T. Curtis, Chairman, Subcommittee on Social Security, and Statement of the Democratic Members of the Subcommittee on Social Security, House Committee on Ways and Means, 83 Cong. 2 sess. (GPO, 1954).

serious underlying contest over policy, because neither the progressive Republicans in the Eisenhower administration nor the more progressive members of the business community wanted to be part of anything so risky and disreputable as "an attack on social security." The progressive Republicans' overweening concern to appear positive and truly presidential colored their approach to social security policy. So did their desire to achieve control of their own party, and to dissociate themselves from its conservative members, such as Curtis, who held power in Congress. The program's partisans shrewdly exploited the intraparty difference among Republicans. Following Eisenhower's State of the Union message, the AFL said that the President had shown a disposition to go along with majority views in Congress instead of asserting affirmative leadership in his own right. The irony is that by rejecting conservative criticism and "asserting leadership in his own right" regarding social security, a Republican President passed up a tentative, fleeting opportunity for sponsoring innovation, endorsed the preferences of the program executives, and reinforced the pattern of incremental enlargement of an established program.

"We are faced with our last good opportunity to make the program sound," Representative Curtis said as he introduced the Chamber of Commerce proposal in the House in 1954.[41] The opportunity passed without the dignity of a public debate. To achieve a debate over what were serious, debatable issues, the conservatives needed unity, force, and momentum because the burden of change was on them. The demands on the defenders of the existing program, precisely because they were defenders, were much less; and their assets—which included clear goals, strategic positions within the executive branch, and the ability to threaten pressure-group counterattack—were more than sufficient to win a struggle that in retrospect was hardly joined.

THE POLITICAL AMBIVALENCE of conservative interests and the political ambiguity of the program together largely account for the failure of conservative pressure groups to oppose the steady expansion of social insurance more actively. Uncertain of their stakes, internally divided, reluctant to appear self-interested or to risk a high level of political involvement in a frequently hostile environment, they settled

41. *Congressional Record* (January 6, 1954), p. 29.

into a pattern of recurrent but limited resistance.[42] When, with the advent of the Eisenhower administration, this pattern was broken and a conservative initiative was finally attempted, it ended quietly in failure and confusion. The complex and ambiguous character of the program made it hard to define or detect a "conservative" course of action. Whereas some conservatives felt that the contributory program worked in a way that obscured (and therefore increased) costs, officials of the Republican administration, reasoning also from conservative premises but under the coaching of program executives, were equally persuaded that it worked to highlight (and thereby control) costs.

Program executives were able to make the most of these circumstances. The differences of opinion among and within conservative interest groups made it possible for program executives to select advice and participation in policymaking from relatively sympathetic representatives of the business community, while the ambiguous content of the program enabled them to emphasize to conservative audiences (including Republican political executives) those program attributes most likely to elicit conservative support. For them, ambivalence among the conservatives and ambiguity in the program created room for maneuver and choice.

42. Readers are again reminded that the singularly intense opposition of the American Medical Association to medical insurance is treated separately in chapter 16.

CHAPTER SEVEN

Expert Critics

ONE of the great assets of social security program executives has been mastery of the apparently abstruse subject matter of their program— their *expertise*, in short. Combined with their strategic position as holders of office in the executive branch, this has given them a great advantage over most other possible participants in policymaking.

Yet, in theory at least, this most valuable of assets is not impregnable. One would expect it to be subject to challenge from rival experts inside the government whose own specialized functions compete with or impinge on the social security program. One would expect also that it would be compromised by differences of opinion and belief among people with equally valid claims to be expert about social security. To be expert is not to agree about policy: differing values, interests, or organizational roles give rise to differing positions among highly knowledgeable persons. It is hard for a single organization or like-minded set of persons to maintain a monopoly on expertise in an educationally advanced society, and impossible in a free society to suppress differences of opinion about policy. The tendency of expert specialists to clash may be relied upon to give generalists many opportunities to choose between rival experts and thereby to assert their own values and preferences in policymaking.

Social security program executives, however, have been remarkably impervious to the challenge of rival experts, and hence have been able to maintain something approaching a monopoly of expertise in policymaking for social security. This is not because expert critics do not exist, but because they have generally lacked an organizational base through which access to policymaking may be secured. There have been no consistent organizational rivals to social security within the executive branch, and individual critics from the private professions of economics and actuarial science have remained just that—individual critics whose criticisms could easily be turned aside by a large, formal organization within the government.

Potentially the most troublesome source of criticism for the Social Security Administration has been internal. There is a pattern of dissent by the system's own actuaries. Both W. Rulon Williamson, the Social Security Board's first actuary, and his successor, Robert J. Myers, left office as open, severe critics either of the system they had served or of the officials who were in charge of administering it. But there was a long interval between these dissenting acts, and in that interval Myers's service as a distinguished professional actuary contributed crucially to construction of the present program. One reason that program executives were able to deflect or ignore much outside criticism is that they had successfully integrated into their organization a source of "outside" expertise drawn from an independent profession.

The Absence of Executive Rivals

Social security program executives have not been challenged by organizational peers within the executive branch. There have been no competitors for their turf, and they have therefore not needed to engage in the kind of intrabureaucratic politics that creates opportunities for, if it does not necessitate, generalist intervention.[1]

If public assistance—the means-tested program that was the concrete alternative to social insurance—had had a bureaucratic existence independent of social security, dating from some year other than 1935 and located in some agency other than the Social Security Board and its successor, then the two might very well have become rivals for the support of presidents, Congresses, parties, and interest groups. Public assistance was the program to which conservatives in the United States gave preference when the initial choice was posed. As it was, however,

1. In the field of unemployment insurance, in contrast to old age insurance, bureaucratic competition did exist. In a reorganization plan in 1949, President Truman transferred the administration of the unemployment insurance program from the Social Security Administration to the Department of Labor. Commissioner Altmeyer was deeply distressed. See Arthur J. Altmeyer, *The Formative Years of Social Security* (University of Wisconsin Press, 1966), pp. 175–78.

the two were created by the same legislation and administered by the same organization. Though separate bureaus were in charge of each, these bureaus were not in fact peers. The Bureau of Public Assistance was in charge of a despised program, which, at least in theory, the Social Security Board intended should wither away, whereas the Bureau of Old Age and Survivors Insurance was in charge of a preferred program that was expected to grow until, again in theory, it virtually supplanted the first. Insofar as decisions about the relative size and importance of these rival programs were made in the federal executive branch, they were made by the SSA, which frankly and unqualifiedly gave preference to social insurance. When public assistance for the aged grew in the late 1930s and the 1940s, the SSA argued in response that it was necessary to extend and liberalize social insurance in order to establish its superiority. Competition between the programs, since it found no organizational outlet in the federal executive branch, was wholly beneficial to social insurance: it provided a justification for expansive action. Eventually (in 1963), public assistance was severed from the parent SSA, but by then the social insurance program was secure.

Another front from which bureaucratic conflict might have been expected to come but did not was the Department of the Treasury. Treasury was not a direct competitor of the Social Security Administration—it did not administer social welfare programs—but it did have a more than routine stake in social security financing. Treasury is the executive department in charge of raising revenue, and, because of its size, social security makes extraordinary demands on the government's capacity to raise revenue. Recognizing this, the Treasury Department became involved in social security policymaking at a very early stage. Conservative officials in the department in 1935 argued for a self-supporting program in contrast to the plan of the Committee on Economic Security, which called for the eventual introduction of general revenues. Possibly at the urging of treasury officials, President Roosevelt decreed that the program should be financed entirely by the payroll tax, and it was Secretary of the Treasury Henry Morgenthau who presented the administration's revised financial plan to Congress. When the 1939 amendments to the Social Security Act were pending, Morgenthau again gave testimony, this time, perversely enough, in support of long-range general revenue financing, to which Roosevelt now raised no objection.[2] Thereafter the Treasury Department proceeded to ignore the program except for some unavoidable involvement in the administrative mechanics of revenue collection, social security trust fund accounting, and issuing benefit checks. The secretary of the treasury did not testify before Congress when the 1950 amendments were pending although these were hardly less important to the government's future fiscal condition than were the amendments of 1939 or the original legislation.

Administrative mechanics, of course, usually contain the seeds of more important matters, and Treasury might have gained access to social security policy by this route if it had wanted to. Very early in the program, Treasury had responsibility under the law for making an annual report on the actuarial status of the program. If this arrangement had persisted, the Treasury Department might have seriously challenged SSB estimating procedures and even program principles. An unsympathetic Office of the Government Actuary in the Treasury Department, if it had had the backing of the secretary of the treasury, could have been troublesome; the seeds of bureaucratic conflict were surely there.[3] Perhaps in recognition of this, SSB officials secured a revision of the law in 1939, before the payment of monthly benefits actually got under way, that diluted the Treasury Department's responsibility. A social security trust fund was then created and placed

2. Morgenthau's position probably changed because in the interim conservative interests expressed vigorous opposition to the original financing plan, under which a large reserve fund would have been created. Liberals and conservatives came together between 1935 and 1939 in opposing this plan, thus laying the basis for the 1939 amendments (see chapter 11). Within the Treasury Department in the 1930s, the social security program had critics from the right and the left. According to Edwin Witte: "There were two groups among the Treasury Department officials, neither of whom cared very much for the social security program: one a group of conservatives, who were anxious to keep down expenditures and to avoid alarming business; the other a group of radicals who felt that the measures proposed by the [Committee on Economic Security] had little value." *The Development of the Social Security Act* (University of Wisconsin Press, 1963), pp. 72–73.

3. For example, see the comments by R. R. Reagh, the government actuary, Department of the Treasury, on Robert J. Myers's paper, "Cost Estimates for the Old Age Insurance System of the Social Security Act," in *The Record*, American Institute of Actuaries, vol. 28 (1939), pp. 337–43, and the testimony of W. Rulon Williamson in *Social Security Act Amendments of 1949*, Hearings before the House Committee on Ways and Means, 81 Cong. 1 sess. (GPO, 1949), pt. 2, p. 1485, in which Williamson urges the committee to consult government actuaries outside the Social Security Administration.

under management of a three-man board consisting of the secretary of the treasury, the secretary of labor, and the chairman of the Social Security Board. This board, rather than the secretary of the treasury alone, had responsibility for issuing annual reports on the financial condition of the fund. With responsibility formally dispersed, the function fell to the agency that was actually in charge of the program. Financial reports were prepared by the office of the social security actuary and reviewed perfunctorily in the Treasury Department. A Hoover Commission task force report prepared by the Brookings Institution in 1949 objected to the lack of independent actuarial estimates and argued that the actuarial function should be lodged in the Treasury, the Bureau of the Budget, or the Bureau of the Census, but it brought no response.[4]

Official expertise is not necessarily confined to the executive branch. Congress may be expert, too, either through employing specialized staffs or through the members' own longevity, diligence, and committee specialization. Congress developed its own expertise in social security, but this expertise was not used to rival or criticize that of the SSA. The differing institutional perspectives of the legislature and the executive were successfully reconciled, and the specialized committees of Congress joined with the SSA in shared proprietorship of a program to which both were fundamentally committed. Within Congress, expert criticism surfaced only when a dissenting committee member sponsored it, and this was a rare occurrence.[5] Because the congressional committees were fundamentally in agreement with the program executives, they felt no need to create expert staffs of their own. The House Committee on Ways and Means and the Senate Committee on Finance sometimes received help on social security from one or two staff members of the Legislative Reference Service of the Library of Congress or from their own small generalist staffs, but mainly they relied on the SSA for information and advice. In effect, the staff of the SSA was also the staff to the committees, so that this potential source of expert criticism was eliminated.

4. *Task Force Report on Public Welfare [Appendix P]*, prepared for the Commission on Organization of the Executive Branch of the Government by the Brookings Institution (GPO, 1949), pp. 490–91.

5. The outstanding example is Representative Carl T. Curtis's minority report in *Social Security Act Amendments of 1949*, H. Rept. 1300, 81 Cong. 1 sess. (GPO, 1949), pp. 173–84.

The Private Professions

No one who had not devoted his career to constructing the social security program could exactly match the expertise of the leading program executives. No one else could achieve an equivalent mastery of the legal, financial, and administrative details. On the other hand, that degree of mastery was not essential to constructing a logically sound analysis of the program and the possible alternatives to it. Training in economics or actuarial science, combined with study of the operational principles of the program and a few readily accessible facts, could lay the basis for a competent critique.[6]

The two professions in which relevant expertise was concentrated were well established by the time the Social Security Act was passed. The American Economic Association and the Actuarial Society of America were founded within four years of each other in the late 1880s and had been holding professional meetings and publishing journals for decades. Professional actuaries were very quick to show an interest in the new program. The analogy between public and private insurance intrigued the more inquiring and studious minds in the profession, and several private actuaries participated in the planning of the program in 1934–35. Those who did participate came away thoroughly convinced that the plan of 1935 was ill conceived in calling for the creation of a huge reserve fund. The actuarial profession produced some remarkably penetrating papers and discussions on social insurance in the late 1930s, the quality of which was praised by foreign visitors. However, critical discussion occurred infrequently after the founding period. Except for receiving regular reports on social security legislation from Myers, the SSA's actuary, who was very active in professional affairs, actuarial conventions in general ceased to pay much attention to the subject. Economists produced a few general books on social insurance and some articles on financial issues in the program's founding years, but it was not until the late 1960s, when the program was well

6. Nor was it absolutely essential to be an economist or an actuary, as the work of Leonard Calhoun, a lawyer who developed the Chamber of Commerce proposal, showed. SSA officials would argue that the advisory councils provided Congress with a source of independent expertise, but the advisory councils were never critical, for the reasons explored in chapter 4.

enough developed to have a significant impact on income distribution, that a substantial amount of economic analysis began to appear.[7]

Because interest in social insurance among the private professions was sporadic, influence on official policy could not be sustained. The private professions, as professions, did not make it their business to maintain a regular scrutiny. They were not organized for the purpose of overseeing public policy; they organized (loosely) to exchange knowledge and reinforce a sense of professional community. Whether their members had anything to say to one another about social security was largely a matter of chance. It depended on whether anyone in the profession had lately decided to do some work on the subject.

If professional criticism was intermittent in time, it was also inconsistent in content. Expert critics who did not agree with the Social Security Administration did not agree with one another either. Among them were libertarians such as Milton Friedman, who argued that the government could not legitimately compel people to provide for their old age;[8] Keynesians, who thought that the program should be designed

7. Sherwin Rosen dates the start of "fundamental economic analysis" of social security from the appearance of Paul Samuelson's article, "An Exact Consumption-Loan Model of Interest with or without the Social Contrivance of Money," *Journal of Political Economy*, vol. 66 (December 1958), pp. 467–82. (Sherwin Rosen, "Social Security and the Economy," in Michael J. Boskin, ed., *The Crisis in Social Security: Problems and Prospects* [Institute for Contemporary Studies, 1977], pp. 87–106.) I know of no comprehensive bibliography of the economic literature on social security, but for an introduction, see Joseph A. Pechman, Henry J. Aaron, and Michael K. Taussig, *Social Security: Perspectives for Reform* (Brookings Institution, 1968), pp. 328–40, and the citations in *The Crisis in Social Security*. For a long time the most prolific academic writer on social security was a social economist, Eveline M. Burns, who taught at Columbia University for more than thirty-five years, the last twenty-one of them (1946–67) at the School of Social Work. Burns wrote several books on social security, including *Toward Social Security: An Explanation of the Social Security Act and a Survey of the Larger Issues* (London: Whittlesey House; New York: McGraw-Hill, 1936); *The American Social Security System* (Houghton-Mifflin, 1949); and *Social Security and Public Policy* (McGraw-Hill, 1956). Among her many articles, two are particularly significant for their analysis of the principles of the American social insurance program: "Social Insurance in Evolution," *American Economic Review*, Supplement, vol. 34 (March 1944), pp. 199–211, and "Social Security in Evolution—Toward What?" *Social Service Review*, vol. 39 (June 1965), pp. 129–40. A complete list of Eveline Burns's publications through 1968 is contained in Shirley Jenkins, ed., *Social Security in International Perspective: Essays in Honor of Eveline M. Burns* (Columbia University Press, 1969), pp. 229–41.

8. Milton Friedman, *Capitalism and Freedom* (University of Chicago Press, 1962), pp. 182–89.

so as to respond flexibly to the demands of fiscal policy; and conservatives—predominant among the actuaries, less frequently found among the economists—who thought it should be designed so as to maximize the control of costs.

With their values and policy goals differently ordered, these critics had very different prescriptions for policy, yet there was also a common strand to their criticism. This was a strand of purism. The critics were rationalists. Conservative or liberal, they sought to strip the program of its propaganda and to correct public misperceptions. (The motto of the actuaries, borrowed from Ruskin, is, "The work of science is to substitute facts for appearances and demonstrations for impressions.") As rationalists, they consistently criticized the program, too, for the inconsistency of its goals. Invariably they began by asking what its purpose was, and invariably they concluded that the goals were mixed and conflicting. Their instinct was to replace the confusion with an internally consistent design and to secure coordination of social security with budgeting and other activities of the federal government. They wished to take a comprehensive view of affairs so as to facilitate the comparisons that lie at the foundation of rational choice. Finally, they thought abstractly. They thought in terms of models and averages, whereas the social security program, like government programs in general, responded to political realities and therefore contained all sorts of anomalous features that were designed to cater to some obscure subset of the population or to particular interests and that had no place in a purely rational program. In many cases these anomalies were introduced by Congress at the behest of a particular member.

All of this put expert critics at odds with the program executives, who were, in the manner of officeholders, highly pragmatic. Wilbur Cohen often rejected outright the critical arguments of expert analysts, sometimes seemed to resent the very process of analysis, and ridiculed the unrealistic (because abstract and apolitical) views of public policy held by the analysts. He believed that economists erred in ignoring psychology as well as politics. In a debate with Friedman, who had characterized the program as "a triumph of imaginative packaging and Madison Avenue advertising," he replied by lashing out sarcastically at economists in general:

And as to the fact that he [Friedman] doesn't agree with it [the social security system]—well, he's not Congress, he's not the American people. He's only an economist.

Mr. Friedman calls a lot of the things he doesn't like about social security rhetoric. And that gets me to a point I want to stress. My point is that economists do not determine all of the choices and options and attitudes prevailing in this nation. People do live by rhetoric. . . .

I believe in rhetoric because it makes a lot of things palatable that might be unpalatable to economists. . . .

True, if you are an economist, you may exclude all matters of politics from your thinking. But to do so is not reality.[9]

Economic analysts who exposed what they regarded as the myths of social security learned to expect a swift, vigorous response from program executives, especially if the critics were liberals and could therefore be regarded (unlike Friedman) as "natural friends" of the system. Then they would be charged with heresy and made to feel that they were endangering the system. Jodie Allen, an economist who wrote a critical article for the *Washington Post* in 1976 ("Social Security: The Largest Welfare Program"), described the response:

I was deluged by calls and letters from the guardians of the social security system—you know, from Wilbur Cohen on down—saying, "Gee, Jodie, we always liked you, but how could you say this?" I acted very politely, and I said, "Well, what's the matter with this; isn't it true?" And they said, "Oh, yes, it's true, but once you start saying this kind of thing, you don't know where it's going to end up." Then I came to perceive that social security was not a program; it was a religion. It's very hard to reform a religion.[10]

Cohen was not much troubled if there was an element of myth in social insurance; he recognized that successful societies make frequent use of myths. If the program had inconsistent goals, again he was unperturbed. Human nature, in Cohen's view, was full of inconsistencies, and so therefore were the works of humankind in the real world. In his eyes, the beauty of the program was that it could be made to serve many purposes; ambiguity made it flexible, adaptable, and widely appealing. Autonomy was of course altogether desirable from the program executives' point of view—and proper, too. All of those who shared in the program proprietorship, whether through the executive, Congress, or the advisory councils, were prepared to argue that social security was unique—not an ordinary government program, but a trust involving inviolable obligations to contributors and beneficiaries, which

9. Wilbur J. Cohen and Milton Friedman, *Social Security: Universal or Selective?* (Washington, D.C.: American Enterprise Institute for Public Policy Research, 1972), pp. 26, 69, 54–55.

10. "Opting Out of Social Security—Is It Smart and Is It Fiar?," SSA, Office of Management and Administration, OHR/DPTO Pub. No. 134 (5–77), p. 13.

ought not to be made to serve exogenous purposes, including the purposes of macroeconomic policy.

How much of a threat expert criticism posed, and what kind of action it therefore evoked from program executives, depended very much on whether the criticism was linked with a source of political power. Purely private debate was one thing; what was said at the annual meetings of the actuarial society did not matter much as long as it was only speech in an academic setting. But expert critics of the program—those who were economists, mainly—had a way of turning up in public or quasi-public offices, from which their criticism could more easily enter into the stream of actual discussion over public policy, creating unwelcome crosscurrents. Thus, for example, Keynesian economists located in the Treasury Department in 1939 wanted President Roosevelt to consider an old age pension program that would benefit all of the aged immediately with flat payments financed out of general revenues. They planted critical questions with a member of the Senate Committee on Finance, and tried to persuade, not only the President, but organized labor, to support this position; for a time they succeeded with the CIO.[11]

Nearly three decades later, midway through Lyndon B. Johnson's presidency, economic analysts with a specialized interest in welfare programs suddenly sprang up at many points in an active and growing executive branch. They could be found in the new Office of Economic Opportunity; the Office of the Assistant Secretary for Program Coordination, also new, in the Department of Health, Education, and Welfare; the President's Council of Economic Advisers; various White House task forces; and the President's Commission on Income Maintenance Programs (called the Heineman commission) that Johnson appointed early in 1968. Many of them were critical of the irrationalities of the social security program and its inefficiency as a means of reducing poverty, which was then the leading rhetorical goal of domestic policy. Some among them favored a negative income tax, a measure designed specifically to relieve poverty that logically implied a substantial revision of social security.[12]

Social security program executives had to improvise their responses

11. Altmeyer, *The Formative Years of Social Security*, pp. 107–08; interview with Murray W. Latimer, September 16, 1977.

12. Daniel P. Moynihan, *The Politics of a Guaranteed Income: The Nixon Administration and the Family Assistance Plan* (Random House, 1973), pp. 124–36; Vincent J. and Vee Burke, *Nixon's Good Deed* (Columbia University Press, 1974), pp. 14–39.

to such criticism because they could not know where it might come from. To counter the ad hoc criticism of individual critics is different from waging a continuing contest with rival parts of a permanent bureaucracy. Arthur Altmeyer responded to the activities of the Keynesian critics in several different ways. He invited them to his home to discuss their differences, with unsatisfactory results. "There was no compromise at all," he recalled. He got President Roosevelt to reconstitute the Committee on Economic Security so as to assert control over policy discussions within the administration, but neither he nor the secretary of labor, who was his ally in this maneuver, ever found it necessary to activate the committee. He also succeeded in having the White House hurriedly intervene in 1940 when the FSA administrator, Paul V. McNutt, a putative presidential candidate, was about to give a speech in New York advocating universal old age pensions. The President's support was crucial, of course. In a meeting with Altmeyer, Roosevelt had rejected a proposal of the Keynesians, calling it a "baby Townsend Plan which would be sure to grow up."[13]

When the analytic challenges of the late 1960s arose, Wilbur Cohen held high office in the Department of Health, Education, and Welfare, as under secretary and, then, in the last months of the Johnson administration, as secretary. From this position, simply by withholding his support he undermined much of the criticism. One critical study that came to him from within HEW he is said to have disposed of by throwing it away. The authors had to have it retyped before publication was possible. When he was to present testimony to the Heineman commission, he solicited it from Social Security Commissioner Robert Ball and rejected it from economic analysts in the Office of Program Coordination. When the White House solicited proposals for new legislation to alleviate poverty, Cohen responded with social security benefit increases.[14] The program executives promised politicians that they would deliver a familiar form of benefits to particular sets of people at a particular (typically preelection) time—political language that gave them an immense advantage over the analysts, whose propensity to think in ideal, abstract terms was a critical political flaw.

13. Altmeyer, *The Formative Years of Social Security*, pp. 107–08, 114–15, 122–23. The Townsend plan originated with Dr. Francis E. Townsend in 1934. It was a widely popular proposal to give monthly income grants of about $200 to all citizens sixty years old or older. For a full discussion, see chapter 8.

14. *Nixon's Good Deed*, pp. 15–16, 36–39.

When not on their own ground—that is, when the issue was not the nature, purpose, or operation of their program—social security executives were more vulnerable to expert critics. Whereas the rationalizers of income support policy could win no victories at the expense of social security in the late 1960s, rationalizers of the federal budget did. They secured adoption of a "unified budget" in which trust fund transactions were included. Before 1969, the omission of social security expenditures from the federal government's "administrative budget"—that budget, among three, that received most attention from Congress and the press —helped to insulate the program from generalists' scrutiny. The budget rationalizers hoped that integration would make the programs that were financed out of trust funds—highway construction as well as social security among them—more susceptible to evaluation and control through budget analysis.[15] This change was unwelcome to social security program executives, but they could not prevent it. The decision was taken by the President alone, without resort to legislation, in response to recommendations of a commission he appointed, in which fiscal experts predominated.

The adoption of the unified budget in combination with the steady development after 1965 of the Office of Program Planning and Evaluation in HEW meant that by the early 1970s, which is to say very late in the history recounted here, rival experts inside the executive branch were beginning more or less regularly to look over the shoulders of social security program executives. Inside the Office of Management and Budget, fiscal experts were taking an interest in social security finance and asking what effects surpluses or deficits in the social security program would have on the budget as a whole.[16] Inside the secretary's

15. *Report of the President's Commission on Budget Concepts* (GPO, 1967), pp. 26–27.

16. Eventually, this led to proposals for reducing certain elements of the program, principally student benefits. Social security benefits paid on account of a dependent child normally end on the child's eighteenth birthday, but if the child is unmarried and a full-time student they continue until age twenty-two. This feature was enacted in 1965. In the 1976–77 school year, it accounted for $1.2 billion in social security expenditures and benefited over 700,000 students, the dependents of dead, disabled, or retired workers. Because other federal programs have since developed to aid college students and are better designed to do so in an equitable fashion, budget analysts have begun to suggest that student benefits under social security should be cut. The fiscal 1978 budget of the Ford administration proposed that they be eliminated, and the Carter administration proposed that they be limited to the amount payable under the basic educational opportunity grant program for students ($1,400 in fiscal 1978). Such proposals show why program executives

office in HEW, economists were beginning to ask questions about the actuary's assumptions and to urge SSA to take an open-minded look at fundamental policy questions rather than be guided by the symbolism of social insurance and the habitual routines of the established program.

Not all outside experts have been critical, however. The social security program has also had friends among experts in the private professions. Some professional economists thoroughly sympathized with the program, such as Harvard's Sumner Slichter and Princeton's J. Douglas Brown. From the actuarial profession there was the Metropolitan's Reinhard Hohaus. The ad hoc, unpredictable confrontations with critical experts were counterbalanced by a deliberate, continuing collaboration with sympathetic experts. It was the sympathetic ones, of course—Hohaus of the Met rather than the acerbic Ray Peterson of Equitable, Brown or Slichter rather than Friedman—whose participation in policymaking was solicited. They were appointed again and again to advisory councils, though many of the critics had comparable claims to expertise. Viewed in their entirety, then, the program executives' relations with experts from the private professions mixed confrontation with collaboration.

The Outsider as Insider: The Role of the Actuary's Office

Even in the most cohesive organizations, occasional dissidents are likely to appear, and so it was with the Social Security Administration. There was the case, already described, of Leonard J. Calhoun, the Southern lawyer who started as an assistant general counsel of the Social Security Board but later joined the conservative resistance, to

---

want to keep social security out of the unified budget. The unified budget, Ball recently wrote, "is leading to confusion about just how separate from other government programs social security really is. Recommendations to change social security benefit provisions in ways that are completely unacceptable in terms of social security policy are often made by the Executive Branch solely to conform to short-term budget policy." The conceptual issue is fundamental. Outside of the social security proprietorship, other officials persist in supposing that social security should be analyzed and managed as if it were a government program like any other, whereas social security officials insist that it is unique and inviolable. See Robert M. Ball, *Social Security: Today and Tomorrow* (Columbia University Press, 1978), p. 459. For analyses of social security student benefits, see Congressional Budget Office, *Social Security Benefits for Students* (GPO, May 1977), and Chester E. Finn, Jr., *Scholars, Dollars, and Bureaucrats* (Brookings Institution, 1978), pp. 73–74.

which he brought formidable expertise and a powerful analytic mind. There was, too, the curious and very conspicuous case of Marjorie Shearon, a member of the Bureau of Research and Statistics who became a zealous opponent of the health insurance legislation proposed by the SSB and a zealous personal critic of I. S. Falk and Wilbur Cohen, its principal authors. She had prepared the economic brief that the solicitor general's office used in defending the constitutionality of the old age insurance program before the Supreme Court, and her belief that SSB officials unfairly deprived her of credit for this work and maliciously suppressed its publication apparently was at the root of her extreme disaffection.

There was nothing in either of these cases or in subsequent events to suggest that the dissents were not purely personal—the one rooted in philosophy, the other, apparently, in emotional distress. Nothing suggests that they originated in tension between the demands of the organization and the performance of a particular professional role. Lawyers in general did not become dissidents in the Social Security Board, nor did members of the Office of Research and Statistics.

It was different, however, with a third dissident of the early years, W. Rulon Williamson, the SSB's first actuary. It was not that Williamson was antagonistic to the SSB's leading personalities, although he did become quite critical of them as a group. (In contrast to Marjorie Shearon, who named names, Williamson's denunciations were impersonal.) Nor was it just that Williamson disagreed with the principles of the program, though emphatically he did. It was that, in Williamson's case, there was tension between his organizational obligations and his professional conscience. Even before he left the organization, he found it very difficult to perform the task that was expected of him, and even after he left and was replaced by a very different man, tensions between the actuary's office and the rest of the organization recurred, culminating in a second dissident parting in 1970. The system, it would seem, tends to reject its actuaries. Why?

To someone outside the profession, the work of an actuary appears quite esoteric. The profession is small. (The Society of Actuaries has only 6,600 members, compared to the 17,900 who belong to the American Economic Association.) To enter it, the main requirements are ability and training in mathematics. It is at least plausible that persons who are drawn to this profession may be temperamentally unsuited to policymaking or administrative roles in large, formal organizations.

Actuaries, it might be supposed, are good at abstraction and the manipulation of figures, but not good at weighing competing intangible values (policymaking) or at leading and motivating men in organizational settings (administration). When asked to describe Williamson, veterans of the early SSB recall him as "eccentric." It was his personality, not his dissenting views on social insurance, that inspires the characterization. He was a solitary figure. For amusement, he climbed mountains. To the staff of the Social Security Board, whose interests were passionately social, he seemed a strange fellow.

The notion that actuaries in general fit poorly into large, formal organizations is intriguing but probably far-fetched. The vast majority work for private insurance companies, many of them become company officers, and a sizable proportion of those become high-ranking officers with generalist functions. M. Albert Linton, for example—an industry leader who was long interested in social insurance—was an actuary who had become the chief executive officer of his company, Provident Mutual. (Interestingly enough, Linton too climbed mountains, and perhaps went Williamson one better in that he watched birds, which likewise is not a gregarious sport.) However others may see them, actuaries tend to see themselves as eminently practical men. Reinhard Hohaus once reminded an interviewer of a classic Scottish definition of an actuary: "He's not a mathematician; he's not a statistician; he's a businessman with a flair for mathematics. In other words, fundamentally he is not geared to the academic world. He's not geared to doing a lot of theory and research in higher math. He's mostly in the world of business."[17]

It seems unlikely, then, that the tensions between SSA actuaries and their organization are characteristic of the relations between professional actuaries and large, formal organizations in general. More likely, the sources are to be found in the relation between the actuarial profession and the particular public organization (or the particular insurance program) that Williamson and later Myers, from among the profession, chose to serve.

The professional actuary is a calculator of risks and probabilities. He estimates the future liabilities of the insurer against the sufficiency of financial assets with which they are to be met. The solvency of an insurance business depends upon the reliability of such estimates. Be-

17. Interview with Reinhard A. Hohaus, Oral History Collection, Columbia University (1965), p. 89.

cause so much depends on actuarial judgments, actuaries are likely to be conservative: they are inclined to be prudent calculators. As Dorrance Bronson, one of the most thoughtful of American actuaries, once remarked: "While our techniques must be available for a variety of purposes and problems, . . . we are, most of us, 'reservists.' We feel uneasy if the equations do not balance, if liabilities for promises (actual or implied) are unprovided for, or are without a prudent structure for building such security. Sometimes I meditate on whether they all *can* be provided for under the usual actuarial philosophy."[18]

What actuaries do for private insurance companies, they have also been expected to do for the Social Security Administration. The actuarial function was embedded in the original Social Security Act, which stated that the amount to be appropriated each year to the government's Old-Age Reserve Account should be "determined on a reserve basis in accordance with accepted actuarial principles, and based upon such tables of mortality as the Secretary of the Treasury shall from time to time adopt."[19] It also provided for an annual report on the "actuarial status" of the account. But Williamson, whom the Social Security Board employed to perform this function, very early developed doubts about the propriety and feasibility of performing it in a social insurance program. More, he concluded that the actual program being developed in the United States was unacceptable to a prudent man. He rebelled.

"No one should pretend," Williamson wrote in 1938, "that the precedents of the relatively simple problems of the insurance business . . . permit the determination of any accurate costs today for our program of old age benefits."[20] He argued that a high degree of uncertainty was inherent in a social insurance plan, and that to pretend otherwise was wrong and dangerous. By the mid-1940s, Williamson also had become highly critical of anomalies in the developing system, among them the inequity as between covered and uncovered persons and variations in benefits for similar contributions, and was arguing for something very different and in the short run more costly: a comprehensive national program that would have given a uniform monthly benefit to all the aged, widowed mothers and their children, and persons with long-term

18. Dorrance C. Bronson, "Pensions—1949," in Society of Actuaries, *Transactions,* vol. I (1949), p. 239.

19. 49 *Stat.* 622.

20. W. R. Williamson, "Cost Factors in Old-Age Insurance," *Social Security Bulletin,* vol. 1 (July 1938), p. 15.

disabilities—parts of the population that could be presumed to need public support. Williamson would have financed such benefits out of a tax on everyone who earned income.[21]

This advice put Williamson very much at odds with the New Deal liberals who were in charge of social security, committed as they were to a contributory, wage-related, gradually maturing program, the full costs of which would not be evident for many years to come. Bound to the analogy with insurance, they were determined to act as if future costs *could* be calculated. "No insurance plan, private or public, ought to be operated on any other basis than an actuarial basis," Altmeyer told Congress in 1949, "which means the best estimates that trained actuaries can make as to future costs."[22] Wishing to demonstrate the "actuarial soundness" of the social insurance program, Altmeyer needed an actuary who would cooperate in doing so. A break with Williamson was inevitable, though the actual departure was managed so discreetly that it is impossible to tell from the public record whether he left voluntarily or Altmeyer had to fire him.

There was no doubt about who would take Williamson's place. Robert Myers, then in his mid-thirties, was thoroughly schooled in social insurance. As a very young man fresh from actuarial studies at the University of Iowa, he had prepared the old age insurance cost estimates for the Committee on Economic Security in 1934, and then stayed on to work for the Social Security Board. Myers did much of the technical work for which Williamson had no taste. A fellow actuary speculated years later that Williamson would never have left his job with the Travelers Insurance Company for Washington if he had liked the actuarial "nitty-gritty."[23] His main interest had always been the larger issues, the social philosophy of social insurance, and it was this interest that cost him his job when his philosophy proved very different from that of the program's leadership.

Myers did like the nitty-gritty, and he was very good at it. His technical virtuosity impressed other actuaries almost as much as it dazzled the members of Congress. And, while Myers was not indifferent to the larger issues, he approached them in a pragmatic spirit. Memoranda

21. American Institute of Actuaries, *The Record*, vol. 34 (1945), pp. 336–38; *Social Security Act Amendments of 1949*, Hearings before the House Committee on Ways and Means (GPO, 1949), pt. 2, pp. 1484 ff.

22. *Social Security Act Amendments of 1949*, Hearings, pt. 2, p. 1316.

23. Interview with Charles A. Siegfried, November 3, 1976.

that he wrote soon after he succeeded Williamson show that he agreed with his criticisms of the social insurance program and favored something virtually identical to his substitute for it, but, unlike Williamson, was willing to compromise. "I do not believe that the present OASI system is bad," Myers wrote in 1948, "but rather that a universal system would be much better."[24]

It was perhaps these two qualities—the technical proficiency and the pragmatism—that enabled Myers to do with aplomb what Williamson had refused to do at all. Williamson declined to respond to the program executives' wish for a single cost estimate for the program or proposed enlargements of it—a "most probable" cost or an "intermediate" cost lying between two hypothesized extremes. Toward the end, he declined even to dignify his various cost calculations by the name "estimates." Myers did supply such estimates—and with an air of confidence and mode of exact expression that seemed the very denial of uncertainty. The actuary's formulas could be made to yield precise mathematical answers. If one credited the assumptions on which they were based, one could also credit the answers. Whereas Williamson had brooded over the assumptions, Myers was lightning quick with the answers.

Myers's performance greatly enhanced the acceptability of the program among public officials, who liked having the uncertainty removed from policymaking and the "actuarial soundness" of their actions vouched for, and among professional actuaries, who liked having one of their own inside the Social Security Administration. They esteemed him for professional integrity as well as competence, for he was generally judged to be independent of partisan or organizational pressures. In the actuarial society as in Congress, Myers's estimates were credited as the work of a neutral expert. Given Myers's reassuring presence inside the administration, the perceived integrity of his work, and the growing general acceptance of social security as time passed, the actuarial profession tended to suspend criticism of the program.

But it did not withhold criticism altogether. The tension between the program and the actuarial profession persisted despite Myers's moderating influence as a bridge between the two. There was lingering resentment over the official use of insurance terminology and of actuarial procedures to elicit public confidence. In a biting analysis delivered to

24. Memo, "Mr. Immerwahr's Memorandum to the Advisory Council," March 4, 1948 (File 025 Social Security, acc. no. 62A-82, R. G. 47, Box 26, Washington National Records Center, Suitland, Md.).

the Society of Actuaries in 1959, Equitable's Ray Peterson charged that official assurance of "actuarial balance" in the system had "anesthetized" the public and "intoxicated" program executives such as Wilbur Cohen. Actuarial calculations, Peterson warned, were less reliable and significant than they had been made to seem. They could not measure the public's future willingness or capacity to pay taxes, judge intergenerational inequities, or assess the broad social and economic effects of a compulsory insurance program. The charge was not that Myers's estimates were wrong or biased, but that too much reliance was being placed on them. Peterson implied that Myers had failed to stress their limitations.[25]

Myers's response to this sort of criticism from professional colleagues was eminently practical. He conceded that his long-range cost estimates were highly uncertain, but argued that, with them, Congress's behavior was more prudent than it would have been without them, and that even if they could not reliably state the cost of any particular proposal, they facilitated comparison of alternative proposals. Myers implied that, except for his estimates, the politicians might not pause to consider long-run costs at all, and how could a professional actuary be in favor of that?[26] There was no good reply to Myers's reply. His was a paradoxical role in the program. He made it *seem* conservative. By his very presence, the weight of his professional authority, and his use of conservative estimating techniques, he did exert a restraining influence. Yet, by imparting to policymaking an appearance of fiscal rectitude, he also helped to secure acceptance for a program that many fiscal conservatives continued to believe was fundamentally wrong—at best unwise and at worst immoral—because misleading. The only way truly to restrain costs, such conservatives believed, was to reveal them to the taxpaying public immediately, by covering all the aged and other groups of beneficiaries. In their view, a professional actuary's calculations might give an appearance of restraint, but this was "anesthetic" only—it lulled the mind. Real restraint could come only through politics, when taxpayers began to feel the full burden of this gradually maturing program.

In the spring of 1970, Myers resigned from the Social Security Ad-

25. "Misconceptions and Missing Perceptions of Our Social Security System (Actuarial Anesthesia)," Society of Actuaries, *Transactions*, vol. 9 (1959), pp. 812–51. See also the ensuing discussion and Peterson's reply, pp. 852–919.

26. Society of Actuaries, *Transactions*, vol. 3 (1951), pp. 502–03.

ministration. Commissioner Ball, while praising his technical competence, explained to the press that Myers was no longer willing to serve as a technical, objective civil servant, but wanted to be a policy spokesman. In his letter of resignation to HEW Secretary Robert H. Finch, Myers denounced the "expansionist" policies of top SSA officials, who he said wanted social security to supplant private pension programs, and warned of their infidelity to Republican administrations.[27]

Myers had always been a latent dissident. Even as he was succeeding Williamson early in 1948, he privately criticized his bosses in the SSA for their unwillingness to consider policy choices. He wrote: "Unfortunately, I think we might say, almost all of the thinking in the Social Security Administration . . . is along the line that the present system is not only the best one possible but also the only one possible. There is little consideration given to various alternatives, such as Meriam's relief approach, the Townsend bountifulness, or Mr. Williamson's social budgeting basis, which, incidentally, I quite strongly favor."[28] He had come to terms with the program; though he did not think it the best policy choice, it was the choice that Congress made, and he therefore accepted it—more, committed his career to it. Yet, even in government service, he retained his professional standing with fellow actuaries, and he was sensitive to (in some degree sharing) the concerns of the insurance industry and of fiscal conservatives generally about the program. He maintained an independent relationship with Congress, and, during Republican administrations at least, cultivated an independent relationship with political appointees in HEW. "Bob Myers was always whispering in my ear," one such official recalled. In Myers's disapproving view, there was plenty to whisper about; he was convinced that others in the SSA were disloyal to Republican administrations.

Whether Myers's dissidence became overt because *he* changed, as Ball implied, or because the "expansionists" were running away with the program, as Myers's public speeches said, is a hard point to settle. Myers did forsake his technician's role to seek appointment as social security commissioner in 1969, or at least to seek the removal of Ball. Yet it is unlikely that he would have done this had not the enactment of medicare in 1965 and the SSA's subsequent pursuit of a much-

27. *Congressional Record* (June 3, 1970), pp. 18059–60, and ibid. (June 10, 1970), p. 19348.

28. Myers to A. J. McAndless, January 23, 1948 (File 025 Actuarial, acc. no. 62A-82, R. G. 47, Box 26, Washington National Records Center, Suitland, Md.).

expanded cash benefits program put his pragmatism to a severe test. He had been able, as conservative interest groups had been able, to come to terms with a cash benefit program that had provided a "floor of protection" to elderly people and raised it along with rises in the cost of living. However, when, on top of medicare, SSA leaders began pressing for a much bigger cash benefit program—one that he believed would eventually supplant private insurance and pension plans—Myers started to protest publicly against this threat to the private sector.[29] Thus his resignation may be interpreted as a conservative's response to policy changes initiated by the SSA leadership rather than the outgrowth of personal ambition.

The change in party control of the federal executive branch that followed the presidential election of 1968 helps to account for Myers's defection and heightens its significance. He began making critical speeches about social security policy soon after the Republicans took office, believing, apparently, that as between two competing policy views high in the SSA, a Republican administration would back his own: it would support the conservative dissident rather than the incumbent liberal commissioner, Ball. He was wrong, and when the Nixon administration declined to remove Ball, Myers had no choice other than to resign. His letter of resignation to the Secretary of HEW is worth quoting at length, bearing as it does on the crucial question of relations between program executives and political executives.

I have previously talked with you about my strong personal beliefs and have given you much supporting factual evidence to substantiate my views— namely, that certain of the top policy-making officials of the Social Security Administration (who are holdovers from the Johnson Administration) have strong beliefs in the desirability—even the necessity—of the public sector taking over virtually all economic security provisions for the entire population and thus eliminating private efforts in this area. It seems to me that this viewpoint is completely alien to that of the Nixon Administration.

Further, and equally important, it is my deeply-held conviction, as I have expressed to you a number of times in the past, that these officials of the Social Security Administration have not—and will not—faithfully and vigor-

29. See, for example, his *Expansionism in Social Insurance* (London: Institute of Economic Affairs, 1970); "Government and Pensions," in *Private Pensions and the Public Interest* (Washington, D.C.: American Enterprise Institute for Public Policy Research, 1970); and "The Future of Social Security—Is It in Conflict with Private Pension Plans?" an article from *Pension and Welfare News* that appears in *Medicare and Medicaid,* Hearings before the Senate Committee on Finance, 91 Cong. 2 sess. (GPO, 1970), pt. 1, pp. 37–43.

ously serve the Nixon Administration. Rather, they will exert their efforts to expand the Social Security program as much as possible by aiding and supporting any individuals and organizations that are of this expansionist conviction. Such anachronistic actions took place extensively during the Eisenhower Administration—against its political views. Such working at cross purposes with the Nixon Administration has occurred in the past year, and is still occurring, although to a somewhat limited extent so far. . . .

Evidently, no credence is placed in what I have related to you personally or in other evidence that I have furnished you on this matter, which has such an important effect on the future of the Social Security program. Therefore, I must, in good conscience and personal integrity, resign. It is especially dismaying to me to have to take this action, because I had hoped to serve the Nixon Administration not only with competence and integrity—as I had tried to serve all previous Administrations—but also with great enthusiasm, since I strongly believe in its philosophy and goals.[30]

Myers's dissent ended, as Williamson's did, with the departure of the dissenter from the SSA. Policy differences among high-ranking experts within the SSA did not persistently keep debate alive within the organization or open recurrent opportunities for generalist intervention from outside. That Williamson's dissent ended in this way is not surprising in view of the fact that it occurred during a Democratic administration and that the dissenting expert did not have much support from outside the organization. Williamson was not well known. Myers, on the other hand, was a major figure in the upper ranks of the federal civil service, greatly admired by Congress and his professional peers, the winner of innumerable awards for distinguished professional service—and had good reason to suppose that the incumbent administration agreed with his policy views. That his dissent was ineffective is far more puzzling and more significant.

Analytically, it is more logical to compare Myers's dissent with the Chamber of Commerce policy proposal of 1952–53 than with the departure of his predecessor. Both came as Republicans took over the executive branch, and both, though in very different ways, raised conservative alternatives for the incoming Republicans to consider. Both had the same outcome—rejection of the alternative. As the Eisenhower administration turned down the Chamber of Commerce plan, the Nixon administration rejected Myers and kept Ball.

In a general way, the two events have the same explanation. As in 1953, a new Republican administration was unwilling to bear the costs of change and ambivalent about the need for it. There were presidential

30. *Congressional Record* (June 3, 1970), p. 18059.

staff members who did want to remove Ball, but Republicans at the top of the Department of Health, Education, and Welfare, especially Under Secretary John G. Veneman, insisted on keeping him. If Ball had been removed, Veneman later said, "it would have been a signal that the Nixon administration put politics over competence—and the press would have written it that way."[31] Republicans at the top of the Bureau of the Budget believed that Ball should stay on. Richard P. Nathan, the assistant director in charge of human resources programs, recommended to Director Robert P. Mayo that Ball should remain despite complaints from private sources that he was an "expansionist." Nathan believed Ball to be "a fair . . . player—a sound hitter, but not an 'expansionist' . . . an excellent man and easy to work with."[32] Ball was so much admired in the Social Security Administration and in the wider community of the capital city that removing him was certain to provoke a critical outcry. At the same time, the liberal Republicans who headed HEW were not greatly concerned about the policy risks inherent in retaining him. "They *wanted* to expand social security," was the conclusion of a disillusioned private insurance executive, one of a group who urged Secretary Finch to replace Ball.[33]

As in 1953, there was a considerable divergence between the attitudes of conservative critics located in private organizations, whom Myers would join in dissent, and a new administration that was nominally conservative but actually mixed different ideologies and mixed all ideologies with pragmatism. The Nixon administration, like the Eisenhower administration, needed a legislative program, and, again like the Eisenhower administration, it advanced one for social security that was quite consistent with the objectives of program executives. Besides tying benefit increases automatically to increases in the cost of living (an idea advanced by conservative Republicans in Congress), the administration proposed to liberalize benefits for the disabled and for widows and widowers.

31. Interview with the author, December 7, 1976.
32. Memo, Nathan to Director, January 27, 1970, Nathan's personal files. However, after more experience in office Nathan came very definitely to the conclusion that immediately upon taking office a president should appoint cabinet and subcabinet officials who share his own policy goals. In retrospect, he believed that the Nixon administration erred in not removing Ball in 1969. Richard P. Nathan, "The 'Administrative Presidency,'" *The Public Interest* (Summer 1976), p. 53, and interview with the author, October 13, 1978.
33. Interview with Charles A. Siegfried, November 3, 1976.

The form in which choice was put to the Republicans in 1969–70 made it possible to deny the policy stakes. Ball told the press that he and Myers had no important philosophical differences. According to Veneman, the central issue was Myers's insubordination. The Washington community, which personalizes issues and is preoccupied with the distribution of offices, saw Myers's dissent as an attempt to get Ball's job. So interpreted, his resignation had no significance. It became simply one man's loss in a narrow contest over the social security commissionership. Conceivably the Nixon administration would have replaced Ball in 1969 if there had been a more plausible candidate for the job than Myers, but even the warmest admirers of Myers's technical skills had doubts about his suitability as an administrator. The private insurance company executives who appealed to the administration to remove Ball could suggest no one to put in his place. But even if Myers's candidacy was weak on its merits, his policy dissent need not have been ineffectual. It did pose a choice; if not Myers himself, the administration could have sought a competent man of conservative temper rather than continue in office a social security executive whose whole career demonstrated a commitment to program expansion and who had served six years as commissioner under the Democrats. An expert's dissent created the occasion for change, but political will to use the occasion was lacking.[34]

Out of office, both Williamson and Myers continued their dissents, but with differences in manner that affected the receptivity of their audiences. Both appeared before congressional committees, which could not fathom Williamson's vague and verbose testimony but welcomed Myers's characteristically direct and lucid statements. Both remained active in professional affairs, Williamson as a jeremiah delivering broadsides against social security, Myers to be honored with the presidency of the Society of Actuaries. Myers, but not Williamson, was retained as a consultant and congressional witness by trade associations such as the American Life Insurance Association and the National Association of Manufacturers. Deprived of his office, however, not even Myers could sustain influence on the course of events. A change in official actuarial

34. According to a contemporary account of the Nixon administration by two Washington journalists, Rowland Evans, Jr., and Robert D. Novak, Secretary Finch agreed to replace Ball but backed off when Wilbur Mills threatened retaliation. They interpret this as but one instance of a general failure of the first Nixon administration to secure control of the executive branch through the use of appointments. *Nixon in the White House: The Frustration of Power* (Random House, 1971), pp. 66–74.

techniques to which he was profoundly opposed took place in 1972, making possible a big increase in benefits that he wished to forestall (see chapter 17). Congress showed no disposition to discuss in general terms the issue his resignation raised, which was how to draw the line between social security and private measures of income protection. Indubitably an important event in the history of policymaking for social security, his resignation was not a dramatic one. It had little effect on public or political discourse, and was hardly noted by the press.[35]

EXPERT CRITICS have not played an important role in policymaking for social security, and expert criticism, even when present within the Social Security Administration, has not compelled consideration of major alternatives to the preferred program. Program executives could reject such criticism because it was intermittent, inconsistent, and generally without an organizational base, and because their own control of executive office enabled them to influence the flow of information to political executives and to select from among outside experts, as participants in policymaking, those most sympathetic to the program.

At the same time, the integration of "outside" expertise through the SSA's Office of the Actuary contributed crucially to the consensual mode of policymaking. It muted criticism from the actuarial profession and the insurance industry. It also elicited support from members of Congress and other attentive persons, such as those on advisory councils, who were impressed, or acted as if they were impressed, by expert assurances of an "actuarial balance."

35. The *New York Times*, on May 27, 1970, reported Myers's resignation at the bottom of page 47, the obituary page, in three paragraphs taken from the Associated Press wire.

CHAPTER EIGHT

Public Opinion

ONE of the most conspicuous features of policymaking for social security is the preoccupation of policymakers with public psychology. They have been enormously concerned with the public's perceptions and subjective experience of the program. Nonetheless, public opinion directly expressed has not had much influence on policy. Political parties, mass movements, and organized pressure groups with a mass membership—the channels through which public opinion normally is expressed —have not often made demands that policymakers had to take into account, and, in the rare event that they did make such demands, as with the Townsend movement in the 1930s, the policymakers' response was negative. The influence of public opinion on the program, though real, is manifested indirectly, in actions of the policymakers that anticipate public reaction and respond to what they believe the public prefers; and even then influence runs in both directions. Policymakers have presented the program so as to induce a favorable mass response.

Presidential Elections

National political campaigns, such as are conducted every four years in the contest for president, may be a medium through which policy choices are advanced by the contending political parties and resolved by the voting public. Political parties, which organize for the purpose of winning office, advance policy positions as one way of satisfying those members whose motive for participation is mainly ideological, and as a way of competing with one another for the people's votes. So expressed, such positions enable the voting public to play a central role in policy-making, at least in theory. Popular choice of some sort (regarding candidates and parties, if not issues) is inherent in a democratic system, in which officeholders gain authority and legitimacy through victory in competitive elections.

On the other hand, it may be argued that national election campaigns are not a very useful medium for making choices about policies or programs. For one thing, the parties are sometimes hard to tell apart. The dynamics of electoral competition usually drive them to the center, where their positions may be hardly distinguishable and, even if distinguishable, are so general that popular choices in national elections can give very little guidance to those who will make policy and design government programs in the ensuing four years.[1] The choices made by the public, according to this interpretation, apply to the general direction or pace of government action, but not to legislative particulars. Officeholders are left with a good deal of discretion.

The truth regarding social security is more complex than either of these contrasting general statements suggests. Some national elections have been much more pertinent to social security than others. In most elections since 1932, party platforms and candidates have had little to say about social security, and differences between the parties have been differences of degree rather than principle. But in a few elections—1936, 1960, and 1964—positions have been unusually detailed; differences have been starkly drawn and have extended to fundamentals. Results therefore could very easily be interpreted (whether correctly or not) as expressing a popular choice in this particular policy area—an endorsement of one specific alternative, the rejection of another.

Though it was not, in any strict sense, a creation of the Democratic party, the social insurance program developed under Democratic sponsorship. A Democratic president proposed it, a Democratic Congress enacted it, and the Democratic platform of 1936 claimed credit for it in a very general way. Thereafter, Democratic platforms intermittently called for extensions of the social insurance principle. The Democratic party supported this particular program, which granted benefits by "right" in return for "contributions" without resort to a test of need,

1. For a summary of political science literature stating this view and a critique of it, see James L. Sundquist, *Dynamics of the Party System: Alignment and Realignment of Political Parties in the United States* (Brookings Institution, 1973), chap. 14.

to protect the old, ill, and disabled. If any political party were to advance an alternative, it would have to be the Republicans.

The Republican party wasted no time in doing so. In the presidential campaign of 1936, when the Social Security Act was only a year old and the social insurance provisions were not yet operative (taxation would not start until 1937), the Republicans made a frontal attack on social insurance. Anyone who believes that party platforms deal in platitudes only, avoiding specifics, should contemplate the Republican plank of 1936 on the subject of social security:

Real security will be possible only when our productive capacity is sufficient to furnish a decent standard of living for all American families and to provide a surplus for future needs and contingencies. For the attainment of that ultimate objective we look to the energy, self-reliance, and character of our people, and to our system of free enterprise.

Society has an obligation to promote the security of the people by affording some measure of protection against involuntary unemployment and dependency in old age. The New Deal policies, while purporting to provide social security, have, in fact, endangered it.

We propose a system of old-age security, based upon the following principles:

1. We approve a pay-as-you-go policy, which requires of each generation the support of the aged and the determination of what is just and adequate.

2. Every American citizen over 65 should receive the supplementary payment necessary to provide a minimum income sufficient to protect him or her from want.

3. Each State and Territory, upon complying with simple and general minimum standards, should receive from the Federal Government a graduated contribution in proportion to its own, up to a fixed maximum.

4. To make this program consistent with sound fiscal policy the Federal revenues for this purpose must be provided from the proceeds of a direct tax widely distributed. All will be benefited and all should contribute.

The unemployment insurance and old-age annuity sections of the present Social Security Act are unworkable and deny benefits to about two-thirds of our adult population, including professional men and women and all those engaged in agriculture and domestic service and the self-employed, while imposing heavy tax burdens upon all. The so-called reserve fund estimated at $47,000,000,000 for old-age insurance is no reserve at all, because the fund will contain nothing but the Government's promise to pay, while the taxes collected in the guise of premiums will be wasted by the Government in reckless and extravagant political schemes.[2]

2. John J. Corson and John W. McConnell, *Economic Needs of Older People* (New York: Twentieth Century Fund, 1956), pp. 133–34. See pages 133–36 for a comparison of all the Democratic and Republican party planks on social security from 1932 through 1952.

On top of that, the party's candidate, Alf M. Landon, made a major speech on social security in which he attacked the law as "unjust, unworkable, stupidly drafted, and wastefully financed." He criticized the old age insurance program for imposing a tax immediately on payrolls, thereby raising the cost of employment, while delaying benefit payments for five years (under the original program monthly benefit payments would not have begun until 1942). "I say the saving it forces on our workers is a cruel hoax," he said, in a phrase that historians and program partisans have found highly quotable. Consistent with the platform, Landon proposed repealing the compulsory insurance plan and substituting grants-in-aid to the states to assure a sufficient minimum income for the needy aged.[3]

This Republican opposition did not persist. The 1940 platform said virtually nothing about old age insurance, and the 1944 platform endorsed it by calling for extension of coverage to all employees not yet covered. Not until 1960 was another issue of principle joined. In the interim, Democratic platforms promised variously to expand social insurance and so did Republican platforms, though with language far briefer and narrower. If Republicans were opposed to what Democrats proposed, they did not say so outright. They were distinguished from the Democrats by what they declined to promise.

The 1960 platforms once again set forth sharply opposing partisan views. The issue was health care for the elderly, which reached the public agenda in the late 1950s through the combined efforts of organized labor, officials of the Social Security Administration, and their liberal Democratic allies in Congress. The Democratic platform promised medical care for the aged through social insurance: "We shall provide medical care benefits for the aged as part of the time-tested Social Security insurance system. We reject any proposal which would require such citizens to submit to the indignity of a means test."[4] The Republican platform pledged to "provide the aged needing it, on a sound fiscal basis and through a contributory system, protection against the burdensome costs of health care." Beneficiaries would be given the choice of purchasing private health insurance, and provision would be

3. *Vital Speeches,* vol. 3 (October 15, 1936), pp. 26–29.
4. John P. Bradley, "Party Platforms and Party Performance Concerning Social Security," *Polity,* vol. 1 (Spring 1969), pp. 337–58, compares platform statements and subsequent actions. I have relied on this article for platform data from 1956 through 1964. The standard source is Kirk H. Porter and Donald B. Johnson, *National Party Platforms, 1840–1968* (University of Illinois Press, 1970).

made for participation by state governments. By linking benefits to need and making participation voluntary, the Republican plan departed fundamentally from that of the Democrats and from the principles of the social insurance program. Beyond that, differences between the presidential candidates on this issue were dramatized in a congressional session that followed the nominating conventions. A health care bill backed by the Democratic candidate, John F. Kennedy, came to a vote in the Senate, where a majority of Democrats supported it and all Republicans but one were opposed. A rival Republican bill, backed by candidate Richard M. Nixon, evoked an even more partisan response. All of the Democratic members voted against it, while a majority of the Republicans were in favor.

This basic difference in approach was reiterated in 1964, when the Democrats promised to "continue to fight until we have succeeded in including hospital care for older Americans in the Social Security program," whereas the Republicans promised "full coverage of all medical and hospital costs for the needy elderly people, financed by general revenues through broader implementation of Federal-State plans, rather than the compulsory Democratic scheme covering only a small percentage of such costs, for everyone regardless of need." Besides defending his party's position on medicare, the Republican candidate, Barry Goldwater, casually suggested in a press conference that social security might be made voluntary. Though this was not the party's position and not even clearly the candidate's position, it was transformed by media coverage and the ridicule of rival candidates (including other candidates for the Republican nomination) into a symbol of Goldwater's radical conservatism. As such, it figured conspicuously in the campaign. T. H. White, the chronicler of presidential campaigns, reported, "Out of the vast mass of his many statements and speeches, [the Democrats] chose to hook and hang him on one issue: Social Security."[5]

Intermittently, then, party competition served to put clear choices about social security before the electorate, and, as it happens, on all three of these occasions the Democrats won the election, twice (1936 and 1964) by very large margins. Inevitably, program partisans argued that the public "chose" social insurance. There is a prima facie case for this interpretation, given the election history just described, but both a priori logic and evidence from opinion polls suggest that such interpretations

5. *Making of the President, 1964* (Atheneum, 1965), pp. 302–03.

are highly simplistic. By ignoring the uncertainty and complexity of expressions of electoral opinion, they exaggerate the policy content of the voters' choice.

No presidential election in this century can safely be interpreted as a referendum on a single question, however prominently it may have figured in party platforms, candidate rhetoric, or media coverage. When millions of voting decisions are made and each decision is subject to many influences—party identification; the opinions of family, peer groups, and neighbors; the personalities of the candidates; current social and economic conditions; the candidates' presentation of a variety of issues—it becomes impossible to ascribe the result to any one factor, or to interpret it as a verdict on any one issue. Analyses of electoral behavior have generally shown that, while voters are not entirely ignorant of or indifferent to issues, most view them in broad and simple terms. Thus they may identify with the Democratic party because they trust the Democrats "to help the working man," "to do something about unemployment," to be "more likely to avoid a depression," but mass knowledge does not extend to the particulars of government programs.[6]

Regarding social security, evidence from public opinion polls fully confirms this finding. The evidence has been summarized in a study prepared for the Social Security Administration by a historian, Michael E. Schiltz, who reviewed all poll data bearing on the social security program between 1935 and 1965. Schiltz concludes from these data that public understanding of even the most rudimentary differences between social insurance and public assistance (the means-tested alternative, providing benefits only to the poor) was remarkably low. "As a consequence," he states, "it remains forever moot whether during the Depression the public understood or endorsed the principle of social insurance."[7] Polls between 1936 and 1944 showed overwhelming and steadily increasing support for some sort of government program to support the incomes of the aged. By 1944 the level of support had reached 96 percent. But "the most likely inference from these [surveys]," Schiltz notes, "is that public response simply did not differentiate between the insurance and assistance orientations."[8] Schiltz also concludes that the early

6. For rigorous analyses, see V. O. Key, *Public Opinion and American Democracy* (Knopf, 1961), chap. 18, and Angus Campbell, Philip E. Converse, Warren E. Miller, and Donald E. Stokes, *The American Voter* (Wiley, 1960), chap. 8.

7. Michael E. Schiltz, *Public Attitudes toward Social Security 1935–1965*, U.S. Department of Health, Education, and Welfare, Social Security Administration, Office of Research and Statistics, Research Report 33 (GPO, 1970), p. 29.

8. Ibid., p. 37.

participants in old age insurance had a very limited understanding of it: "During the first decade of the program's life, a substantial proportion of those paying social security payroll deductions did not understand that their participation would entitle them to a retirement benefit regardless of need. In effect, they did not have even the most elementary understanding of what the OAI program was all about."[9]

Regarding health insurance, Schiltz reaches similar conclusions. It was impossible to infer from poll data of the 1940s, when national health insurance was an issue, or the early 1960s, which were the climactic years of the medicare campaign, that the public favored health care through social insurance. He writes:

Both the low level of public understanding and the imprecise questions in the literature make it impossible to draw from the health insurance controversies any conclusions about public attitudes toward social insurance as a principle. Considerably less than half of the population during each of the two controversies knew that the programs were to be financed through the social security system, and presumably many of those who were incorrect on this detail thought the programs involved a means test as well as noncontributory financing. The survey questions themselves never raised the issue of social insurance directly, and the alternative posed to respondents was itself an insurance program, albeit a private one. Upwards of 70 percent of the American population felt that some action was necessary, and about as large a proportion specifically endorsed the principle of Government responsibility for medical expenses of the poor. But these trends do not directly touch the issue of social insurance. Thus data available on the health insurance issues neither affirm nor deny public support for the principle of social insurance.[10]

The picture that emerges from these rather elliptical and unsatisfactory data is that of a public generally in favor of some sort of action, but confused and undecided about alternatives and ignorant about the working of actual programs. Public opinion, if these data are a guide, left the policymakers with all their options open except the option to do nothing about helping the aged poor after the Depression. When juxtaposed with the poll data, party competition and electoral results can be seen to have had the effect of narrowing policy alternatives rather than widening them. Elections coming after programmatic platforms or campaigns make the electorate seem more decided than it is. Election results render in clear and highly simplified form mass opinion that is actually confused and conflicting. The net effect of such elections is to eliminate options that on the face of it have been defeated. Policy, as John Kingdon has observed, is arrived at largely by a series of *nega-*

9. Ibid., p. 53.
10. Ibid., p. 147.

tive decisions, which successively narrow the range of choice.[11] As a means of providing expression for popular opinion, elections in which differing party programs are advanced are best understood as a part of this narrowing process. That rival proposals are generated in the course of party competition guarantees that one proposal will be defeated. And, having once met popular defeat, a course of action may well be forever eliminated from the public agenda.[12]

But suppose the Republican party had won election after advancing an alternative to social insurance. Its presidential candidate came very close to winning in 1960. Had he won, would health care policy have followed a very different course? And would the dynamics of party competition not then have served to widen the range of policy choice? That party competition has not widened options may be merely because the minority party has been persistently weak. Imbalance in the party system has produced an almost unbroken succession of Democratic congresses since 1936 and a preponderance of Democratic presidencies. Perhaps a highly competitive and well-balanced party system is the essential condition for maintaining a range of choice. Frequent alternations of party regimes might encourage flexibility among program executives.

This is an intriguing possibility that is impossible to test. Most of the time, Republicans have not won election; when they have won, their victories have been partial (the presidency but not the Congress); and their winning platforms have not called for major changes in social

11. John W. Kingdon, "Dynamics of Agenda Formation in Congress," in James E. Anderson, ed., *Cases in Public Policy-Making* (Praeger, 1976), pp. 35–49.

12. How important defeat is depends on the stage of program development and on the margin of defeat, which is important not just in itself but because of its long-term effect on the party composition of the government. The defeat of Landon's proposal of 1936 was conclusive because it confirmed a program that was already enacted, because the Republican loss was numerically devastating, and because it coincided with a party realignment that favored the Democrats. The defeat of the Republican position in 1960 was inconclusive because action on medical care was prospective and the margin of the electoral outcome was narrow. The Republicans did not abandon their position in 1964; they reaffirmed it. The election of 1964 was conclusive because it brought in a big enough Democratic majority to pass the Democrats' proposal. In their 1968 platform statements regarding medicare, the parties reverted to a familiar pattern in social insurance. Republicans acquiesced silently in what the Democrats had done, neither calling for repeal of medicare nor proposing to enlarge it. The Democrats proposed to enlarge it in two significant ways: medical care should be extended to disabled beneficiaries in the same way it had been extended to the aged, and medical care for the aged should be expanded to include the cost of prescription drugs.

insurance. This is not a history from which to draw firm inferences about the effects of party alternation on policy, yet the limited effect of the small amount of alternation that has taken place casts doubt on the effectiveness of party change in general. Republicans have taken the presidency from the Democrats twice in the history of social insurance, and kept it for eight years both times. Both Republican presidencies confirmed established social insurance policy and accepted, even when they did not intend, significant enlargements in the program. The Republican platform of 1952 promised to "make a thorough study of universal pay-as-we-go pension plans." The actual Republican administration of 1953 dismissed most of these plans out of hand and found little merit in the U.S. Chamber of Commerce's well-considered proposal. The 1968 Republican platform promised to "take steps to help improve and extend private pension plans." But the actual Republican administration of 1969–72 declined to remove from office a Democratic social security commissioner who was committed to increasing the relative importance of social security.

In a different way, the fate of Democratic platforms also calls the importance of party into question. What Democratic platforms have called for has generally been done sooner or later, but the delay of the responses casts doubt upon the strength of the causal connection between party proclamation and government action. In 1948 and 1960 the Democratic party made specific promises regarding social insurance on which it failed to deliver despite its control of the government. Among other things, the 1948 platform promised disability and health insurance and benefits for women at age sixty instead of sixty-five. The 1960 platform promised medical care for the aged through social insurance. But party platforms, as a leading study of presidential nominating procedures says, are pronouncements of the presidential wing of the party.[13] Written for use in presidential campaigns, they promise congressional action to which the party's congressional wing may not assent. Neither in 1949–52 nor in 1961–64 was there enough Democratic support in Congress to enact the party's social insurance platform.[14]

13. Paul T. David, Ralph M. Goldman, and Richard C. Bain, *The Politics of National Party Conventions* (Brookings Institution, 1960), p. 498. For discussion of platforms, see pp. 407–09, 497–98.

14. See Wilbur J. Cohen, *Retirement Policies under Social Security* (University of California Press, 1957), 77n, where Cohen cites several instances in which party actions in Congress diverged from party platforms; and, for a contrasting argument, see Bradley, "Party Platforms and Party Performance Concerning Social Security."

Beyond that, analysis of party platforms raises the provocative question of whether parties as such—parties as a distinct form of organization—have had positions on social security policy at all. If they did, one would expect these positions to be quite consistent over time, with each platform reiterating the positions and perhaps even the precise language of earlier platforms, making due adjustment for intervening legislative events. Yet the platforms show a remarkable inconsistency in style and content, especially those of the Democrats. The Democrats' 1944 platform, coming at a time when a national health insurance bill had already been drafted and introduced in Congress, was astonishingly empty on social insurance, promising only the postwar enactment "of such additional humanitarian, labor, social and farm legislation as time and experience may require, including the amendment or repeal of any law enacted in recent years which has failed to accomplish its purpose." The 1948 platform, going to the other extreme, embodied the entire legislative program of the Social Security Administration in a series of highly specific promises. The 1952 platform swung back again to brief generalization, omitted disability and health insurance although neither had passed, and, quite contrary to the SSA's position, promised to eliminate retirement from work as a condition for receipt of social security benefits. In 1956 the position on the retirement test was reversed, and the platform introduced two new proposals—an increase in the wage base and an increase in benefits for each year of covered employment—which were goals of the SSA leadership. This fluctuation suggests that the composition of a party platform is a haphazard affair. Party factions and leading personalities vie for control, with outcomes that may vary considerably from one campaign to the next. When an incumbent President is running, the White House staff takes an active part in the drafting, and the President's program, to the extent that he has one (as Truman had one in 1948), becomes the party's program. Otherwise, the platform is up for grabs. There is no permanent party machinery to maintain control of it through successive elections.

If the parties were formally organized, with a permanent central bureaucracy, they might become an important rival to program executives as a source of policy proposals.[15] Because they could claim mass followings and the backing of electoral majorities, they could be a

15. But see Hugh Heclo, *Modern Social Politics in Britain and Sweden: From Relief to Income Maintenance* (Yale University Press, 1974), pp. 293–97, for an argument that this has not occurred in those two countries.

powerful rival. As it is, the absence of permanent party organizations with programmatic interests leaves program executives with a relatively clear field. They have to deal with transient party figures in the White House and the Department of Health, Education, and Welfare in ad hoc fashion, and they have to adapt proposals to the partisan and ideological composition of Congress, but party organizations as such— party organizations as an independent link to mass opinion—are not a significant part of their environment.

Mass Movements

Constitutionally limited terms for officeholders, in combination with a system of competitive parties, provide for expression of mass opinion in a regular, predictable way through elections, but this is not the only way in which mass opinion can be expressed. Less predictably and more spontaneously, opinion finds outlets in mass movements that coalesce around a cause or charismatic figure, often with panacean objectives.

One such movement, led by a California doctor named Francis E. Townsend, is important in the history of the social security program. Begun in 1934, it survived nominally for some twenty years and was at a peak in the 1935–41 period, during which the old age insurance program was founded. Though it had particular strength in the Far West, it claimed a nationwide membership of 3.5 million, organized in 7,000 clubs. It published a weekly newspaper and was able to mount massive letter-writing campaigns. In the congressional debates of 1935 and 1939, the Townsend movement provided the principal alternative to proposals of the Committee on Economic Security and the Social Security Board.[16]

The nature of the Townsend proposals changed over time, becoming more realistic as the initial mass base of the movement eroded. The original Townsend plan, embodied in a bill introduced by a California congressman in January 1935, would have provided a monthly pension of $200 to every citizen sixty years or older who had not been convicted of a felony. Pensioners would have been prohibited from wage-earning and would have been required to spend all of their pension within thirty

16. Abraham Holtzman, *The Townsend Movement: A Political Study* (Bookman Associates, 1963); Committee on Old Age Security of the Twentieth Century Fund, *The Townsend Crusade* (New York: the Fund, 1936); Corson and McConnell, *Economic Needs of Older People*, pp. 117–18, 406–08.

days. The plan would have been financed by a 2 percent tax on the gross dollar value of every commercial and financial transaction, with discretionary power lodged in the president to raise the tax to 3 percent or lower it to 1 percent. Responsible economic analysts concluded that the plan was utterly fallacious. It would not restore prosperity and employment. Expenditures would be many times greater than revenues. Many of the nation's self-supporting families would be forced into poverty by the cost. One-third of the earnings of the nation's workers would have been absorbed. In short, the plan was preposterous. Revision began immediately. A second version, introduced in April 1935, called for pensions of no specified amount, but not to exceed $200 monthly, and added other sources of taxation in an effort to balance revenue and expenditure.

By 1953 it was hard to tell the Townsend proposals from those of conservative critics of social insurance except for the size of the monthly payment. The Townsend plan of 1953 called for pensions paid by right, administered by the federal government on a uniform, nationwide basis, with current (pay-as-you-go) financing, from taxes borne by "the entire American community, including all individuals and all business and industry." Pensions should be high enough to enable the aged and disabled to live in "modest comfort and dignity," an amount that Townsend leaders estimated to be in the neighborhood of $150 a month.[17]

In the Townsend movement, as in certain of the presidential elections, public opinion was organized and expressed in a way that seemed to pose a fundamental choice. Through "Townsendism," an alternative to the officially endorsed program welled up from the grass roots. Paradoxically, though, the net effect of the movement over the long run was probably to narrow choices.

The choice initially posed by the Townsend movement was so irresponsible and extreme that it was not a real choice. This was no accident, but arose from the utopian tendencies that are typical of mass movements. The utopian character of Townsendism in turn had a powerful effect on the perceptions of the early program executives, who reacted to the movement intensely. It was the most important political phenomenon in their immediate environment, and it became for them the epitome of error. The Townsend plan was the false, corrupt religion to which their own true religion was opposed. That they developed a

17. Ibid., pp. 407–08.

"religion"—which is to say an intense dogmatism about their program—was in some significant measure a response to the messianic character of this early rival.

The nature of the rival also affected the perceptions of the program executives' larger audience in Congress and elsewhere. Congressmen feared the Townsend movement. Responsible men in general recoiled from its extreme irrationality. Townsendism was dangerous, and anything that resembled it in any respect was discredited to the extent of the resemblance. The result was that rational plans from more respectable sources—plans that called for giving uniform flat grants to all the aged, and thereby resembled the Townsend plan in important respects—suffered from the association. Social insurance program executives were quick to label such proposals Townsendism, and Townsendism tainted everything to which it was applied.

The initial Townsend plan posed no serious threat to the proposals of the Committee on Economic Security and the Social Security Board. By contributing greatly to the momentum in support of some sort of action while providing a specific alternative that was patently absurd, it contributed to congressional acceptance of the official proposals from the executive. The idea of flat, noncontributory grants, which the Townsend movement had popularized, persisted for some years, but lacked mass support after 1940–41, by which time the Townsend movement as a mass phenomenon came to an end. Whatever positive influence the Townsend movement may have had in support of a specific alternative to social insurance was dissipated quickly. This is the nature of such movements. Spontaneous and unpredictable in their origins, they are also ephemeral. Their effects on policy, if any, are bound to be episodic.

Organized Groups with a Mass Membership

The more so because of the Townsend movement, social security program executives needed a source of mass support. The verdict of the 1936 election helped them greatly, but that did not put the Townsend movement to rest or satisfy their need for recurrent, reliable expressions of popular approval for what they were trying to do. The best place to look for such support, they believed, was organized labor.

The elderly might have seemed the natural constituency for the social security program, but, as the Townsend movement showed, they were prey to panacean appeals. Besides, on purely rational grounds they could hardly be expected to show much interest in the 1930s in a program that did not promise to pay benefits until 1942, and then only to persons who made tax payments. It is no wonder that the aged flocked to the Townsend movement, which promised utopia right away to everyone over sixty. Even if the elderly had been more conventionally organized, without the messianism and impermanence of the Townsend movement, their immediate interest in benefits and their relative indifference to the tax burden would have made them a very demanding constituency, hard to resist or restrain. The manifest imbalance of their stakes and the self-interestedness of their demands would have undermined their credibility and legitimacy.

Organized labor as a mass base of support for the program did not have these defects. While the insurgent CIO had some of the messianic fervor of a movement, the constituent units of the AFL and the national federation itself were large and durable organizations, even if in a turbulent state. While their members were potential beneficiaries of old age insurance, more immediately they would be taxpayers. Through the payroll tax, they would bear much of the cost of the program. Here, then, was a mass constituency that *had* to be won—and which, if won, might function effectively as the mass base for the program by reason of its size, organizational stability, political legitimacy, and the direct yet balanced stakes of its members in social insurance (payroll taxpayers initially, beneficiaries later).

The steps by which organized labor became allied with social security program executives are described in chapter 5. In this evolution, the election campaign of 1936 was important in that it failed to elicit resistance to the payroll tax from industrial workers. Some industrial employers (how many is not clear from historical accounts) joined with Republican party leaders to appeal to the working class with an attack on the payroll tax. Messages were inserted in payroll envelopes and placards were posted in factories warning that a compulsory tax was about to be imposed ("You're sentenced to a weekly pay reduction for all your working life") with no assurance of a return ("You might get this money back . . . but only if Congress decides to make the appropriation for this purpose. There is NO guarantee").[18] The Social Security Board joined in this propaganda war with a pamphlet distributed

18. Arthur M. Schlesinger, Jr., *The Age of Roosevelt*, vol. 3, *The Politics of Upheaval* (Houghton Mifflin, 1960), pp. 635–38.

through AFL unions and promising that workers would always get back more than they paid in taxes. It is hard to know what effect this flurry of propaganda had on the election, but obviously there was no working-class revolt intense or widespread enough to prevent the massive shift of that year to the Democratic party. At the next AFL convention, Arthur Altmeyer thanked the AFL for help in repelling the "dastardly attack." "I can say to you truthfully that the Social Security Board owes to organized labor a great deal for that service," he said.[19]

Yet it was not until the 1940s that the leadership of organized labor was won over wholeheartedly to support of the social insurance program, and only then could program leaders begin to feel secure in possession of the mass base that they sought. For years thereafter they could count on labor support for all of their measures. Union members acquiesced in their leadership's commitment to social security—passively for the most part, yet sometimes actively, for example, by passing resolutions appealing to Congress to increase the payroll tax in the late 1940s at a time when program executives were trying to prevent successive congresses from postponing scheduled increases. The value of this mass base increased as organized labor became more active politically, more united, more closely bound to the Democratic party, and more widely recognized as a powerful and legitimate political force.

So committed was organized labor to constructing the social insurance program that eventually, in the drive for health insurance, it took over much of the work of propaganda and public relations. It was the AFL-CIO that built support at the grass roots for enacting health insurance for the elderly. (Quite possibly the uneven distribution of labor's influence accounts in some measure for Schiltz's finding that support for medicare was much higher in urban than in rural areas. Schiltz speculated, plausibly enough, that the perception of need for publicly subsidized health care for the aged increased with the availability and sophistication of medical care facilities, and that availability and sophistication in turn were functions of size of place. The influence of organized labor on public opinion probably also increases with size of place.)

It was labor, too, in the course of the medicare campaign, that took the initiative in finally organizing the social security program's "natural" constituency. The National Council of Senior Citizens, a federation of senior citizen clubs growing out of union locals, was created in the early

19. *American Federationist,* vol. 44 (November 1937), p. 1208.

1960s with labor's financial backing. After Nelson Cruikshank retired as social security director of the AFL-CIO, he was elected president of the National Council of Senior Citizens. Like its parent organization, the NCSC became a faithful, uncritical supporter of the established program and of expansions certified by program executives to be consistent with it.

Social security program executives were conspicuously grateful for labor's support. They often paid tribute to the American worker for his willingness to pay payroll taxes. They believed that labor's support was crucial to constructing their program. Yet they did not rely solely on this organized, private intermediary for the management of their public relations.

Influencing the Public

Inasmuch as their organization's own clients included a sizable and ever-increasing number and proportion of citizens, there was much that social security executives could do directly to influence public opinion and to elicit mass support for their program.

The SSA's leaders tried hard to give dependable, efficient, client-oriented service, and Arthur Altmeyer claimed that their success in doing so accounted for the popularity of the program. Because there was a lag between enactment (1935) and inauguration of monthly benefits (set at 1940 by the 1939 amendments), there was ample time to make administrative preparations. "That gave us a chance to really dig in and set up an effective and comprehensive program," Altmeyer told an interviewer. "I think it's unquestionably been the major reason why social security became so popular. There was little maladministration or whatever you want to call it. But, more importantly, the people who came into contact with the public had been so thoroughly drilled in their attitudes."[20]

The SSA's public relations, however, were not confined to routine administrative contacts in field offices. They consisted, not just of what was done for the public there, but what was said to the public every-where—in law, official speeches, press conferences, congressional testimony, and descriptive brochures that were distributed to social security

20. Interview with Arthur J. Altmeyer, Oral History Collection, Columbia University (1967).

taxpayers and beneficiaries. "Insurance" was the central symbol of all these messages, and it was stressed precisely because it was expected to secure public acceptance. Because insurance implied a return for work and investment, it preserved the self-respect of the beneficiaries; because it implied a return in proportion to investment, it satisfied a widely held conception of fairness; and because it implied the existence of a contract, it appeared sound and certain. (Insurance industry executives complained privately that leaders of social security were hostile to their industry but eager to exploit its good name for their own purposes.)

For constitutional reasons, there was some delay in instituting the term. It implied a link between the tax title (title VIII) of the Social Security Act of 1935 and the benefits title (title II), which the drafters had separated so as to reduce the risks of constitutional challenge. But once the test of constitutionality was passed in 1937, social security executives were quick to proclaim the unity of taxes and benefits and to say that the result was "insurance." Wilbur Cohen has recaptured the moment:

I recall walking down the steps of the Supreme Court building in a glow of ecstasy with Mr. Winant and Mr. Altmeyer. We had hoped and prayed for this day, and yet when it occurred it was still unbelievable to us. When I came back to the office, I obtained Mr. Altmeyer's approval to send out a memo to the staff stating that because of the decision we could now call the old age benefits program "old age insurance." . . . The American public was and still is insurance-minded and opposed to welfare, "the dole," and "handouts." [21]

The analogy was thereafter elaborated and insisted upon. Taxes became "premiums" or "contributions." Workers had "old age insurance accounts" in Baltimore. They were "paying for their own protection, building up insurance for their old age." To challenge the insurance analogy or resist using the terms was to show oneself an enemy of the program. Quarrels with conservative critics over semantics persisted for years, as in this politically revealing exchange between Cohen and two Republican senators in 1961:

Senator [WALLACE F.] BENNETT. My idea of contribution is something I myself take out of my pocket and hand to somebody. It is not, it does not apply to what somebody else takes out of my pocket, and I think this is a tax. . . .

21. *Congressional Record* (September 16, 1957), p. 28874.

Mr. COHEN. You have to change the law then because it says it is the Federal Insurance Contributions Act.

Senator CARL T. CURTIS. Who told us to do that, Wilbur? I remember the day it happened.

Mr. COHEN. I think it was a good idea, Mr. Curtis.

Senator CURTIS. Well, it happened over in the Ways and Means Committee, and I was there.[22]

It is hard to judge what the effects of this official terminology have been. It would be reasonable to infer that the insurance analogy has made a profound impression on the public.[23] Congress has joined with program executives in fostering the analogy, which is embedded as deeply in statutory terminology as in the SSA's pamphlets. With the exception of a very few conservative dissidents (Curtis mainly), all official policymakers have encouraged the public to think of the program as insurance. Judging from their own public statements, they believe that the public does think of it that way. And in their own choice of policies and program changes, as well as language, they have acted as if it were very important to preserve the public's perception. Hence they have eschewed courses of action, such as immediate coverage of all the aged or heavy reliance on general revenue financing, that could destroy the public's perceptions. In the constraints that policymakers feel—the courses of action they reject—it is possible to see the effects of public opinion on the program: not public opinion directly

22. *Social Security Benefits and Eligibility*, Hearings before the Senate Committee on Finance, 87 Cong. 1 sess. (GPO, 1961), p. 102. Curtis's statement is puzzling in one respect. The Federal Insurance Contributions Act was enacted in 1939. Although he was a member of Congress then, having been elected in 1938, Curtis did not become a member of the Ways and Means Committee until 1945.

23. There are very few data on public attitudes toward social security, but clues may be found in the results of a small pilot survey directed by a social psychologist, Leonard Goodwin, in the summer of 1974, and reported in the *American Psychologist*. Questionnaires were administered to 615 persons in three cities (Baltimore, Cincinnati, and Denver) stratified by age, sex, income level, and employment status. Goodwin found a high level of support for social security. Respondents generally showed a high willingness to pay into a mandatory system. He also found support for the founders' assumption that linking benefits to contributions enhances public acceptance. Oddly enough, given the very favorable benefit-cost ratios in the early program, Goodwin's respondents on the average did not believe that they were getting a good return on their investment. There was a slight tendency for them to agree with statements that the money paid into social security would be better invested elsewhere. Leonard Goodwin and Joseph Tu, "The Social Psychological Basis for Public Acceptance of the Social Security System," *American Psychologist*, vol. 30 (September 1975), pp. 875–83. I also benefited from correspondence with Goodwin.

expressed, but public opinion as the policymakers presume it to be, having themselves tried to shape it.

Even if the public fully credits the implied analogy to private insurance, it is hard to assess how this has affected its political behavior regarding the program. To what extent does the perception that the program is insurance account for popular acceptance of it? Here the practical question—the question ever in the minds of policymakers—is how large a tax rate the public will tolerate. The effort to woo public opinion is at bottom an effort to elicit public acquiescence to taxation.

Holders of political office often talk as if there is some absolute limit to the amount of social security taxation the public will stand for, and warn that the employee tax is at or approaching the limit of public tolerance.[24] Such warnings were heard from Republicans for many years, with each increase in the rate. Less predictably, Democratic secretaries of HEW were susceptible to the same anxiety, as Abraham Ribicoff showed in the Kennedy administration. In testimony before the Senate Committee on Finance, he argued in 1961 that the combined employee-employer tax should not be allowed to rise above 10 percent, 1 percent above the level then attained.[25] For a short while, this 10 percent was taken seriously; insiders called it "Ribicoff's rubicon." Yet if one looks at what policymakers did rather than what they said, the notion that here is an absolute limit to taxation appears problematic. Ribicoff's rubicon was crossed in 1971, as other rubicons had been crossed before (6 percent was for a long time regarded as the absolute limit, probably because that was the plateau set by the 1935 law). Policymakers acted as if the public would accept tax rate increases if they were small and if they were accompanied by increases in benefits.

24. For example, see the remarks of Wilbur Mills in *Medical Care for the Aged,* Executive Hearings before the House Committee on Ways and Means, 89 Cong. 1 sess. (GPO, 1965), pt. 1, p. 29.

25. *Social Security Benefits and Eligibility,* Hearings, pp. 78–79. In 1976, a member of the House Committee on Ways and Means harked back to the 10 percent standard. James Burke of Massachusetts observed that "I support the Ribicoff rule that was designed by the Senator when he was Secretary of Health, Education, and Welfare. He said the social security tax should never go above 10 percent but now it is going above 12 percent—that extra 2 percent is raising cain with industry in this country." Robert Ball, who was the witness before the committee, replied that he had as commissioner "reinterpreted the Ribicoff Rule to 10 percent for cash benefits." *President's Social Security Proposals,* Hearings before the Subcommittee on Social Security of the House Committee on Ways and Means, 94 Cong. 2 sess. (GPO, 1976), p. 147.

Here again it is possible to detect the indirect effects of public opinion. Fear of adverse public reaction limited the size of tax increases and made them contingent on granting added benefits. On the other hand, the fact that a taxpayers' revolt was constantly feared but never came raises intriguing yet imponderable questions about the content and the political efficacy of public opinion. Did the public not resist rising taxes because it believed it was getting a fair and valuable return for its money (a belief presumably encouraged by the insurance analogy)? Did it not resist because the rate, though rising, did not become absolutely intolerable? (Where then does the barrier lie, assuming that at some point a limit of tolerance will be reached?) Or did the public not revolt because it was unable to? Social security taxpayers constitute the principal potential source of resistance to program expansion, but they are an unorganized and unorganizable mass, which includes nearly all adult Americans who are employed. It is a group so large, so heterogeneous, and so amorphous as to be incapable of forming direct expressions of opinion on a single aspect of a single government program. This means that its influence will be felt only indirectly, in the policymakers' anticipation of public reactions. But the limited ability of an unorganized public actually to react to specific tax increases raises the question of how and whether (as well as at what level of taxation) public opinion would impose an effective barrier to continual expansion of the program.[26]

26. Several critics viewed this passage about the inefficacy of public opinion very skeptically. They argued that the American political system is sensitive even to murmurs of public discontent and that to protest the cost of social security effectively and block expansion taxpayers would only have to write their congressmen or complain to them during members' visits home. In fact, such protests seemed to occur early in 1978, following passage of the Social Security Amendments of 1977, which raised social security taxes beginning in 1979. They formed part of a growing protest against tax burdens that was finding an outlet chiefly in actions limiting the amounts that state governments could collect or spend. I continue to doubt that the present social security program will be curbed by taxpayer protest even as the cost of sustaining it grows with increases in the retired portion of the population. When taxpayer revolts do occur, as in the late 1970s, they find their most efficacious outlets at the level of state and local governments, where mechanisms of direct democracy are much more readily available than at the national level and where it is constitutionally feasible to impose spending and taxing limits. In recent years, property taxes have been falling as a percentage of gross national product, whereas the social security payroll tax has been rising. I doubt that this is simply because the social security tax is more popular than property taxes or the social security program more popular than the local services that are financed with property taxes. I believe it is partly because opposition is easier to organize and express effectively at the

The fact that the taxpaying public as a whole is not organized—and, as a practical matter, cannot be—has increased the importance of such organized expressions of mass opinion as exist on the subject of social security. Organized labor, though it represents only part of the public, tends to be treated by program executives as a surrogate for the tax-paying public as a whole. No comparable surrogates exist. In view of this fact, organized labor's highly sympathetic support of the program becomes all the more significant. If organized labor can be said to speak for social security taxpayers generally, not just for labor, then social security taxpayers generally can be said to have supported construction of the program.

Whatever the explanation of it, the taxpaying public's failure to impose a barrier to tax increases meant that policymakers had recurrent opportunities for expansion above and beyond those that economic growth would have given them anyway. Each of these expansions in turn created a new obligation to the public as a beneficiary of the program. And the public-as-beneficiary is highly influential in policymaking, again as a latent, potential actor—one whose reactions the active policymakers anticipate—rather than being organized and active itself.

In section 1104 of the Social Security Act, Congress explicitly reserved "the right to alter, amend, or repeal any provision of this Act" (49 Stat. 648). Those are hollow words. Abraham Ribicoff, who had suggested, as secretary of HEW, that the public would not stand for a combined tax rate higher than 10 percent, later declared, as a senator from Connecticut, that the public would stage a revolution if the social security program were tampered with. Nor could sunset laws—laws that would automatically terminate government programs so as to compel reexamination of them—apply to social security, he said. "How," he asked rhetorically, "are you going to terminate a retirement program that

---

local level. Even if strong opposition to social security costs does develop, the most likely response in the short run will be to shift some of the burden to general revenues (mainly the income tax) because the income tax is less visible than the payroll tax. Reduction in expenditures is even less likely in social security than in other government programs because the benefits provided for in law are widely interpreted as solemn, unbreachable promises on the government's part (see the discussion later in this chapter and in chapter 20). Proposed legislative *additions* to social security can be expected to suffer when taxpayers are in revolt; partly for that reason, national health insurance for all members of the population has been stymied in the late 1970s. But I would argue that even in a situation of intense and widespread citizen pressure for retrenchment, social security would be the last public program to suffer cuts.

people have been paying into for decades with the expectation of receiving money back?"[27]

The anticipated reactions of the public prevent social security policymakers from seriously considering, let alone adopting, alterations of the social security program of a kind that would entail reduction of benefits for any portion of the constituent public. The withdrawal of a benefit or privilege once granted, which is difficult for the government to do in any of its programs, is uniquely difficult in the social insurance program because of the implied contractual content of the government's promise. Here the public psychology associated with insurance becomes very important. The public presumably believes, for it has been encouraged by policymakers to believe, that the benefits authorized in the law belong to it by right, as a just return for contributions. For the government to withhold or revise any of these benefits violates an implied moral contract, even if not a legal one. The usual political risks that accompany withdrawal of benefits are much compounded by the introduction of moral and psychological stakes peculiar to the program. The very integrity of the government, not just the election chances of incumbent officeholders, is put at risk.

The bond of obligation creates a special relation between the Social Security Administration and the public as beneficiary of its programs, and tends to foreclose opportunities for those who might wish to change the content of social insurance or advance alternatives that might substitute for it in some degree. As one party to a moral contract, the public-as-beneficiary helps to sustain the existing program, whatever the program's stage of development. This the public can do effectively without being organized or activated at all. The effect, then, of the public's latent, indirect influence is to constrain, not widen, policy choice. What exists, the public has a stake in.

THE INFLUENCE of public opinion on social security policy has been paradoxical. In latent form, it limited the size of program increases, discouraged serious consideration of alternatives that would have broken commitments implicit in the existing program, and inhibited actions and speech that could have diminished the public's presumed receptivity to an "insurance" program. Thus latent opinion was an important influence in establishing the policymaking pattern of incremental change along a

27. *Welfare Reform: Why?* (Washington, D.C.: American Enterprise Institute for Public Policy Research, 1976), p. 41.

familiar path. Public opinion had least effect on policy when it was expressed in an active, direct form, as in the Townsend movement, the effect of which was to elicit an intense, dogmatic resistance from program executives.

However expressed, public opinion left a good deal of discretion and initiative to policymakers at the center of government. As expressed through parties and elections, it appeared to endorse the program executives' preferences (though poll data leave the public's actual preferences very much in doubt). As expressed in a spontaneous mass movement (the Townsend movement), public opinion was so utopian as to have no real and substantial effect on policy. As expressed through a private, organized pressure group with a mass base (labor), public opinion was subject to cooptation. And though public opinion in its latent, unorganized form imposed limits on official action, these limits changed frequently as policymakers tested them and found the public to be adaptable and responsive. Most importantly, the public proved willing to accept small, steady increases in the tax rate.

CHAPTER NINE

The Policymaking System: A Summary Analysis

P RECEDING CHAPTERS have emphasized the initiating, energizing role of the executive leadership of the program. These leaders had a deep commitment to development of social insurance in the United States and confidence that in time this country would do the things that other industrial countries had done before it. They were catalysts in the formative process—actors whose influence and perceptions were applied to matching institutionalized provisions for social security and the political system of a particular country. Important as they were, they could not create a social security program by themselves. They lacked the authority that comes with elective office—the right to decide that, in a democracy, belongs to people who have won constitutional offices through a competitive struggle for votes. Some of them occasionally lacked office altogether (Wilbur Cohen from 1956 through 1960 and again after 1968), and always some degree of constraint was inherent in the various offices they did hold. Whether as political appointees or as civil servants, they could not publicly and avowedly pursue courses of action that the President had not approved of. If they were to build the structure of social protection they believed the nation needed, they had to adapt to their environment without sacrificing essential objectives, and they had to manipulate it without jeopardizing their own legitimacy. They exercised influence by encouraging and facilitating the actions of others.

Their adaptations to the external environment took many forms, of which the incremental mode was probably most important. They learned not to ask for everything at once. They asked for a piece at a time, and then trimmed the pieces. They forwent goals that were not urgent or immediately feasible, such as the introduction of general revenues. They assimilated program changes that Congress valued even at the cost of doctrinal consistency. Despite a seeming dogmatism, they were ingenious and adept at compromise, and willing to search for the particular measure that could win the marginal vote in a congressional committee.

Manipulation of the environment took the form mainly of persuasion. Executive leaders conceived proposals and presented them in a way that enhanced acceptability to the public in general, the public's elected representatives, and diverse private interests. Pursuing welfare ends that were valued primarily by liberal interests with a commitment to expanding the public sector, they cast them nonetheless in conservative terms, calculated to appeal to a society that valued individual work and sacrifice. While creating a social institution, they justified it largely in individualistic terms, with analogies drawn at least by implication to the private insurance industry.

Policymaking routines were a subtle blend of adaptation and manipulation. Program executives nurtured the advisory councils as a forum in which the legitimacy of the program could be affirmed regularly and the acceptability of particular proposals could be tested before being introduced into the critical arena of Congress. The norm of fiscal soundness, ritually invoked in congressional committee reports and institutionalized through the SSA's actuarial techniques, assured advisory councils and congressional committees of the soundness of their choices.

Politics, as social security program executives ordinarily sought to practice it, did not consist primarily of the mobilization of allies, although they did what they could to encourage labor to participate. It consisted primarily of averting conflict through anticipating others' preferences and minimizing the costs of action for those relatively few political actors who insisted on getting into the act of policymaking, or were invited to get in, or were necessarily involved because they had the authority of office. Program executives minimized cost in the narrow, obvious sense that they designed proposals with low initial tax rates (a point that is taken up more extensively in later chapters), but the costs that they minimized were not alone the costs that fell immediately and directly on the taxpayer and then were likely to be converted, in inhibiting fashion, into resentment directed at officeholders. They also minimized the other sorts of cost that are normally associated with public policymaking, including especially the psychological and political costs associated with innovation, uncertainty, and disagreement. Their proposals were invariably extensions of a familiar program; the actuary's techniques appeared to remove all uncertainty about financial cost; and, as much as possible, disagreements were worked out at an early stage, primarily through the medium of the advisory councils.

As it happened, only a few political actors were ordinarily engaged in policymaking. Congress, which was by far the most important of them because it did have authority to decide policy questions, on the whole deferred to its specialized committees and, in the House, even accepted a procedure, the closed rule, that institutionalized deference. The specialized few in Congress, particularly in the House, in time reached a shared understanding with program executives about how policy was to be made and what doctrines should guide it. The president, who was the hierarchical superior of the social security leadership within the executive branch, was a busy generalist little inclined to trouble any part of any domestic department that did not trouble him, and the same could be said of the secretary of health, education, and welfare. The Social Security Administration, perhaps because of competent leadership, perhaps because its tasks were benign and readily routinizable, caused no trouble. Generalists in both Congress and the executive branch were additionally deflected by the program's financial autonomy; omitted from the budget process, social security was omitted from the politics of budgeting and appropriations.

Private pressure groups did not consistently demand to be part of the act. Labor had to be urged by the SSA leadership to get in, and even after it did, social security continued to be peripheral to the interests of the labor leadership. That labor's activity regarding social security was managed almost entirely by labor's specialist on the subject meant that labor's participation did not extend the range of interests or enlarge the diversity within the policymaking arena very much. It meant merely that a labor member had joined the proprietary core of policymakers. Business interests were too divided, uncertain of their own stakes, and diffident in the face of the growing power of the national government and persistent Democratic majorities to risk aggressive action, or to insist on a larger role than was offered through the advisory councils. The one clear effort to take an initiative—the Chamber of Commerce proposal of 1952–53—failed even to mobilize business interests, still less to win support among officeholders. Political parties, as permanent, formal organizations, did not exist, and public opinion was not otherwise organized in a way that impinged directly on policymaking except for the ephemeral movement led by Francis Townsend.

Bureaucratic rivals to the SSA did not exist within the executive branch; the Treasury Department chose not to intervene after the late 1930s. Deferral to specialists prevailed in the executive branch as well as Congress. Disagreement among specialists produced some conflict and potentially enlarged social security politics, but W. Rulon Williamson as the dissident actuary was too quixotic a figure to attract attention, and Robert J. Myers turned into a dissident only after several decades had elapsed and the program was well established. Then his dissent too was ineffectual, though he was a more imposing figure than his predecessor. Intrabureaucratic contests, even between high-ranking and relatively important bureaucrats (as both Myers and Ball were) do not necessarily mobilize rival interests outside the bureaucracy. Outsiders may or may not pay any attention.

Program executives functioned in an institutional milieu that was ordinarily characterized more by deference to specialists than by widespread and sustained mobilization of interests. Eager to avert conflict, they did not have it thrust upon them by vigorous opponents and competitors or by a political system supercharged with combative energy. In particular, they were fortunate to be linked to a set of institutional arrangements in the legislature—the House, specifically—that was a model of consensual decisionmaking. Under the chairmanship of Wilbur Mills and even to a degree before then, the House Committee on Ways and Means managed to settle questions internally, successfully restraining partisanship and anticipating what the House would accept, a mode that left little for the House to debate and nothing for it to choose, given the effects of the closed rule.

On the other hand, averting conflict was only an incidental, tactical aim of the program executives, valuable insofar as it facilitated achievement of their social goals. To realize those goals, action was needed, and in a political system that made consensus a condition of action, action could be hard to achieve. Recognizing this, program executives approached their task of construction with patience as well as tactics designed to keep the costs of action low.

Forward movement was slow in the American political system, and yet there was, in this case at least, something inexorable about it. Program executives could afford to be patient because they were confident that patience would be rewarded, and they derived this confidence both from the example of social security development in other countries and an understanding of the political system of the United States. American political institutions combined slowness to act with a powerful will, nonetheless, to do so. The underlying dynamic of the system has its source, presumably, in what David Mayhew has called "the electoral connection," the desire of politicians to secure election and reelection.[1] This desire impels presidents to advance legislative programs, Republicans hardly less than Democrats, and impels Congress to enact, often in a much-revised form, some of what a president proposes. Elected officeholders wish to provide benefits to voters for which credit may be claimed. Also, officeholders are likely to be activists by nature. While some persons may acquire power simply for the love of it or for personal gain, most probably wish to do something to or for the collectivity. Indeed, that is their constitutional function and, to put it in moral terms, their duty. The imperatives of office are such that they can hardly avoid acting.

The latent will to act means that action will occur when proposals pass tests of political acceptability. For a supply of proposals that will do this, political officeholders depend very much on others; though possessed of a will to act, generalist politicians have a limited capacity to initiate proposals for action. This gave social security program executives their opportunity to contribute to policymaking. Program specialists in executive bureaus are one of the principal sources of supply for politicians who are looking for ideas for things to do. In the case of social security, for several decades they were almost the only source of supply.

Because program executives in social security were purposeful and adroit, they were able to make good use of the opportunities latent in the political system, but it would be easy to attribute too much to their ingenuity and manipulative skill. If the program grew and grew without serious opposition, this was not just because its leaders were brilliant tacticians and merchandisers. It was also because they had something very attractive to sell. If congressional committees joined them in a commitment to program maintenance, this was not just because of institutional barriers to formulation of alternative choices. It was also because social security had a powerful intrinsic appeal to elected holders of office and to the people who elected them.

Part 2 reviews the characteristics of the program that are most salient to politics. It describes major policy choices embedded in the social security program and analyzes how they have been arrived at.

1. David R. Mayhew, *Congress: The Electoral Connection* (Yale University Press, 1974).

PART TWO

The Program

CHAPTER TEN

The Balance of Equity
and Adequacy

THE CENTRAL POLICY choice connected with social insurance is the purpose to be served, which determines (or is determined by) the principle by which benefits are distributed. The basic choice is between giving benefits according to need and giving them in proportion to individual tax payments; in the American program, policymakers came to phrase this choice as one between "adequacy" and "equity." In practice, the two purposes have always been mixed, but the mix changed substantially over the years. Without disappearing altogether, equity yielded to adequacy.

The mixture of purposes underlies much expert criticism of the program. "It falls between two stools," Milton Friedman remarked. "It gives too much attention to 'need' to be justified as return for taxes paid, and it gives too much attention to taxes paid to be justified as adequately linked to need."[1] Many economic analysts would have preferred consistency. Program executives, on the other hand, being pragmatic rather than rationalistic, did not view inconsistency and ambiguity as inherently bad, but did view the corollary qualities of the program— flexibility, adaptability, a broad appeal—as inherently very good.

The Shift toward Adequacy

Under the program that Congress enacted in 1935, monthly benefits would have been paid starting in 1942 to retired workers in commerce

1. Wilbur J. Cohen and Milton Friedman, *Social Security: Universal or Selective?* (Washington, D.C.: American Enterprise Institute for Public Policy Research, 1972), p. 36.

and industry who had made payroll tax payments to the government. The amount of the benefits would have been related to the cumulative wages on which taxes had been paid; the effect was to relate benefits and total tax payments.[2] If a person did not pay enough in taxes to qualify for benefits, he was to get back a lump sum upon retirement, in proportion to his total taxed wages. If he died, the lump sum was to be paid to his estate. By stipulating a minimum monthly benefit ($10) and a progressive benefit formula (proportionately, benefits declined as total wages rose), this first law gave considerable recognition to adequacy, but the relation between taxes paid and benefits was much stronger in this initial design than it would later be in the actual program.

This initial plan was substantially changed in 1939 before payment of monthly benefits began. Under the revised program, the start of monthly benefits was advanced two years to 1940, and payments were based on average monthly wages instead of on the total amount of wages. Dependents of the beneficiary were made eligible. If he had an aged wife or dependent child, for example, a supplementary benefit was added equal to half of the basic benefit. If he died, monthly benefits were authorized for certain of his surviving relatives (widows over sixty-five, widows with children, orphans, dependent parents over sixty-five). The progressivity of the benefit formula was also increased. The original large "money-back" payments in case of death were sharply reduced, and the lump-sum payments for those who paid taxes for too short a time to qualify for benefits were eliminated. In all, the relation between taxes and benefits was much weakened.

In 1950 the next round of major amendments weakened the relation further. Current beneficiaries received increases to compensate for increases in the cost of living, independently of their tax payments. Ten million additional workers including many of the self-employed and farm and domestic workers—who had originally been excluded on administrative grounds—were brought under the act and given the advantage of a "new start," which made it possible for them to qualify for

2. Basing benefits straightforwardly on taxes might have been more logical, but its drafters believed that the Social Security Act would be less vulnerable to constitutional challenge if the two were sharply separated. See *Helvering* v. *Davis* (301 U.S. 61), in which the Supreme Court held that payment of old age benefits by the federal government did not violate the rights of the states defined by the Tenth Amendment of the Constitution and was legitimate under the general welfare clause. Opponents did not question Congress's power to impose the payroll tax, but argued that the tax was plainly meant to support a purpose—old age benefits—that was unconstitutional.

benefits promptly (a minimum of six calendar quarters in covered employment was required). A provision for an annual "increment," which rewarded workers for the number of years spent in covered employment, was removed.

The tax rate, meanwhile, had stayed very low. Set by the original act at 1 percent each for employer and employee, it went into effect in 1937 and was scheduled to rise in steps of 0.5 percent every three years until it reached a plateau of 3 percent in 1949. However, the initial step to 1.5 percent was repeatedly postponed and did not take effect until 1950.

These legislative developments, with still others that followed, made of old age and survivors insurance a very mixed and confusing program, full of anomalies no matter what underlying principle was posited. It did not distribute benefits according to need. For a long time many elderly people were left out altogether because they had not been in the work force, had not been in the covered portion of it, had not been in long enough to qualify, or were not married to someone who did qualify. Among these were a large number of persons who had to fall back on public assistance. Those who did get benefits got them whether they needed them or not, and those who presumably needed them the most—the workers who had low average monthly wages—got the smallest monthly amounts, even though they got a higher return for their tax dollars than high-wage earners. On the other hand, this was not a program, either, that related benefits closely to tax payments. Low-wage earners got more for their money than high-wage earners and short-term participants more than long-term participants; but everyone retiring in the early years, no matter what his wages or tax payments, got much more in protection than the tax payments would have "bought." The actual basis of benefit payments was a very bewildering business that no one could rationalize and only the very expert could even begin to understand.

Mixed as the results might be, the direction of change nonetheless remained clear. Although adequacy never became the sole guiding principle, it consistently gained in relation to equity. Behind this change lay two driving forces: the program executives' will to achieve welfare objectives, and the congressmen's will to secure reelection through immediate gratification of taxpayers. It was the program executives who initiated measures for bigger benefits and wider coverage of categories of persons, while it was Congress that wished to minimize the current tax burden. Speaking from experience, Arthur Altmeyer once remarked that "if there's anything that Congress likes to do it's to avoid levying new taxes or increase taxes."[3] Seven times in nine years, Congress declined to let the social security tax rise despite the most strenuous pleas from program executives. This too contributed to the increasing discrepancy between the value of taxes paid and benefits bought.

It would be hard to say whether program executives or members of Congress were more willing to compromise the benefit-tax relation for the sake of their own objectives. Although the program executives were primarily responsible for initiating changes, they were in some respects more faithful to the original concept than was Congress. Altmeyer and Cohen, but not Ball, argued in 1949–50 for the "increment," which would have rewarded social security recipients for length of time in covered employment. (Ball, as staff director of the advisory council of 1947–48, was willing to sacrifice this feature of the program for the sake of increasing benefits in the short run and securing agreement between business and labor inside the advisory council.) Program executives would not have gone as far as Congress did in 1950 in lowering the eligibility requirements for newly covered workers. They argued for higher taxes partly on the ground that this would preserve the relationship between taxes and benefits. They steadily resisted proposals for blanketing in elderly persons who had paid no taxes at all. Yet even when they were defending "equity," it was hard to tell whether they valued it for its own sake or merely thought it served the strategic purpose of preserving the public's perception of the program as insurance.

Constraints on Change

Despite change social security remained contributory; it was financed by a payroll tax. Those who benefited had paid taxes or were dependent on someone who had paid them.[4] A relation between wages and benefits

3. Arthur J. Altmeyer, Oral History Collection, Columbia University (1967), p. 66. (Hereafter Altmeyer, OHC.)

4. There was a brief, limited exception in the late 1960s. The Prouty amendment to the Tax Adjustment Act of 1966 provided monthly payments of $35 (plus $17.50 for a spouse) beginning October 1, 1966, for all persons seventy-two or over who were not otherwise eligible for social security, but after January 1, 1968, eligibility was limited to persons who had paid payroll taxes and had acquired at least three quarters of coverage for each year between 1966 and the year in which they became seventy-two. Also, these payments were reduced by the amount of payments received under government programs such as veterans' or civil service pensions and were not to be paid to persons receiving public assistance.

persisted, and, with it, a rough and remote relation between taxes paid and benefits. If, from their very different perspectives, program executives and Congress had the will to turn the original social insurance program into something else, one wonders why they stopped short of transforming it completely, or why they did not pick something different to start with. If program executives wanted to help people in need, why did they not concentrate public funds on the poor? Or, if that was undesirable, why did they not choose to distribute public funds for old age support equally among the aged rather than be responsible for a program so full of anomalies? As for Congress, if it wanted to give benefits in a hurry on favorable terms, why did it approve a program that imposed taxes in 1937 but deferred benefit payments until 1942? Surely nothing could have been less compatible with congressional interests than that.

Rejection of Alternatives by the Program Executives

It was a dictum of program executives that "a program for the poor is a poor program." By this they meant that it would degrade the beneficiaries and that it would lack sufficient public support to command a substantial share of public resources. They assumed that the poor in the United States are despised by themselves and by others, and that a government program designed for their benefit would be despised too. Hence the ideal program for old age security should benefit everyone, poor and nonpoor. Benefiting all classes, it would have the support of all classes, and it would avoid stigmatizing beneficiaries with a "means test."

So strong was the founders' aversion to a means-tested program that one must ask why they chose nonetheless to rely on one for a number of years. Old age insurance started slowly, and therefore had to be supplemented by a program for the poor. For this purpose, the Social Security Act included grants-in-aid to the state governments for old age assistance. After the Social Security Act was passed, the number of OAA recipients jumped sharply, whereas insurance benefits did not begin until 1940 and then grew very slowly at first. Not until after the 1950 amendments were there more insurance recipients than OAA recipients. "The proponents of the present program . . . claim to prefer insurance payments to assistance and a contributory program to a noncontributory one," a penetrating critic wrote in 1949. "What they propose, however, is just the reverse of this stated preference. They favor a program which would leave for large numbers of needy persons only needs-test assis-

tance, while at the same time favoring others with virtually noncontributory insurance benefits."[5]

Instead of the combination of slow-starting old age insurance with
means-tested public assistance, program executives could have chosen
to support flat payments to all the elderly without regard to need, paid
for out of general revenues. Many such proposals were put forward in
the two decades (1935–54) during which the old age insurance program
was founded, coming from sources as oddly disparate as the Townsend
movement, the CIO, Keynesian economists in the Department of the
Treasury, conservative economists at the Brookings Institution, and the
dissident actuary of the Social Security Administration. Social security
program executives rejected them all.

Their resistance to universal flat pensions was so rigid, and the reasons
for it were so little articulated in public, that the logical content is hard
to summarize. They were reluctant even to consider such proposals, but
at one point, just before World War II, when interest in flat pensions
appeared to be mounting in Congress and the administration, they
reluctantly prepared a two-decker plan that would have superimposed
wage-related benefits upon flat pensions. President Roosevelt included
this idea in a speech to the teamsters' union in the fall of 1940, but to
the relief of program executives did not adopt it. Altmeyer later explained that they feared that "political pressures" would force increases
in the flat payment until it displaced the superstructure of wage-related
insurance, and that flat payments to everyone would deprive exempt
occupational groups such as farmers of all incentive to submit to
insurance coverage.[6]

Flat pensions, the program executives believed, would intensify the
politics of old age support. Movements of the aged—witness the Townsend phenomenon—would bring irresistible pressure to bear on the
elected politicians in the legislature. In the face of such pressures, pensions would get "too big." Spending would get out of control and disrupt
the economy and society. By contrast, a contributory program financed
with earmarked payroll taxes would impose its own discipline by limiting expenditures to whatever payroll-taxpayers would tolerate. The

5. *Social Security Act Amendments of 1949*, H. Rept. 1300, 81 Cong. 1 sess.
(GPO, 1949), p. 181.

6. Arthur J. Altmeyer, *The Formative Years of Social Security* (University of
Wisconsin Press, 1966), pp. 126, 205–06.

public would be taught the salutary lesson that benefit payments depended on revenue from "contributions."

Before long, conservative critics turned this argument upside down. It was the contributory program that was fiscally irresponsible, they said, because it created a misleading revenue surplus in the early years when the ratio of taxpayers to beneficiaries was artificially high. In their view, the only way to discipline the spending impulse was to highlight costs by enacting universal coverage. Pressures from the aged to spend more for pensions would be met with counterpressure from taxpayers. In the normal course of politics, a process of checks and balances would develop.

Whether the hurly-burly of politics would produce uniform pensions that were "too big," as seemed likely in the heyday of the Townsend movement, or "too small," as they later judged, program executives feared the contest itself as well as a particular outcome. The normal course of politics was precisely what they wished to avoid. Political debate meant uncertainty—uncertainty for the beneficiaries, the size of whose pensions would depend on the results of the contest, and uncertainty too for the program executives, who would be drawn into this conflict rather than being able to maintain an autonomous stance such as independent financing through the payroll tax made possible.

The great value of the contributory program, in the program executives' view, was that it bound the elected holders of public office. It increased the likelihood that benefits would be paid as promised. More precisely, it *created* a promise—an obligation on the government's part, in return for the taxpayer's contribution.

Congressional Preferences

Congress was not at all enthusiastic about old age insurance in 1935. Both the House Committee on Ways and Means and the Senate Committee on Finance came very close to voting against it; no other part of the bill was so much in jeopardy.[7] Frances Perkins would recall in 1962 that Senator Pat Harrison, who was the Finance Committee chairman, "didn't know the first thing about this bill," and that his counterpart on

7. Edwin E. Witte, *The Development of the Social Security Act* (University of Wisconsin Press, 1963), pp. 93–94, 102–03; "The Development of the Social Security Act: An Interview with Dr. Edwin E. Witte" (Wilbur J. Cohen was the interviewer), SSA, Office of Administration, OMA-TCD Pub. No. 083-75 (3-75), p. 6.

Ways and Means, Robert Doughton, "knew even less about it because he was deaf and couldn't hear what was said to him about it."[8] Left to itself, the Democratic majority would have enacted something else. That it approved old age insurance was due to the executive's influence.

The executive put old age insurance inescapably on the congressional agenda with a presidential message early in 1935. The proposal was prepared by a small staff attached to the Committee on Economic Security, the cabinet-level committee that President Roosevelt had appointed in 1934 at Secretary Perkins's urging to make legislative recommendations. Roosevelt accepted the proposal along with other recommendations of the committee, including programs of unemployment insurance and grants-in-aid to the states for old age assistance and aid to dependent children. Leading members of the Ways and Means Committee sounded him out about omitting old age insurance only to be told very firmly that it must stay. Reaction in the Senate was similar. Without much liking the proposal, Harrison loyally committed himself to enacting it on the President's behalf. Only his adroit tactics saved old age insurance inside the Finance Committee. When the time to vote came, he held the proxies of three Democrats and the ranking Republican, who was in a hospital, seriously ill.

Congress clearly preferred to start paying benefits to the aged right away. By themselves in 1935 congressmen would probably have chosen OAA grants and OAA grants only. Many bills for such grants but none for insurance had been introduced, and one—the Dill-Connery bill—had passed the House in 1934. But for being linked to this highly acceptable program, old age insurance would surely have been unacceptable to the legislature. President Roosevelt's crucial tactical contribution was to insist that the link be maintained. (A lesser tactical move conceived in the executive branch was to make OAA grants title I of the bill so as to capitalize on congressional support for them. Executive drafters expected that congressmen would read title I, if nothing else, and be convinced.) Congressmen in general did not share the program executives' deep, principled aversion to means-tested public assistance. Later they would choose to begin aid to the disabled in this way, and then aid to the aged who needed medical care.

There was a great deal of support for the Townsend plan in the late 1930s among the rank and file in Congress and, as late as 1953–54, 160

8. Frances Perkins, "The Roots of Social Security," SSA, Office of Administration, OA-DTC Pub. No. 88-72 (11-72), p. 18.

congressmen signed a discharge petition to bring a Townsend-sponsored bill to the floor of the House.[9] But this support did not extend to the legislative leadership. Altmeyer explained some years later:

The congressmen were beset by these old age pension groups, for example, and many of them were committed. Many of them signed discharge petitions to bring out bills for flat pensions paid out of general funds. You couldn't convince a large proportion of them that insurance was a good idea. From a political standpoint they had these groups on their neck. They represented important blocs of votes, and no matter how desirable contributory insurance might be in the long run, nevertheless they had to respond to immediate pressures. But you'd always find some leaders in key positions who recognized the dangers of the general pension approach, and that you had to have something that was self-regulating, so to speak; so that the revenues would be coming in to meet the expenditures. Well, we were fortunate that the committees with which we had to deal were money-minded committees. Otherwise we would have had a flat general pension. There's no question about that. And so I found it rather easy to convince the key legislative committees— Ways and Means and the Senate Finance Committee—that contributory social insurance was the only safe kind of a system that we could adopt.[10]

There is no telling how the congressional leadership would have reacted to a plan for universal flat payments if one had come to it carefully worked out, from a responsible and credible source, rather than from the Townsend movement. Never compelled by executive initiative to confront the idea, which program executives treated as heresy, congressional leaders clearly had no great enthusiasm for it, and never encouraged any of the responsible proponents to perfect their plans.

After 1940, when monthly payments of old age insurance benefits began, the choice for Congress would have been between flat pensions as a hypothetical alternative to old age insurance and the actual benefit program then in operation.[11] And not just one benefit program, it is important to remember, but two, for old age assistance, on which the federal government spent nearly $500 million in 1947, must also be taken into account. The question, then, is not how universal flat payments compared with a fledgling insurance program, but how they compared with the combination of a small insurance program having huge future potential and a large OAA program that insurance was eventually expected to replace but which was in fact growing too.

9. Altmeyer, *The Formative Years of Social Security*, p. 243.
10. Altmeyer, OHC, pp. 122–23.
11. Altmeyer later judged that flat pensions would have been approved had it not been for the 1939 amendments, which got old age insurance off the ground in a hurry.

A universal program would have cost much more in the short run because it would have covered more people. There were approximately 10.3 million persons aged sixty-five or over in the United States in 1947, of whom fewer than half received either insurance or OAA payments. If each of them had been paid $20 per month, an amount roughly comparable to old age insurance and the federal share of OAA payments in 1947, federal expenditures would have totaled $2.5 billion compared to the $906 million that was actually spent. Besides being higher, costs would have been more visible. Expenditures divided between two programs would have been combined in one budget item, and it would have been necessary to abandon the officially propounded fiction that insurance expenditures, handled through a "trust fund," were not really government expenditures at all, but individual savings for the collection and management of which the federal government was merely a convenient agent.[12]

Of course, benefits would also have been more visible and more widely distributed, but while this might have been welcomed by rank-and-file politicians in Congress, it was feared by the legislative leaders who had responsibility for the program. Like the program executives, though for rather different reasons, they persisted in fearing the politics of flat pensions. It was not that they wished to bind the politicians of the future but that they wished to deflect constituency pressures from politicians of the present. That a proposal of the SSA's dissident actuary, indubitably a fiscal conservative, was "a whole lot like the Townsend plan" was enough to make Wilbur Mills very wary of it even though it called for much smaller monthly payments.[13] The memory of the Townsend movement survived even after the mass phenomenon had dissipated.

Political Properties of the Hybrid

The actual benefit program that emerged was a hybrid: hybrid in purpose, in that it balanced equity with adequacy, and hybrid too in its balancing of the goals and institutional imperatives of the leading policymakers in the legislative and executive branches.

12. The politics, logic, and propaganda associated with use of the payroll tax are explored more fully in chapter 11.

13. *Social Security Act Amendments of 1949*, Hearings before the House Committee on Ways and Means, 81 Cong. 1 sess. (GPO, 1949), pt. 2, p. 1499.

In choosing insurance, program executives had to sacrifice in the short run some of the welfare objectives they sought. Insurance could not do immediately everything that they wanted it to do. They could come to terms with it, though, because they had a long time horizon. They anticipated what it would be eventually. As did their conservative critics, they recognized that its initial incompleteness could in the long run serve their goals. By doing less initially, insurance would do more when mature, because artificially low initial costs would foster liberalizations the full burden of which would not be felt for many years.

In contrast, congressmen had short time horizons. Some of them would have maximized distribution of benefits in the short run; others sought to minimize short-run costs, and on the whole the latter prevailed. Just as the slow-starting nature of social insurance served the program executives' long-run interest in achieving welfare goals, it served the legislators' short-run interest in keeping individual tax rates low. Differing time perspectives, which might have been a source of tension between the two branches, instead were reconciled by the properties of the program. What was sacrificed in this process of reconciliation was a close relation between benefits and tax payments.

In coming together to nurture this hybrid, the program executives and the "program" legislators in the committees did not so much agree on a purpose as on a symbol ("insurance") and a process of policy-making—an incremental process. They agreed on a program the essence of which was that it would grow gradually and could be enlarged frequently in small steps at their own discretion. Both costs and benefits would creep up on the public; as costs and benefits grew gradually, the public could adjust to them gradually, and policymakers could judge the public's response as they went along.

Agreeing implicitly on this approach, leading policymakers showed a notable reluctance to debate fundamental premises and purposes, as their critics wished to do. These critics wanted to go back to first principles to reveal the inconsistencies and injustices in the developing program. The program executives' reaction to this is nicely epitomized in an exchange of letters in 1948 between Wilbur Cohen and George Immerwahr, an actuary who had worked in the Bureau of Old Age and Survivors Insurance. Major amendments were under consideration, and the 1947–48 advisory council was preparing to issue its report. Immerwahr had urged the council to delay the report long enough to analyze the philosophy of the program and to consider fundamentally different alternatives, including flat pensions or a double-decker plan. He sent a copy of his statement to Cohen, with a cordial and tactfully worded covering letter. The reply, in its entirety, was as follows:

Thank you very much for sending me a copy of your statement to the Advisory Council. I appreciate very much your thoughtfulness.

I regret to say that I would have to disagree with you on the Council's delaying making a report on old-age and survivors insurance for a more fundamental re-examination. I have always been an "institutionalist." I believe that to be practical we must always start from where we are now, not from where we would like to be.

While I believe that the old-age and survivors insurance system will change during the course of the years, I believe that this will only be possible in an evolutionary way rather than a basic change at this time. With all best wishes.[14]

The dissenters from gradualism were either men of populist temper who did not shrink from the radical implications of the Townsend plan or fiscal conservatives of firm principle who felt that a large, immediate, and overt increase in expense would evoke discipline. Thus, in these early debates over income support for the aged, conservative Republican congressmen and professional actuaries were paradoxically aligned with the Townsendites in calling for immediate, universal coverage, although the two had different ideas about the size of payments.

The Symbol and the Reality

As the link between tax payments and benefits grew more and more tenuous, the program became less and less like insurance, and the less like insurance it became, the more its executive leaders insisted that that was what it was.[15] In 1935 they did not call it by that name for

14. Letter from Wilbur J. Cohen to George E. Immerwahr, March 24, 1948 (File 025 Advisory Council 1948, acc. no. 56-A533, R. G. 47, Box 6, Washington National Records Center, Suitland, Md.).

15. Not all forms of private insurance make the amount of protection depend directly on the amount of premiums paid. Insurance purchased by an individual works that way, but group insurance, arranged by employers for employees as a class (with or without employee contributions), does not. Program executives therefore reject the suggestion that social security is not "insurance" because it does not relate benefits closely to taxes. In their view, it is a means of pooling the costs of risk—and that is the essence of "insurance." Whether the program is "like insurance" is a highly debatable point, if only because private insurance takes a variety of forms, but there can be little doubt that to the average person the term "insurance" has conveyed the idea that he would get from social security what he had paid for.

fear of increasing its vulnerability to constitutional challenge. Then it was dissenting Republicans who insisted on the terminology of insurance: "The tax imposed under Title VIII is not a tax at all," the ranking Republican on Ways and Means insisted, "but an enforced insurance premium for old-age annuities."[16] In 1939, after the constitutional challenge had been surmounted, the language of insurance began to be inscribed in the law as the substance began to be removed. By 1950, with the discrepancy grown great, the Republican party's clearest minds and plainest speakers were protesting strenuously. "I think social insurance is not, in fact, insurance," said Senator Robert A. Taft. "It is not anything in the world but the taxing of people to provide free services to other people. . . . It is not insurance, and, at least up to date, this system has not been very social either, because it has covered only a very small portion of the total number of people who are over 65 years of age."[17] In the House, John W. Byrnes of Wisconsin complained of this "so-called insurance," this "fictitious insurance." He did not object to raising the benefits, he said. "But, I do complain when you try to make the American people and everybody else feel that they have paid for what they are getting. It just is not honest and it is playing politics with the old people of this country."[18]

Unable to draw program executives into a debate on first principles, critics in the late 1940s and early 1950s freely questioned their integrity. Convinced equally that the conception of the program was wrong and that its public presentation was false, the critics grew acrimonious; beneath the rational surface of their statements lay political frustration and moral outrage. "Although the Government has in various ways suppressed false advertising by private individuals and organizations, there appears to be no agency to prevent the Government itself from supplying misleading information or withholding significant facts," a task force report of the Hoover commission said in 1949.[19] It questioned the ethics and legality of the SSA's use of public funds to promote the extension of its program and charged the SSA's leaders with suppressing information about the long-run costs of their program while publicizing the benefits and the need for extended coverage.

16. *Congressional Record* (April 12, 1935), p. 5530.
17. *Congressional Record* (June 14, 1950), p. 8586.
18. *Congressional Record* (October 5, 1949), p. 13939.
19. *Task Force Report on Public Welfare* [Appendix P], prepared for the Commission on Organization of the Executive Branch of the Government by the Brookings Institution (GPO, 1949), p. 491.

The anomalies in the program that troubled or infuriated expert critics were unknown to the public at large, and, even if known, might not have stirred much reaction. That all of the beneficiaries were receiving big windfalls was not a circumstance to incite rebellion even if some windfalls were bigger than others. That many elderly people were left out altogether seemed unjust to a number of expert analysts in Washington who understood that no one had really paid for his benefits, but to a public that was encouraged to believe that benefits were a reward for contributions, the exclusion of noncontributors must have seemed reasonable.

Only in one respect did the public obviously have a hard time reconciling its understanding of the program with its experience. That was in regard to the retirement or "earnings" test, which limits the amount that a social insurance recipient can earn. The public reasoned that what a person paid for he should get when he reached the age of eligibility. Program executives said no—that the program provided insurance against loss of earnings, not an annuity to the elderly. This was a persistent source of tension between congressmen and their constituents on one side and the SSA on the other. The following exchange in 1949 between Representative Walter A. Lynch of New York and Commissioner Altmeyer is typical:

Mr. LYNCH. Do you think the average American workingman knows that he is being insured against a wage loss, or do you believe the average American man feels, when he is contributing to OASI, that he is going to get, as a matter of right, an annuity when he reaches the age of 65 or retires from work?

Dr. ALTMEYER. I think most of the workers understand that they must retire in order to draw this old age retirement benefit.

Mr. LYNCH. They do when they try to get the benefits; they realize it. But I mean up to that time do you feel they know they must retire? . . .

Dr. ALTMEYER. Yes; I think so.

Mr. LYNCH. In my experience in my own district, I can tell you frankly they have not any such idea until they apply for their insurance.[20]

No other aspect of old age insurance so aroused congressmen. Members who otherwise showed relatively little interest in the program would sponsor bills to repeal the earnings test. Had the leadership of the Ways and Means Committee not agreed with the executive that the test should be retained, Congress would certainly have repealed it.

20. *Social Security Act Amendments of 1949*, Hearings, pt. 2, p. 1214.

IN ITS ACTUAL OPERATION, old age insurance was a complicated, confusing program. The promise of benefits in return for contributions implied a close relation between the two. In the initial design of the program, there was a moderately close relation, but it weakened as the program underwent changes. These changes reflected the overriding interest of the executives in enlarging benefits and the overriding interest of the legislature in minimizing the current burden of taxation.

A program that gave benefits in return for contributions differed from a universal program for the aged in that it started small and grew gradually. Hence the costs became apparent gradually. Also, a program that gave benefits in return for contributions could plausibly be said to give benefits "by right," whereas in a program financed by general revenues, entitlements would have been much more open to debate.

The confusing mixture of purposes and benefit principles, the widely appealing symbolism of insurance, the low initial cost, the assurance of benefits as a matter of right, immune to debate, all help to explain the popularity of the old age insurance program. In making the choice for a program that based benefits on contributions rather than some other type of program, the executive founders intended to avoid politics as conflict. That was one of their principal reasons for preferring it to other alternatives.

CHAPTER ELEVEN

Financing

WHEN POLICYMAKERS considered how to pay the costs of social security, more than a method of finance was at stake. The whole philosophy of the program and the psychology of its public relations rested on the proposition that benefits were earned through the "contributions" of individual workers. Financing was more than a means to an end. It was central.

It is of course important to understand why this was so and why policymakers became committed to the payroll tax as the sole source of revenue. It is puzzling that a program created and led by New Deal liberals with support from organized labor should be financed by a regressive tax.[1]

Besides their choice of a tax source, it is also important to understand the policymakers' choice of a rate. In this they initially had a wide range of discretion. They could choose to set a fairly high rate and build up a big reserve fund to meet future costs, or they could minimize the rate by basing it on current costs, which began low. Their choice was more nearly the latter, and it was a choice with profoundly important consequences for the politics of social security.

1. For discussion of the regressivity of the tax, see Joseph A. Pechman, Henry J. Aaron, and Michael K. Taussig, *Social Security: Perspectives for Reform* (Brookings Institution, 1968), pp. 178–83; Dorothy S. Projector, "Should the Payroll Tax Finance Higher Benefits under OASDI? A Review of the Issues," *Journal of Human Resources*, vol. 4 (Winter 1969), pp. 60–75; Benjamin A. Okner, "The Social Security Payroll Tax: Some Alternatives for Reform," *Journal of Finance*, vol. 30 (May 1975), pp. 567–78; and John A. Brittain, *The Payroll Tax for Social Security* (Brookings Institution, 1972), esp. chap. 4.

The Choice of a Payroll Tax

The Committee on Economic Security staff members who planned old age insurance within the executive branch did not propose to rely exclusively on the payroll tax. They believed that the combined payroll tax rate (the employee tax and the employer's matching share) should not be allowed to rise above 5 percent, and that when that rate was reached, estimated to be in 1965, general funds of the government should be introduced. They reasoned that a rate higher than 2.5 percent might impair the living standards of workers and that the employer's 2.5 percent share might actually fall on workers. Given these risks, they were reluctant to endorse more than a limited use of the tax. Though the payroll tax would have been used exclusively in the short run—a short run lasting nearly thirty years, to be sure— the program would have been frankly based on the assumption that it would cease to be self-supporting someday.[2]

It was President Roosevelt who committed the government in 1935 to an uncompromising policy of payroll tax financing. Arthur Altmeyer suspected that conservative officials in the Department of the Treasury were behind the President's decision, yet Altmeyer also testified in his memoirs that from the very start of planning for old age security, Roosevelt had favored a contributory program rather than one financed with general revenues. He recognized that general revenues might have to be used in the short run to aid people who were already old and who could not build up the necessary contributions, but in the long run he favored payroll tax financing. When he discovered that the Committee on Economic Security had presented him with something else, he insisted that it be changed. This occurred at the last minute of the committee's planning in 1935, and executive branch planners had to work out the new financing provisions after the bill reached Congress. To suit the President's orders, the committee's staff and the Treasury Department agreed on a payroll tax that would rise in stages until it reached 6 percent in 1949, which was expected to be enough

2. *Social Security in America: The Factual Background of the Social Security Act as Summarized from Staff Reports to the Committee on Economic Security* (GPO, 1937), pp. 204–06.

to support the program indefinitely when combined with the interest from a very large reserve fund.[3]

Altmeyer believed that the President preferred a contributory system both because it was financially safe and because it would make the protection an earned right, but Roosevelt himself later stressed the second point to a visitor who complained of the regressive nature of the tax:

I guess you're right on the economics, but those taxes were never a problem of economics. They are politics all the way through. We put those payroll contributions there so as to give the contributors a legal, moral, and political right to collect their pensions. . . . With those taxes in there, no damn politician can ever scrap my social security program.[4]

Like the executive planners of 1934–35 and the program executives who followed them, the President favored the payroll tax because it would make the payment of benefits certain. The government would be put under obligation. The executive policymakers of 1935 did not argue—perhaps they did not believe—that society was obligated to support its elderly members whether or not they had made tax "contributions" for that purpose in their productive years. They certainly did not believe that Congress or the majority of the public believed it. They assumed that Americans would readily approve giving benefits only to those who had "earned" a "right" to such benefits by work and sacrifice.

The argument that using the payroll tax would make benefits more certain became the argument of the American Federation of Labor, too, as it was drawn into close collaboration with program executives in the 1940s, but the AFL also told its members that benefits would be higher under a contributory plan (if financed with general revenues, they would "irresistibly be pulled down to relief standards") and that labor's political influence would be greater. "When the money goes directly out of our pay," an AFL bulletin said, "people realize that it is our insurance and we can have a strong voice in advising on the way the insurance system works. The more social security protection we try to build up, the harder it will be for us to get it and to see that it

3. Arthur J. Altmeyer, *The Formative Years of Social Security* (University of Wisconsin Press, 1966), pp. 11, 29; Edwin E. Witte, *The Development of the Social Security Act* (University of Wisconsin Press, 1963), pp. 72–75, 147–51; Arthur M. Schlesinger, Jr., *The Age of Roosevelt*, vol. 2, *The Coming of the New Deal* (Houghton Mifflin, 1959), pp. 309–10.

4. Schlesinger, *The Coming of The New Deal*, pp. 308–09.

works properly unless right in the books it shows that we are paying our share."[5]

Finally, there was the psychological argument for payroll taxes, in which program executives and their allies in the AFL put much stock. Given the laissez-faire, individualistic ethos of American society, it was hard for the citizen to accept government aid without feeling guilty. Payroll tax financing relieved him of guilt. He was told that he was getting a return from his own "savings."

Although the AFL's social security staff was not indifferent to the tax's regressive character, it believed that the intangible gains were worth the tangible costs. Nelson Cruikshank felt very deeply about this. He told an interviewer:

Now, the labor movement was committed to [contributory social insurance] largely because, going all the way back to our experience with workmen's compensation, we felt that there were great values here in terms of human dignity and self-respect, in having a system where the entitlement to benefits was a matter of legal right.

. . . Just yesterday and this morning I had a long telephone call from an old associate of mine who, for reasons I won't go into, . . . his wife is not eligible for disability insurance. He's an old labor business agent. He practically wept, yesterday and this morning. He said, "Nelson, you just don't know what you're asking me to go through. You have no idea what these people ask you about your personal life and all that, things that I'd have to reveal that I've never. . . ." But people do know this. Poor people know about it. And when the working man agrees to pay a payroll tax, he's buying not just medical benefits, but he's buying his dignity and self-respect, which to him is very real and worth money.[6]

The notion that social security recipients were not getting government benefits had a twin in the notion that spending for social security was not government spending. Program executives spoke as if spending for social security, which was financed by a payroll tax and accounted for in a separate fund, was money that the federal government "saved" because it was spending that, in the absence of social insurance, would have had to be financed from general revenues and accounted for conventionally in the federal budget. In the mythic construction begun in 1935 and elaborated thereafter on the basis of the payroll

5. Cited in Raymond E. Manning, *Financing Social Security*, Public Affairs Bulletin No. 46 (Washington, D.C.: Legislative Reference Service of the Library of Congress, 1946), pp. 10–11.
6. Interview with Nelson H. Cruikshank, Oral History Collection, Columbia University (1967), pp. 188, 393. (Hereafter Cruikshank, OHC.)

tax, social security was a vast enterprise of self-help in which government participation was almost incidental. "Never has the system once cost the Federal Government a red penny," a South Carolina senator declared in 1956. "Every cost of the system, from administration to retirement, is paid for out of contributions by participants. Millions have participated in social security; millions have retired with social security; millions have benefited from social security, and millions more will continue to do so of their own volition and at their own expense."[7]

To deny that social security was a government program and to assert that the payroll tax was an insurance premium, not a tax, made it cease to seem regressive. This too entered into organized labor's rationale for accepting it. As Cruikshank explained to an interviewer, a low-income workingman would pay exactly the same premium for a private life insurance policy worth $5,000 as would his far wealthier boss, assuming they were of the same age and physical condition, but under social security the low-income workingman would pay less in taxes. "So, as insurance, it's the least regressive of the insurance premiums in America," Cruikshank concluded.[8]

Such was the logic of the payroll tax, on which this program was founded.

The Early Debates

The financing plan that had been improvised in 1935 to satisfy the President's instructions gave rise very quickly to partisan controversy, which was not put to rest by the election of 1936 even though Landon's defeat was taken in Washington as a conclusive popular endorsement of social insurance. It was not the principle of a self-supporting program that came under Republican attack in 1937. It was the prospective result—the planned accumulation of a reserve fund of $47 billion by 1980. This was "the most fantastic and the most indefensible objective imaginable," Senator Arthur H. Vandenberg, a Republican member of the Finance Committee, declared. "It is scarcely conceivable that rational men should propose such an unmanageable accumulation of funds in one place in a democracy."[9] Republican criticism of

7. *Congressional Record* (July 17, 1956), p. 13041.
8. Cruikshank, OHC, p. 394.
9. *Congressional Record* (March 17, 1937), p. 2324.

the reserve plan precipitated intense consideration of financial questions in 1937–39.

The reserve would have accumulated because payroll tax collections in the early years of the program would have greatly exceeded expenditure. Its purpose was to yield future income for the program. The funds would be invested in obligations of the federal government, interest from which would eventually constitute a very important supplement to payroll tax revenue. The cost of the mature program was expected to approach 10 percent of payrolls. Of this, 6 percent would be raised from the payroll tax and the rest from interest on the reserve fund.

The conservative attack on the reserve fund was led by M. Albert Linton, president of the Provident Mutual Life Insurance Company of Philadelphia, who had been an adviser to the Committee on Economic Security in 1934 (see chapter 6). An active Republican, he wrote often and forcefully to the *New York Times,* and published articles in the *Atlantic Monthly* as well as actuarial society proceedings. His criticisms therefore cut a wide swath. Social Security Board officials assumed that Vandenberg got his advice from Linton.

Though he did not suppose that a large fund would actually be created, Linton nevertheless feared the political and economic consequences of trying to create one. He thought that Congress would either disregard the actuarial calculations submitted by the Social Security Board and fail to allot excess revenues to the fund or that it would use the excess as an excuse for liberalizing benefits. The essential problem was political, not actuarial, he told the Actuarial Society of America. "Enough experience has been gained in the field of pensions to make it clear that the politician has but scant appreciation of the significance of a reserve fund and of the necessity of foregoing the expenditure of current revenue in favor of investing it to benefit voters of the more or less distant future."[10] Given political voice through Vandenberg, Linton's attack gave rise to formation of the 1937–39 advisory council, in which the issue of financing was joined.

In this debate, the key council members were Linton; Edwin E. Witte, a University of Wisconsin economics professor who had been staff director of the Committee on Economic Security; and Alvin H. Hansen, a Keynesian economist from the Harvard faculty. Representatives of organized labor, as yet uninterested in old age insurance, took

10. "Reserve Provisions of the Federal Old Age Security Program," *Transactions of the Actuarial Society of America,* vol. 36 (1935), pp. 363–80.

little part. The council chairman was Professor J. Douglas Brown, one of the three CES staff members who had planned the program in 1934, and the staffing was provided by the Social Security Board.

The participants in this debate all recognized that the huge reserve, still an imaginary thing, was only superficially the source of dispute. What was really to be decided was how to distribute benefits, how to raise taxes, and how to relate the two—in short, what kind of program to have. Put simply, the question was whether to preserve the relation between tax payments and benefits in something like its initial relatively pure form or further to compromise it for the sake of welfare goals. The participants also recognized that a crucial feature of the program, highly salient to politics, was that the cost would rise drastically in the long run. Another issue in 1939 was how to respond to this fact in a responsible fashion. How big should the future program be, and who should decide how big it should be—policymakers of the present or of the future?

Among the advisory council and the SSB leadership, everyone except Witte was willing to increase benefits in the short run. It was generally agreed that they could be paid sooner than 1942 and extended to dependents and survivors of covered workers. In the case of liberal council members such as Paul H. Douglas of the University of Chicago, as in the case of SSB officials, this position is readily comprehensible. It was consistent with their welfare goals. It is the support from conservative council members that presents a puzzle. Not that they were indifferent to the welfare objectives of public policy; the "conservative" members of the advisory council, after all, were very "liberal" representatives of the business world. Linton, Marion Folsom, Gerard Swope, and other businessmen on the advisory council sincerely believed in the need for government to provide financial assistance to the aged. But for that belief, they would never have been named to the council. Still, it does not suffice to explain their support for broadening and accelerating benefit payments in the old age insurance program. That position can be understood only if one understands their concern about long-run costs.

The more he studied social security, Linton told the advisory council, the more he feared the danger of creating an excessive, intolerable burden on future generations. He noted that the program was eventually expected to cost 10 percent of taxable payrolls, perhaps 20 percent if survivors and disability benefits were added, as Altmeyer's public speeches were hinting. "We of this generation," Linton admonished, "do not propose to pay out any such proportion of our earnings to provide current benefits under the Social Security Act but we blithely assume that our children and grandchildren will be able to do so without serious disturbance to the economic life of the country. This whole philosophy needs to be reconsidered." Each generation, he argued, had necessarily to support the aged of its own time and therefore could not really commit any distant generation to a specified level of old-age support.[11]

Linton's logic implied a noncontributory program, either public assistance to the needy poor or flat pensions to all the aged, but he did not make that argument. This first advisory council, like all its successors, took the basic program as given and failed to consider fundamental alternatives. Instead Linton proposed changes in the insurance program that would produce a better balance between short-run and long-run costs.

Witte shared Linton's acute concern for the future economy. But, in opposition to Hansen, who was concerned above all with the deflationary consequences of excessive taxation in the early years, he discounted the fiscal harm from a large reserve, arguing that it served the crucial function of alerting the country to the size of its future obligation. He rejected Linton's argument that a big reserve would stimulate the demand for benefits. He thought the pressure for increased benefits would exist quite independently of the size of the reserve, "particularly if we adopt the method of financing under which only enough money is raised to meet current disbursements, in complete disregard of future liabilities."[12] Whereas Linton wished to keep the options of a later generation open, Witte wished to give that generation fair warning of what was in store for it.

Other council members were more inclined than Witte and Linton to worry about the long run when they got there. *"Après nous le deluge,"* Chairman Brown had remarked during one of Witte's presentations. It is safe to say that neither Witte nor Linton was much amused. Hansen expected economic growth to ease the insurance burden in the long

11. Theron F. Schlabach, *Edwin E. Witte: Cautious Reformer* (State Historical Society of Wisconsin, 1969), p. 165; M. A. Linton, "Observations on the Old Age Security Program Embodied in the Social Security Act," November 5, 1937 (File 025 Advisory Council, R. G. 47, Box 137, National Archives).

12. Edwin E. Witte, "Thoughts Relating to the Old-Age Insurance Titles of the Social Security Act and Proposed Changes Therein" (1938), p. 16 (File 025 Advisory Council on Social Security, R. G. 47, National Archives).

run. He was strongly opposed to Linton's proposal to reduce ultimate benefits, as was Witte. Within the council only Walter Fuller, president of the Curtis Publishing Company, supported Linton on that point.

The advisory council settled on what they could agree on and postponed the rest in pragmatic fashion. They agreed on a quick increase in benefit outlays. This resolved the immediate issue—the pseudo issue, actually—regarding accumulation of a large reserve. The total estimated cost of the system would be unchanged; benefits had merely been redistributed, over time and among social units (early retirees benefited at the expense of later ones and families benefited at the expense of single persons). Conservative critics who opposed creation of the big reserve were mollified, as were liberal critics who wanted bigger benefit outlays, but the fundamental premises of a financing plan had yet to be agreed on. The advisory council recommended that the tax schedule in the act be considered later in the light of experience. It said that if and when the schedule was amended, the principle of distributing the eventual cost of the system in tripartite fashion—one-third from the tax on employers, one-third from the tax on employees, and one-third from general revenues—should be introduced. Since the nation as a whole would benefit, it was appropriate that general revenues of the federal government should be used.[13] Neither Witte nor Linton objected to this, though Linton later changed his mind and Witte warned that the "wish or hope" of general revenues some time in the future should not become an excuse for lowering the size of the payroll tax or the reserve account in the short run; if general revenues were introduced, they should be introduced right away, without jeopardy to the principle of full financing.[14]

Congress approved the advisory council recommendations, which were also the recommendations of the administration, regarding benefits, but in an early confirmation of Witte's fears, it elected to cancel a 0.5 percent increase in the payroll tax rate scheduled for 1940. Thus with the 1939 amendments Congress was able to increase benefits in the short run yet lower taxes, which may explain why both committees and both houses approved the act overwhelmingly. In contrast to 1935, Republicans in Ways and Means did not dissent, but filed supplemental

13. Advisory Council on Social Security, *Final Report*, S. Doc. 4, 76 Cong. 1 sess. (GPO, 1939).
14. *Social Security Act Amendments of 1949*, Hearings before the House Committee on Ways and Means, 81 Cong. 1 sess. (GPO, 1949), pt. 2, p. 1387; Witte, "Thoughts Relating to the Old-Age Insurance Titles," p. 27.

views claiming credit for abandoning the big reserve and deferring the scheduled tax increase, warning of long-range costs, and questioning the fairness of changes adverse to single persons.[15]

A few years afterward, in a talk to SSB employees, Wilbur Cohen summarized the politics and policymaking of 1939 in succinct and revealing fashion. No one had been opposed to survivors insurance, he said, and no one except the advisory council was for it. There had been a lot of talk that the system ought to be changed "to avoid the hocus-pocus of the $47 billion reserve," and "we came through with a great idea about changing it." There had not been a complete appreciation of the problems of social security in 1939, Cohen observed, and this had given the board and the advisory council an opportunity to advise. "Congress wanted something done," and "we gave them something." Cohen thought that the situation was unlikely to be repeated.[16]

Freezing the Tax Rate

Monthly old age insurance payments began in 1940, and two years later the United States entered World War II, sending actuarial forecasts awry. Benefit payments in the first years of the program were lower and payroll tax collections much higher than anyone had expected in 1939. Congress responded by repeatedly deferring a scheduled increase in the payroll tax, which remained at 1 percent each for employer and employee all through the war and for several years thereafter. Senator Vandenberg again led the legislative criticism, again with encouragement and expert advice from Linton, but the votes to retard payroll tax increases were bipartisan. Without regard to party or ideology, elected representatives of the people were not willing to argue for increases in an earmarked tax if a current need for them could not be demonstrated.

Altmeyer sought to demonstrate the program's long-run need. High levels of employment and low rates of retirement during the war were decreasing short-run costs but increasing long-term liabilities of the system. In 1944 Altmeyer estimated that the system's deficit—the excess

15. *Social Security Act Amendments of 1939*, H. Rept. 728, 76 Cong. 1 sess. (GPO, 1939) pp. 113–21.

16. *Analysis of the Social Security System*, Hearings before a Subcommittee of the House Committee on Ways and Means, 83 Cong. 1 sess. (GPO, 1954), app. 2, pp. 1417–18.

of long-run obligations over trust fund assets—stood at $16.5 billion.[17] He conceded that no matter what went into the trust fund in the short run, future workers would have to pay the cost of supporting future retirees, either through payroll taxes or other taxes. There was no way to lighten the load on subsequent generations, but he argued that building up the trust fund would make future benefit payments more certain. He implied, without actually saying, that this method of finance would reliably establish the program's claim on future revenue-raising capacity, since revenues would come to the program largely in the form of interest on the trust fund, an obligation that the government could be counted on to meet, whereas Congress's willingness to provide general revenues directly to the program was much more problematic. The trust fund, then, must be seen as a device to depoliticize the program, a way of avoiding future contests over funds. Against Linton's argument that a growing reserve would constitute a standing invitation to excessive liberalization, Altmeyer argued that the failure to raise tax rates would foster liberalization by obscuring the true costs of the program.

Despite repeated and carefully argued testimony, Altmeyer was unable to convince Congress that the tax rates should be increased right away and the trust fund built up for the sake of making the payment of old age insurance benefits more certain in a distant future. His sole victory was to secure an amendment promising that if payroll taxes proved insufficient to meet benefit obligations—a far-off prospect—general revenues would be used. This amendment was prepared by the Social Security Board and introduced in the Senate by one of its allies, James Murray of Montana, after having been agreed to by Vandenberg. It was contained in the Revenue Act of 1943. Neither the Ways and Means Committee nor the Finance Committee considered it. This early authorization of general revenues was a tactical concession to the administration rather than a considered policy.[18]

Congress's Choice: A Self-Supporting Program

When Congress enacted the 1950 amendments and substantially increased social security benefits, there was no escaping the issue of

17. *Freezing the Social Security Tax Rate at 1 Percent,* Hearings before the House Committee on Ways and Means, 78 Cong. 2 sess. (GPO, 1944), p. 2.

18. *Congressional Record* (January 19, 1944), p. 374.

finance. What had been left to executive planners in 1935 and finessed by the advisory council in 1939 had now to be faced by the legislature. And, though it was slow to be made, Congress's choice was firm and clear when it finally came. The program must be self-supporting. It would be financed exclusively by payroll taxes, which would rise in stages over a long period. The recommendation of the Social Security Board and of two successive advisory councils—the council of 1947–48 as well as that of 1937–39—for the introduction of general revenues was rejected.

The Ways and Means Committee, in which the choice originated, did not explain its logic. Several objections to using general revenues were adduced by committee members in hearings and on the floor: that it would be unfair to persons who were not covered by the system; that it would lead to imposition of a means test, which was undesirable; and that it would remove all restraints on spending. The committee's choice can probably be understood only if one appreciates the fact that the committees in charge of social security legislation were also the tax committees of the Congress. As such, they had several reasons for liking the social security program's link between benefits and taxes. This link made taxes easier to raise because the public could see that it would get something for its money. The link also disciplined the demand for benefits, because congressmen in general and their constituents could be admonished that they must pay the costs, and this in turn relieved the committees of the need either to raise general revenues for the program, a relatively unpopular course, or to accept responsibility for increases in the national debt. Perceiving these advantages at an early stage of the program's development, the committees committed themselves unequivocally to the payroll tax.[19]

The choice of a tax rate was to some extent determined by the choice of a type of tax. If the payroll tax were to support the program exclusively, it would have to be higher than if the direct use of general revenues were planned for. (The recommendation of the 1947–48 advisory council and of the administration was that the payroll tax be allowed

19. The committee reports in 1949–50 affirmed the principle of self-support without elaborating the rationale. See *Social Security Act Amendments of 1949*, H. Rept. 1300, 81 Cong. 1 sess. (GPO, 1949), p. 31; *Social Security Act Amendments of 1950*, S. Rept. 1669, 81 Cong. 2 sess. (GPO, 1950), pp. 33–34. For a recent statement of the rationale, see the remarks of Senator Russell B. Long, Finance Committee chairman, in *Social Security Financing Proposals*, Hearings before the Subcommittee on Social Security of the Senate Committee on Finance, 95 Cong. 1 sess. (GPO, 1977), pp. 21–23.

to rise to 2 percent each on employer and employee and that general revenues be introduced when that rate proved insufficient to support the program.) The Ways and Means Committee rejected a "level-premium" rate—the single rate that would cover the full cost of the program if charged from the beginning. Estimated in 1949 to be about 6 percent, this rate would have resulted in the accumulation of an absurdly large reserve fund. No one was in favor of that. Instead the committee chose an ascending tax schedule that would begin at 1.5 percent in 1950 and rise to 3.25 percent in 1970. It was a modified pay-as-you-go plan. Because the tax would yield more than enough revenue in the early years to support the program, a sizable trust fund was expected to develop (estimated to be $35 billion in 1960) and to yield interest that would eventually constitute a substantial supplement to payroll tax revenue.[20]

Here again, as with its choice of a tax source, Congress rejected executive advice. In hearings, one Ways and Means Committee member asked Altmeyer what the tax rate should be on the assumption that general revenues would not be used. Altmeyer recommended that it be 3 percent and that it be reached by January 1, 1956. Whereas he would have reached the theoretical peak in six years, Congress preferred to take twenty and to make the ultimate rate higher.[21] Congress's choice approximated a pattern that Robert Ball, in an article in the *Social Security Bulletin,* had scorned. "A pay-as-you-go system financed exclusively from pay-roll contributions makes little sense in an old age retirement program," Ball had written. "From the standpoint of persons who spend a working lifetime under the program, it seems somewhat absurd to charge first a combined employer-employee rate of only 1.0 or 1.5 percent and then gradually to increase the rate to perhaps as much as 11 percent. For social insurance just as for private annuities, it is much easier for both workers and employers to pay a more or less level rate over a working lifetime." He recommended a fairly low rate, to be combined with general revenues.[22]

Yet SSA officials did not put up much of a fight for their own financing plan. Both because the need for general revenues was remote in time (they guessed 1965 or 1970) and because methods of financing were less important to them than building the coverage and benefit base, they

20. *Social Security Act Amendments of 1949,* H. Rept. 1300, pp. 32, 35.

21. *Social Security Act Amendments of 1949,* Hearings, pt. 2, p. 1316.

22. Robert M. Ball, "What Contribution Rate for Old-Age and Survivors Insurance?" *Social Security Bulletin,* vol. 12 (July 1949), pp. 3–9. Ball was out of office when he wrote this article.

did not view introduction of general revenues as an urgent objective. Years later, Wilbur Cohen recalled that in 1949–50 he had collaborated with Wilbur Mills in removing the Murray amendment, the ad hoc language of 1943 that authorized general revenues whenever payroll taxes proved insufficient.[23]

Among leading policymakers, the only dissent from Congress's choice came from a few conservative Republicans in the House. Carl T. Curtis, the Ways and Means Committee member from Nebraska, analyzed the implications of the financing plan at some length in a separate minority statement, concurred in by John W. Byrnes of Wisconsin and Noah Mason of Illinois. Curtis's statement was an outstanding example of what a later generation is pleased to call policy analysis. It was as powerful and penetrating a brief critique of the social insurance program as has ever been published.

Curtis's statement argued that because of the artificially low initial ratio of beneficiaries to contributors, no suitable method of financing the insurance program could be found. For Congress to require contributions of the "level actuarial type" would be politically impossible, and even if it could be achieved it was undesirable because in the early years of the program much more would be taken out of the economy than would be put back into it in the form of benefits. On the other hand, not to require level actuarial contributions meant that early entrants would pay for far less than the value of their benefits and hence the public would not perceive the true costs of the program. Curtis urged that a realistic program be established in which the number of beneficiaries would be roughly comparable to what could be expected in future years. That is, there should be universal coverage of the aged. Costs should be met currently, and, because the payroll tax was regressive, they should be met from the income tax.[24]

On the floor it was Curtis's colleague Byrnes who led the criticism. Though he was only the junior member of the Republican minority in Ways and Means and only in his third term in the House, Byrnes already commanded wide respect. He raised the central issue clearly and cast it in moral terms:

The thing that is more important than anything else is to try to answer this question, and I think it is a question that we should all ask. . . . Would we vote

23. *Financing the Social Security System*, Hearings before the Subcommittee on Social Security of the House Committee on Ways and Means, 94 Cong. 1 sess. (GPO, 1975), p. 625.
24. *Social Security Act Amendments of 1949*, H. Rept. 1300, pp. 173–84.

for this bill today if it carried with it [a] 6½ percent pay-roll tax, which is necessary to pay actually for the benefits going to be granted by it? If we are not willing to do that, if we are not willing to impose that tax, which is necessary to pay for these benefits, on ourselves and the present generation, how can we vote to place it on the next generation? Yet that is just what we will be doing in voting for this bill. We will be saying that we will charge this generation only 1 or 2 or 3 percent, but the next generation—and there will be no backing out of it—this is not something that you go into one day and back out the next—we will tax at the rate of 6½ percent. . . . That is one thing I have to consider. As I said in the beginning, it would be the easiest thing in the world to vote for this bill, because you are giving the beneficiaries who are now on the rolls and who will go on the rolls within the next 20 or 25 years something for nothing; but you are not giving something for nothing to future generations. Those future generations will pay for what you are giving away today for nothing. I just do not believe it is honest or sound to burden my children or your children on that basis. Remember we give them no voice whatever in what we are committing them to.[25]

The next speaker complimented Byrnes on his statement and then proceeded to ask him to clarify the law's definition of an employee, especially in regard to the lumber and paper industries. The point Byrnes raised was not one that the House much wished to discuss.

The Republican party as a whole had no fundamentally different alternative to offer to the committee proposal in 1949–50. In the House, most minority members of the Ways and Means Committee voted to report the committee bill and then offered a Republican alternative that was essentially similar but of lower cost. In the Senate, all Republican members of the Finance Committee but one (Hugh Butler of Nebraska) backed the bill to liberalize and enlarge the insurance program and to finance it with a payroll tax rising gradually over a long future span. In the House, only twelve Republicans voted against the committee bill. Not even Curtis, who defended his own minority statement poorly when Democratic members of Ways and Means challenged him on the floor, was among them. (Byrnes and Mason both voted no.) In the Senate, the vote for passage was 81 to 2. Only Harry P. Cain of Washington kept Butler company in the minority.

Fiscal conservatives in the party continued to be uneasy about social insurance. They would have preferred a pay-as-you-go system with universal coverage on the ground that it would have given the public a plainer guide to costs, besides being fairer; but by 1949 it was clear that they would have to accept social insurance instead. Their leader rationalized acceptance of the 1950 legislation by citing the improvements

25. *Congressional Record* (October 5, 1949), p. 13940.

in coverage and benefit levels. "I feel that the bill carries out general pledges which have been made by both parties." Robert A. Taft said in the Senate. (The Republicans had pledged extension of coverage and more realistic benefits in 1948.) "The only thing I do not like about the bill is the fact that it still adheres to the so-called social insurance program. I do not believe it is insurance, and I think the sooner we recognize that old-age pensions are desired by the people on a pay-as-you-go basis, on a universal basis, the better off we shall be."[26]

Organized labor did not protest Congress's decision in favor of payroll tax financing. Acting, as was now their custom, in cooperation with the Social Security Administration, both the AFL and the CIO testified in 1949 that general revenues should eventually be used. In connection with the Wagner-Murray-Dingell bill in the early 1940s, both organizations had endorsed tripartite financing (employer payroll taxes plus employee payroll taxes plus general revenues). However, Wilbur Mills shrewdly led William Green, the AFL president, to give this position up:

Mr. MILLS. We shall have the support of your great organization in taking a position that every benefit enacted in the future must be paid for.

Mr. GREEN. Oh, yes. That is the sound, uncompromising position of our great organization.

Mr. MILLS. But it causes some, perhaps, to have some doubt as to whether or not these payments of benefits and the costs will be paid by the taxes imposed under the social-security program when it is suggested to the committee that appropriations from general funds might well be made for the purposes of the social-security program.

Now, you make that statement on the fourth page of your prepared statement to the committee, that the Federal Government might well contribute to this fund. It is such statements as that which cause certain individuals in the Congress to be concerned as to whether or not the argument that I have just submitted is a valid one.

Mr. GREEN. I can appreciate that fact. It would create grave concern.

Mr. MILLS. Congress should in the future go very slowly, should it not, in making available from general funds amounts of money for the purpose of OASI and should, on the other hand, attempt to maintain a rate of taxation on employer and employee that will pay the costs.

Mr. GREEN. Yes; that is our purpose; that is our objective. That is what we favor.

Mr. MILLS. And we can expect a continuation of that purpose on the part of your organization?

Mr. GREEN. You can rely on that.[27]

26. *Congressional Record* (June 14, 1950), p. 8586.
27. *Social Security Act Amendments of 1949*, Hearings, pt. 2, pp. 1994–95.

Self-support took on the quality of dogma. This was Congress's contribution to programmatic doctrine, and program executives bent to it. Just as Congress "learned" from the executive the sanctity of benefits by right and benefits related to wages, program executives "learned" from Congress the sanctity of a self-supporting program. They did not revive their proposal for using general revenues even as the payroll tax rate rose well above the 2 or 2.5 percent that they had originally judged to be appropriate. Like the congressional committees, the executives came to treat finance as if the issue were settled for all time.

The finality with which Congress seemed to assert its decision in 1949–50 was misleading. The Eighty-first Congress could not bind its successors. General revenues could still be introduced whenever politicians judged the payroll tax to be "too" high. But by the emphatic language of committee reports, the decision to remove the Murray amendment, and the concern to elicit supporting commitments from the AFL, this Congress—led in the matter by Mills—left no doubt about its intentions. Just as social security program executives maneuvered in these early years to close the options of future politicians and compel them to pay the promised benefits, Mills maneuvered in 1949 to compel them to pay the benefits out of payroll taxes. Because so much of the impact of social security lay in the future, policymaking consisted, not just of bargaining among present contestants, but of calculating the burdens of future contestants, anticipating their reactions, and contriving constraints on them.

Self-Support in Practice

While actual and prospective tax rates changed with virtually every new piece of social security legislation, Congress adhered to the policy of self-support. Current tax rates were kept high enough to cover current expenditures (plus a bit in most years to add to the trust fund), and the law embodied a schedule of rising tax rates planned to cover the future's rising costs. In a symbol-laden, self-congratulatory phrase, Congress habitually termed this a policy of "fiscal soundness" or "actuarial soundness." The actuary's projections, on which Congress relied in setting future tax rates, protected it against the charge that it cared only for the short run. To those who said that Congress looked

Table 11-1. *Scheduled OASDHI Tax Rates under the Social Security Act Amendments of 1950 and Actual Rates, 1951–73*[a]

Percent

Year	1950 scheduled tax rate	Actual rate
1951	1.5	1.5
1954	2.0	2.0
1957	. . .	2.25
1959	. . .	2.5
1960	2.5	3.0
1962	. . .	3.125
1963	. . .	3.625
1965	3.0	. . .
1966	. . .	4.2
1967	. . .	4.4
1969	. . .	4.8
1970	3.25	. . .
1971	. . .	5.2
1973	. . .	5.85

Source: Robert J. Myers, *Social Security* (McCahan Foundation, 1975), pp. 116–27.
a. Both employers and employees pay the rates shown.

to the next election, Congress could reply that it had an actuary who could see forever. Actuarial estimates stretched to perpetuity.[28]

Congress could claim that it took costs scrupulously into account; and yet the fact was that the theoretical plateau of taxation remained always on the horizon, a distance of six to twenty-one years away, depending on Congress's latest plan, and this meant that the current costs of the program were always misleadingly low. The public's willingness ultimately to pay them was necessarily problematic. Just how "sound" the program was, only time could tell.

Also, even assuming the accuracy of the actuary's estimates, on which Congress totally depended for its claims to actuarial soundness, any given tax schedule was a poor guide to what future taxpayers would be called on to pay because Congress steadily raised both present and future rates in the course of program expansion. Table 11-1 compares

28. Had the system not had a suitable actuary—one in whom Congress had confidence and who had confidence in his own estimates—the financing method chosen by Congress would have been much less feasible. The departure in 1947 of the dissident W. Rulon Williamson, who had said that highly reliable estimates could not be made, followed by his replacement with Robert Myers, was the necessary precondition to the policymaking routine that the program legislators in Congress and the program executives in the SSA together settled on in 1949–50. (See chaps. 2 and 7.)

the increases scheduled in the law of 1950 with those that actually occurred. Instead of going up by a sizable fraction, on the order of 0.5 percent, every five years or so, tax rates went up by smaller amounts every year or two as the protection of the program was liberalized.

The Ways and Means Committee made a virtue of linking benefit and tax increases. Mills as chairman often said that the public should be taught that benefits necessarily bring higher costs. However, to link the two had the effect of obscuring another lesson that would also have contributed to the public's understanding of the program. Not every increase in tax rates was caused by an increase in benefits. Rates would have risen even had no benefit increases occurred. To link them with rising benefits presumably helped to win acceptance of rising rates, and to obscure the fact that rising rates were inherent in the program. From one point of view, this link was fiscally responsible; from another, it was politically expedient.

A significant breach in the policy of self-support came when medicare was passed. Congress then decided to use general revenues to pay the costs of health care for elderly persons not otherwise covered by social security and to match the premiums paid by participants in the voluntary portion (part B) of the program, which covers the cost of doctors' services.[29] Mills had told an interviewer in the early 1960s that the reason for his opposition to health insurance for the elderly was that it would probably lead to the use of general revenues, but when, in the heat of the moment, Mills accepted medicare legislation in 1965 he also accepted a substantial measure of general revenue financing. The major breach was still confined, though, to this new and distinct part of the program, and two years after the medicare legislation, Mills was as

29. Congress has also made general revenues available for certain limited and specific purposes: to pay for wage credits granted for active service in the armed forces between 1940 and 1956; to pay for wage credits granted to Japanese Americans who were interned during World War II; and to pay the cost of special benefits to persons seventy-two and over to whom Congress in 1966 granted benefits of a flat amount if they were not otherwise eligible. These exceptions do not add up to very much. In fiscal 1975, out of OASDI trust fund income of $50.4 billion, $447 million came from general revenues, not counting interest payments. Social Security Administration officials maintain that interest payments should not be counted as income from general revenues. Such interest payments, they reason, are not for the purpose of paying social security benefits. Rather, they represent the cost of the government's borrowing to pay for general expenses; if the interest did not go to the trust fund, it would go to other (presumably private) investors.

adamant as ever that general revenues not be used to finance the basic program of old age insurance.[30]

For the time being, Mills need not have worried. A brief test in 1967 proved that the policymakers' consensus in support of payroll tax financing remained firm. During debate on social security legislation in the Senate, Winston L. Prouty of Vermont sponsored an amendment that would have halted the rise in payroll taxes and begun general revenue financing. After an opposing speech by Finance Committee Chairman Russell B. Long, the Senate voted no by the very large margin of 62 to 6.

Nor did social security program executives respond at this time to a growing call from liberal economists, who were concerned about the regressivity of the payroll tax, to reduce their reliance on it. What seemed a stubborn dogmatism had a strategic foundation. A background paper prepared by a social security executive for a Brookings conference in 1966 argued that the most important reasons for not using general revenues were "institutional." In other words, they were rooted, not in principle, but in the need for program maintenance and enlargement. According to this remarkably candid analysis:

The notion of earned rights, absence of the means test, the wide acceptability of the system, were made possible in large measure by the decisions to make OASI a self-contained system financed by payroll taxes. . . .

It is not uncommon for economists who are unimpressed by the institutional features of the social security system to refer to the contributory aspects of the system as a "myth" or to deride the notion that rights have been built up by beneficiaries, or to debunk the insurance features of the system. But it can scarcely be contested that earmarking of payroll taxes for OASDI reduced resistance to the imposition of taxes on low-income earners, made feasible tax increases at times when they might not otherwise have been made, and has given trust fund programs a privileged position semi-detached from the remainder of government. Institutionalists foresaw these advantages as means to graft the new programs into the social fabric.[31]

30. Dan Cordtz, "Social Security: Drifting Off Course," *Fortune*, December 1967, p. 210; Mills's views on health insurance were obtained in an interview with Gary L. Filerman on August 10, 1962, when the latter was a graduate student at the University of Minnesota. For a copy of the interview protocol, I am indebted to my Brookings colleague James L. Sundquist, to whom Filerman gave copies of this and many other interviews on medicare.

31. John J. Carroll, for the Social Security Administration, Office of Research and Statistics, "Social Security Financing Revisited," a background paper for the Conference on Social Security Financing held at the Brookings Institution, June 17, 1966, pp. 26–27.

This appraisal of the political significance of payroll tax financing requires scrutiny.

Consequences for Politics and Policymaking

The decision to rely exclusively on payroll taxes and to impose an automatically rising tax rate were policy "outcomes." Like all outcomes, however, they in turn had an effect on policymaking. They contributed to the depoliticization of social security—the dampening of dispute and debate that would normally have been expected to accompany a government program of such magnitude.

They made social security highly attractive to Congress as an institution. With a slight tax on many, Congress offered the promise of future benefits to all taxpayers and gave current benefits to several million of the aged in amounts far out of proportion to the social security taxes they had paid. At the same time, with the policy of self-support, Congress renounced the very notion of debt. Rhetorically, it elevated fiscal responsibility to a first principle of the program while in practice it incurred a huge, incalculable, and largely unacknowledged future debt. Once Witte's insupportable notion of full reserve financing was abandoned, the absolute size of the accruing obligation was lost from view.

Ordinary people apparently credited the official statements that they were earning their own retirement benefits by paying payroll taxes and accepted the taxes uncomplainingly because they believed they would get back what they put in.[32] There is much evidence that this view of the matter prevailed among the leading policymakers in Congress, not unmixed with cynicism.

There was, for example, Mills's presentation of old age insurance to the House in 1949. He scorned the charge that it was a step toward the "welfare state." Flat pensions given without regard to need might bring the welfare state, he said:

But when we call upon the individual during his productive years to lay aside, in the form of a contribution, out of his wages and earnings an amount of

32. One cannot be sure just which properties of the program best account for the public's liking it. The favorable early benefit-cost ratios presumably were important, even though the public was probably not conscious of them. It is quite safe to suppose that if the reverse had been true—if, that is, individual benefit-cost ratios had been highly unfavorable—the program would have been unpopular.

money which will enable an agency of the Government to provide him with benefits after he becomes 65 years of age . . . how can it be said that we are doing something for that individual for nothing?

Certainly he is at least entitled to say he is buying and paying for that security against need in his old age.[33]

John Byrnes was quick to point out that current taxpayers came nowhere near buying and paying for their security against need. Mills, of course, had conceded as much by claiming no more than that the taxpayer was "entitled to say" he had bought and paid for his benefits—not that he had actually done so.

As another example, there was a revealing exchange in Senate hearings in 1950 between Robert Kerr of Oklahoma and a witness from the U.S. Chamber of Commerce, who was suggesting immediate maturation of social security as a way of revealing the costs. Kerr pointed out that this would require abandoning the notion that people paid for their own benefits:

Senator KERR. Now, under the suggestion you have just made, he [the taxpayer] would become aware of the fact that he was contributing to a pension system for the benefit of others, and that no part of it was being kept for a system that would be for his benefit. . . .

Mr. MARSHALL. Of course, Senator, I recognize that problem. It is largely a matter of presentation.

Senator KERR. Could a rose by some other name be presented so as to smell as sweet, or any more?[34]

Not all members of Congress liked social security because the public appeared to like it. To the conservative Robert Taft, it was a drawback that the public liked insurance so much. He foresaw that other welfare measures would gain politically from bearing that name. But not even Taft would carry conservative principles as far as John Byrnes did and actually vote against the 1950 amendments. A pragmatic spirit prevailed within both parties.

Even though exclusive reliance on a payroll tax contravened their early judgment, program executives came to like such a tax because Congress and the public accepted it. It fostered program maintenance and enlargement. "The financing of social security," Arthur Altmeyer once told a meeting of SSB employees, "important as it is, is of secondary

33. *Congressional Record* (October 5, 1949), p. 13905.
34. *Social Security Revision,* Hearings before the Senate Committee on Finance, 81 Cong. 2 sess. (GPO, 1950), pt. 3, p. 1485.

importance . . . if all people are covered, it follows automatically that ways and means will be found to finance that adequate protection."[35]

Organized labor's prolonged support for the payroll tax also had a basis that was partly strategic. "We in the AFL-CIO have ridden along with this, over the years," President George Meany told the Ways and Means Committee in 1967, "for the sake of the greater objective which we know you share."[36] In other words, organized labor believed that self-support through the payroll tax had been essential initially, but Meany warned that labor's view was being revised now that the program was well established. In 1969 the AFL-CIO proposed that general revenues be introduced until they paid for a third of the cost of the program, which had been the original (pre-1950) position of the program executives.

Publicly, program executives interpreted the payroll tax as a device of fiscal discipline. To a Republican senator who worried about expansion, Wilbur Cohen could reply, "That is why, Senator, it is good to stress this as a contributory program. The ultimate safeguard you have against all those potentialities is that the employer and the employee have to contribute to meet the cost under a program that relates the total income and the total outgo."[37] The proffered theory was that when the earmarked payroll tax got "too" high, public resistance would put a limit on expansion, and this provided much of the rationale for conservative acceptance of the program. That the tax did not necessarily work that way—both because future commitments were being incurred while the rate was still misleadingly low and because Congress could introduce general revenues whenever intense opposition to the tax actually developed—was a truth that it took perspicacity to grasp and much courage to declare in public. Whether in the Democratic party or the Republican, the executive branch or the legislature, public officials in general were not equal to this dual test.

35. *Analysis of the Social Security System*, Hearings, app. 2, p. 1407.

36. *President's Proposals for Revision in the Social Security System*, Hearings before the House Committee on Ways and Means, 90 Cong. 1 sess. (GPO, 1967), pt. 2, p. 576. Several years before, Nelson Cruikshank had told an interviewer that organized labor had accepted the financing plan in the 1950 amendments "as a practical move to get the benefits we wanted." Robert M. Clark, *Economic Security for the Aged in the United States and Canada: A Report Prepared for the Government of Canada*, vol. 1 (Ottawa, 1960), p. 154.

37. *Social Security Benefits and Eligibility*, Hearings before the Senate Committee on Finance, 87 Cong. 1 sess. (GPO, 1961), p. 102.

THE DECISIONS to finance social security entirely from a payroll tax (aside from the interest on the trust fund) and to keep the tax at a low (nearly pay-as-you-go) rate had important effects on the politics of social security. These were congressional decisions primarily, and they reflected the profound aversion of the revenue committees and of Congress as a whole to raising general purpose revenues or payroll tax revenues if the latter were not absolutely required to meet current social security expenditures.

No important participants in policymaking maintained opposition to these choices. Organized labor, which might have been expected to object to the payroll tax as regressive, came to accept it on its merits (the principal merit being its guarantee of benefits by right without regard to need) and for strategic reasons (it contributed to the building of the program). Conservative interests, which might have been expected to oppose pay-as-you-go financing and favor the accumulation of a large reserve as a measure of fiscal discipline, instead believed that any such reserve would only encourage profligate spending. It would be dissipated as fast as it accumulated.

Program executives did favor higher early tax rates in order to secure the program's claim on public resources, and they also preferred a more progressive plan of financing, such as would have been produced by the introduction of general revenues, but they placed importance above all on establishing the program and expanding the scope and size of its benefits. Financing arrangements, however ordered, were in their eyes an instrument to this end, and it happened that the arrangements preferred by Congress served that end very well. It was, after all, the nature of Congress to prefer what was popular.

CHAPTER TWELVE

Who Wins, Who Loses

Distributive choices—in brief, decisions about who wins and who loses—are embedded in every government program. Policymakers cannot avoid them, yet policymaking for social security has not been characterized by much competition between potential or actual winners and losers.

While severe distributive biases arise out of social security—especially between participants and nonparticipants, early entrants and late entrants—they are artifacts of the program, without foundation in enduring social differences. They therefore did not give rise to conflict in the early years of the program. Conflict developed when a real or alleged bias of the system coincided with otherwise existing political cleavages or social bases for cleavage, such as social class, sex, age, or marital status. This kind of conflict was rare, however, because compromise and ambiguity in the program blunted it, and because not all of the affected and potentially active groups were actually organized for political purposes. Distributive bias was either eliminated by compromise and balancing of interests; obscured by official rhetoric and the complex, highly technical character of the program; or rendered politically irrelevant by the indifference and inactivity of its victims.

The Public Stance of the Policymakers

From studying what the leading policymakers said, whether in the executive or in Congress, one can hardly discern the existence of distributive choices. Their conceptual language does not contain the terms of group conflict, and it may be that their terminology influenced the political realities. Words and symbols influence perceptions, and political activity is inspired as much by perceptions as by actualities.

To the extent that perceptions were within their power to shape, leading policymakers encouraged an apolitical view of the program. Robert Ball once remarked, for example, that "income security after retirement is not a matter of one group—those of working age—helping another group—the retired. It is a matter of everyone planning for a continuing income during the latter years of life."[1] When a young member of the Senate, John F. Kennedy of Massachusetts, observed in debate that social security treated many groups unfairly—citing in particular discrimination against high-income persons—the chairman of the Finance Committee, Eugene Millikin, replied that he had "some opinions on that subject which I cannot express publicly."[2] To conceive of social security as essentially a system of individual activity, not a matter of groups at all, and to decline to talk in public about group biases, drains it of political significance, and political content is further drained by the official assertion that individual participants invariably gain by their participation. Program executives have repeatedly said that everyone gets back more from social security than he puts in. There are no winners and losers because everyone is a winner.

On the face of it, this poses a political puzzle. How can everyone gain? If some get more out of the system than they put in, do not others inevitably get less? The official answer to this is no, because the funds that are used for redistributive or "social" purposes come out of the employers' share of the payroll tax rather than the share of individual employees. This implies a much more exact accounting than actually takes place, and disregards the belief of many academic analysts that employer taxes are actually borne by employees.

Even if the official statements are accepted at face value, and even if everyone is a winner (which happened in the early years to be true, though not for the reasons officially given),[3] distributive questions are

1. "The 40th Year of Social Security in America," *Congressional Record* (September 17, 1975), p. 29063.
2. *Congressional Record* (August 13, 1954), p. 14429.
3. This was true initially because, among other reasons, early participants paid taxes for only a fraction of their working lifetimes; received benefits related to average monthly wages rather than to cumulative wages in covered employment; and received periodic benefit increases from Congress to compensate for increases in the cost of living independent of their tax payments. The economist Paul A. Samuelson has argued that social security will always pay everyone more than the tax he has

not satisfactorily disposed of, for one must still ask if some are bigger winners than others. Though program executives did not emphasize the point, they often acknowledged in congressional testimony that the benefit schedule is progressive: low-wage workers get back more for tax payments than high-wage workers. Especially after the legislative changes of 1939 they never pretended that the system was run on strict principles of individual equity. And, once it is conceded that the individual does not get back benefits exactly in proportion to payments, it is hard to escape the fundamental political question: how are costs and benefits distributed?

The following analysis considers the differential effects of the program on various categories of the population. Some of these categories (those based on differences in social class, age, sex, and marital status) are common to social analysis. Others are pertinent specifically to the social security program (participants and nonparticipants, early entrants and late entrants).

Social Classes

To judge from the public record, policymakers for social security have taken very little account of class cleavages—those divisions in society that arise out of the unequal distribution of income and property. Even in 1935, a time of deep economic distress, though their public justifica-

---

put in. In academic form, his argument appears in "An Exact Consumption-Loan Model of Interest with or without the Social Contrivance of Money," *Journal of Political Economy,* vol. 66 (December 1958), pp. 467–82. In popular form, it was rendered as follows in a column in *Newsweek:*

The beauty about social insurance is that it is *actuarially* unsound. Everyone who reaches retirement age is given benefit privileges that far exceed anything he has paid in. And exceed his payments by more than ten times as much (or five times, counting in employer payments)!

How is this possible? It stems from the fact that the national product is growing at compound interest and can be expected to do so for as far ahead as the eye cannot see. Always there are more youths than old folks in a growing population. More important, with real incomes growing at some 3 percent per year, the taxable base upon which benefits rest in any period are [sic] much greater than the taxes paid historically by the generation now retired. And social security, unlike actuarially funded insurance, is untouched by inflation....

Social security is squarely based on what has been called the eighth wonder of the world—compound interest. A growing nation is the greatest Ponzi game ever contrived. And that is a fact, not a paradox. (*Newsweek,* February 13, 1967, p. 88.)

tion for social welfare legislation sometimes referred obliquely to the potential for class conflict, they nevertheless cast the objectives of legislation in terms of security, not equality. The goal was to provide protection against misfortune—"certain hazards and vicissitudes of life," such as the unemployment that accompanies depression—and not to reduce the inequalities of income that persist through good times and bad. The President's statements and those of his Committee on Economic Security were devoid of the ideology of class conflict.[4] A decade later, Arthur Altmeyer remarked to a 1945 meeting of Social Security Board officials that while income redistribution among social classes would be a good thing, it was not the purpose of social security. "That problem," he said, "has to be attacked frontally and frankly through progressive taxes."[5]

Yet even the most obtuse political analyst would infer from their actual behavior that social security policymakers were not insensitive to class cleavages when designing their program. Social security combines a regressive tax with a progressive benefit schedule. When criticized for the regressivity of the tax, program executives have replied that the progressivity of the benefit schedule compensates for it; and while they have not been publicly criticized for the progressivity of benefits, one suspects that the regressivity of the tax is understood to be a political condition for acceptance of this progressivity. There would seem to be a quid pro quo here, a big bargain at the heart of the program, arranged by leading policymakers to reconcile the conflicting interests of the better-off and worse-off participants.

This interpretation, however, makes the latent politics of social security seem simpler, more straightforward, and more transparent than they are. The compromises and accommodations that have forestalled an open, class-related contest go deeper than this apparent bargain, for it is not just the combination of the payroll tax with progressive benefits that makes them acceptable. Each element separately is politically ambiguous, and for that reason has proved acceptable to interests that might be thought antagonistic.

4. The phrase cited is from the opening sentences of *Message of the President Recommending Legislation on Economic Security*, H. Doc. 81, 74 Cong. 1 sess. (GPO, 1935), p. v. See also *Report to the President of the Committee on Economic Security* (GPO, 1935).

5. Transcript of meeting appears in *Analysis of the Social Security System*, Hearings before a Subcommittee of the House Committee on Ways and Means, 83 Cong. 1 sess. (GPO, 1954), app. 2, p. 1407.

Organized labor, which might have been expected to oppose the payroll tax, accepted it because the contributory principle was believed to protect the right to benefits, to preserve the dignity of recipients, and to serve a variety of strategic ends including labor's access to policy-making (see chapters 5 and 11). And, just as certain attributes of the payroll tax helped to make it acceptable to progressive interests, the benefit schedule has had attributes that won support among the better-off, who presumably were opposed to redistribution among income classes. Though progressive, the benefit schedule was wage-related: low-income earners got proportionately more for their payroll taxes than high-income earners, but still got less absolutely.[6]

The ideology of wage-related benefits had a powerful appeal. Program executives presented variable benefits to the public—and evidently believed in them—as the American way, consistent with an economic system fueled by individual enterprise. Because benefits were related to wages, the worker covered by social security would always have an incentive to work and earn more. The system of economic incentives that underlay American capitalism would be preserved. This argument was widely accepted and widely appealing, since Americans who would admit to rejecting the work ethic were few and far between in the founding years of social security. When Dorrance Bronson, an actuary who had worked for the Social Security Board and was one of the most astute critics of social security, suggested in congressional testimony that flat benefits were not more socialistic than wage-related ones, a Democratic committee member was downright incredulous:

Mr. BRONSON. If we had this thing to do all over again, I would favor the flat system, flat benefits, flat contributions.
Mr. CARROLL. But the flat system is the socialistic system, is it not?
Mr. BRONSON. I tried to point out here that I feel this system is more socialistic.

6. This has been achieved by the use of a benefit formula that divides average monthly earnings into steps or brackets and reduces the proportionate social security benefit with each additional step. For example, the formula of 1939 promised benefits amounting to 40 percent of the first $50 of average monthly earnings (AME) plus 10 percent of the next $200 (53 Stat. 1376). By 1976 this relatively simple, two-step formula had grown far more complicated, and consisted of eight brackets: 137.77 percent of the first $110 of AME; plus 50.11 percent of the next $290; plus 46.83 percent of the next $150; plus 55.04 percent of the next $100; plus 30.61 percent of the next $100; plus 25.51 percent of the next $250; plus 22.98 percent of the next $175; plus 21.28 percent of the next $100.

Mr. CARROLL. Do you mean to say that the contributory system is more socialistic than the flat system? . . . There is nothing socialistic about [benefits] based upon each individual worker's ability and his earnings.[7]

Policymakers were at least as sensitive to the reality of wage related-ness as to the symbolism of it. They usually kept the ratio of the maximum to the minimum payment at around four to one. "Let's keep it as much wage-related as we can," Wilbur Mills admonished Wilbur Cohen in the late 1960s, warning that otherwise public support would be lost.[8] Cohen was hardly one to argue the point. Only a few years before, he had remarked in congressional testimony that "if you do not have what . . . the country thinks is an adequate spread between the minimum and the maximum, then the enthusiasm for a wage-related contributory system is dampened."[9] In his view, the difference "should be great enough to ensure psychological as well as financial support from a majority of taxpayers and beneficiaries."[10]

Here as elsewhere in the design of the program, policymakers were preoccupied with the need for public acceptance, which was the indispensable condition of program maintenance and growth. Cohen was quick to concede as much in an exchange with Milton Friedman regarding the class biases of social security. Friedman had said that social security benefited the middle class. "Actually I think he is probably right about that," Cohen replied. "But, that is part of the system's political sagacity. Since most of the people of the United States are in

7. *Social Security Act Amendments of 1949,* Hearings before the House Committee on Ways and Means, 81 Cong. 1 sess. (GPO, 1949), pt. 2, p. 1635. Bronson had argued that the whole tendency of the system was to obscure costs and to build up "the benefit largesse in contrast to the facts of normal pay levels, of actual recent coverage and of actual wages on which tax was paid." He interpreted the administration's request for a much-increased wage base as a highly expansive and redistributive measure. High-income people were not asking for bigger benefits, he said. The sponsors of legislation wanted to cover the higher incomes in order to get the tax proceeds (pp. 1625–32).

8. *President's Proposals for Revision in the Social Security System,* Hearings before the House Committee on Ways and Means, 90 Cong. 1 sess. (GPO, 1967), pt. 1, p. 314.

9. *Social Security Amendments of 1961,* Executive Hearings before the House Committee on Ways and Means, 87 Cong. 1 sess. (GPO, 1961), p. 88.

10. Milton Friedman and Wilbur J. Cohen, *Social Security: Universal or Selective?* (Washington, D.C.: American Enterprise Institute for Public Policy Research, 1972), p. 12.

the middle income, middle class range, social security is a program which appeals to them."[11]

The only reliable information contained in this exchange is political, not economic. The truth is that no one knows how social security affects income distribution. Despite much sophisticated analytic work on the program by economists, there is no consensus about its class impact. Pechman, Aaron, and Taussig, after a careful analysis, declined to render a judgment.[12]

If the analysts are uncertain, so are interest groups, and uncertainty inhibits political action. To raise an issue requires singling out some one element of the program as unjust, as academic economists have done in their critique of the payroll tax. Policy processes, however, have developed in such a way that this is difficult for active participants, such as organized labor, to do. The founders of the program have insisted that it is an organic entity—an "integrated social mechanism" in J. Douglas Brown's phrase. Program elements, such as taxation, are to be evaluated for their contribution to its functioning, and not by exogenous criteria.[13] Interest group leaders accept the compromises embodied in the social security program because they *are* compromises—that is, the complementary elements of what policymakers insist is a distinct and internally integrated system.

Age

An age-based bias is inherent in social security because it is basic to its social function. Costs are borne by active workers and benefits go to elderly nonworkers. Nothing would seem more probable than that the politics of social security should pit elderly recipients demanding

11. Ibid., p. 54.

12. "In short," they wrote, "the degree of net progressivity of OASI, as measured by its effects on the lifetime distribution of individual or group income, is uncertain." Joseph A. Pechman, Henry J. Aaron, and Michael K. Taussig, *Social Security: Perspectives for Reform* (Brookings Institution, 1968), pp. 246–47.

13. J. Douglas Brown, *An American Philosophy of Social Security: Evolution and Issues* (Princeton University Press, 1972), p. 86. See also Wilbur J. Cohen, "Memorandum of Comment, Reservation, or Dissent," in Richard A. Musgrave, ed., *Broad-Based Taxes: New Options and Sources* (Johns Hopkins University Press, 1973), pp. 286–88, which is a succinct statement of the political and psychological functions of the payroll tax within the system and of the organic unity of the system, in response to a fiscal economist's critique of the payroll tax.

more benefits against active workers resisting higher taxes, yet nothing of the kind took place.

To be sure, this presumed intergenerational conflict might have been mitigated by the active generation's sense of moral obligation. The active young bear responsibility for support of the old privately if not publicly. Active workers could reason that a public program, rather than creating a new and unwelcome burden, would merely shift a responsibility hitherto privately borne, and, to that extent, would warrant their support. Also, intergenerational conflict could be mitigated by the inescapable dynamism of age. While age categories in the abstract are fixed, real individuals move along inexorably into the aged category. Thus, AFL President William Green insisted in 1934 that employers bear the full cost of unemployment insurance because it was employers who laid men off, but he told one of the planners of old age insurance that the American labor movement would go along with "fifty-fifty" contributions in that program "because everyone gets old."[14] This commonsense perception tends to undermine intergenerational conflict. Individuals recognize that time will change their position in the social security system.

Nonetheless, even after these mitigating factors are taken into account, it remains remarkable that the program did not get caught up in intergenerational politics—and this despite the fact that at the time of the program's founding the aged were at a peak of political activity, having been aroused by various individual demagogues and mass movements that sprang up in the perfervid politics of the Depression.

One reason why conflict did not develop is that policymakers designed a program that, in principle, denied that there was any basis for it. Old age insurance was presented to the public as a means by which the individual put aside funds for his own future. When pressed in congressional testimony, program executives would concede that this notion did not fit the fiscal realities very well, but they almost never were pressed, since congressmen liked the notion as much as if they had thought of it themselves.

It was also important that the social security program started small, with a limited number of initial beneficiaries, and grew by stages. The elderly did not become instantly and en masse a client group of the program. Whereas government programs often have the effect of mobiliz-

14. Brown, *An American Philosophy of Social Security*, p. 83.

ing clients and creating an active political interest group where little
or none existed before, social security may well have had the reverse
effect; by giving benefits to some but not all of the elderly in the short
run, it may have helped to demobilize the Townsend movement. To the
extent that the aged did remain politically active after the start of social
security, they focused on what was in the short run the larger program—
old age assistance—and sought to influence state governments, which
were mainly responsible for determining the size of its benefits. In some
states—such as Massachusetts, Louisiana, Oklahoma, California, Oregon, and Washington—the elderly were for some years a powerful and
effective political force, whereas in others their influence was negligible.
Thus the fragmentation of governments in the federal system combined
with the initial fragmentation of old age income support programs in
the Social Security Act to inhibit the formation and maintenance of a
nationwide political organization of the elderly.

If the elderly had been mobilized on a national scale by social security
legislation, an opposing force of active workers might have been mobilized too; politics often works that way, with force eliciting counterforce.
As it was, active workers became the principal organized source of
support for the program through the medium of the AFL and CIO,
whose locals in the 1940s perversely passed resolutions calling on
Congress to let the payroll tax rise. Here again, one sees the political
significance of the program executives' success in coopting organized
labor. What might easily have been the leading source of organized resistance to old age benefits became the program's faithful promoter.
When the National Council of Senior Citizens developed in the early
1960s to campaign for medicare, organized labor was its sponsor. Such
was the irrelevance of the potential cleavage between active workers
and elderly dependents.

Sex and Marital Status

The social distinctions toward which policymakers showed least
sensitivity were those of sex and marital status, presumably because
they had little political relevance. The women's suffrage movement ex-
cepted, neither sex nor marital status had proved a source of political
consciousness, and here alone the policymakers consciously introduced

an avoidable bias into the program for the sake of welfare objectives and without evident fear of the political consequences.

By introducing dependents and survivors benefits, the amendments of 1939 gave a substantial advantage to married workers, and actually reduced the long-run benefits promised to single workers with relatively high incomes—a rare instance of benefit reduction. As usual, official statements promised that every worker whether single or married would get more for his money than he could buy privately ("except possibly in a very few extreme cases" among single persons);[15] but they did not disguise the fact that married persons gained a relative advantage. Economic analysts eventually concluded that the advantage was probably unfair. Pechman, Aaron, and Taussig found in the late 1960s that the differential in replacement income between married couples and single persons was much larger than could be justified by a couple's need for more income.[16] "Among social security beneficiaries," Robert Ball observed after leaving the commissioner's office, "the worst off are the non-married."[17] Single persons, however, were a small and politically inactive portion of the population—a statistical category, not an organized interest group—and so the program's bias against them was not translated into a political issue.

On the other hand, sexual bias in the program did eventually become a political issue even though the factual basis for it was tenuous by comparison. When the women's movement of the late sixties and early seventies scrutinized social security, a number of anomalies came to light. For example, social security law provided survivors benefits to widows but not to widowers unless they could prove dependency. Similarly, monthly benefits for aged wives of insured male workers were payable automatically, without requiring proof of dependency, whereas proof of dependency was required of aged husbands. But, though the fact of discrimination was clear, who was discriminated against was not. Did the burden fall on the men who were deprived of benefits or on the women whose taxes bought less protection for their husbands than did men's taxes for their wives? Some of the more obvious differences in treatment of the sexes were attacked in court and struck down.

Workingwomen had much more cause for complaint against the

15. *Social Security Act Amendments of 1939*, H. Rept. 728, p. 7.
16. Pechman and others, *Social Security*, pp. 84–86.
17. *Congressional Record* (September 17, 1975), p. 29064.

system than women in general. Inequity arose from the decision in 1939 to pay a benefit to an insured worker's elderly spouse (in the usual case, the wife) who became eligible for one-half of the monthly benefit of the retired worker (usually the husband) upon reaching a specified age. The typical working wife got half of her husband's benefit or the amount to which her own work entitled her, whichever was higher. With justification, married women workers complained that they were not getting very much for their taxes. The added benefit gained from working and paying taxes was usually slight, and the sense of grievance spread as women joined the work force in greater numbers. Here, too, the women's movement brought discrimination to light, even if the discrimination was against employed women rather than all women (and technically not against women at all, since male spouses were treated the same as female spouses).[18]

The instinctive response of program executives to such issues was to alleviate conflict by making adjustments in the program. "I think the time has come," Robert Ball testified in 1973, "when it is much more important, from the standpoint of the health of the program, to focus on the correction of inequities" than to spend funds on general benefit increases.[19] To alleviate the bias against single persons and the anomalous treatment of working spouses he proposed to reduce the benefit of the nonworking spouse from one-half to one-third of the worker's benefit, but simultaneously to increase the worker's benefit by 14 percent. This would have substantially improved the position of single workers and

18. Ella J. Polinsky, "The Position of Women in the Social Security System," *Social Security Bulletin,* vol. 32 (July 1969), pp. 3–19; Dalmer Hoskins and Lenore E. Bixby, *Women and Social Security: Law and Policy in Five Countries,* Social Security Administration, Office of Research and Statistics, Research Report No. 42, DHEW Publication No. (SSA) 73-11800; Robert J. Myers, "Social Security and Sex Discrimination," *Challenge,* vol. 18 (July–August 1975), pp. 54–57; *Social Security Inequities against Women,* Hearings before the Subcommittee on Retirement Income and Employment of the House Select Committee on Aging, 94 Cong. 1 sess. (GPO, 1975); *Women and Social Security: Adapting to a New Era,* prepared by the Task Force on Women and Social Security for the Senate Special Committee on Aging, 94 Cong. 1 sess. (GPO, 1975); *Future Directions in Social Security,* Hearings before the Senate Special Committee on Aging, pts. 18 and 19, *Women and Social Security,* 94 Cong. 1 sess. (GPO, 1975); Rita Ricardo Campbell, "The Problems of Fairness," in Michael J. Boskin, ed., *The Crisis in Social Security* (San Francisco: Institute for Contemporary Studies, 1977), pp. 125–45; Marilyn R. Flowers, *Women and Social Security: An Institutional Dilemma* (Washington, D.C.: American Enterprise Institute for Public Policy Research, 1977).

19. *Economic Problems of Women,* Hearings before the Joint Economic Committee, 93 Cong. 1 sess. (GPO, 1973), pt. 1, p. 331.

working couples in relation to the couple with only one earner while assuring that no couples would suffer a reduction of benefits. It would also have very much increased the cost of the system.[20]

Participants and Nonparticipants

In addition to the distinctions existing in society independently of the program, the operation of the program created some of its own between participants and nonparticipants and early entrants and late entrants. It was here that the most severe biases developed, but because these biases were program-based only, they had a very limited potential for generating conflict.

Social security gives a great advantage to categories of workers whom it does not cover in their usual occupation. The program can be fair to everyone only if it covers everyone. Workers not regularly covered can get large windfall benefits by entering covered employment just long enough to become eligible. Because of the progressivity of the benefit schedule, which gives disproportionate benefits to persons with low covered earnings, such persons may get very large returns from a limited "investment" of taxes.

Universal coverage of the work force has always been the goal of program executives, but they had to approach it by stages. The original law covered only workers in commerce and industry. The Committee on Economic Security had recommended covering all privately employed wage-and-salary earners except for those covered by the Railroad Retirement Act, but Congress omitted agricultural workers and domestic servants after hearing from Secretary of the Treasury Morgenthau that it would not be feasible to collect payroll taxes for them. Edwin Witte believed that in this instance Congress was quite ready to follow custom. Agriculture and domestic service had usually been excluded from all types of laws regulating employment conditions. The House Committee on Ways and Means also exempted nonprofit organizations such as churches, colleges, hospitals, and charities after receiving objections from some of their representatives.[21] Thereafter, it became a central pur-

20. *Congressional Record* (September 17, 1975), pp. 29063–66. Ball later revised this proposal to call for a 12.5 percent increase for workers.

21. Edwin E. Witte, *Development of the Social Security Act* (University of Wisconsin Press, 1963), pp. 152–57.

pose of program executives to recover these initial losses and to reach as well into the self-employed and publicly employed sectors of the work force.

Against pockets of resistance from interest groups and the ingrained reluctance of Congress to extend or increase taxation, they made slow but steady progress. One obstacle was the chairman of the Ways and Means Committee, Robert L. Doughton, who once told Altmeyer that he would consider coverage for farmers "when the first farmer with manure on his shoes comes to me and asks to be covered."[22] For a time, an even more formidable obstacle was Senator Walter F. George of Georgia, a member of the Committee on Finance, who became an implacable opponent of compulsory coverage of the self-employed in the early 1950s on the ground that they should provide for themselves. George decided that it was "creeping socialism" to cover them.[23] A final obstacle, as Altmeyer saw it, was the "individualism, reactionism, independence—whatever you want to call it" of the nation's farmers. When Congress agreed in 1950 to cover regularly employed farm and domestic workers, Altmeyer felt that "we'd really crossed the mountain."[24] Thereafter, extensions occurred every few years for the next two decades until virtually every occupational group was covered except federal civil servants. Participation remained voluntary for state and local governments and nonprofit organizations, but they entered the system steadily and by the early 1970s it covered 90 percent of the employees of nonprofit organizations and 70 percent of state and local government employees. (Numerically, however, the remaining 30 percent of state and local employees were as significant an exception as federal employees.)

There was monumental irony in this outcome. In this biggest of federal government programs, only the federal government's own employees remained exempt. Yet many of them did participate as individuals. In 1972, 58 percent of federal civil service retirees were also receiving social security benefits, presumably as the result of holding secondary jobs or jobs taken after retirement from the government.[25] By combining benefits in the civil service retirement system with benefits under social security, they were able to secure higher retirement pay

22. Arthur J. Altmeyer, *Formative Years of Social Security* (University of Wisconsin Press, 1966), p. 103.

23. Ibid., pp. 245–48.

24. Interview with Arthur J. Altmeyer, Oral History Collection, Columbia University (1967), p. 210.

25. Robert J. Myers, *Social Security* (McCahan Foundation, 1975), p. 580.

than if they had been covered by one system only or if civil service retirement benefits had been designed to supplement social security rather than to stand as an independent system.[26]

Federal civil servants did not remain outside of social security for want of proposals to the contrary. Successive advisory councils, a special presidential committee to study retirement policy for federal personnel (the Kaplan committee), and studies by the SSA (in which the Civil Service Commission was sometimes a reluctant collaborator) all repeatedly recommended either outright coverage or transfer of credit plans that would have improved coordination.[27] The Eisenhower administration made a particular effort in the mid-1950s to cover federal employees. All such efforts foundered on the opposition of the civil service unions, which believed that their members could get more generous retirement benefits by staying out of social security than by coming in. The civil service retirement system was superior to social security in several respects, and continued separation, of course, preserved the possibility of pyramiding coverage and receiving windfall benefits under social security.

Nonparticipation of federal civil servants did not stimulate group conflict. The participants in social security, consisting of nearly all employed workers outside of the federal government, were so large and diffuse a group that counterorganization against the nonparticipants would not have been feasible. Besides, the stakes were obscure. Participants could hardly have known that the nonparticipation of federal employees imposed an unfair cost on them. For most people, surely, their relative position in the social security system was not salient to political activity.

Early Entrants and Late Entrants

Social security can be fair to everyone only when the system has fully matured and covers everyone from the time of his entry into the work

26. *Background Material on Social Security Coverage of Governmental Employees and Employees of Nonprofit Organizations,* prepared by the staff of the Subcommittee on Social Security of the House Committee on Ways and Means, 94 Cong. 2 sess. (GPO, 1976), pp. 13–14.

27. The various studies and proposals are summarized in ibid., pp. 14–20, and in "Relating Social Security Protection to the Federal Civil Service," A Report to the House Committee on Ways and Means and the Senate Committee on Finance by the Social Security Administration, January 1969.

force until retirement, disability, or death. Even then, costs and benefits may be unevenly distributed among generations, depending on the relative size of successive generations (how many workers are called on to support how many retirees) and on the condition of the country's economy, especially the maintenance of economic growth; but such differences may be regarded as "accidents"—the chance results of demographic and economic events—rather than intrinsic biases of the social security system. An immature system, on the other hand, is unavoidably biased unless policymakers are willing to give some participants minuscule benefits and tax other participants at far higher rates than maintenance of the system requires. It is biased, that is, in the sense that the relation between benefits and costs is warped; early entrants have higher benefit-cost ratios than later entrants.

A young social security system is biased in favor of workers who are relatively old when it starts. If they qualify for benefits at all, and if a reasonable monthly minimum is stipulated, they will get more in return than their limited tax contributions will have "bought." Founders of the social security system in 1935 acknowledged this, but argued that a reasonable minimum monthly benefit was necessary on psychological as well as administrative grounds. It made no sense to issue checks in paltry amounts. Edwin Witte made the case as follows before the Ways and Means Committee for a monthly minimum of $10 or $15:

This man at $40 [in wages per month] will get a pension of around 20 cents a month after 5 years of contributions, which is such a small amount that it certainly would not be satisfactory. . . . After this man has contributed 5 years, although the actuaries compute that his contributions would buy a monthly annuity of only 20 cents, he is apt to think that he has earned a pension of $10 or $15 at least. It is that psychological factor you have to take into account. A pension of such a small amount as people who are in the system only a short time can buy, will never be satisfactory to them. It will seem to them that they are being cheated.[28]

Congress in 1935 set the minimum at $10 monthly, and while this was not a large amount, it created benefits far out of proportion to what many workers had "earned."

Policymakers were much less ready to acknowledge the second form of bias that characterizes an immature system, perhaps because this bias would have been easier to avoid. Because a social insurance system starts small, covering the aged by slow stages as they become eligible through contributions and then retire, the costs develop gradually. Be-

28. *Economic Security Act*, Hearings before the House Committee on Ways and Means, 74 Cong. 1 sess. (GPO, 1935), p. 102.

cause an immature system is characterized by a high ratio of active, tax-paying workers to retired beneficiaries, it is possible to charge the tax-paying members artificially low rates (that is, less than what their own benefits will cost) and yet sustain the system. This bias could have been wholly avoided by charging a level-premium tax rate—a course of action against which there were powerful economic as well as political arguments—or largely avoided by charging what Ball in 1949–50 iden-tified as an "actuarial rate"—that rate that would have been sufficient to finance the average benefit for members of a generation of workers. Under the executives' plan for an actuarial rate, payroll taxes would eventually have been supplemented with general revenues, but payroll taxes would have been nearly the same for early and late entrants into the system (see chapter 11).

This was not the plan that Congress chose. Instead, Congress in 1950 elected a graduated schedule of payroll taxes, starting at a low rate (1.5 percent in 1951) and rising in later years to much higher levels that were specified in law but in truth could only be guessed at. Early entrants who paid the low rates therefore had a substantial advantage over later entrants who would pay much higher rates; and this advan-tage was periodically renewed by acts that extended the system to cover additional occupational categories. As additional occupational groups were drawn in—say, farmers or self-employed professionals such as lawyers or doctors—the short-run effect was to draw in many more tax-payers than beneficiaries and thus prolong the immaturity of the system and the possibility of sustaining artificially low tax rates for early entrants.

Economists and actuaries who have attempted to project individual benefit-cost ratios have arrived at very different results, depending largely on their assumptions about interest rates and the incidence of the employer tax, but all such estimates agree that such ratios will drop sharply as the system matures. In the mid-1960s, for example, the chief actuary of the Social Security Administration estimated that the benefit-cost ratio for a married man retiring in 2010 would be one-tenth what it was in 1962, though still favorable. Private estimates showed less favor-able results, but the difference was only in the steepness of the trend.[29]

29. Colin D. Campbell and Rosemary G. Campbell, "Cost-Benefit Ratios under the Federal Old-Age Insurance Program," in *Old Age Income Assurance*, A Com-pendium of Papers on Problems and Policy Issues in the Public and Private Pen-sion System Submitted to the Subcommittee on Fiscal Policy of the Joint Economic Committee, pt. 3, *Public Programs*, 90 Cong. 1 sess. (GPO, 1967), pp. 72–84.

Table 12-1. *Number of Taxpayers per Beneficiary, Old Age and Survivors Insurance, Selected Years, 1950–70*
Thousands of people

Year	Beneficiaries	Taxpayers	Number of taxpayers per beneficiary
1950	3,477	48,283	13.9
1955	7,961	65,203	8.2
1960	14,157	72,530	5.1
1965	19,128	80,681	4.2
1970	23,564	92,700	3.9

Source: Robert J. Myers, *Social Security* (McCahan Foundation, 1975), tables 10.26 and 10.27, pp. 386–87.

Table 12-2. *Taxable Earnings Base, Tax Rate, and Maximum Employee Tax Payable, by Period or Year, 1937–72*
Amounts in dollars

Period or year	Taxable earnings base	Tax rate (percent)			Maximum employee annual tax
		OASDI[a]	Health insurance	Total	
1937–49	3,000	2.00	...	2.00	30.00
1950	3,000	3.00	...	3.00	45.00
1951–53	3,600	3.00	...	3.00	54.00
1954	3,600	4.00	...	4.00	72.00
1955–56	4,200	4.00	...	4.00	84.00
1957–58	4,200	4.50	...	4.50	94.50
1959	4,800	5.00	...	5.00	120.00
1960–61	4,800	6.00	...	6.00	144.00
1962	4,800	6.25	...	6.25	150.00
1963–65	4,800	7.25	...	7.25	174.00
1966	6,600	7.70	0.7	8.40	277.20
1967	6,600	7.80	1.0	8.80	290.40
1968	7,800	7.60	1.2	8.80	343.20
1969	7,800	8.40	1.2	9.60	374.40
1970	7,800	8.40	1.2	9.60	374.40
1971	7,800	9.20	1.2	10.40	405.60
1972	9,000	9.20	1.2	10.40	468.00

Source: Myers, *Social Security*, table 3.5, p. 120; table 7.1, p. 270.
a. Old age, survivors, and dependents insurance.

A simpler, less speculative way of demonstrating the bias of the immature program is to show the ratio of taxpayers to beneficiaries, as in table 12-1. In a mature program, assuming universal coverage, this ratio is essentially a function of demographic factors—that is, of the number of people in different age groups. In an immature program, it is artificially enlarged because of the time lag in reaching beneficiaries. In the two decades from 1950 to 1970, the number of taxpayers per beneficiary dropped from 13.9 to 3.9.

Another way to portray the relatively light burden on early participants is to show tax obligations. Table 12-2 shows increases in the wage base, tax rate, and maximum individual tax payable from the start of the program through 1972. Not until twenty years after benefit payments began did the maximum annual tax reach $100. As late as 1964, on the eve of medicare, it was still below $200.

From a political point of view, this bias in favor of early entrants was the most important one in the system. It gave rise to no conflict. Early entrants paid low taxes and realized superb returns while late entrants who were victims of this bias could have no consciousness of it in the program's founding years. Also, the inherent dynamism of the system and the problematic, highly technical character of benefit-cost calculations made it impossible even for expert analysts to draw a sharp line between advantaged early entrants and relatively disadvantaged later ones.[30]

For the ordinary individual, economic prospects in the system are unknown, and they are hardly knowable because the elements that must enter into a calculation are arcane and changeable, and the calculation itself is technically so complex that only highly trained persons can perform it. Prospects change with changes in the law and in the economic and demographic environment. Furthermore, if it is hard to know where one stands in the system (that is, as to prospects of a return on investment), it is still harder to know where one stands in relation to others. The dynamism of the system and of individual life experiences is such that one does not *stand* anywhere; the individual moves through a constantly changing system in a constantly changing socioeconomic environment, first as a taxpayer and then as a beneficiary.

There is some stability in the relation among age cohorts—that is, in the relative advantage or disadvantage of generations as they move through the system—but only specialists can perceive it, and age cohorts are statistical categories, not bases for developing a sense of shared

30. Whether later entrants would be absolutely disadvantaged by participation in social security—that is, whether their benefit-cost ratios would fall below one— began to be at issue in the late 1960s. The projections of expert analysts disagreed. See John A. Brittain, "The Real Rate of Interest on Lifetime Contributions toward Retirement under Social Security," in ibid., pp. 109–32.

interest and hence of political organization. Even if, despite the dynamism of the system and its technical mysteries, the individual could detect his "place" in it, that place is probably not important enough in his experience to provide a motive for joining with others similarly placed in an effort to pursue common interests.

Even elderly, retired persons—whose stakes in the system are large and manifest—when they do organize cannot sustain organization simply on the basis of a shared status as beneficiaries of social security That is only one of several interests that bind the members of the National Council of Senior Citizens or the American Association of Retired Persons (founded in the late 1950s), and lobbying for bigger social security benefits, while very important, is only one of many services that such organizations offer their members.

THIS CHAPTER has analyzed the distribution of social security costs and benefits among various categories of the population to explain why distributive issues have not inspired a more intense conflict. Answers varied from one category to another, but the point of greatest analytic interest is that the most pronounced bias in the system—that which favored early entrants with much higher benefit-cost ratios than late entrants—inevitably helped to secure acceptance of the system in its early years. If early tax rates and benefit-cost ratios had been more realistic, and had represented the long-term rather than the short-term costs of the program, popular acceptance would presumably have been much harder to obtain.

CHAPTER THIRTEEN

The Level of Benefits

SOCIAL SECURITY replaces income that is lost because of a worker's retirement, disability, or death. Obviously, one of the leading policy choices posed by this program is how much income it should provide. By what standard should the sufficiency of benefits be judged? The individual worker's previous earnings? The society's prevailing wages? An ideal standard of living? The minimum required for subsistence? Though these questions go to the heart of the social function of social insurance, they have not been much illuminated by the policymakers' public discussion.

For years, the short, standard, official answer to such questions was that social security was designed to provide a "floor of protection," but that was no answer at all. It did not say where to locate the floor, or, to borrow a metaphor from Wilbur J. Cohen, whether the floor should be covered with quality carpeting. Far from settling anything, this standard phrase was ambiguous in the extreme. "Undoubtedly," Cohen once remarked, "its great attractiveness and usefulness has been that it can mean different things to different people. Its value is in what it conceals rather than what it reveals."[1]

The notion of a floor implies a uniform benefit, whereas the program always scaled benefits to earnings. Wage relatedness, in fact, was the one fixed and clear principle by which benefits were determined— favored by policymakers because it seemed consistent with an economic system based on incentives to work; because it facilitated adaptation of

1. "Proceedings of the Social Security Conference," Labor and Industrial Relations Center, Michigan State University, and Institute of Labor and Industrial Relations, University of Michigan and Wayne State University (East Lansing, Mich.: 1958), p. 10.

the program to regional differences in income and the cost of living; and because it was expected to win political support from the better-off. But even with this as settled dogma, it still had to be decided how high benefits should be, granting that they would be related to wages.

To that basic question, policymakers responded pragmatically, with an eye, as usual, to the requirements of program maintenance. They finally agreed on two guides: social insurance benefits should be set high enough so that that program, rather than public assistance, would be the predominant public means of supporting the aged; and benefits should be increased to at least keep up with the cost of living. But while they found it easy to agree that social insurance should prevail over public assistance at the lower end of the income scale, they found it hard to agree on how to draw a line between social insurance and the private provision of pensions and annuities at the upper end of the income scale. Decisions about benefit levels inevitably raised this question, and it proved to be the most tendentious of policy choices in the basic program of cash benefits for the retired elderly.

The Public Assistance Comparison

The planners of old age insurance in 1934–35 did not pretend in later years to have paid a great deal of attention to the benefit structure. They were above all concerned with establishing the principle, and, quite specifically, the constitutionality of the program, which was much in doubt in those early New Deal days. Besides, payments of benefits were not supposed to start until 1942, and that gave time for a second look.[2]

When the advisory council of 1937–39 took that second look, the need to get the program securely established was still the first priority of executive planners, and one way to do this was to expedite the payment of benefits. J. Douglas Brown, who was the council chairman, recalled that it was the idea of the Social Security Board staff to do two or three things at once: "We would get benefits up faster by using the average [monthly wage], regardless of how long contributions have been made; two, we would hold down the reserves by getting benefits paid out;

2. J. Douglas Brown, *The Genesis of Social Security in America* (Princeton University, Industrial Relations Section, 1969).

third, we would make the system viable politically. In other words, we'd get insurance benefits out faster and better, over against old age assistance."[3]

Again ten years later, establishing social security remained the prime goal for program executives who were at work on the 1950 amendments, which constituted the program's third and final statutory "founding." At this time it still seemed possible that means-tested public assistance, not social insurance, would emerge as the predominant means for public support of the elderly. In June 1950, more elderly people were getting old age assistance than were getting insurance (2.8 million as opposed to 2.1 million). OAA rolls were growing steadily, and at a pace fast enough to stay ahead of insurance. The average OAA payment in 1949 was 70 percent more than the average primary insurance benefit. "So long as benefits under the contributory insurance program remain at totally inadequate levels while the noncontributory assistance payments steadily increase, the contributory program is threatened," the Social Security Administration declared in its annual report for 1949.[4] The SSA recommended a wide range of legislative measures to establish the primacy of insurance, including a large increase in benefits.

Both the House Committee on Ways and Means and the Senate Committee on Finance accepted the administration's argument that insurance must prevail, though with rather different reasoning. The House committee's report of legislation in 1949 echoed the executive's litany in celebration of insurance: that it would preserve self-reliance and initiative, reward individual ambition and effort, preserve the worker's dignity and independence, encourage the accumulation of private savings, and achieve fiscal discipline by basing benefits on contributions.[5] The Senate committee stressed the merits of insurance less and the burden of public assistance costs more, perhaps because of a greater sensitivity in the Senate to the interests of state governments, which bore nearly half of assistance costs. "Your committee is greatly disturbed by the increasing burden on the general revenues caused by dependency in the United States," the Senate report says. "Your committee's impelling concern . . . has been to take immediate, effective

3. Interview with J. Douglas Brown, Oral History Collection, Columbia University (1965), p. 48. (Hereafter Brown, OHC.)

4. Annual Report of the Federal Security Agency, 1949 (GPO, 1950), p. 80.

5. Social Security Act Amendments of 1949, H. Rept. 1300, 81 Cong. 1 sess. (GPO, 1949), pp. 2–3.

steps to cut down the need for further expansion of public assistance, particularly old age assistance."[6] The Senate committee recommended a much greater liberalization of eligibility requirements for social insurance than did the House committee. The Senate's preference in regard to liberalized eligibility prevailed, and, along with a big benefit increase, this change made social insurance the predominant program in less than half a year.

The change involved a shift in functions from one level of the federal system to another and from one public program to another—adjustments within the public sector to which there was no opposition. Significantly, the American Public Welfare Association, in which state public assistance administrators were organized, never opposed the growth of social security. However, conservative critics, watching what they took to be a process of competition between insurance and assistance, concluded that costs would be easier to control if only one federal program existed. Hence the interest of the Chamber of Commerce in the late forties and early fifties in blanketing in all the elderly under social insurance and ending federal grants to the state for OAA.

Quarterly claims for social insurance benefits doubled in volume after the 1950 amendments were passed. In February 1951, the number of aged on insurance passed that on OAA. Expenditures for insurance benefits doubled between 1950 and 1951 (rising from $727 million to $1,498 million), while combined federal and state expenditures for OAA dropped slightly (from $1,559 million to $1,549 million). Having achieved their basic objective of reducing old age assistance to a residual program, program executives could consider other criteria for setting benefit levels. Trends in wages and prices became the benchmark for change, with the 1950 levels serving as the base.

The Cost of Living Criterion

Between 1952 and 1971, Congress enacted increases in social security benefits seven times, applying to both current and future retirees. This was done by changes in the benefit formula and in statutory "conversion tables" that were used in applying the changed formulas to current bene-

6. *Social Security Act Amendments of 1950*, S. Rept. 1669, 81 Cong. 2 sess. (GPO, 1950), pp. 1–2.

ficiaries. To illustrate, the formula changed as follows between 1950 and 1965:[7]

Year change enacted	Benefit as percentage of average monthly wage
1950	50 percent of first $100 plus 15 percent of next $200
1952	55 percent of first $100 plus 15 percent of next $200
1954	55 percent of first $110 plus 20 percent of next $240
1958	58.85 percent of first $110 plus 21.40 percent of next $290
1965	62.97 percent of first $110 plus 22.90 percent of next $290 plus 21.40 percent of next $150

In general, these changes were justified as the necessary response to increases in wages and prices. The following statements from reports of the Ways and Means Committee state the rationale:

The rapid rise in wages and prices during the last few years makes immediate benefit adjustments imperative.—1952.[8]

The level of benefits [proposed] . . . will represent a realistic floor of protection in line with current price and wage levels.—1954.[9]

Your committee has not been able to recommend benefits at as high a level as, in our opinion, would be justified if one considered solely the need for this protection. The increase of approximately 7 percent provided by the bill is actually somewhat short of the rise in the cost of living that has taken place since 1954. We believe, however, that it is essential that a significant part of the additional contributions to the system that we are recommending be used to strengthen the financing of the system rather than to improve benefit protection.—1958[10]

Your committee believes that a benefit increase at this time is obvious. . . . The last general benefit increase was enacted in 1958 and was effective with benefits payable for January 1959. Since that date there have been changes in wages, prices, and other aspects of the economy.—1965[11]

To say that benefits increased with wage and price changes is not very satisfying inasmuch as wages and prices typically rose at different rates, the former faster than the latter. With minor exceptions in 1958

7. 64 Stat. 506; 66 Stat. 768; 68 Stat. 1062; 72 Stat. 1013; 79 Stat. 361.

8. *Social Security Act Amendments of 1952,* H. Rept. 1944, 82 Cong. 2 sess. (GPO, 1952), p. 2.

9. *Social Security Act Amendments of 1954,* H. Rept. 1698, 83 Cong. 2 sess. (GPO, 1954), p. 15.

10. *Social Security Amendments of 1958,* H. Rept. 2288, 85 Cong. 2 sess. (GPO, 1958), p. 2.

11. *Social Security Amendments of 1965,* H. Rept. 213, 89 Cong. 1 sess. (GPO, 1965), p. 84.

Table 13-1. *Percentage Increases in OASI Benefits, Prices, and Wages,
by Effective Date of OASI Change, 1950–71*

Date of change[a]	Increase in OASI benefit		Increase in consumer price index		Increase in average wages, each amendment
	Each amendment[b]	Since January 1940	Each amendment	Since January 1940	
September 1950	81.3[c]	81.3	75.5[c]	75.5	148.8[c]
September 1952	14.1	106.9	9.3	91.8	12.5
September 1954	13.3	134.3	0.5	92.8	7.7
January 1959 (1958)	7.7	152.4	7.9	108.0	19.4
January 1965	7.7	171.9	7.9	124.5	22.3
February 1968 (1967)	14.2	210.5	9.3	145.4	18.0
January 1970 (1969)	15.6	258.9	10.8	171.8	12.2
January 1971	10.4	296.2	5.2	185.9	5.3

Source: *Future Directions in Social Security,* Hearings before the Senate Special Committee on Aging, 93 Cong. 1 sess. (GPO, 1973), pt. 1, p. 84. The data on wage increases were supplied to the author by Robert J. Myers.
a. Year of enactment, if different from year in which change took effect, is in parentheses.
b. Average increases for current beneficiaries, that is, people who were on the rolls. At the same time, increases approximately equal to these were promised, by statutory formula, to active workers.
c. Percentage increase since January 1940, when OASI benefits were first paid.

and 1965, Congress enacted increases that were at least equal to price increases, and sometimes, as in 1954, considerably in excess of them. In relation to wage increases, no clear pattern is discernible. Sometimes benefit increases were greater than wage increases and sometimes they were less, as table 13-1 shows.

Cumulatively, social security benefit increases between 1950 and 1971 far exceeded price increases but lagged behind wage increases. The effect was that the purchasing power of a retired worker's benefit was substantially improved over time, but not directly in proportion to the overall improvement in the standard of living. Also, because the benefit increases were intermittent and ad hoc, there was ordinarily a lag between price increases and the subsequent adjustment of benefits.[12]

That the rate of benefit increases for retired persons lagged behind the rise in wages should not be taken to imply that social security benefits in absolute terms fell farther behind absolute wage levels. Mainly as a result of increases in the wages of covered workers and changes in the benefit formula, the average monthly benefit more than tripled between

12. There are few analyses of the relation between benefit increases and wage increases, but see Daniel N. Price, "OASDHI Benefits, Prices, and Wages: Effect of 1967 Benefit Increase," *Social Security Bulletin,* vol. 31 (December 1968), pp. 28–35.

Table 13-2. *Relationship of Average Wages to Average Old Age Benefits, Selected Years, 1950–71*

Dollars

Years	Average monthly old age benefit	Average weekly earnings of privately employed workers
1950	43.86	53.13
1955	61.90	67.72
1960	74.04	80.67
1965	83.92	95.06
1966	84.35	98.82
1967	85.37	101.84
1968	98.86	107.73
1969	100.40	114.61
1970	118.10	119.46
1971	132.16	126.91

Sources: Robert J. Myers, *Social Security* (McCahan Foundation, 1975), p. 387; *Monthly Labor Review*, vol. 95 (August 1972), p. 98.

1950 and 1971, steadily narrowing the gap between old age benefits and the wages of currently employed earners. In 1971, for the first time the average monthly benefit passed the average weekly earnings of privately employed workers, as is shown in table 13-2.

Actuarial procedures of the Social Security Administration were designed to facilitate periodic increases in benefits. As Commissioner Ball explained it, "we almost always are in the position of finding some long-range [financial] surplus under a new evaluation. . . . In a sense, what I am saying is that the present way of evaluating the program takes into account benefit increases on an ad hoc basis. It is assumed that the Congress will, from time to time, increase the benefits, at least to keep up with the cost of living." To allow for that, he said, the SSA based its financial estimates on the assumption that earnings would not increase.[13] The "level earnings assumption" was a technician's device that had important political implications.

To understand the importance of this assumption, it is necessary to understand the importance of actuarial estimates in policymaking for social security. Congress never acted without having the actuary's long-range estimates of revenue and expenditure before it. It was Congress's policy that the system should be self-supporting (that is, revenues from

13. *Social Security and Welfare Proposals*, Hearings before the House Committee on Ways and Means, 91 Cong. 1 sess. (GPO, 1970), pt. 1, p. 172.

the payroll tax and from interest on the trust fund should meet costs) and that it should be kept in "actuarial balance" (revenues should meet expenditures both currently and as far into the future as the eye of actuarial man could see). Congress enacted a schedule of tax rates sufficient to meet projected expenditures; in deciding what rates were sufficient, it accepted the actuary's estimates. The assumptions that underlay these estimates—assumptions regarding such things as mortality rates, birth rates, immigration, employment, earnings, decisions to retire, interest rates, and the size of benefits—in large measure defined the choices before Congress. Not that proposals for changes in the program originated with the actuary, but all such proposals were weighed according to his estimates of revenue and expense. Also, he regularly evaluated the financial condition of the program as a whole. His long-range projections, with updated judgments on whether the system showed a surplus or deficit, were published frequently in a series of actuarial studies.

These periodic updatings of the program's financial condition ordinarily revealed a surplus as long as the actuary based his projections on the assumption that earnings would not rise, an assumption that was used in long-range projections until 1972. The assumption was arbitrary and unrealistic, of course. Policymakers knew this—they knew that earnings *would* rise—but they found the assumption useful nonetheless. As Commissioner Ball explained, it virtually guaranteed the development of (technically unanticipated) financial surpluses that policymakers could use for periodic benefit increases. But that was not the only reason for using it. It also satisfied the actuary's preference for fiscal prudence. It was a procedure, he once explained to the Finance Committee, that utilized actuarial gains "only after they have materialized." When earnings in fact rose, actuarial calculations were revised to show a surplus in the system—but not before. To attempt to project increased earnings, the actuary pointed out, would "count on profits arising from future economic changes over a long future period before such changes occur."[14]

14. *Social Security Amendments of 1971*, Hearings before the Senate Committee on Finance, 92 Cong. 1 and 2 sess. (GPO, 1972), pt. 2, p. 863. Although technically unrealistic, the estimates incorporating the level earnings assumption yielded good predictions of the system's financial performance as long as that performance was expressed as a percentage of taxable payroll (that proportion of all wages and salaries

The level earnings assumption satisfied the policymakers' preference for avoiding political conflict. In the context of the American economy of the 1950s and 1960s, it was a conservative assumption with liberalizing consequences, and, because it was ambiguous in practice, it was a convenient instrument of compromise and hence of policymaking. It was conservative because it constrained the size of benefit increases. If the actuary had assumed that wages would rise, he would have projected rising returns from the payroll tax, and these higher anticipated yields could have been used to justify higher benefits. The method was conservative also in the sense that it made prudent provision for error; if other elements of the actuarial calculations went awry, the (technically) unanticipated yield from rising wages could be used to compensate. But in a growing economy—and in an economy in which wages almost always increased faster than prices—it enabled Congress at least to keep benefits up to date with increases in the cost of living, and sometimes, as in 1954, to do a good deal more than that, to the satisfaction of liberal interests that wished to expand the protection offered by the program.

Besides containing the element of compromise, the level earnings assumption was a superb artifice for harnessing the political advantages of economic growth. Economic growth has generally served to ameliorate conflict in American politics; distributive decisions, such as government has to make, are made more easily in a context of increase and abundance than of stagnation and scarcity. Through the technical device of the level earnings assumption, program growth in social security was made to depend directly upon economic growth. To the extent that benefit increases were made possible by economic expansion, they came to policymakers as actuarial windfalls, which could be distributed to the

subject to taxation for social security). This was sure to be so because the actuarial surpluses produced by increases in earnings levels (and hence in the size of the taxable payroll) strongly influenced the bounds of benefit increases voted by Congress. In his defense of the level earnings assumption, the actuary had conceded that "the dollar figures of [the] estimates might not be realistic in the face of dynamic economic conditions," but argued that "the resulting benefit costs expressed as percentages of taxable payroll would very likely be good indications of what the actual costs in the future under dynamic conditions and resultant possible congressional action would likely be." Robert J. Myers, "Study of Actuarial Assumptions as to Social Security Tax Rate Schedules," appendix I to F. J. Crowley, "Financing the Social Security Program—Then and Now," in *Studies in Public Welfare*, Paper No. 18: *Issues in Financing Retirement Income*, prepared for the Subcommittee on Fiscal Policy of the Joint Economic Committee, 93 Cong. 2 sess. (GPO, 1974), p. 95.

populace at no added cost in taxes. Here was a paradigmatic case of the beneficent political economy that is associated with growth.[15]

Social security benefit increases became a means by which politicians gratified constituents and sought to elicit their votes. In the 1950s, increases were enacted in election years with perfect regularity. (In 1956, although there was no benefit increase, the program was liberalized in other ways.) Republican members of Congress, in the minority most of the time, sometimes commented caustically on the political motive for Congress's acts, but along with the Democrats they supported the increases.

The Public-Private Controversy

At the lowest income levels, the question for social security policy was how to divide responsibility with another public program—public assistance. That government was responsible for supporting the incomes of the very poor was not in dispute; the questions were how much should be done by the different kinds of public programs and by different levels of government in the federal system. At higher income levels, the policy question involved rather the division of responsibility between public and private organizations. Should social security cover everyone, even those who presumably had enough income to protect themselves against the risks that social security was designed to cover? At one extreme, social security might not cover the better-off at all. At the other extreme, it might tax and undertake to replace, upon retirement, all of their earned income. (No one has ever suggested that social security should replace the loss of unearned income—that from savings or investments.) Or, between these two extremes, it could offer voluntary, partial, or contingent coverage—contingent, that is, on the failure to make private

15. The actuary's office consistently estimated that half of the increased revenue yield from increased earnings must be used to pay the higher benefits that inevitably resulted from higher earnings in a wage-related program, but the other half could be used to finance immediate benefit increases or other liberalizations. This half was the windfall. It was not usually sufficient to pay the whole of the cost of benefit increases or other liberalizations. To finance liberalization between 1950 and 1971, Congress used some combination of three techniques: capturing new revenues through extension of coverage to additional population groups; increasing taxes (through an increase in the rate, the wage base, or both); and the use of actuarial gains that followed from using the level wage assumption. Two benefit increases, those of 1952 and 1969, were financed wholly with the actuarial windfall, as was a package of miscellaneous liberalizations in 1960.

arrangements. The public-private division of responsibility proved to be unusually contentious. This controversy divided liberals from conservatives, labor from business, Democrats from Republicans, as no other policy choice did during the early years, but even here the divisions after 1935 were usually confined within the constricted, specialized, and detached world of social security policymaking.

The most difficult issues in 1935—difficult in that they divided Congress internally or divided Congress from the administration—all had a public-private dimension. There were three: whether to enact an old age insurance program at all; whether such a program should provide for the sale of voluntary annuities by the government; and whether industrial employers with their own employee pension plans should be exempt.[16]

The Republican party in Congress opposed the compulsory old age insurance plan on the ground that it was an illegitimate invasion of the private sphere. The Republican minority of the Ways and Means Committee charged that the bill would destroy the retirement plans of private industries, establish a public insurance bureaucracy in competition with the private insurance business, and violate the Constitution. Though Republicans in the Finance Committee did not file a separate report, most of the party's senators voted to kill the old age insurance title on the floor. Despite some lack of enthusiasm for old age insurance, the Democratic majority in Congress backed the Democratic administration on this basic question.

The old age insurance title would not have passed, though, if the administration had not been willing to sacrifice a provision for the sale of voluntary annuities. This provision was meant to assist persons not covered by the act such as the self-employed, and to provide supplementary protection for those who wanted more benefits than the compulsory program promised. A direct threat to private insurance, it was eliminated initially by the Ways and Means Committee; restored by the Finance Committee on a narrow vote after heated argument; and eliminated on the Senate floor on the motion of a Democratic senator from Connecticut, which is home to much of the insurance industry.[17]

16. The plan for financing, which was difficult conceptually, divided the Treasury Department from the Committee on Economic Security staff, but this particular issue was resolved within the executive branch. See chapter 11.

17. Edwin E. Witte, *Development of the Social Security Act* (University of Wisconsin Press, 1963), pp. 93–94, 102, 105.

The third issue—whether to exempt from payroll taxes industrial employers having government-approved pension plans—was much the hardest to resolve. It caused a deadlock between the House and Senate and delayed passage of the Social Security Act for several weeks in the summer of 1935. The proposal for exemption came from an official of a Philadelphia insurance brokerage firm that specialized in group annuity contracts. The Ways and Means Committee rejected the proposal and so, by a narrow margin, did the Finance Committee, but when Senator Bennett Champ Clark of Missouri offered it as an amendment on the floor, the Senate backed him, 51 to 35, with the Democrats divided and Republicans solidly in favor. Debate had escalated steadily as opposing forces gathered allies. In the end, the bill's passage could only be achieved by deferring that particular issue. The conference committee reported the bill without the Clark amendment, but with an understanding that the chairmen of the Ways and Means and Finance committees would appoint a special joint committee to study the question and report to the next Congress. Curiously, in view of the intensity with which the issue had been fought, it did not revive. The special committee held two meetings, took about thirty pages of testimony, and then quit without making a report. The original sponsor stopped his quest, causing friends of social security to speculate that he lost interest when he found that passage of the act did not harm his brokerage business. Industrial employers who would have benefited from the exemption apparently had mixed feelings about it. They recognized that it would burden them with government regulation.[18]

Strangely, there was no conflict in 1935 over what would eventually become the focal issue, the size of the wage base. The very concept of such a base—the amount of earnings subject to taxation for old age benefits—appears to have been arrived at casually. The Committee on Economic Security initially proposed that salaried employees earning more than $3,000 a year be exempt from old age insurance, but this was dropped. Instead, the law provided that only the first $3,000 of annual earnings would be taxed and taken into account in computation of benefits. The program would simply ignore earnings above that amount.

In retrospect this was a significant change, with important implications for the size, social function, and class and distributive character of

18. Ibid., pp. 102–08, 160–62; Merrill G. Murray, "Social Insurance Perspectives: Background Philosophy and Early Program Developments," *Journal of Insurance,* vol. 30 (June 1963), pp. 183–96.

social security, yet it received little notice at the time. It did not figure in debates and is mentioned perfunctorily or not at all in memoirs and histories. J. Douglas Brown, asked by an interviewer why the change occurred, gave a thoroughly pragmatic explanation. He said it was necessary to simplify administration and to assure coverage for people with sharply fluctuating incomes. "Let me put this to you," Brown replied. "If you had an absolute break point, say of $3,000, persons would be entering and going up and down below that figure. One year they'd be over $3,000 [and] uncovered. The next year they'd be below $3,000. That would add a great administrative difficulty in universal coverage. How would an employer keep track, especially of men working on commission or overtime, that kind of thing? You'd have all kinds of administrative problems. Secondarily, you'd have men who were well over $3,000 and then in a depression would fall below." There is a hint—but only a hint—of a broader motive in Brown's added statement that universal coverage without regard to income level would be "more democratic in a country like ours."[19]

The outcome of 1935 was a compromise. There would be an old age insurance program, it would be compulsory, and there would be no exemption for those few employers who had created private pension plans for their employees. This much was victory for proponents of a public program. On the other hand, the federal government would not go into the business of selling annuities, and that was a victory for the defenders of private insurance. It protected what social security policymakers came to call the "third tier"—the zone of voluntary, private protection that was to come on top of a "second tier" of old age insurance for all workers, which came on top of a "first tier" of public assistance for the very poor. The sum of the early decisions, then, was that public and private insurance would coexist, but the boundary between them was unclear. It would be determined by some combination of chance events, deliberate choices in the private and public sectors, and future clashes between the two.

Setting the Wage Base

Within the public sector, where policy for old age insurance was made, the wage base came to be regarded as the crucial determinant of

19. Brown, OHC, pp. 62, 66–67.

the public-private boundary. The lower the wage base, the more income the worker was free to dispose of voluntarily and the more he was likely to invest in the private sector (assuming that he wished to protect himself against the risks that social security was addressed to). "Keeping this base up to date," Commissioner Ball observed in 1966, "is the factor that determines how much of the job of providing retirement security is to be done by social security and how much of the job is to be either left undone or left only partially done by private pension plans."[20] The tax rate and the benefit formula clearly are factors as well, but at the upper income levels, the wage base is fundamental. It is not surprising, therefore, that the wage base became a focal point of contention.

Program executives wanted to maintain a high wage base for several reasons. For political reasons, they did not want social security to be a program for the poor only ("programs for the poor are poor programs"). If coverage of the better-off was not to be merely trivial or symbolic, the wage base had to be fairly high. Also, a high wage base sustained wage relatedness, which executives regarded as essential. If the base were allowed to stabilize at a low level, most wage earners would sooner or later attain that level and qualify for the same benefit. Raising the wage base contributed to maintenance of the system in other ways, too. It contributed directly, by yielding higher tax revenues. Although raising the base increased benefit obligations and therefore was by no means pure gain, because of the progressive benefit formula it increased revenues more than it increased obligations.

As a source of additional revenue, raising the wage base was more attractive to program executives than an increase in tax rates: to raise the rate would affect everyone, whereas to raise the base would affect only those at the upper-income margin of the system. It is the more progressive way of increasing revenue. A high wage base is, in fact, essential if the program is to be progressive, which is a final reason for the program executives' concern about it. They were supported, as usual, by organized labor, and opposed by all conservative interests—by the insurance industry, of course, and the business federations.

A critical clash of these rival forces occurred in connection with the 1950 amendments, with results that set precedents for some years to come. At $3,000, the base had remained the same since 1935. Program executives had sought no change in 1939. Ten years later, however,

20. Robert M. Ball, "Policy Issues in Social Security," *Social Security Bulletin,* vol. 29 (June 1966), p. 7.

World War II having intervened, wages had soared and program executives proposed to Congress that the wage base be allowed to soar too—to $4,800.

SSA leaders argued that the base should meet the standard set initially, when 92 percent of earnings in covered employment were subject to taxation and 97.1 percent of covered workers had all their wages covered. Among regularly employed males, 93.9 percent had all their wages covered. Yet it was hard to argue the sanctity of that standard, since it had neither been thought about nor fought about in 1935. J. Douglas Brown subsequently attributed the choice of $3,000 to "aesthetic logic," a phrase that he and Wilbur Cohen are fond of using to explain elements of the social security system the rationale for which is less than rigorous. "Three thousand looked very good," Brown told an interviewer. "It was $250 a month. At that time it seemed like a reasonable upper limit, so to speak."[21] Brown and the other planners did not know what proportion of wages or workers they were covering, nor pause to ask whether it was the correct proportion or what the correct one would be. He was not at all disposed in later years to defend as proper "a ceiling set a priori by the planners of an untried program."[22]

The program executives' proposal of a $4,800 wage base divided the 1947–48 advisory council and the congressional committees. The council split three ways, with a majority endorsing $4,200 and separate minorities favoring $3,000 and $4,800. The Ways and Means Committee divided along party lines, with the Democrats supporting $3,600 and the Republicans $3,000. The Finance Committee recommended $3,000 with two Democrats dissenting in favor of something higher (they did not say how much higher), but on the floor changed its recommendation to $3,600, which the Senate adopted. An attempt by liberal Democrats to get support for $4,800 was defeated.

The outcome of 1950 was arrived at by compromise among conflicting interests and opinions. Pressure met counterpressure, faction fought faction, and the result was a figure of $3,600. Except for the program executives, who argued that the original standard should be restored (without, however, explaining why it was proper in the first place), there was not much discussion of a standard and not much acknowledgment of what this patently divisive issue was all about.

21. Brown, OHC, p. 61.
22. J. Douglas Brown, *An American Philosophy of Social Security: Evolution and Issues* (Princeton University Press, 1972), p. 70.

The Republican minority report in Ways and Means was unusual in its willingness to go forthrightly to the heart of the matter: "Raising the wage base . . . brings into sharp focus a basic conflict in the conception of the purpose of the compulsory social-insurance system. This conflict is whether the system should serve to afford economic protection at a basic level appropriate for those least able to provide for their own security, or whether it should now be expanded into a national retirement system of high benefits as a relatively complete means of furnishing retirement and survivors' benefits without any need for supplementation by the individual."[23]

The congressional decision was on balance a conservative victory. When Congress divided the difference between $4,800 and $3,000 and found the answer to be $3,600, it left a sizable space for the "third," or private, tier. With the new base, 81 percent of covered earnings were subject to taxation in 1951, and about 75 percent of covered workers and 64 percent of regularly employed males had all their wages covered. No more reasoned than the original percentages, these nevertheless had political legitimacy, and for the next two decades they were treated as a benchmark. Congress periodically increased the wage base—to $4,200 in 1955, $4,800 in 1959, and $6,600 in 1966—and in doing so restored the proportions of 1950. By thus adhering to precedent, policymakers avoided reopening the issue. Where to draw the public-private boundary—which was potentially the most divisive of questions —was reduced to the single point of where to set the wage base, and that seemingly narrow, nearly technical question was treated as if it had been closed in 1950.

Program executives were gratified that Congress raised the wage base at all in 1950. This precedent-setting action promised to preserve the principle of a wage-related program. On the other hand, so small an increase limited the absolute dimensions and relative significance of their program. They were surprised and delighted in 1961 when Wilbur Mills briefly toyed with the idea of financing a set of program enlargements by raising the wage base to $5,400. It was extraordinary for Congress to propose such a change. However, Mills's Republican counterpart, John Byrnes, reminded the committee that raising the base was a risky thing to do. "A change in the base has always given rise to considerable questions and problems in controversy," Byrnes remarked, and Mills

23. *Social Security Act Amendments of 1949*, H. Rept. 1300, p. 159.

conceded the point: "There is no doubt about it, an increase in base is more controversial than an increase in tax rate." Having no taste for controversy, the committee decided to increase the rate.[24]

The politics of the wage base remained latent until the late 1960s. Then, with successful campaigns for disability coverage and medicare safely behind them, program executives began a drive for a much-expanded cash benefits program.

THE HANDLING of benefit levels was another instance of interests nicely balanced and potential for conflict averted. The practice of holding the line on the wage base (in proportion to total payrolls) assured conservative interests that the program was not expanding in such a way as to threaten the private sector. This practice sustained the notion that social security provided only a "floor of protection." At the same time, the steady elevation of that floor (in relation to consumer prices) satisfied liberal interests that wished to make benefits more generous. In turn, the degree to which this floor was elevated at any given time depended on the use of the level earnings assumption in actuarial estimates, a technique that was conservative in theory but in practice facilitated liberalizations by making it possible to finance them painlessly out of the actuarial windfalls generated by rising wages in an expanding economy.

24. *Social Security Amendments of 1961*, Hearings before the House Committee on Ways and Means, 87 Cong. 1 sess. (GPO, 1961), pp. 110–11.

CHAPTER FOURTEEN

Properties of the Program:
A Summary Analysis

Social insurance had a number of properties that made it extremely appealing, or at least more acceptable than any likely alternatives, to the public, to officeholders in both major parties, and to interest groups (business and labor) that typically were at odds. Three such properties were particularly relevant to politics. First, the program was intrinsically incremental, which meant that costs would start low and grow gradually. Second, it promised taxpayers specific benefits in return for their taxes, which both eased their willingness to pay taxes and alleviated whatever stigma was attached to getting the benefits. Third, it contained many compromises and ambiguities that enabled diverse interests to coalesce in support of it.

Social security started small in at least two senses. Beneficiaries were few in proportion to taxpayers, and only part of the work force was covered. By keeping costs artificially low for a long time, both of these factors worked to ease acceptance. The high early ratio of taxpayers to beneficiaries meant that the program could be sustained with low individual tax rates, and the limited initial coverage of the work force meant that there would be infusions of fresh revenue every time additional groups of workers were brought in. Each such extension of coverage prolonged the immaturity of the system and the period of artificially low taxes.

Besides causing the short-run costs to be artificially low, the intrinsically incremental character of the program meant that the short-run costs of any benefit increases were also artificially low, a circumstance that very much affected the program's politics. In a world where consequences are hard to foresee, policymakers like to take a small step or two and then assess the effects of what they have done. But in social insurance this was not the safe and sound technique it seemed to be because so much of the experience that mattered could only be acquired in the long run. Because the program was itself incremental, the full consequences of incremental additions, in the form of more liberal benefits, could not be assessed until the program had matured and the potential universe of beneficiaries was fully covered. The assurance gained immediately from experience was unreliable, but because it *was* reassuring, further liberalizations in benefits could be undertaken with relative ease.

That social insurance started slowly meant that the public could adapt to it gradually, and this in turn made it very attractive to policymakers. Not that the slow-growing quality of social insurance was their main reason for choosing it: executive officials favored contributory old age insurance primarily because it would establish the principle that the aged were entitled to their benefits without regard to need, in return for tax payments, whereas Congress initially did not like old age insurance at all. Had President Roosevelt not insisted that old age insurance stay in his social security bill, Congress would surely have taken it out rather than accept a program that imposed taxes in 1937 but would not begin to pay benefits until 1942 (or, as turned out to be the case, 1940). On the other hand, as old age insurance took shape neither executive nor legislative policymakers seemed greatly concerned that the full effects—benefits as well as costs, of course would be long delayed. They were not so concerned, anyway, that they were receptive to arguments from both conservative and radical sources that to be fair an old age income support program should cover all of the aged right away. They were unwilling to accept flat grants to all the aged, which would have met this criticism, and it is fair to say that one reason they resisted this alternative is that the cost would have been evident immediately.

Social security was presented to the public as a program in which the worker takes care of his own future, gets back at least what he has paid for, and is entitled to get it back as a right. Because officeholders expected the public to accept it on this basis and because taxpayers never showed any sign of resistance, it is reasonable to infer that this appeal was very effective. Though it is unlikely that taxpayers in general had any idea how big a benefit their payments might have bought,

290 POLICYMAKING FOR SOCIAL SECURITY

or any idea, therefore, that in general they were getting much more than they had bought, the big windfalls to participants in the program's early years can only have helped increase public acceptance. This was a program calculated to appeal to citizens on economic, individualistic grounds, and if citizens responded in the same spirit, they were certain to approve the early program, it was so advantageous to them.

Possibly it was the expectation of a return on taxes that accounts for acceptance of the program even in the very first years, when there were many taxpayers and few beneficiaries—a situation that might have been expected to work to the program's political disadvantage— although I find it more plausible that the public acquiesced in the low tax of that time out of apathy or deference. Just as mutual deference among specialized elites works to contain political conflict, so does the deference of the mass public to authorities. If the government imposed a 1 percent tax on their wages, workers between 1937 and 1949 may well have assumed that there must be a good reason for it to do so without yet having much awareness that they could eventually expect something in return.[1]

Taxpayers were not much encouraged by political leadership to contemplate the social purpose of social insurance—that is, support of the elderly who no longer supported themselves with earnings—but to the extent that taxpayers perceived this as the purpose of the program, they did not object. Public support of elderly, retired persons was not unpopular. Opinion polls revealed overwhelming support for it as early as the 1940s. Here again, though, the relatively low costs of the early program presumably eased public approval. Assuming that the public values economic security for the aged, it is still necessary to ask how much it is willing to pay for the purpose. The early social security program did not require it to pay very much.

Besides the economic realities of the program's operation, which fostered mass acceptance and facilitated incremental enlargements by obscuring their long-term consequences, the many compromises embedded in the program help to explain the low level of political controversy. Benefits were related to wages and a substantial difference was maintained between the highest and lowest benefit, which appealed to the better-off; but a progressive benefit formula nonetheless meant that low-income people got much higher benefits in relation to

1. Poll data, it will be recalled, showed substantial ignorance of the benefits to be gained from paying taxes. See chapter 8.

their wages and tax payments than did the well-to-do. The progressive benefit formula in turn was balanced off against regressive taxes. The steady expansion of benefits, which was achieved, in a growing economy, by actuarial techniques that tied benefits to rising wages, was balanced off against the stability of the wage base, as measured by its proportion of total payroll. There was much here to satisfy the better-off segments of the population and organized conservative interests. There was also much to satisfy people who were less well off and organized liberal interests.

Compromise was compounded by ambiguity. Program executives could argue with some plausibility that because benefits were earned by workers and were wage-related, the program fully preserved incentives to work. Critics could argue with some plausibility that by guaranteeing monthly benefits to virtually everyone in old age (not just workers, but their spouses too), by guaranteeing survivors benefits in the event of a worker's death, and by making the relation between benefits and tax payments very weak, the program undermined self-reliance and discouraged private saving. With much plausibility, it could be argued either that the earmarked tax fostered expansion of the program (because it freed the program from budgetary scrutiny and because the propaganda associated with such a tax facilitated popular acceptance) or constrained expansion (because it guaranteed the visibility of costs). With much plausibility, it could also be argued that the actuarial techniques used in the program were conservative (because they constrained benefit increases by assuming static earnings in the future) or liberal (because in practice this assumption repeatedly made it possible to finance benefit increases out of actuarial windfalls rather than tax increases and to more than compensate for increases in the cost of living).

In all, this was a hard program to classify politically, and a very hard program to understand. Combined with its extreme technicality, compromise and ambiguity helped to render the program incomprehensible to all but a highly expert few at the proprietary core of policymaking, and it helped these few to reach compromises among themselves and to manipulate public presentation of the program in a way that would facilitate acceptance.

As a vehicle for achieving welfare goals, program executives preferred this program to any alternatives partly because of the opportunities it offered for reaching a consensus. Also, they wanted to remove enacted benefits from the realm of legitimate debate, and were able through an insurance program to advance the doctrine that a benefit promised was an unbreachable obligation, a contract between the government and the individual who had paid taxes. This doctrine applied no matter how slight the tax payment or how weak the ultimate relation between the actual tax payment and the statutory benefit. To the extent that program executives could win acceptance for this idea, they had succeeded in containing the politics of social security and in creating a truly uncontrollable program.

It is necessary to end part 2, like part 1, in ambiguous fashion. Part 1 argues the importance of the policymaking system in determining the character of social security politics, especially the influential role of the program executives, but suggests the potential importance of program characteristics. Part 2 argues the importance of program characteristics but closes by suggesting that these were in some measure conceived and advanced by program executives with political ends in view. Part 3, which covers three more cases of policy choice, is designed to weigh both sets of factors by analyzing the response of the policymaking system to three highly controversial issues—the authorization of insurance benefits for disabled persons, authorization of benefits for elderly persons in need of medical care, and a sharp increase in benefit levels in the basic program.

PART THREE

The Politics of Expansion

CHAPTER FIFTEEN

Disability Coverage

EXPANSION of the old age insurance program is harder to define than one might suppose. First, it needs to be distinguished from what might be called "natural increase." As time passed a rising share of the elderly population qualified for benefits, and the elderly population itself increased in actual numbers and as a proportion of the population. Second, it needs to be related to some sort of economic benchmark. By the criteria of most analysts, increases in benefits that merely kept pace with increases in price levels were not expansions.

By a reasonable definition, an expansion is a legislative change that enlarges the scope or function of the program in relation to its social or economic base. So defined, expansion has taken a variety of forms: covering workers in occupational categories initially excluded, such as farmers, domestic servants, and self-employed professionals; liberalizing the eligibility of covered workers for benefits, for example, by lowering the age of eligibility or reducing "insured status" requirements; defining additional classes of eligible dependents, increasing their entitlements, or liberalizing the terms of their eligibility; covering new kinds of risk (disability, medical expense); or raising benefit levels out of proportion to price increases.[1]

1. Defining the expansion of the program by the growth in benefits is particularly problematic. There has been no accepted criterion for measurement. It might be argued that any increase not "earned" by beneficiaries through payment of taxes is an expansion, even if it is sufficient only to compensate for increases in the cost of living. Or it may be argued that expansion occurs when increases exceed increases in the cost of living. Some might argue that even increases in proportion to wage increases (which historically have exceeded price increases) do not constitute expansion of the program as long as the proportion of total earnings subject to social security taxation remains stable. "Replacement rates," which are probably the best single indicator of benefit levels, did not have wide currency as such until the 1970s. Such rates express the relation between the preretirement wage and postretirement pension. See chapter 17 for further discussion.

Such expansions occurred with each new piece of social security legislation. Rather than attempt to describe them all, I concentrate in this and the following two chapters on the three most important instances: disability coverage, coverage of medical care, and a quantum increase in benefit levels. After the establishment of the basic program was completed in 1950, program executives turned in earnest to these major expansions and achieved them all. Disability coverage was enacted only after much conflict and delay and many concessions to the conservative opposition, but, once enacted, it ceased to be so controversial, and a process of incremental expansion set in.

Early Moves

Though it did not recommend a disability program to President Roosevelt in 1935, the Committee on Economic Security did recommend further study of the subject. Upon signing the Social Security Act, the President appointed a committee to study both disability and medical care. This group—the Interdepartmental Committee to Coordinate Health and Welfare Activities—continued for several years after 1935 the social policy planning that the Committee on Economic Security had begun. Most of the members and staff of the new group had been associated with the CES in 1934–35. From its Technical Committee on Medical Care came the earliest proposals for disability and health insurance, which were contained in a report to President Roosevelt and publicized at a National Health Conference called by the interdepartmental committee in 1938.[2]

In later years, Arthur Altmeyer reproached himself for not urging disability insurance on Congress in 1939.[3] The American Medical Association was not then mobilized in opposition. Its house of delegates actually endorsed disability insurance in 1938, and in retrospect it seemed to Altmeyer that a splendid opportunity to move ahead unopposed had been lost. Yet this failure is understandable. Old age insurance payments had not even begun in 1939, and the Social Security Board was anxious to secure the basic program before branching out. By defusing partisan criticism of the big reserve fund and accelerating

2. Wilbur J. Cohen, *Retirement Policies under Social Security* (University of California Press, 1957), p. 44. Chapter 4 of this book summarizes the early history of disability insurance legislation.

3. Arthur J. Altmeyer, *The Formative Years of Social Security* (University of Wisconsin Press, 1966), p. 260.

benefit payments, the 1939 amendments served that end, and though they added survivors coverage, that particular expansion did not pose the definitional and administrative problems inherent in any attempt to cover disability. Nor would the politics have been simple in 1939, even assuming the benign neutrality of the AMA. The advisory council of 1937–39, while agreeing that benefits for permanently and totally disabled persons were "socially desirable," could not agree to recommend them.[4] Conservative council members argued that costs and administrative difficulties required further study.

Study proceeded within the SSB, which began recommending disability legislation in the early 1940s. Its proposal, of course, was for an insurance program, not assistance; benefits would have been paid by right, without application of a means test. To cover temporary disability, the SSB proposed to offer federal inducements to state governments much in the manner of the unemployment compensation program. In contrast to benefits for permanent disability, those for temporary disability would not have been attached to the Old Age and Survivors Insurance program.

Beginning in 1939 disability proposals had won support and sponsorship from liberal Senators James Murray of Montana and Robert F. Wagner of New York, the program executives' main collaborators in the legislature, but they did not get far in the legislative committees. President Roosevelt endorsed disability legislation in his 1942 budget message but did not pursue it. Not until World War II ended and Harry Truman succeeded Roosevelt did the SSB's plans receive firm backing from the President.

Planning for disability insurance intensified as the SSB's postwar preparation of legislation began. In draft legislation, disability insurance was separated from health insurance, which was intensely controversial, and attached to incremental revisions of OASI, where political prospects were much better. SSA officials presented disability but not health insurance to the advisory council of 1947–48 and urged Congress to take action in 1949–50.

The Contest

It became clear as the 1950 amendments were considered that disability insurance would be a divisive issue. The advisory council de-

4. *Advisory Council on Social Security: Final Report, December 10, 1938,* S. Doc. 4, 76 Cong. 1 sess. (GPO, 1939), pp. 19–21.

bated it at length and made many concessions to conservative dissidents, only to lose their votes in the end. In closed sessions, Ways and Means endorsed it by the narrowest of margins, and in the committee's published report the Republicans dissented. The Finance Committee divided between a bipartisan conservative majority that opposed disability insurance and two liberal Democrats who favored it.

"We got a disability proposal and we compromised and compromised on it," labor's Nelson Cruikshank recalled of the 1947–48 advisory council.[5] In the vain hope of winning support from two business dissenters—Marion Folsom of Eastman Kodak and M. Albert Linton of the Provident Mutual Life Insurance Company of Philadelphia—the council kept tightening the language of its proposals. It recommended a strict definition of disability; a six-month waiting period for benefits; no benefits for dependents; reduced benefits for those who received disability aid from another government source (a provision known as the "offset"); and a requirement of "recent, substantial attachment" to the labor force. The council did not propose to cover temporary disability at all. The vice chairman, Sumner H. Slichter, presented the disability plan to Congress as a measure carefully calculated to prevent abuse.[6]

Disappointed by this report, the Social Security Administration proposed a much more liberal measure. The work history requirement would have been less rigorous. Benefits would have been provided for dependents, and there would have been only a minor offset for other government disability payments. In a departure from its earlier plans, the SSA now also proposed to cover temporary disability under the insurance program, a measure so problematic that it apparently had not even been agreed on within the SSA. Oscar Pogge, director of the Bureau of Old Age and Survivors Insurance, declined to testify to its administrative feasibility, saying that the Ways and Means Committee should consult the director of research and statistics, I. S. Falk, if it wanted information about that part of the SSA's plan.[7]

While the SSA occupied a position to the left of the advisory council, the insurance industry and the Chamber of Commerce stood well to

5. Interview with Nelson H. Cruikshank, Oral History Collection, Columbia University (1967), p. 58. (Hereafter Cruikshank, OHC.)

6. *Recommendations for Social Security Legislation,* the Report of the Advisory Council on Social Security to the Senate Committee on Finance, S. Doc. 208, 80 Cong. 2 sess. (GPO, 1949), pp. 69–93; *Social Security Act Amendments of 1949,* Hearings before the House Committee on Ways and Means, 81 Cong. 1 sess. (GPO, 1949), pt. 2, pp. 1555–56.

7. *Social Security Act Amendments of 1949,* pp. 2200, 2219.

the right of it. They objected to disability insurance altogether and proposed instead a program of grants-in-aid to the state governments for support of the disabled who were also poor. This put the issue in terms of principle. A means-tested approach, though it conceded the need for national action, was of course anathema to leaders of the SSA and their collaborators in organized labor except as a residual supplement to insurance.

The conservative argument, as formulated by Linton in a bluntly worded dissent to the advisory council report, was that physical incapacity for work is difficult to determine objectively; that in periods of high unemployment many people of questionable eligibility would attempt to qualify; that in a program offering benefits by right, applicants would feel entitled to such support; and that in a program characterized by a high degree of administrative discretion, administrators would be under pressure to decide borderline claims in the claimant's favor, especially when financing came from a "reserve fund" of several billion dollars in Washington. Costs would be impossible to predict or control, and incentives to work would be seriously undermined with potentially grave consequences for the economy and the society. As an insurance executive, Linton was sensitive to the industry's adverse experience with disability claims in the Depression, when hundreds of millions of dollars had been lost. As an active Republican, he seems also to have feared that the Democratic party would enlarge and solidify its national following through the use of social insurance. He concluded that because of the highly discretionary character of disability administration, "the handling of total-disability cases belongs peculiarly in the realm of the individual States and not in that of the Federal bureaucracy. Turning over to the Federal Government this area of individual care would mean further encroachment of Washington upon State authority, further building up of the Federal pay-roll vote and of the potential opportunity to exert Nation-wide political influence in the handling of benefit payments." Narrow language in the initial law would provide no protection against these dangers, he concluded. Liberalizing changes would soon follow, especially if the economy prospered and claims were few in the first years of the program's operation.[8]

In 1950 Congress enacted the conservative alternative. The Ways

8. *Recommendations for Social Security Legislation,* S. Doc. 208, pp. 85–92, quotation from p. 91.

and Means Committee approved both disability insurance and disability assistance grants, the more conservative Finance Committee approved neither, and their conference approved assistance grants as a compromise. This conservative victory was only temporary, however. The conservatives' intention was that assistance should be a substitute for insurance. Program executives did not accept it as any such thing. They regarded it as a supplement to disability insurance, as OAA was a supplement to OAI, and stepped up their own campaign.

Though program executives had argued for disability insurance in 1949–50, it had not been first among their legislative priorities. Asked by a sympathetic Ways and Means Committee member in 1949 what he valued most in the very large package presented to Congress, Altmeyer unhesitatingly replied that it was of first importance to broaden occupational coverage and increase benefits in the basic program.[9] After passage of the 1950 amendments, which brought 10 million more workers under OASI and increased benefits by 81 percent, disability coverage moved to the top of the program executives' agenda.

Step One: The Disability Freeze

To begin with, the program executives reduced their objectives. Rather than renew right away their failed request for cash payments to the disabled, they decided in 1952 to approach this goal indirectly, in piecemeal fashion, by asking Congress to preserve the OASI benefit rights of disabled workers. Because such benefits were based on average monthly earnings and because a certain amount of time in covered employment was required to qualify for benefits, a disabled worker ran the risk of losing his benefits or having them reduced by reason of his disability. Program executives proposed to avert these risks with a "disability freeze" whereby the years of disability would be excluded when the worker's OASI eligibility and benefits were calculated.

A friendly Republican, Robert W. Kean of New Jersey, sponsored this provision inside the Ways and Means Committee in 1952, as one among a package of relatively modest amendments to the Social Security Act. It moved along smoothly until it reached the floor, and then protest from members of the American Medical Association suddenly caused

9. *Social Security Act Amendments of 1949*, Hearings, p. 1243.

it to ignite as a symbolic issue. Daniel A. Reed, ranking Republican on Ways and Means, took the floor to denounce it as a "sneak attack," an "entering wedge," the "first major cornerstone of socialized medicine in this country."[10]

Though a seemingly small step, the freeze inevitably raised some of the difficult issues inherent in a program of disability benefits. For the freeze no less than for benefit payments, it was necessary to arrive at a definition of disability and to prescribe an administrative method for determining it in individual cases. Determining disability required medical examinations, and it was here that the AMA broke into the contest with charges of "socialized medicine." The bill would have authorized examinations by publicly employed doctors in "existing facilities of the Federal Government" or by private agencies or physicians designated by the federal security administrator. The fees for such examinations would have been stipulated in agreements between private providers and the administrator or his agents. Had socialized medicine not already been a big issue, these provisions might hardly have been noticed, but, having been fully mobilized for opposition to health insurance—a separate campaign—the AMA was prepared to carry its fight to other fronts.

When the AMA joined sides with the insurance industry and the Chamber of Commerce, the disability fight took on added intensity. "We felt we had a real red hot controversy going," Arthur Hess of SSA recalled some years afterwards. "And in fact we did. The disability insurance provisions . . . were fought tooth and nail in the House and in the Senate."[11] Hess, who would later be involved in the medicare fight, thought that business groups—the insurance industry and the Chamber of Commerce—were more active and aroused over disability. Disability politics, he said, was pressure group politics. Organized contestants brought pressure directly to bear on the congressional committees, with less public involvement than in the later case of medicare.

In 1952 the disability freeze carried the House but failed in the Senate, in a repetition of the pattern of 1949–50. The conference then proceeded to decide the issue in a most peculiar way. The disability freeze was included in the 1952 amendments but with an expiration date of June 30, 1953. When combined with another provision, which

10. *Congressional Record* (May 19, 1952), pp. 5471–72.
11. Interview with Arthur E. Hess, Oral History Collection, Columbia University (1966), p. 36. (Hereafter Hess, OHC.)

stipulated that no application from a disabled worker could be received before July 1, 1953, the effect was to nullify what had seemingly been approved. It was the kind of outcome that makes political decisions seem downright absurd. Had the stakes of interest and ideology not seemed so high, a more rational compromise might have been arrived at, but personality played a part too. The outcome owed something to the stubbornness of the retiring chairman of the Ways and Means Committee, who was not for nothing known as "Muley." Hess recalled:

When they finally got into conference, old "Muley" Doughton, who'd been in Congress for forty years or so, and chairman of the Ways and Means Committee for a great many of those years, was riding high. This was his last session of Congress, the last bill, virtually the last conference committee if not *the* last conference committee he was involved in. He was determined that he was going to have something on disability in that bill, not because he personally was sold on disability insurance or the disability freeze, but I think it was a matter of prestige with him that it had passed the House and he didn't want to recede completely to the Senate. And the Senate conferees were equally determined that disability insurance wasn't going to be in there. So they finally ended up with the fantastic compromise.[12]

Concealed beneath this bizarre outcome were solid steps toward agreement. While searching for compromise, the conference committee had hit on the idea of having state agencies make determinations of individual disability. By protecting doctors from direct involvement with the federal government, this could make the bill more acceptable to the AMA. Following from that was another concession to the conservative opposition that provided that the federal security administrator could reverse a positive finding of disability by a state agency but not a negative finding. Hess later credited this "flash of genius" regarding the use of state intermediaries to a Democratic senator from Colorado, Edwin C. Johnson, but he guessed it might actually have come from Wilbur Cohen, to whom ingenious compromises in social security policy are usually attributed.[13]

This was where matters stood when a Republican administration took office for the first time in the history of the social insurance program. The issue of a disability freeze had been fought but not resolved. Congress was committed by the conference report of 1952 to take it up again in 1953. In so volatile and close a contest, the position of the administration could matter a great deal.

12. Ibid., pp. 37–38.
13. Ibid., pp. 84–85.

Oddly, given the timeliness and symbolism of this issue, neither of the major party platforms took a position on it in 1952. Neither made the slightest mention of disability coverage—a sign both of the haphazard quality of the parties' involvement in social security policymaking and of the limited public awareness of the issue. The contest over disability insurance, though intense, was narrow. It involved organizations only: the coalition of the SSA and organized labor on one side against the AMA, the insurance industry, and the Chamber of Commerce on the other. With much freedom to decide its own position—and much appearing to depend on its choice—the Eisenhower administration entered this contest on the side of the SSA.

Roswell B. Perkins, who, as an assistant secretary of HEW, was largely responsible for the administration's position, later explained it as follows:

We were sold on this provision by Wilbur Cohen and others, and at the time we were developing the '54 amendments, it seemed eminently fair not to have your Social Security benefits drop because of a period of nonearning resulting from total disability. It seemed humane. It didn't cost much. It paralleled a common provision in private health insurance.

As a safeguard, Perkins insisted that determinations of disability be made by state agencies for vocational rehabilitation: "people with a constructive and positive approach to disability," as he saw it, rather than "people who simply were interested in adding more recipients to the Social Security benefit payrolls."[14]

Republicans in the Ways and Means Committee, especially John Byrnes, argued bitterly with Perkins when he presented the administration's position. "I had a terrible time defending the disability freeze," Perkins recalled, "because the Republicans kept telling me, 'Perkins, don't you realize this is nothing but a scheme of the New Dealers to pave the way for disability benefits?' " Perkins insisted that it wouldn't be that way—that all the emphasis would be on rehabilitation. " 'We're building up the [Office of] Vocational Rehabilitation,' " he told them, " 'and we're going to funnel all these people through the rehabilitation process. It's going to be a great, huge recruiting system for rehabilitation. We're going to emphasize the positive.' "[15]

Congressional Republicans remained deeply skeptical, but in the end

14. Interview with Roswell B. Perkins, Oral History Collection, Columbia University (1968), pp. 25–26.
15. Ibid., p. 26.

did not dissent publicly from what had unpredictably become the position of their party's executive leadership. That settled the issue. The disability freeze passed in 1954, and the program's leaders then proceeded to concentrate on the next step—cash benefits.

Step Two: Cash Benefits

It did not follow that because the Eisenhower administration had supported the disability freeze it would also support cash benefits for the disabled. Rather the reverse. Because Perkins was genuinely committed to the rehabilitative approach (as he thought of it) and because he had given his word in talks with congressional Republicans, he was determined that the approach be given a fair trial. He did not hesitate to oppose cash benefits a mere two years later when the trial had barely begun. Marion Folsom, who succeeded Mrs. Hobby as HEW secretary in 1955, was much more hesitant, given his long and sympathetic association with the development of social insurance. Robert Ball believed that privately Folsom favored making a limited start on disability coverage and opposed it only on instructions from the White House. But that Folsom, too, had doubts about the desirability of covering disability is shown by his dissent in the advisory council of 1947–48.

The administration's opposition lends significance to the ensuing contest, for this was the first time that the program leaders had sought expansion against the express preferences of the political leadership of the executive branch. A Democratic president might disappoint them by failing to grant formal endorsement, as Franklin Roosevelt did more than once. For strategic reasons, Roosevelt had been reluctant to commit himself to the most ambitious and controversial of their goals, but they could nonetheless be sure that he did not truly disapprove of what they wished to do. The Republican administration, even allowing for the ambivalence of Marion Folsom, really did disapprove of enacting disability insurance in 1955–56.

Had a Democratic Congress not been elected in 1954, the program's leaders might have had to pause in their pursuit of disability legislation. Divided government was one condition of major expansion in these years of Republican rule over HEW. Another was Wilbur Cohen's departure from office. "I could see the clouds rising," he told an interviewer.[16] Not wanting to be in an administration that was opposed to disability insurance, he resigned as of January 1956 to become a professor at the University of Michigan in Ann Arbor, freeing himself from a civil servant's constraints. A third condition was the continuing alliance with organized labor, which did the necessary lobbying.

The climactic contest took place in the summer of 1956, as a presidential election approached, in the Senate, where disability measures had always died before. In 1955 the House had again voted to pass disability benefits and coupled them with another measure long sought by program executives—a lower age of eligibility (sixty-two instead of sixty-five) for women in the basic program. Disability benefits would have been restricted to persons aged fifty or above, a limitation that tended to obscure the threshold nature of the change. Proponents presented the measure as a reduction in the age of eligibility for women and the disabled rather than as a major new program of aid to the disabled. The Finance Committee held hearings on this package early in 1956, at which Secretary Folsom opposed both changes. The administration was campaigning for universal coverage in the basic program (it especially wanted to bring federal civil servants in at this time), but not for expanded benefits.[17]

In the Senate, the tactical challenge for proponents of disability insurance was to unite the Democratic party. That had not been possible in the past; the Finance Committee's opposition to disability coverage had been bipartisan. But by 1956 the political situation had changed. There was divided government, which gave the Democratic party in Congress an incentive to compete with the incumbent administration for legislative leadership. There was a new and very strong party leader in the Senate, Lyndon B. Johnson, who thought his job was to do just that. Finally, there was a new and not very strong chairman of the Finance Committee, Harry F. Byrd of Virginia, to whom the Senate did not defer as it had deferred to his predecessor, Walter F. George of Georgia. George remained on the committee but had given up the chairmanship in order to chair the Foreign Relations Committee. This change of political forces and party leadership presented the partisans

16. Interview with Wilbur J. Cohen by David G. McComb for the Lyndon B. Johnson Library (1968); copy in John F. Kennedy Library, Waltham, Mass.
17. *Social Security Amendments of 1955*, Hearings before the Senate Committee on Finance, 84 Cong. 2 sess. (GPO, 1956), pt. 3, pp. 1225–51.

of the social insurance program with precious tactical advantages. George became the sponsor of disability insurance in the Senate in 1956, and Johnson, as Democratic majority leader, became responsible for assembling a winning coalition.

George's support was as improbable as it was invaluable. Only two years before he had inveighed on the Senate floor against "the reformers in the social security outfit" and appealed to the good Lord to save the world from reformers and get the country out of debt—this as part of his campaign to save farmers from social security coverage.[18] Now, with Southern oratory still reverberating, he cast aside his concern about debt and creeping socialism to join the side of the "social security outfit." Seventy-eight years old, he was facing a difficult contest in the Democratic primary, and perhaps got interested in disability legislation as a way of strengthening his support. In May he announced that he would not run, and the disability measure then became his sentimental parting gift to the country. In another year he would die.

Whatever George's motives, he was the best of all possible sponsors. Everyone listened when this powerful veteran spoke, in veneration of a Southern statesman at the end of his career. Without a sponsor of such stature, it might not have been possible to overturn the committee, which had once again recommended against disability insurance.

The outcome was decided on the floor following George's speech. The narrow vote of 47 to 45 was a final sign of the divisiveness of the issue. Despite strong pressure from the Eisenhower administration, six Republicans joined forty-one Democrats in voting for the George amendment, while seven Southern Democrats defected to join thirty-eight Republicans in opposition. Action was finished in July, on the last day of the second session of the Eighty-fourth Congress, and in August the Democratic party platform boasted of having improved social insurance over the Republicans' opposition. Program partisans had their law, after a long fight, and the Democrats had a campaign issue.

With the government divided and a presidential election impending, party had played a larger than usual part in social security policymaking. Democratic leaders of the Senate—Johnson, in collaboration with George and Robert S. Kerr of the Finance Committee, who in turn were being assisted by Wilbur Cohen and Robert Ball—had worked out a bill that nearly all of their party could support. Besides

18. *Congressional Record* (August 20, 1954), pp. 15409–12.

the George amendment on disability, it included authorization of benefits for women at the age of sixty-two, but at actuarially reduced rates that substantially cut the cost of the original House package and thereby increased its acceptability to Senate Democrats.

There was hard lobbying on both sides by private interest groups, especially the AMA in opposition to disability insurance and organized labor in support of it. Nelson Cruikshank's recollections recapture the closing moments of the campaign and illustrate labor's relation with the Democratic legislative leaders:

In the last episode we thought we had them rounded up. We went into Lyndon Johnson's office and counted noses. The debate was going on, and I saw Johnson stand on the floor and look around in the gallery. I thought he might be looking for me, and I stood up in the gallery, which is against the rules, but as soon as I did, he caught my eye and motioned for me to go downstairs, and I knew he meant in that little private office of his. I went down there and he said, "How many votes do you think you've got?" I told him that I thought we had about 50. He said, "You have like hell. You're about three votes short right now." He said, "I'll tell Walter George to keep on talking for an hour and in that hour you've got to round up those three votes. That's the best I can do, but I think maybe you can get them," and he suggested some names that we see. I went out in the corridors. There were eight or ten labor fellows there, railroad fellows and all, and I talked to them all. We made some assignments. We started talking to these people. One of them was from [North] Dakota, Young. He was against us, and because of the roll call and his name began with "Y," we were still talking to him while the roll call was on, and the railroad boys convinced him that he should go for disability. One of the arguments was that you couldn't administer it. I knew this was Young's argument, and I told the railroad boys, I said, "Tell him, for heaven's sake, you've got disability in the railroad system and have had it for several years; it's being administered all the time. Just bear down on him that this is a theoretical argument." And they did, and he went in and . . . voted "aye," which gave us the vote we needed.[19]

While Johnson and the labor lobbyists were looking for the winning votes, Wilbur Cohen was in an office in Washington responding to telephone calls for information and advice. Cruikshank thought of him as the anchor man. Never out of touch, even when based in Ann Arbor, he came to Washington when the Senate debate drew near and provided his usual combination of technical expertise and tactical ingenuity, crucially complemented at this time by freedom from official constraint.

19. Cruikshank, OHC, pp. 44–45.

After Enactment: Invisible, Incremental Change

The law of 1956 bore many marks from its long and intensely political passage. To accommodate conservative opposition, program executives had made compromises all along the way.

Disability was defined as the inability to engage in any substantial gainful activity by reason of a medically determinable physical or mental impairment that was expected to result in death or to be of long-continued and indefinite duration. Thus disabilities known to be temporary, even if total, were excluded. There was to be a waiting period of six months before benefits began. A showing of recent and substantial attachment to the work force (as evidenced by employment in six out of the preceding thirteen calendar quarters) was required. Benefits were limited to disabled persons aged fifty and over and were reduced by the amount of other government benefits for disability from such sources as workmen's compensation. Benefits were not authorized for dependents. Determinations of disability were to be made by state agencies and were subject to reversal by the SSA only if they were positive. Finally, disability spending was to be accounted for in a separate trust fund so as to increase visibility and improve prospects of control, a technical contrivance that was introduced during Senate consideration in the summer of 1956.

SSA officials estimated that this program could be financed with an additional tax of 0.25 percent each on employers and employees, which was incorporated in the 1956 amendments. That level of cost appears to have been aimed at specifically in 1955 when the Democrats in Congress began to assemble a legislative package. The other item in the package—a lower retirement age for women—was quite costly, and in order to limit the prospective increase in cost to 1 percent of the taxable payroll, the disability proposal was trimmed to fit. It was then that the age limitation of fifty was introduced.[20] (When the package reached the Senate, the rest of it was trimmed, too, so that the lower retirement age for women was achieved in a way that did not raise costs.)

Conservative opponents repeatedly protested that all the trimming was only tactical and that restoration and further expansion would occur after the initial expansion of the program was achieved. They were

20. Cohen, *Retirement Policies under Social Security*, p. 59.

right; the compromises incorporated in 1956 began to be removed in 1958. And their removal, remarkably enough, given so turbulent a history, generated hardly any dispute. The policymaking system, which had expanded under the impact of a divisive issue, contracted again, and further change occurred with little debate or disagreement among the small, dominant group of program-oriented policymakers.

The definition of disability was liberalized in 1965 by removing the prognostic requirement of "long continued and indefinite duration" and substituting a requirement of twelve months' duration, thereby opening the way to the coverage of temporary disabilities. The requirement of six quarters of employment out of the preceding thirteen calendar quarters was dropped in 1958, and other liberalizations of eligibility were enacted in 1960, 1965, 1967, and 1972. The age limit of fifty for payment of benefits was dropped in 1960, and the offset for other government programs was dropped in 1958 (but later partially restored). Dependents' benefits were added in 1958. The six-month waiting period was reduced in 1972 to five months.

Liberalization was also achieved through administrative discretion, which SSA executives had never been loathe to use, and which they could not avoid using in the disability program. A high degree of administrative discretion was inherent in determining disability. That was one reason for the conservatives' opposition to the program, and a reason for their insisting on a major administrative role for the states. They did not trust the SSA. In response to this conservative hostility and a generally contentious atmosphere, program executives were quite cautious at first. But they soon grew less hesitant as the program was established, controversy subsided, and congressmen sought a liberal administration of the law on behalf of their constituents.

Despite the prescription that state agencies should make determinations of disability, BOASI dominated administration. Its central office prepared the standards by which state agencies were guided. Its district offices received applications from claimants and helped them prepare their claims. After the claims were reviewed by state agencies and determinations of disability made, the states' decisions were reviewed by BOASI's central office in Baltimore. If the bureau disagreed with a state's decision, it notified the state, giving reasons for the disagreement and asking for reconsideration. In all but a handful of cases, the state agencies complied with the federal request.

Characteristically, the bureau used these administrative powers in a liberal, client-serving fashion. "I can assure you the general attitude of people in the district office is wanting to pay claims," Robert Ball testified to a congressional committee. "And if there seems to be a likelihood that on reconsideration . . . the individual might be allowed, he would be given every encouragement to have his case reconsidered."[21] The head of the bureau's Division of Disability Operations had set the tone of administration with a warning to his staff not to be paralyzed by fear of conservative criticism. "I would not want to disclaim a concern for improper allowances," he had told them in 1957, as benefit payments got under way. "But, frankly, at the moment I am haunted more by the fear of improper disallowances. . . . Where there is a reasonable doubt in a close case, the disabled individual should be given the benefit of the doubt."[22]

Bureau guidance provided that in determinations of disability, primary consideration should be given to severity of the impairment as shown by medical evidence, but that the individual's failure to meet the prescribed standard of severity was not necessarily conclusive. Nonmedical factors were also to be taken into account, such as the individual's intelligence, psychological adaptability, age, education, work experience and skills, and motivation. This willingness to give weight to nonmedical factors put a liberal gloss on the seemingly strict requirement of the law that disability depend on a "medically determinable" impairment, and administrators became more willing to use discretion as time passed. A study in 1962 showed that 40 percent of the disability cases in a sample universe had been approved on a finding that nonmedical factors contributed crucially to the disability, whereas in 1959 the proportion had been only 10 percent.[23]

The SSA's administrative conduct also all but nullified the provision of law that gave it authority to reverse only positive findings of disability by the states. "Write-backs" or "bureau bounces," as they were called, often occurred in response to negative determinations by the

21. *Administration of Social Security Disability Insurance Program,* Hearings before the Subcommittee on Administration of Social Security Laws of the House Committee on Ways and Means, 86 Cong. 1 sess. (GPO, 1960), p. 38.

22. Ibid., p. 85.

23. George Goldsborough, Jr., William G. Tinsley, and Arnold C. Sternberg, "The Social Security Administration: An Inter-Disciplinary Study of Disability Evaluation," pt. 1, "The Administrative Determination of Permanent and Total Disability," section 1, "The Social Security Disability System" (George Washington University, 1963), pp. 98–100.

states, normally with the result that the state agencies concurred in the federal recommendation. A team of George Washington University law professors who studied the administration of disability benefits in the early 1960s questioned the propriety of this practice while taking care not to question the SSA's motives. Their report concluded that this procedure stemmed "solely from a deep sense of responsibility for proper administration," especially the achievement of nationwide uniformity in application of the disability standards.[24]

The remarkable thing about the post–1956 liberalization of the law was that it encountered so little resistance. An issue that had provoked intense conflict for much of a decade suddenly seemed to lose its political salience. Congressional committees that had labored to write suitably restrictive language could not recall that they had written it, or why, and instead began asking administrators why it took so long to adjudicate disability claims and why seemingly disabled claimants sometimes had their claims denied. This important change stemmed, first of all, from the changed behavior of the hostile pressure groups.

Business groups found it hard to sustain opposition after a disability program had been established in law. Perhaps this was because a principled opposition, as was theirs to disability insurance, is hard to maintain after the principle has been compromised. Yet the Chamber of Commerce explicitly declined to concede the issue of principle after 1956. Its 1957 policy statement said: "Voluntary agencies and state and local public assistance systems, in conjunction with state rehabilitation agencies, are the appropriate means of providing for the disabled who need help. The recent enactment of a federal system of disability benefits . . . does not alter this fundamental concept." The chamber called for "rigorous screening of disability claims" and other administrative measures to control costs and encourage individual rehabilitation.[25] Judging from this statement, the chamber was not indifferent to the legislative and administrative aftermath of the fight.

Perhaps a better explanation for the failure of business groups to sustain the intensity of their opposition is that crowding of the policy agenda compelled them to overlook much that they might have wished to attend to. Besides being incremental, the bits and pieces of disability legislation that passed after 1956 were not isolated. They were invariably

24. Ibid., p. 224.
25. U.S. Chamber of Commerce, *Policy Declarations* (Washington, D.C.: the Chamber, 1957), p. 38.

part of a large and complicated legislative bundle for social security, which was itself just one part of a long agenda of domestic legislation. Pressure groups with limited resources have to choose their targets from a large universe. Business groups, including the insurance industry, concentrated in social security on new issues of principle (health insurance) or continuing issues in which their interests were directly involved (the level of the wage base) rather than on incremental changes in which their direct interest was limited, as with disability.

The American Medical Association had been less concerned than other opponents with the principle of disability insurance and more concerned with the immediate threat of regulation. The AMA feared that the disability program would be the federal government's first step in controlling medical practice. In fact it hardly disturbed the nation's doctors, the AMA calmed down, and the issue lost the intense symbolism that had been imparted by the AMA's earlier cry of "socialized medicine."

The disability program was designed *not* to disturb doctors. In the legislative stage, politics worked to protect them. When they objected to the law, proponents changed it to meet their objections. The law specifically prohibited federal interference with the practice of medicine or with doctor-patient relationships and, more effectively, protected doctors from such interference by assigning disability determinations to state agencies. Because state vocational rehabilitation agencies, which were expected to have this responsibility, already had working relations with doctors, this arrangement imposed the lightest possible burden of innovation. Nor did BOASI leaders invite contest with their conduct of administration. Program executives were thoroughly pragmatic, accommodating, and conciliatory. By their determination to focus on the administrative task, they helped to remove attention from the symbolic conflict. Despite dissent from their own staff subordinates, who distrusted the states and were inconvenienced by having to deal with them, they determined to develop the intergovernmental partnership (recognizing it to be a leading condition of accommodation to the medical profession); and they engaged an advisory committee of doctors to help prepare disability standards. Looking back on the experience, Arthur Hess thought that, beyond easing acceptance of the disability program, it had done much to pave the way for medicare:

I have said it many times—that the way in which we went about administering disability insurance, for example, through the consultations and rapport that we established with organized medicine around the medical subject of disability, was an important precedent for medicare. Almost the sole basis for establishing lines of communication over time and getting into professional dealings with organized medicine that have now paid off in medicare was the fact that we had a specific disability administrative process that we could meet around the table on. . . . We had to demonstrate that it was possible for doctors to talk to Social Security people and still go home and not feel that they had been socialized or regimented. I think disability did this.[26]

As the pressure of doctors and business groups against disability insurance subsided, Congress began to come under pressure from a new group, albeit unorganized, consisting of beneficiaries and potential beneficiaries of the program. Congressmen heard many complaints from individuals whose claims had been handled slowly or denied for what did not seem good reasons, and they began asking why the program was so restrictive. So voluminous were such complaints that they caused the Ways and Means Committee to investigate administration of disability insurance in 1959. Program executives who only a few years before had had to meet conservative objections to their proposal now had to answer complaints about the strictness of administration.[27]

It is clear in retrospect that passage of the law profoundly changed the political milieu in which Congress deliberated, and, as the political milieu changed, so did the role of Congress and its orientation to the program. Initially, it reflected—and, by the working of internal processes, resolved—the pressure group conflict. Subsequently it supplied constituent service by liberalizing the law and legitimating a liberalized administration of it, as well as handling individual cases of complaint.

This change could occur rapidly because Congress is highly responsive to immediate and proximate pressures—the characteristic, presumably, of a body whose members are subject to near-constant tests of their popularity. As Congress in general does not look far into the future, it does not in general remember much of the past. The Ways and Means subcommittee that investigated disability administration in 1959 had to have the politics of 1952–56 explained to it. Most of the members had not been on the committee four years before. Hess recalled with

26. Hess, OHC, p. 44.
27. Besides the hearings cited in note 21, see *Disability Insurance Fact Book* prepared by the staff of the Subcommittee on Administration of Social Security Laws of the House Ways and Means Committee, 86 Cong. 1 sess. (GPO, 1959), and *Administration of Social Security Disability Insurance Program,* Preliminary Report to the House Committee on Ways and Means (GPO, 1960).

some amusement the committee's attitude toward removing the age limitation of fifty for cash benefits:

> One of the funniest things that happened in a long time—I guess it was 1960 or whenever the age fifty limitation for cash payments was repealed—was members of the Ways and Means Committee sort of looking at each other and saying, "Well, there's no logic to age fifty. Whatever made anyone think that that had any sense to it?" When we recalled that some of those very same members just a couple of years earlier had been accepting very logical rationalizations that people were giving them as to why you're much less likely to be rehabilitated after fifty and why it was a much more logical approach to at least go that far if you weren't going to meet the cost of going all the way.[28]

In sum, the explanation for the changed politics of the disability program lies in the changed orientation of Congress, and this in turn is explained by a fundamental change in the pressures brought to bear on Congress after the program was established. To this institutional explanation must be added the point that incremental change in whatever institutional setting has less potential for generating conflict than change that involves an innovation in principle. That is why program executives, even when undertaking an innovation in principle, tried to cut and clothe it in a fashion that made it seem merely incremental.

The Outcome

Though disability assistance was established first, in response to the conservatives' hope that it would be the prime government program for the purpose, it was very quickly surpassed by insurance. In fiscal 1958, the first full year of disability insurance operations, benefit payments exceeded federal disability grants to the states by $45 million. In number of recipients, insurance passed assistance in 1959, soon after dependents' benefits were authorized.

The initial disability tax rate of 0.25 percent each on employer payrolls and employee wages was supposed to be sufficient indefinitely, assuming, of course, no subsequent liberalization. In this part of the social security program, unlike OASI, the tax rate was theoretically a "level premium." That is, instead of being graduated as was the rate in the basic program, it was set in 1956 at a level that was expected to finance the program for all time. It was understood that an early surplus

28. Hess, OHC, pp. 41–42.

would develop in the disability insurance trust fund, and conservatives feared—correctly, as it happened—that this would facilitate liberalizations.

The initial rate proved adequate for almost a decade. In 1966 it was raised to 0.35 percent. Another raise to 0.475 percent followed in 1968, and a third, to 0.55 percent, in 1970. Further increases were in prospect as the program continued to grow. Financial deficiencies had become chronic in the disability insurance program, according to a report of the Ways and Means Committee staff issued in 1974.[29]

29. *Committee Staff Report on the Disability Insurance Program,* prepared by the staff of the House Committee on Ways and Means (GPO, 1974), p. 1.

CHAPTER SIXTEEN

Medicare

FROM DISCUSSIONS by the Committee on Economic Security in 1934–35 through enactment of medicare by a divided Congress thirty years later, the issue of a federal program of health insurance remained extremely controversial. Fearing official regulation of professional practices and privileges, the American Medical Association was implacably opposed to all proposals and waged recurrent wars of propaganda against them. This heightened the ideological and emotional stakes for the proponents of health insurance, who came to include, besides officials of the Social Security Administration, the Democratic administrations of Presidents Truman, Kennedy, and Johnson, the most liberal members of Congress, organized labor, and various associated private and quasi-public groups. Conservative and liberal coalitions were mustered on each side, and millions of dollars were spent on mass persuasion.

Because health insurance was so controversial, it was exceptionally difficult for program-oriented policymakers to manage. Widespread participation complicated the work of bargaining and coalition-building and caused tensions between program-oriented proponents of health insurance and their more partisan and ideological allies. Even among the program-oriented, overriding ideological differences obstructed agreement, and health insurance proved hard to reconcile, both in doctrine and policymaking procedure, with the basic program of cash benefits. The persistent opposition of Ways and Means Committee Chairman Wilbur Mills clearly owed much to Mills's strong sense of proprietary responsibility for the social security program and his fear that the introduction of health care would substantially increase its cost and alter its character.

The Early Campaigns

It is useful to compare disability and health insurance. Both were considered by the staff of the Committee on Economic Security in 1934 but not included in the committee's recommendations to the President or the President's recommendations to Congress. Both were then taken up by the Interdepartmental Committee to Coordinate Health and Welfare Activities, which the President appointed upon signing the act, and by the Social Security Board's Office of Research and Statistics. Bills that they drafted were introduced in Congress by sympathetic liberals—Senators Robert F. Wagner and James Murray and Representative John Dingell—when, for strategic reasons, President Roosevelt withheld sponsorship.[1] Yet the greater controversiality of health insurance very early made it much harder to manage. SSB officials submitted disability but not health insurance to the 1937–39 and 1947–48 advisory councils. Nor did they submit health insurance to the committees that had jurisdiction over social insurance in Congress—Ways and Means in the House and Finance in the Senate. Early health insurance bills omitted or were vague about revenue provisions so that they would be referred to committees having jurisdiction over public welfare. These committees held hearings but never issued favorable reports.

This unpromising political situation, in which they had no active support from the President and practically none from Congress, did not deter the proponents. Nowhere is the aggressiveness of social security program executives better demonstrated than in these early campaigns for national health insurance. Quixotic in retrospect, these efforts were sustained by a wartime hope that great things would be possible in the postwar period; by the inspiring example of England, which had produced the Beveridge plan; and by the native zeal of the prime movers inside the SSB, Wilbur Cohen and I. S. Falk, the director of research and statistics, who, with Altmeyer's backing, drafted the bills and arranged for their introduction by Wagner, Murray, and Dingell.

1. On the early history of health insurance, see Daniel S. Hirshfield, *The Lost Reform: The Campaign for Compulsory Health Insurance in the United States from 1932 to 1943* (Harvard University Press, 1970), and Peter A. Corning, *The Evolution of Medicare: From Idea to Law,* Department of Health, Education, and Welfare, Office of Research and Statistics, Research Report No. 29 (GPO, 1969). The oral history project on social security at Columbia University contains a wealth of material.

Altmeyer later described Wagner and Murray to an interviewer as "pragmatists and liberals" who were not much interested in philosophy or in technical details and who would introduce a bill if their advisers told them it was a good one.[2]

After Roosevelt died, the proponents picked up very important allies in President Truman and Oscar Ewing, Truman's federal security administrator, both of whom seized the issue with a will. Truman used it in his campaign of 1948, and Altmeyer surmised that Ewing, whom he judged to have political ambitions, hoped to use it himself on the way to higher office. There was a time of high hope after Truman's surprise victory in 1948.

This moment passed quickly. Congress was no more willing to act than before. The escalation of the issue into the high politics of a presidential campaign had not mobilized a partisan majority for it but had stirred the organized medical profession to a newly active opposition, which was carried across the nation in a massive grass-roots campaign against "socialized medicine." The defeat of several liberal members of Congress in the elections of 1950, men whom the AMA had actively opposed, was widely interpreted as a definitive popular rejection of national health insurance.[3] Democratic party leaders were intimidated for the time being, and social security program executives were chastened. Although it was probably no more a "referendum" on social insurance than the election of 1936, the election of 1950 was the only such "referendum" that the program executives ever "lost."

They did not give up, but changed their tactics completely. An incremental approach was substituted for a comprehensive one.[4] In the Wagner-Murray-Dingell bills of 1943, 1945, and 1947, health insurance covered virtually all kinds of care for virtually the whole work force and their dependents; it was advanced simultaneously with other major

2. Interview with Arthur J. Altmeyer, Oral History Collection, Columbia University (1967), p. 165. Similarly, Wilbur Cohen recalled that "Senator Wagner heard us out and, after five minutes' discussion, gave us his O.K.," according to Richard Harris's account of medicare politics. ("Annals of Legislation," *New Yorker,* July 2, 1966, p. 40.) Harris's study, which focuses heavily on the lobbying of the AMA, appeared initially in four issues of *New Yorker* (July 2, 9, 16, and 23, 1966) and later as a book, *The Sacred Trust* (New American Library, 1966).

3. The AMA's campaign activity is described in Stanley Kelley, Jr., *Professional Public Relations and Political Power* (Johns Hopkins Press, 1956), chap. 3.

4. Theodore R. Marmor, *The Politics of Medicare* (Chicago: Aldine Publishing Company, 1973), chap. 1.

changes in the social insurance program when it was not actually combined with them in one omnibus piece of legislation. After 1950 health
insurance proposals were cut back and made to wait upon disability
insurance.

Disability Insurance as a Prelude to Medicare

Much in the contest over disability insurance anticipated the later
struggle over medicare and helped to prepare program executives for
it. There was the same process of cutting and trimming in an effort to
mollify opposition and make the change seem a modest addition to old
age insurance rather than a big new departure. There was the same
responsive, pragmatic accommodation to intermediary organizations
that would have a role in administration—state vocational rehabilitation
agencies in disability insurance, hospitals and insurance carriers in the
later case of medicare. There was the same decision in Congress to
enact first the public assistance alternative—a categorical grant-in-aid
program for the disabled in 1950, and a program of medical assistance
for the aged in 1960.

More than a political trial run for medicare, the passage of disability
insurance was a necessary prelude. The drive for health insurance would
not be resumed until disability coverage was safely out of the way, but
once it was out of the way, program executives did not lose a moment.
"It was probably in the fall of 1956," a leading medicare planner recalled
for an interviewer, "[that] we had a work plan meeting with Bob Ball,
and he said at that time that the next big item we would have in the
social security field would be this health insurance fight."[5] Ball himself,
when asked to explain why the effort got started in 1957, said he could
think of no explanation "except possibly that '56 saw the passage of a
good disability program; and the people interested in expanding social
security I think quite logically turned to what's next."[6] The opposition
of an incumbent Republican administration was a disadvantage but
not a deterrent. The experience with disability insurance had shown

5. Interview with Irwin Wolkstein, Oral History Collection, Columbia University (1966), p. 2. (Hereafter Wolkstein, OHC.)

6. Interview with Robert M. Ball, Oral History Collection, Columbia University
(1967–68), p. 14. (Hereafter Ball, OHC.)

that, thanks to a Democratic Congress, the alliance with organized labor, and the free-floating advocacy of Wilbur Cohen, major expansion could be achieved even during a Republican presidency.

The Pro-Medicare Coalition

With three years of the Eisenhower administration remaining, social security program executives began in earnest to prepare a passable piece of health insurance legislation. More than one office of the Social Security Administration worked at this task: the Division of Research and Statistics and the Division of Program Analysis in the Bureau of Old Age and Survivors Insurance contested for this prize. In 1957 they worked on more than one bill, but the one that made history as the antecedent of medicare was the Forand bill, so called for Representative Aime J. Forand of Rhode Island, who introduced it. It would have provided surgical expenses and hospital and nursing-home care for the recipients of old age and survivors insurance. Thus it was closely tied to the established program.

According to the best contemporary account of the passage of medicare, the Forand bill was prepared by Nelson Cruikshank, Robert Ball, Wilbur Cohen, and I. S. Falk in a period of a few months during which they communicated mainly by letter and telephone.[7] Only Ball, as an official of the SSA, and Cruikshank, as social security director for the AFL-CIO, were based in Washington. Though often in Washington, Cohen was living in Ann Arbor, and Falk had moved to New Haven as a Yale faculty member after the Eisenhower administration removed him as director of research and statistics. To say that the four of them wrote the bill is doubtless an oversimplification and probably overstates the role of both Falk, whose participation diminished when he left office, and Ball, who was constrained by his office. The SSA staff worked on it, too, and there was much back-and-forth between the SSA staff and Cruikshank's staff as details were worked out and successive versions were prepared after 1957. Whatever the precise composition of the original drafting group, it is true that at this early stage the work was being done by the inner core of program proprietors—current or former officials of the SSA and their close allies in organized labor—who were invariably the prime movers on behalf of expansion.

7. Harris, *New Yorker,* July 9, 1966, p. 35.

Once prepared, the bill was offered to high-ranking Democrats on the Ways and Means Committee for sponsorship, but those above Forand turned it down. Cruikshank later recalled for an interviewer how Forand's sponsorship came about:

We naturally tried to get the chairman, who was Jere Cooper at the time, and he didn't want to do it because it was a touchy thing; he was from Tennessee; it was near the end of the session, and he didn't want to become involved. Now, he was a pretty liberal man. Jere Cooper had carried a lot of liberal legislation and had strong support from the railway unions in his district, but he just didn't want to get another chairman's bill in at that time. And then the next in line, of course, was Wilbur Mills, and Wilbur Mills didn't want to touch it, which we rather expected. . . . Jere Cooper was not well, and it was thought generally at that time that Mills would soon be chairman of the committee, and he was already the power on the committee. So the next in line was Aime Forand, and we went to him three or four times as soon as we had the bill drafted, and he said he'd look it over and decide what he wanted to do. Finally, when we were pressing him, it was near the end of the session, he said, "Well, you boys assure me that this is soundly drawn?" and we said, "Yes." He said, "All right, I'm just not going to have time to read it, but I'll put it in and I'll read the speech." That's how it became the Forand bill.[8]

Though a liberal, Forand had no particular identification with the social insurance program. He had shown more interest in public assistance. Nor did he have influence within the committee, but to have sponsorship in Ways and Means at all was an asset to the proponents—one that they had lacked a decade earlier and that made it possible to get a hearing. They were far, however, from having the support of a committee majority or of Mills, its most powerful member, who would soon begin a seventeen-year reign as chairman. Mills's opposition was the biggest single obstacle to their success, and they would struggle against it for the next eight years.

In the ensuing campaign, program executives remained prime movers as always, but they had to share power and action with many others in a broad coalition. In its truncated form, designed to benefit only the aged, health insurance proved far more attractive to politicians than it had been a decade earlier. There were more liberal politicians in national office than in 1949, there were more aged members of the population, and the aged constituted an appealing group, a natural object of public sympathy. As the 1960 election approached, these elements combined in such a way that health care for the aged suddenly became a major

8. Interview with Nelson H. Cruikshank, Oral History Collection, Columbia University (1967), pp. 425–26.

national issue, one that figured prominently in the presidential campaign and caused the medicare coalition to burgeon into a varied and formidable political force.[9]

One politician who sensed the potential of this issue was Senator Pat McNamara of Michigan, who in 1959 was named chairman of a new Senate subcommittee on problems of the aged and aging.[10] McNamara was to be up for reelection in 1960 and was trying to increase his visibility. The Senate leadership named him to the new position rather than John F. Kennedy, whose request for it followed McNamara's by a few days and who in any case would not have to defend his Senate seat until 1964. (Kennedy, of course, had other plans.) Served by an aggressive staff, this committee held nationwide hearings at which elderly citizens testified to their plight. The hearings got immense publicity, helped to make a national issue of medical care, and ended early in 1960 with a recommendation to expand the social security program to include health benefits.

Organized labor also helped to push the issue to national prominence. No newcomer to the campaign for health insurance, labor had backed the Wagner-Murray-Dingell bill, but neither the leadership nor the membership had been much aroused in the 1940s. Other issues central to the very existence of labor organizations had competed for attention. More secure by 1960, labor was also more deeply engaged in issues of social policy generally. Much of the impetus came from the United Auto Workers, politically the most militant of the major national unions. In March 1960 the UAW sponsored a rally for health insurance at the State Fair Grounds in Detroit at which the candidates for the Democratic nomination for the presidency appeared. Kennedy led off with a fiery speech praising the Forand bill and condemning the Republican opposition. There was an excellent response, and Kennedy, who had already shown much interest in the issue, was thereafter committed to it.

9. For a detailed account of the burgeoning of the issue, see James L. Sundquist, *Politics and Policy: The Eisenhower, Kennedy, and Johnson Years* (Brookings Institution, 1968), pp. 296–308.

10. Without setting up a specialized subcommittee, the Senate Committee on Labor and Public Welfare had begun to get involved in problems of the aging in 1956, when it hired Cohen as a consultant on the subject. Under authority of a Senate resolution, he prepared a ten-volume report. Creation of the subcommittee followed and the subcommittee in turn evolved into the Special Committee on the Aging, authorized by Senate Resolution 33 of the Eighty-seventh Congress (1961). The initial authorizing resolution contemp'ated only a temporary existence for the special committee, but the authorization has been regularly renewed.

After Kennedy won the election, the medicare coalition automatically expanded to include the leaders of the new administration—partisan figures in the White House and in the top appointive positions in the Department of Health, Education, and Welfare. One of these was Cohen, who had long advised Kennedy on social welfare matters, headed a postelection task force for him on health and social security, and in 1961 received appointment as assistant secretary of health, education, and welfare for legislation, which ended his not-so-inhibiting exile in Ann Arbor. Health insurance was now high on the official agenda of the administration, and the leading legislative strategist of social security was now highly placed in a crucial administrative post.

All this created a radically different situation from the late 1950s, when the Forand bill, with little fanfare, received hearings from the Ways and Means Committee and adverse reports from the Republican administration. To have all these fresh participants, high-spirited and hungry for legislative victories, added immeasurably to the force of the health insurance campaign, but also burdened program executives, Cohen especially, with the task of managing a coalition in which motives and orientations were quite mixed. The program-oriented members at the core of the coalition now had to reconcile their objectives and tactics with others who were constituency-oriented (and dedicated above all to serving the aged), party-oriented (and dedicated to building a mass electoral following for the President), or ideological (and dedicated to winning a contest of principle against profit-making adversaries in the private sector). Tensions erupted at many points.

The staff director of the McNamara committee sensed that the program proprietors were apprehensive about the committee. He told an interviewer:

. . . those involved in the social security field over the years (and this included people in the SSA and . . . guys like Nelson Cruikshank in organized labor) were very much concerned about this new committee coming into the field of health insurance and perhaps unsettling the sensitive relationships that had been built up in the Ways and Means Committee and in the Finance Committee. So we had this matter to contend with of these brash new guys who wanted to come in and kind of revolutionize the publicity situation and upset a lot of these working relationships.[11]

The uneasiness was mutual. Cohen's pragmatism made him suspect to some of the more ideological members of the coalition. There were

11. Interview with Sidney Spector, Oral History Collection, Columbia University (1966), pp. 18–19.

insinuations that he had "sold out" in 1960 by cooperating with Representative Mills and Senator Robert Kerr in preparing a piece of public assistance legislation for the aged who could not afford medical care. Senator McNamara, among others, regarded this as treachery. Because of his long association with Cohen, Cruikshank was likewise suspect to some of the more militant elements in organized labor. Ideological liberals were purer about the social insurance principle than program executives, who had concluded from experience that a categorical public assistance program would not long stand in the way of the progress of social insurance. It had not done so in regard to old age or disability insurance.

There were also differences over tactics. The program executives, fundamentally accommodationist, favored negotiations with interested groups and with holders of power—Mills, to wit—in the legislature, an approach that would preserve the working relations and cohesion of the programmatic network. Those with a partisan or ideological orientation, who had no interest in preserving that cohesion, wanted to rouse the public and bring electoral defeat to, or pressure upon, their legislative opponents and shame to opposing pressure groups. The latter group, in which the central figure was HEW Under Secretary Ivan Nestingen, bore considerable animosity to Cohen, who later told an interviewer that it had been almost impossible for him to conduct negotiations "without having to spend a lot of time always looking behind me to see if somebody was cutting my throat while I wasn't looking."[12]

Both tactics were necessary and both worked slowly. The 1960 election narrowed the anti-medicare majority in the Ways and Means Committee and so did that of 1962; two Democratic vacancies on the committee occurred in 1962, and the President and party leaders in the House cooperated to fill both with medicare supporters. Meanwhile, Cohen, Ball, and their planning staff in the SSA were constantly testing new proposals and compromises in order to woo the various health interest groups, especially the American Hospital Association; meet the arguments of the AMA, even if it was not possible to negotiate directly with this dogmatic opponent; and win over the liberal Republican or conservative Democratic votes that could make the difference. They tried to do all this without alienating organized labor, which resisted such measures as voluntary options, introducing large deductible amounts

12. Interview with Wilbur J. Cohen by David G. McComb for the Lyndon Baines Johnson Library (1968); copy in John F. Kennedy Library, Waltham, Mass.

into the benefit schedule, or giving a large administrative role to private organizations, especially if they were profit-makers.[13] Much progress was made between 1960 and 1964, but not enough to win a congressional majority or, crucially, to win over Mills.

The Opposition

Two factors made the opposition to health insurance formidable: the persistence and ardor of the AMA, which threw all the considerable resources it could muster into the propaganda fight, and the relative cohesion of the bipartisan conservative coalition in Congress.

The AMA was the arch opponent of the expansion of social insurance, incomparably more active and committed than the insurance industry ever had been. Whereas the insurance industry seemed uncertain of the effects of government action on its interests, the organized medical profession believed itself to be fundamentally threatened. And with good reason. The first Wagner-Murray-Dingell bill, which was introduced in Congress in 1943, would have radically restricted the freedom of doctors and reduced their incomes. While it would have permitted doctors to remain outside the program, it would have required patients to select a doctor from among participating physicians and given the Surgeon General extensive powers to set fee schedules and limit each doctor's number of patients.[14] Subsequent bills were steadily modified to reduce the threat until finally, in bills of the early 1960s, physicians' services were omitted altogether and the SSA proposal was confined to hospital and nursing-home care, but the doctors were not placated by compromise. Alarmed by the example of England, where medical practice had been socialized, distrustful of officials in the SSA, and fearful of the long-run consequences of any federal action no matter how limited the initial provisions, the AMA maintained a rigid and vociferous opposition.

In the health insurance fight, Southern and border-state Democrats in general lined up with the Republican opposition. Politically, this was the big difference between disability and health insurance. The leading opponents of health insurance in the two houses, Mills and Kerr, had

13. Ball and Cohen themselves disagreed over voluntary options—Cohen was for and Ball against them, and President Kennedy settled the difference in Cohen's favor.

14. "The American Medical Association: Power, Purpose, and Politics in Organized Medicine," *Yale Law Journal*, vol. 63 (May 1954), p. 1009.

been leading proponents of disability insurance, and whatever side they were on gained greatly by having them. When Kerr died in 1963, Senate opposition was critically weakened, and a medicare bill passed the next year, as an amendment to a social security bill that came from the House. Mills's resistance then became more important than ever.

Proponents struggled unsuccessfully to understand Mills's motives and to find some formula, some concession, that would win him over. Some of the proponents believed that he was influenced by the doctors in his own district, but Robert Ball, who is as thoroughly experienced, shrewd, and credible a witness on Mills's motives as anyone but Mills himself could be, had a much less simplistic explanation for the latter's position. It was partly tactical, Ball thought. He told an interviewer that Mills was not "ordinarily one, particularly as chairman of that committee, to take the lead in a brand-new development with as many departures and as many complications as this had. I think one would kind of expect him to come along with it when there was a significant consensus for it." But Ball also acknowledged that Mills was concerned about the substance of the proposal and its effects on social security. "He's a middle-of-the-road type person, very conscientious, and very much concerned about the stability of the program generally and the financing of it, and there was enough doubt about this [proposal] to be disturbing."[15]

Mills feared the costs of health insurance and the effects of unanticipated costs on the basic program. Also he was reluctant to graft payments for services, which bore no necessary relation to individual wages or tax payments, onto a program in which benefit payments had been systematically related to the individual's wages.[16] Sensing Mills's concern that health insurance was fundamentally incompatible with the basic principles of old age insurance, program executives did their best to argue that it was a logical and necessary extension. Without it, they said, too many of the aged would be forced by the cost of health care to resort to public assistance, contrary to the basic policy choice made in 1935 and 1950. To protect the dignity of the nation's elderly and to avoid burdening the general taxpayer with the cost of their health care, "we must once again place our main emphasis on social insurance," the

15. Ball, OHC, pp. 19–20.
16. Interview with John W. Byrnes, Oral History Collection, Columbia University (1967), p. 3.

administration said.[17] Here was the familiar if dubious claim that money raised from the payroll tax was money saved.

It is testimony to the power of programmatic doctrine that both Mills and the executive proponents of medicare appealed to such doctrine at this time, and it is a testimony to its inconsistency and ambiguity that, from opposite sides of the contest, each could do so. Both maintained a programmatic perspective, but whereas the executives' welfare objectives implied expansion, Mills's preference for fiscal responsibility and for consistency in relating benefits to wages implied merely maintenance. As the principal legislative proprietor of the program, Mills wished to keep his options open and to protect a set of arrangements that had (as he believed) successfully balanced the public's appetite for benefits against the need for fiscal discipline. Health insurance, with its highly unpredictable costs, could upset this balance. Before long it might compel the introduction of general revenues, which Mills feared would remove all fiscal restraint; require frequent increases in the wage base, which was always controversial; jeopardize the biennial increases in cash benefits, which members of Congress had come to take for granted as election-year offerings to their constituents; and undermine the politically useful (because popular) idea that benefits were based on wages and tax payments. Whereas program executives discounted or even welcomed these risks (they would have been quite pleased to raise the wage base and would not have been much troubled by the use of general revenues), Mills was disturbed. Health insurance threatened to undermine precisely those attributes of old age insurance that he valued most.

The legislative opponents of health insurance followed two strategies: delay and preemption. Mills held hearings on health insurance bills but did not bring them to the floor for a vote. He also contrived alternative measures that he hoped would make health insurance unnecessary or unfeasible.

The first such measure was the Kerr-Mills Act, passed in 1960 when the pressure to do something suddenly increased in the heat of the presidential campaign. This act provided grants-in-aid to the states for a new category of public assistance called Medical Assistance to the Aged. Like public assistance programs generally, it gave benefits only to those who proved financial need, and use of it varied greatly from state to state.

17. *Medical Care for the Aged*, Hearings before the House Committee on Ways and Means, 88 Cong. 1 and 2 sess. (1963 and 1964), pt. 1, p. 27.

After 1960, much of the health insurance debate consisted of arguments about whether the Kerr-Mills approach was working. Backers of the act said it should be given more time and hinted that the Social Security Administration was sabotaging it. Backers of health insurance, speaking for this purpose through the McNamara committee, said that it was failing because many states were not participating and because those that did participate often gave inadequate coverage.[18] No matter how well the Kerr-Mills Act had worked, it would not have satisfied the proponents of an insurance program. To them, the issue was one of principle. The "better" Kerr-Mills worked, the more recipients of assistance there were, and the more insistent were they that insurance must be enacted instead. Program executives like Cohen and Ball could accept assistance only as a residual program, whereas less pragmatic proponents of health insurance could not accept it at all.

The other effort at preemption occurred in 1964, when opponents of health insurance tried for a cash benefit increase so large that it would have used up all the tax revenue on which health insurance planners had been counting. Health insurance might not have been dead, but the proponents would have borne the burden of arguing for a higher tax rate than was thought feasible or desirable at that time. The tactic failed. Surprisingly, Congress in the election year of 1964 accepted no social security benefit increase rather than a large increase that would have jeopardized health insurance. The deciding votes came in the Senate, where the opposing forces were weakened by the loss of Kerr, and in the House-Senate conference, where the Senate conferees, under pressure from the Johnson administration, stood by the Senate's position.[19]

As 1964 closed, health insurance had not yet passed, but the option of passing it remained open. The strategy of preemption had failed.

Enactment

Mills had known all along that the moment might come when he must enter into negotiations with the administration over a bill. As support for legislation increased in Congress he took a larger part in committee

18. *Performance of the States: Eighteen Months of Experience with the Medical Assistance for the Aged (Kerr-Mills) Program*, a report to the Senate Special Committee on Aging, Committee Print, 87 Cong. 2 sess. (1962).

19. In addition to the sources already cited, see Eugene Feingold, *Medicare: Policy and Politics* (San Francisco: Chandler, 1966), chapter 3 of which is a comprehensive legislative history of medicare.

hearings, and when the lopsided Democratic victory of 1964 settled the issue, he quickly took charge.

Debate then subsided, and the policymaking structure reverted to its familiar, constricted form. The Ways and Means Committee went into executive session and invited witnesses to discuss technical matters only. When the AMA persisted in opposing the bill on the ground that its defects were not merely technical, Democratic committee members were incensed. Even organized labor, close as it was to the proprietary core, found negotiations inaccessible. Negotiations were dominated by Mills and Wilbur Cohen, who was now firmly in charge on the executive side. A member of the AFL-CIO staff recalled the situation:

In many ways we were in the same position with regard to Wilbur Cohen as some of the committee members were in respect to Wilbur Mills. We were very much dependent on his judgment, and he was really the man. . . . He had the power that comes with a tremendous amount of technical know-how. He really knew his stuff, and he had the relationship with Wilbur Mills. And that was an absolutely crucial component. . . . If we had been in on all the meetings between Wilbur Mills and Wilbur Cohen, then it would be very easy to say, "But, gee, Wilbur Cohen, Mills doesn't seem to feel very strongly about this, and I think you could get him to maneuver on that." We never had that kind of information. And so when Wilbur said, "Look, this is what Mills will take," we had to believe him. I don't think Wilbur ever lied to us. I think there were days when he just wanted this issue settled or that issue settled, that he might have exaggerated in his own mind his conviction that one couldn't get any further movement out of Wilbur Mills on that.[20]

By creating a majority for medicare in the House, the 1964 election had assured a liberal victory on the basic issue, but by drawing Mills into active command of the negotiations and confining them to a narrow, program-oriented arena, it paradoxically diminished the immediate influence of the liberal, pro-medicare coalition, except for the program executives who were at its core and who now sat down with Mills and his committee to decide what should go into the bill.

Substantively, Mills was concerned above all with the financing. His dilemma, once enactment became inevitable, was how to reconcile the impending expansion with the norm of fiscal soundness.[21] Old age insur-

20. Interview with Leonard Lesser and Lisbeth Bamberger Schorr, Oral History Collection, Columbia University (1967), pp. 79–80.

21. See the speech by Mills, delivered in his district, that is the fullest explanation of his position on medicare in *Congressional Record* (October 30, 1964), pp. 24014–16. I have also relied on "Memorandum Reporting a Meeting with Representative Wilbur Mills, August 10, 1962," by Gary L. Filerman, a graduate student in political science who interviewed Mills.

ance had rested on the premise that costs could be predicted accurately and contained through use of an earmarked payroll tax and actuarial techniques that provided a margin of safety. However, even before health insurance was enacted it became clear that costs would be very hard to predict. Costs of hospitalization were rising faster than the cost of living, and as successive bills were submitted the SSA found it necessary to make substantial changes in its estimates. This made Mills very uneasy, as did the realization that the historic safety device in the actuarial estimates—the level wage assumption—could not serve the same purpose in health insurance. In the cash benefit program, to assume that wages would not rise typically had the effect of generating an "unanticipated" surplus of tax revenues when wages in fact rose. By contrast, in the hospital insurance program if wages unexpectedly rose expenditures would rise too, because expenditures depended directly on the cost of medical services. To make the estimates suitably conservative, Mills urged Robert Myers, the SSA actuary, to devise other safety factors.[22] (For his part, Myers did not mind coming under this kind of pressure. Other officials in the SSA suspected that some of the criticism that came from Mills had actually been planted by Myers, who was dissatisfied with his own estimates but could not easily have revised them in the absence of external pressure.)[23]

In view of Mills's overriding concern for fiscal conservatism and his mastery of the legislative situation, it is not surprising that the liberal sponsors of health insurance failed to enlarge their proposals after the big election victory of 1964. For them, it was enough that legislation long delayed was at last in sight. What is surprising is that enlargement of the administration's bill occurred in the Ways and Means Committee, on the initiative of members (Mills himself and John W. Byrnes) who until that moment had opposed all expansion of social insurance for the provision of health care.

Successive compromises had turned the administration's bill into a relatively modest proposal even if it was still quite controversial in principle. It did not cover doctors' fees, but was confined to the costs of hospitalization, skilled nursing-home care for recuperation, home

22. U.S. Department of Health, Education, and Welfare, SSA, Office of the Actuary, "History of Cost Estimates for Hospital Insurance," Actuarial Study No. 61 (SSA, December 1966), pp. 51–53; *Medical Care for the Aged*, Hearings, pt. 1, pp. 139–146.
23. Wolkstein, OHC, p. 67.

health services after hospitalization, and outpatient diagnostic services. The Forand bill had been broader without being comprehensive. It had covered surgeons' fees, but this provision was dropped in the early 1960s in an effort to undercut the opposition of the AMA. If doctors' services were not covered, the AMA could hardly cry "socialized medicine" or expect to be believed if it did. (Besides, some proponents of the bill feared that to pay surgeons' fees would encourage unnecessary surgery.) Conservative opponents of the health insurance bill often attacked it for being inadequate when their real objection was to the principle; tactically, they thought it better not to take a thoroughly negative stance. Presumably it was in this spirit that Byrnes, ranking Republican on the Ways and Means Committee, offered a more comprehensive alternative to the administration's bill in 1965. Modeled after the federal government's employee health benefits program, Byrnes's bill would have paid for hospitalization and nursing-home care and 80 percent of other medical expenses, including doctors' fees and prosthetic devices. In contrast to the administration's approach, participation would have been voluntary, and financing would have come both from general revenues of the federal government and monthly "premiums" paid by elderly participants. Half-facetiously, Byrnes called the Republican alternative "better-care."

No one expected the Byrnes bill to pass. Inside the SSA, no one thought that Byrnes or other Republican leaders in the House really wanted it to pass. When Mills, in executive session, proposed to combine Byrnes's plan for payment of doctors' fees with the administration's plan for hospitalization insurance, SSA officials were astounded. They guessed that Mills was calling Byrnes's bluff, and that Byrnes might decide to back off. When he did not back off, Mills told them to prepare a new draft consolidating the two approaches. The administration's proposal became part A of Medicare (Hospital Insurance Benefits for the Aged) and Byrnes's proposal, minus hospitalization, became part B (Supplementary Medical Insurance Benefits for the Aged).[24]

Mills's move was consistent with his consensual style of leadership. Typically he tried to build bipartisan support for committee bills with concessions to Republican views. What was anomalous, and therefore puzzling, was that the concession to Byrnes entailed an expansion that neither Byrnes nor Mills "really" wanted, judging from their recent

24. 79 Stat. 290 and 79 Stat. 301.

behavior. But it was an expansion that Mills knew was bound to come: if health insurance were enacted without coverage of doctors' fees, it was only a matter of time (and probably very little time) until pressure from the elderly, from organized labor, and from the SSA made action unavoidable. The Byrnes proposal was a way of forestalling such pressures. Tactically, it was preemptive, and it was much more acceptable to conservative interests than compulsory coverage of doctors' services under social insurance would have been; it was voluntary in principle, placed most of the responsibility for administration in the hands of "carriers" (that is, private organizations under contract to the government) rather than the SSA, and promised to pay physicians' "reasonable" charges with few and vague tests of what was "reasonable."[25] It would also meet the desire of program executives and allied interests for government action, yet do so in a way that minimized disruption of existing private arrangements for the provision of physician care.

So interpreted, Mills's acceptance of Byrnes's proposal remains puzzling in only one important respect. For years Mills had been firmly opposed to the use of general revenues in social insurance on the ground that it would open the fiscal floodgates, yet he now accepted it in one part of medicare. But this too ceases to be puzzling if Mills thought of the Byrnes proposal as a buffer against further changes in social insurance rather than as an addition to it. As an addition, it was incompatible. It undermined the principle of self-support (and hence "actuarial soundness") through the payroll tax. However, given Mills's view that the whole scheme of health insurance was a threat to the actuarial soundness of social security, it made just as much sense to accept the proposal as to confront eventually the payment of doctors' fees through the basic system. In Mills's view there would have been risks to the program either way.

Surprising as Byrnes's expansive proposal seemed, it was consistent with one strand of conservative Republican thought on the subject of social security. Byrnes had been one of a handful of Republicans to vote against the 1950 amendments on the ground that the insurance analogy was false and likely to undermine fiscal restraint.[26] He would have provided benefits to all the elderly, without regard to work history or payroll tax payments, and financed them out of general revenues, a plan that

25. Interview with Robert J. Myers, Oral History Collection, Columbia University (1967), p. 19; Ball, OHC, p. 24.

26. See pp. 225, 241–42.

would have left benefit levels much more open to debate than they were under contributory social insurance. In 1965, Byrnes harked back to this old argument. "Under the payroll tax," he told the House, "an erroneous concept has been sold to the people that they have paid for their benefits, that they have bought something as a matter of right, under such a concept there is no flexibility to make changes because the people tell you, 'We have bought this, and you cannot make any change except to liberalize it.' "[27]

Mills rose to counter Byrnes's argument. "A payroll tax," he said, "will tend to limit the growth of the benefit and will tend to do so to a greater extent than will be the case if that benefit cost is placed in the general fund of the Treasury"—to which Byrnes replied quite simply that he disagreed.[28] Expert and knowledgeable, with forty-six years of experience in the House and forty-one years on the Ways and Means Committee between them, the two men could not agree on the actual consequences of one or the other method of financing. Such was the political ambiguity inherent in social security financing; it confounded even the most canny and experienced men.

Mills's decision to incorporate a portion of Byrnes's proposal did not win Republican support for the whole bill. Republicans on Ways and Means continued to oppose the incorporation of hospitalization in the social insurance program. The central fact, according to the minority, was that because the costs of this service benefit were unpredictable, they threatened to undermine the "soundness" of old age insurance. (To drive the point home, the minority quoted from a speech in 1964 by Chairman Mills.)[29] The Republicans put forth Byrnes's voluntary plan whereby health care for the aged would be financed with a combination of general revenues and individual premiums. When Byrnes offered this to the House as a substitute for the committee bill, 191 members voted for it and 236 against, a surprisingly close vote in which many Southern Democrats joined Republicans in favoring the Byrnes proposal. Northern Democrats favored the committee bill, which covered hospitalization under social insurance. This remained to the end the liberals' overriding objective, and to the end it was a divisive issue. Even on final passage, after the Republican attempt to substitute the Byrnes proposal had

27. *Congressional Record* (April 7, 1965), p. 7223.
28. Ibid.
29. *Social Security Amendments of 1965*, H. Rept. 213, 89 Cong. 1 sess. (1965), p. 247.

failed, a majority of Republicans voted no in both the House and Senate, persisting in a degree of partisanship unusual in issues related to social security.

The partial adoption at the last minute of a Republican alternative to the insurance approach raises the intriguing question of whether such an alternative would have been seriously considered had it been proposed earlier. No alternative comparable to Byrnes's comprehensive bill had been offered. Among proponents of action, program executives monopolized the initiative. For nearly a decade, they and their allies sustained a campaign for expansion of the insurance program. They were able to sustain it until, through electoral fortunes, it was won. However, it was not until the election of 1964 assured them of victory that the Republican party in Congress ceased to resist at the public-private boundary. Not until it was certain that the boundary would be breached in a massive way, and that a federally financed program of health care for all the aged would be enacted, did the Republicans offer a distinctive way to do it, different in principle from social insurance.[30]

The Aftermath

Opponents of the administration's proposal of hospitalization insurance had argued that it would just be the beginning. "It will grow; it will expand; it will increase," Robert Kerr had said, with senatorial re-

30. Over the years, Republicans had developed a variety of answers to the Democrats' plan for compulsory health insurance. In the 1940s, Senator Robert A. Taft had submitted bills that would have authorized federal grants to the states for support of the medically indigent. Somewhat later, the Flanders-Ives proposal, sponsored by two liberal Republicans, would have encouraged a voluntary nationwide prepayment program for the whole population, with a federal subsidy where needed. In the mid-1950s, the Eisenhower administration advanced a proposal to permit insurance carriers to pool substandard health risks, and another that would have created a federal reinsurance corporation for health insurance carriers. In the early 1960s, when the issue heated up, both Arthur S. Flemming, as Eisenhower's secretary of HEW, and Senator Jacob Javits of New York led a liberal Republican search for an alternative that would involve the participation of state governments or make individual participation voluntary. None of these alternatives ever had widespread or wholehearted support from the Republican party or from conservative interest groups, let alone from the Democrats who controlled Congress, if not the administration, most of the time. For a summary of the innumerable array of health care proposals advanced from all sources between 1935 and 1957, see Agnes W. Brewster, *Health Insurance and Related Proposals for Financing Personal Health Services* (GPO, 1958).

dundancy. "We are not staring at a sweet old lady in bed with her kimono and nightcap," said Louisiana's Russell Long. "We are looking into the eyes of the wolf that ate Red Riding Hood's grandma." The aged would get ever broader coverage until the federal government was paying for eyeglasses and false teeth. Beyond the aged, coverage would be extended to the disabled, and then to other groups, and finally to everyone. Long predicted that the average wage earner would soon be paying more in social security taxes than in income taxes.[31]

This was a plausible fear given the pattern of expansion that had characterized other parts of the social insurance program and the manifest potential of medical care. Nothing seemed more predictable in 1965 than that the incremental pattern would be repeated after enactment. Yet this pattern was much less pronounced in medicare than in other parts of the insurance program.

In regard to the coverage of physician care, the Byrnes proposal successfully preempted the program executives' logical next move. Whereas the politics of disability insurance worked to lay the logical foundation for next steps, the politics of medicare worked to preclude them. In disability politics, compromise had taken the form of marginal reductions of program elements, and, when the fight was over, the reductions promptly began to be restored. In the politics of health insurance, compromise had instead taken the form of enacting an alternative to social insurance. At least in the short run, this act of preemption was effective. Rather than a vacuum inviting further action, program executives were faced with an anomalous adjunct to their program. Their initial reaction was to integrate rather than expand it. Through the medium of the 1969–71 advisory council, they recommended that part B of medicare (Byrnes's discordant contribution) be consolidated with part A (hospitalization insurance) and that the whole be financed through a combination of employer payroll taxes, employee payroll taxes, and general revenues. Payment of premiums by the beneficiaries of part B would have been eliminated.[32]

Regarding part A, program executives did develop a substantial agenda of expansion, consisting of proposals to cover the disabled and to cover the cost of drugs prescribed outside of the hospital. Congress approved the first of these proposals after several years of delay and flirted with, but failed to act upon, the second. It also enacted a few

31. *Congressional Record* (July 16, 1962), pp. 13631, 13664–66.
32. H. Doc. 92-80, pp. 54–55.

relatively minor liberalizations of coverage under both parts of the program, such as a slight addition to the number of patient-days covered under hospitalization insurance and the addition of physical therapy and speech pathology services under part B, but it considered many more such liberalizations than it actually approved. Nor did it take action to consolidate parts A and B.[33]

Along with measures of expansion, several measures of contraction also appeared on the agenda of medicare policymaking in the early 1970s. By increasing deductibles and coinsurance, the Nixon administration in 1973 proposed to shift more of the cost of medicare to the beneficiaries, and the Ford administration made similar proposals two years later. Such measures found no congressional support whatsoever, yet their very appearance under official sponsorship represented a significant deviation from the deeply imprinted pattern of automatic, incremental expansion.

The explanation for the relatively weak repetition of the incremental pattern is that the initial enactment proved far more costly than anyone expected. Mills had been right in fearing that costs would be unpredictable, and wrong in supposing that he and Myers had contrived an adequate margin for error. Hospital admission rates were much higher and hospitalization costs rose very much faster than expected, with the result that Myers had to keep correcting his estimates and Congress had to keep increasing the tax rate merely to finance the original program of hospitalization insurance. The 1965 law had imposed a modest initial tax of 0.35 percent on both employers and employees and stipulated increases to 0.5 percent in 1967, 0.55 percent in 1973, 0.6 percent in 1976, 0.7 percent in 1980, and 0.8 percent in 1987. In reality, the rate reached 1 percent in 1973. Meanwhile, the monthly premium paid by participants in part B had risen from $3.00 to $5.80. Instead of urging the SSA to expand coverage for the benefit of aggrieved constituents, Congress criticized it for failing to control costs. A report of the Senate Finance Committee staff in 1970 charged the SSA with following a "costly policy of laissez-faire with respect to physicians' fees under medicare."[34]

33. For a comprehensive review of legislative developments in medicare, see Robert J. Myers, *Social Security* (McCahan Foundation, 1975), chap. 7, and Myers, *Medicare* (Irwin, 1970).

34. *Medicare and Medicaid: Problems, Issues, and Alternatives,* Staff Report to the Senate Committee on Finance, Committee Print, 91 Cong. 1 sess. (GPO, 1970), p. 62. See also *Medicare and Medicaid,* Hearings before the Senate Committee on Finance, 91 Cong. 1 sess. (GPO, 1969), and *Medicare and Medicaid,* Hearings before the Senate Committee on Finance, 91 Cong. 2 sess. (GPO, 1970), pts. 1 and 2.

There was something startling and perverse about this congressional stance. The insistence on stricter supervision was coming from a Congress that for years had been immobilized by the protests of the AMA. The pattern of boundary politics, which had for so long pitted the medical profession and its allies in business against the SSA and its allies in labor, had crumbled quickly. The AMA no longer resisted measures of expansion and intervention so strongly or successfully. "There is a completely different atmosphere," Robert Ball remarked in 1973. He detected an opportunity to use the social security program to change the system of health care whereas only seven years before it had seemed necessary to adapt medicare to the system.[35]

Here, in the sharp discontinuity between pre-enactment and post-enactment politics, there was a parallel of sorts to the disability case. In health care as in disability, the ideological intensity seemed to go out of politics once the threshold of innovation was crossed. In place of boundary issues—issues of principle that had stirred passions and mobilized interest groups on a massive scale—there appeared issues of cost control and of technique that baffled minds more than they excited emotions. Demoralization of the medical profession in the wake of defeat may account for this, or, conversely, the pleasing discovery that the welfare state did not necessarily work to the doctors' disadvantage. Doctors' fees rose much faster in 1966 and 1967, the two years after enactment of medicare, than did the cost of nonmedical services.[36] Yet the change cannot be accounted for simply by the changed political behavior of private interests. It stemmed as well from a change in the role of political officials once the government took on major responsibility for the provision of health care. Before the enactment of medicare, political officials had been objects of pressure in the struggle over legislation; after enactment they became, inescapably, managers of the government's health business, and it was a business that urgently demanded the management's attention. This unpredictable budget item in the social insurance program threatened other parts of the same program (increases in cash

35. Robert M. Ball, "Managing the Social Security Program," a special issue of SSA Vista, vol. 16 (January 29, 1973), pp. 48–50. See also Lawrence D. Brown, "The Formulation of Federal Health Care Policy," in New York Academy of Medicine, Bulletin (December 1977) (Brookings Reprint 334). Judith M. Feder, Medicare: The Politics of Federal Hospital Insurance (Heath, 1977) describes the post-enactment adaptation of the SSA to hospital administration.

36. Executive Office of the President, Council on Wage and Price Stability, The Complex Puzzle of Rising Health Care Costs: Can the Private Sector Fit It Together? (the Council, December 1976), pp. 71–77.

benefits might have to be forgone); other parts of the HEW budget (including, for example, an item as popular with Congress as biomedical research); and, more remotely, other parts of the federal budget altogether. Without regard to party or ideology, Congress and the administration cast about for techniques of control.

Because the unanticipated costs of medicare had effects far beyond the program, the interest in control extended far beyond the program-oriented officials who normally dominated policymaking for social security. Health insurance had been hard to fit to the programmatic mold while enactment was impending, and it continued to be a poor fit after enactment.

CHAPTER SEVENTEEN

Bigger Cash Benefits

CONCEIVABLY, the momentum for expansion could have been lost when the campaign for medicare was won. The fight for health insurance was long and hard, and it might have exhausted men less purposeful than the executive leaders of social security. But in 1967 they moved on to a campaign for a much-expanded program of cash benefits. When it was over in 1972, Robert Ball could say that "in truth we have a new social security program—a program that provides a new level of security to working people of all ages and to their families."[1]

Like other expansionary efforts before it, this one proved divisive. The issue here was how big a part the public program should play in providing retirement income. What should be its relation to private pensions and savings? Like earlier boundary, or public-private, issues, this divided business groups from labor and Republican party members from Democrats. Once again, resolution depended very much on the pivotal figure of Wilbur Mills, who in the end unpredictably supported expansion. In 1972 Mills sponsored a 20 percent increase in benefits that climaxed the expansionary campaign. He did this even though it flouted precepts of social security policymaking that he had stood for throughout his career, and violated the practice of consensual decisionmaking in the Ways and Means Committee.

The Aims of Expansion

In the spring of 1966, soon after the enactment of medicare, Commissioner Ball described the goals of social security policy in a speech to the

1. *Future Directions in Social Security,* Hearings before the Senate Special Committee on Aging, 93 Cong. 1 sess. (GPO, 1973), pt. 1, p. 2.

American Society for Public Administration. He said that the first priority was an increase in benefit levels, and this increase was needed throughout the range of incomes, not just for the poor. Ball conceded that other approaches than social security, such as public assistance or a negative income tax, could do a better job of supporting the very poor, but "why," he asked rhetorically, "would we want to limit our economic security objectives to such a goal? A 'minimum income for all' might have been a stirring objective when it was proposed by Sidney and Beatrice Webb about 1910, but we can do much better than that in the United States in 1966."[2] The central, abiding concern of program executives was with expansion of the program as a whole.

To finance the bigger benefits, Ball acknowledged that higher payroll tax rates were possible, but he gave more attention to two other methods. He revived the idea—hardly uttered in public by program executives since 1950—of using general revenues, and he appeared to attach great importance to raising the wage base while conceding that this would not suffice to finance a big increase in general benefits. He argued that a bigger wage base was needed to keep the program progressive as well as to strengthen its financing. "Keeping this base up to date," Ball said, "is the factor that determines how much of the job of providing retirement security is to be done by social security and how much of the job is to be either left undone or left only partially done by private pension plans."[3]

The changes in benefits, taxes, and the wage base were a means to a more fundamental end—higher "replacement rates." This term denotes the relation between the retirement benefit and the preretirement wage. It is an important and useful indicator of the size and social function of a retirement system, yet it had not been much used before in the policymakers' public discussions. The staff of the Committee on Economic Security in 1934 had suggested that insurance benefits, in contrast to public assistance, could be "ample for a comfortable existence, bearing some relation to customary wage standards." It envisioned an eventual replacement rate of 50 percent, while conceding that the insurance program could not begin at any such level.[4] Thereafter, however, policymakers had settled on the phrase "floor of protection" to denote the

2. Robert M. Ball, "Policy Issues in Social Security," *Social Security Bulletin,* vol. 29 (June 1966), p. 5.

3. Ibid., p. 7.

4. *Social Security in America: The Factual Background of the Social Security Act as Summarized from Staff Reports to the Committee on Economic Security* (GPO, 1937), pp. 190, 202–03.

function of social security. This minimized contention by leaving dollar amounts and replacement rates vague while implying a circumscribed role for the public program. In Ball's post-medicare enunciation of policy on cash benefits, the aim was a "more adequate" program, and replacement rates emerged as a measure of adequacy. He stipulated no goal, but called for an increase in existing rates, which he said stood at about 50 percent of earnings for a married man earning average wages and about 67 percent for a married man earning at the level of the federal minimum wage. (In the case of a married man, the spouse's benefit, amounting to half of his own, raised the ratios well above those for a single man.)

More fundamentally still, the changes in all these program features— benefits, taxes, wage base, and replacement rates—were a means to secure the primacy of social security as the nation's system for providing retirement income. Ball argued that social security should be used to supply the major part of retirement income for workers at all income levels rather than counting on private pensions "to play a larger and larger role."[5] It should not be transformed into a program for the poor, as might happen if private sources of retirement income continued to grow for the better-off. However, except to say briefly that it would give greater pension security and facilitate the mobility of labor, Ball did not explain why the public program should be paramount.

Ball's statements made the proposed changes sound as if they were no more than a means of preserving the status quo in public-private relations or, at most, reversing a moderately unfavorable trend. By contrast, the dissenting speeches of Robert J. Myers, the SSA actuary, beginning in 1969 portrayed the aims of "expansionists" in dramatic terms, as virtually unlimited and profoundly threatening to private pensions and savings. He said that their goal was to use the public program to provide complete economic security for the vast majority of the retired population. Summoning private interests to their own defense, Myers warned that they must "devote more time to the general situation and thus possibly less time to their own personal business. Or else, they will, in the long run, not have any personal business."[6] Even in retrospect it is hard for the outside observer to assess the stakes precisely, if only because the

5. "Policy Issues in Social Security," p. 5.

6. "Where Will the Pending Social Security Amendments Take the Program?", *CLU Journal*, September 1971; reprinted in *Social Security Amendments of 1971*, Hearings before the Senate Committee on Finance, 92 Cong. 1 and 2 sess. (GPO, 1972), pt. 2, p. 887.

interdependence of public and private pensions is highly problematic, but it is clear that an important issue was being raised.[7]

The Legislative Program

President Johnson was at least as eager to raise social security benefits as were the leaders of the program. When, as under secretary of HEW, Wilbur Cohen came to him with a proposal for a 10 percent increase, the President's reaction, according to Cohen, was " 'Come on, Wilbur, you can do better than that' "—and then he kept urging him to do better as Cohen returned with successive proposals. More than any of the other presidents in Cohen's experience, Johnson reacted to the program with a passionate spontaneity. He really cared about the aged, and his administration's proposals to Congress in 1967 reflected his caring.[8] Included were a general benefit increase of 15 percent, a small increase in the tax rate (an additional 0.1 percent in 1969 and 0.15 percent in 1973), a big increase in the wage base (from $6,600 to $7,800 in 1968, $9,000 in 1971, and $10,800 in 1974), and a big increase, from $44 to $70, in the minimum benefit.[9]

7. Ball commented as follows: "I've never argued for taking over virtually all economic security provisions for the entire population and thus eliminating private efforts in this area. My views are . . . that there needs to be a social security program that in itself is adequate for average and below-average earners, but that for above-average earners, it is necessary to have a combination of social security and a private pension plan to give a reasonable replacement rate. I've never thought that social security should or would do anything like the whole job. . . . The problem was that social security wasn't growing sufficiently to keep its relative position stable." (From tape-recorded comments addressed by Robert M. Ball to the author, May 6, 1978.)

On the general subject of the relation between public and private pensions, see Merton C. Bernstein, *The Future of Private Pensions* (Free Press of Glencoe, 1964); Peter F. Drucker, *The Unseen Revolution: How Pension Fund Socialism Came to America* (Harper and Row, 1976); President's Committee on Corporate Pension Funds and Other Private Retirement and Welfare Programs, *Public Policy and Private Pension Programs: A Report to the President on Private Employee Retirement Plans* (GPO, 1965); Norman B. Ture, with Barbara A. Fields, *The Future of Private Pension Plans* (Washington, D.C.: American Enterprise Institute for Public Policy Research, 1976).

8. Interview with Wilbur J. Cohen, December 29, 1977.

9. *Social Security Amendments of 1967,* Hearings before the Senate Committee on Finance, 90 Cong. 1 sess. (GPO, 1967), pt. 1, pp. 417 ff.; and *President's Proposals for Revision in the Social Security System,* Hearings before the House Committee on Ways and Means, 90 Cong. 1 sess. (GPO, 1967), pt. 1, p. 220.

The social security proposals of the Johnson administration had taken shape in the second half of 1966. In July, Joseph A. Califano, Jr., the President's special assistant, had set up an interagency task force on income maintenance "to formulate a comprehensive income maintenance policy for the nation as a whole."[10] The task force had been chaired by the chairman of the Council of Economic Advisers, Gardner Ackley, and had included representatives of the Bureau of the Budget, the Departments of the Treasury, Labor, and Health, Education, and Welfare, and the Office of Economic Opportunity. In November this task force had recommended a 10 percent increase in social security benefits and a change in the benefit formula to make social security more progressive. When the recommendations were discussed at the White House, Wilbur Cohen had argued for a bigger increase and against concentrating it at the bottom income levels. The President had sided with Cohen, apparently preferring comprehensive expansion of a generally popular program to overt redistribution of income among social classes. Also, the President had been under heavy pressure from organized labor and organized groups of the elderly to back a big increase in social security. The unusually large increase in the minimum benefit was included in an effort to do something specifically for the poor, although it was an inefficient instrument for the purpose (recipients of the minimum benefit were not necessarily the most needy social security beneficiaries). According to Robert A. Levine, who headed research and planning for OEO at this time, the President and his staff never seriously considered any measure for income maintenance except an increase in social security.[11]

SSA officials testified that under the administration's proposals 87 percent of covered workers would have all their earnings covered in 1974, a figure far exceeding the plateau of 75 percent that had been accepted since 1950. Replacement rates would be increased by 5 to 15 percent,

10. Memo, Joseph A. Califano to Gardner Ackley, "To Establish a Task Force on Income Maintenance," July 11, 1966 (Box 1, Legislative Background, Social Security Increases of 1967, Lyndon Baines Johnson Library, Austin, Texas).

11. For a summary of these events, see Memo, James C. Gaither for the files, "Social Security Increases of 1967," November 15, 1968 (ibid., LBJ Library). The administration's proposal appears in *President's Proposals for Revision in the Social Security System*, Hearings, pt. 1. Robert A. Levine's observation is from his essay, "How and Why the Experiment Came About," in Joseph A. Pechman and P. Michael Timpane, eds., *Work Incentives and Income Guarantees: The New Jersey Negative Income Tax Experiment* (Brookings Institution, 1975), p. 17.

Table 17-1. *Comparison of Actual and Proposed Increases
in Replacement Rates for a Couple Aged Sixty-five and over, 1965*[a]

Average monthly earnings (dollars)	Replacement rate (percent)	
	Actual	Proposed
100	94.8	109.1
200	67.5	77.6
300	56.2	64.7
400	51.0	58.6
500	47.1	54.1
550	45.8	51.5
650	38.8	47.8
750	33.6	45.1
900	28.0	42.0

Source: *President's Proposals for Revision in the Social Security System*, Hearings before the House Committee on Ways and Means, 90 Cong. 1 sess. (GPO, 1967), pt. 1, p. 224.
a. Retired worker and spouse.

depending on the income level (see table 17-1). The administration made no proposal for the use of general revenues, but organized labor served notice on the Ways and Means and Finance committees that it would soon begin asking for that.

Congress gave the administration only part of what it asked for. It granted a benefit increase of 13 percent and provided for a small increase in the tax rate. It raised the wage base to $7,800 but made no promise of further steps. At that figure, the base in 1968 covered 81.7 percent of earnings in covered employment and was closely comparable to the base of $3,600 in 1951. Nonetheless, Commissioner Ball professed great satisfaction. The increases of 1965 and 1967 together brought the base from $4,800 to $7,800 in less than three years. Ball told a conference of SSA employees that this was in many respects the most important accomplishment in that time—striking testimony to the significance that program executives attached to the wage base, given the fact that the same period also included the enactment of medicare.[12]

Congress had little to say about replacement rates except that the Ways and Means Committee suggested that the rate for a couple at the top of the wage base should be approximately 50 percent. It was the Republican minority, led by John Byrnes, that urged a 50 percent replacement rate at higher income levels. This was a somewhat

12. Robert M. Ball, "Remarks," *SSA Vista*, vol. 11 (January 12, 1968). *Vista* was an internal publication of SSA "to share management and program matters with supervisory and administrative staff."

higher rate—implying a less progressive system—than the administration's proposals had contemplated.[13]

The administration's proposals for expansion divided the Finance Committee from Ways and Means and Democrats from Republicans inside the Finance Committee. In contrast to the 1950s liberal Democrats now had control of the Finance Committee, and they would have given the administration all that it asked for, including the 15 percent benefit increase, a three-step increase (to $10,800) in the wage base, and a minimum monthly payment of $70. Dissenting Republicans in the committee endorsed the Ways and Means Committee recommendations, which would have limited the benefit increase to 12½ percent and the wage base to $7,600.[14] The final choice of a 13 percent increase and a wage base of $7,800 was a conference compromise that favored the Ways and Means position.

Unlike Finance, Ways and Means was cohesive. That it could reach bipartisan agreement on this potentially quite divisive issue is powerful evidence of the effectiveness of Mills's leadership and of the consensual norm under which the committee had come to operate in policymaking for social security. One liberal member (Jacob H. Gilbert of New York) and one conservative member (Thomas B. Curtis of Missouri) filed supplemental views, Gilbert to argue for a bigger benefit increase, Curtis to argue that any increase in retirement benefits should come from private sources, but no member declined to sign the committee report.[15]

In sum, the opening of the campaign for bigger cash benefits produced only modest gains in 1967, and when the Republican candidate won the presidential election in 1968, it seemed likely that the campaign would be thwarted.

The Advent of the Nixon Administration

The Eisenhower years had shown that Republican control of the executive branch did not necessarily interrupt the progress of expansion.

13. *Social Security Amendments of 1967*, H. Rept. 544, 90 Cong. 1 sess. (GPO, 1967), p. 23; Wilbur J. Cohen and Milton Friedman, *Social Security: Universal or Selective?* (Washington, D.C.: American Enterprise Institute for Public Policy Research, 1972), p. 86.

14. *Social Security Amendments of 1967*, S. Rept. 744, 90 Cong. 1 sess. (GPO, 1967), pp. 7–8, 340.

15. *Social Security Amendments of 1967*, H. Rept. 544, 90 Cong. 1 sess. (GPO, 1967), pp. 197–201.

Beginning in 1969, the Nixon administration provided a second test. There was no reason to suppose that a reversal of past gains would occur—less reason even than in 1953, when the Chamber of Commerce was calling for a serious reexamination of social security policy and conservative Republicans in Congress might have liked to engage in one. The Republican platform of 1968 promised to provide automatic adjustment of benefits to the cost of living, an increase in widows' benefits, and liberalization of the retirement test, a plank not likely to alarm the program's partisans. (The Democratic plank called for extending medicare to cover the disabled and to pay the cost of prescription drugs for the aged.)[16] Still, a political analyst would probably have predicted that expansion would slow down, and few, surely, would have predicted the explosion in social security benefits that was to occur between 1969 and 1972. Big increases were enacted in 1969, 1971, and 1972, each far exceeding the increase in the cost of living. Real benefit levels—benefits adjusted for inflation—rose by 23 percent. More significantly, there were also big increases in the proportion of earnings subject to social security taxation and in replacement rates. By any definition, a big expansion occurred.

Party rivalry in a divided government was one cause of this extraordinary escalation. The Republican administration consistently proposed benefit increases in proportion to increases in the cost of living, and the Democratic Congress consistently outbid it, raising the Republican offer in 1969 from 10 to 15 percent, in 1971 from 6 to 10 percent, and in 1972 from 5 to 20 percent.[17] In defense of the administration's record, Secretary of Health, Education, and Welfare Elliot Richardson remarked to a congressional committee in 1972 that a Republican president facing a Democratic Congress could expect "to be outbid no matter what he might propose."[18] All of the increases were attached to "veto-proof" legislation—a tax reform act in 1969 and acts to increase the ceiling on the national debt in 1971 and 1972.

A second cause was the Nixon administration's own ambivalence and internal division, which inhibited it from applying heavy and consistent

16. Kirk H. Porter and Donald B. Johnson, comps., *National Party Platforms, 1840–1968* (University of Illinois Press, 1970), pp. 736–37, 754.

17. 83 Stat. 737, 84 Stat. 407, and 86 Stat. 406.

18. *Older Americans Act Amendments of 1972*, Hearings before the Subcommittee on Aging of the Senate Committee on Labor and Public Welfare, 92 Cong. 2 sess. (GPO, 1972), p. 235.

pressure against the increases. It could not be indifferent to the aged as a political constituency or to the possibilities for credit claiming inherent in social security benefit increases. Nor did it fail to include committed advocates of more spending for welfare purposes. Finch, Richardson, and Veneman, at the top of HEW, were very liberal by Republican standards, as was Arthur Flemming, who served as a consultant to the President on aging, as chairman of an active cabinet subcommittee on the aging, and then as commissioner of the Administration on Aging in HEW. Before entering the Nixon administration, Flemming was chairman of the Social Security Advisory Council of 1969–71.

It is important, too, to note that this Republican administration was not more determined or more able than its predecessors of the 1950s to assert partisan control of the executive apparatus for social security. Shortly before his departure as chief actuary, Myers remarked to a newspaper reporter that Wilbur Cohen might as well still be running HEW.[19] Afraid to replace Ball as commissioner, the Republicans ironically accepted the resignation of Myers, whose increasingly vocal attacks on "expansionist" policy made his position in the SSA untenable while Ball remained. The Republican arrival, far from installing a conservative leadership, removed the only important conservative influence from the upper ranks of the SSA. Yet, without daring to remove Ball, the Nixon White House deeply distrusted him. The President's staff believed that he worked for the Democrats in Congress, or they for him. Republicans at the top of HEW, Richardson especially, admired his competence and trusted his integrity (and for that reason among others were themselves distrusted by the White House), but they also knew that he was on close terms with Wilbur Mills and other Democrats in Congress, and they did not delude themselves that a Republican presence in the department would make him any less close.

Much of the explanation, then, for the system's expansion in this period is to be found in the nature of the Republican administration and its relations with Congress, the voting public, and high officials of the "permanent government." The administration could not manage these relations in a way that promoted the objectives it professed, and what it professed it was not always uniformly and wholeheartedly committed to. But this is not the whole explanation of the escalation. Beyond looking at the role and external relations of the Republican administration,

19. *Congressional Record* (March 12, 1970), p. 7168.

it is necessary to consider the nature of the social security program and the policymaking arrangements associated with it.

Insofar as expansion was linked to rising wages, the tendency to expansion was built in. It derived from the actuary's practice of basing his long-range cost estimates on the assumption that earnings would remain level.[20] When earnings rose—as invariably they did—an actuarial surplus was "discovered." The SSA thereupon proposed benefit increases or other expansions, and Congress enacted them if an election was impending—as invariably one was. Thus the program was geared to the economic and political systems in a way that guaranteed its growth, and guaranteed that growth would be linked at least partially to wage increases rather than price increases, which typically were smaller.

The potential capriciousness of this arrangement was never more evident than in 1969. Prices were rising rapidly and wages more rapidly still. The annual report on the status of the social security trust fund, released early in the year with updated actuarial projections, said that receipts had exceeded expenditures by $2 billion in 1968 and that the program was substantially overfinanced in the long run.[21] Confronted with a "galloping surplus," as *Business Week* called it, Congress did what it had always done.[22] Topping the recommendations of the administration, which wanted to tie benefit increases to cost of living increases, it used up the surplus on bigger benefits. So large was this surplus in 1969 that Congress was able to enact a 15 percent increase without imposing any increase in taxes and without jeopardizing the perennial claim, based on Myers's estimates, that the program was "actuarially sound." Replacement rates for individual workers rose by 4 or 5 percentage points.

Even before 1969, some in the governing community in Washington were coming to believe that there might be a better way to set social security benefits. After 1969, interest in finding alternatives intensified. Two different ideas were afloat, coming from two very different sources. Republican officeholders, assisted by Myers, liked the idea of tying social security benefits automatically to increases in the cost of living.

20. See chapter 13.
21. *The 1969 Annual Report of the Board of Trustees of the Federal Old-Age and Survivors Insurance and Disability Insurance Trust Funds*, H. Doc. 91-46, 91 Cong. 1 sess. (GPO, 1969).
22. *Business Week* (October 18, 1969), pp. 41–42.

The other idea, which was advanced by economic analysts outside the SSA and promoted as well by Commissioner Ball, was to abandon the level wage assumption. In 1972 both ideas were adopted, and another big increase in benefits took place.

Changing the System

Republican officeholders thought of indexing social security benefits as a way to contain the biennial pressure for expansion and to depoliticize social security to their own advantage. They hoped to get credit for introducing the automatic feature and to deprive the Democratic majority of future opportunities to act. John Byrnes promoted the idea, which was included in the 1968 party platform and then became the centerpiece of President Nixon's proposals to Congress.[23] In Congress, it divided the normally cohesive Ways and Means Committee along party lines. Mills, who did not want to give up the ad hoc biennial increases, was very much opposed to it.

Fiscal conservatives who did not hold public office and who therefore were not engaged in rival credit claiming with the Democrats were afraid of the idea. The National Association of Manufacturers and the Chamber of Commerce opposed it, and four conservative members of the 1969–71 advisory council strongly dissented from the council's endorsement. They argued that the change would make inflation harder to control, that it was unnecessary because Congress kept benefits on a par with cost of living increases anyway, and that it would not forestall political pressures for even larger increases. Inside the Nixon administration there were dissents from some of the President's economic

23. Byrnes's interest in this idea was at least ten years old. In debate on Social Security Act amendments in 1958, he told the House: "I am not so sure but what the committee and the Congress should give consideration to the advisability of a provision which would automatically make the basic benefit payments consistent with changes in cost of living or in general economic conditions; a provision in the nature of an escalator clause to be financed by a change in the wage base. Average wages constantly change as your general economy goes on an upward trend. In this way we might possibly avoid the problem which has presented itself during the last 3 election years; the idea that no Congress can adjourn before an election without at least making some changes in the Social Security Act. In my book, if we want to ruin the Social Security Act, [we can] start making it a political football to be used to try to garner votes in an election year." *Congressional Record* (July 31, 1958), p. 15746.

advisers, including Arthur Burns and Paul McCracken, chairman of the Council of Economic Advisers.[24]

Leading program executives, who had contemplated an indexed system for some time, were receptive to the Republican proposal except that they and their allies in organized labor preferred to postpone the beginning of such a system until after a major increase in benefit levels had been achieved. When the idea came up in 1967 under Republican sponsorship, Wilbur Cohen as under secretary of HEW had advised President Johnson to outbid the Republicans by sponsoring an indexed formula *plus* a big benefit increase. Program executives would also have liked to consider the possibility of basing benefit increases on wage rather than price increases. Indexing to wages would be the more expansive method.[25]

The idea of automatic increases proved so popular in Congress that the House approved it in 1970 over Mills's opposition, an extraordinary event. The Senate approved it too as part of an omnibus bill on welfare and social security, but the two houses failed to complete action on social security legislation that year. By the time the Senate finished on December 29 Mills decided that it was too late to go to conference. Hence this measure with which Republican officeholders hoped to contain future benefit increases was not yet law when the social security advisory council issued its report in the spring of 1971—a report that had become the vehicle for an attack on the level earnings assumption.

24. *Reports of the 1971 Advisory Council on Social Security,* H. Doc. 92-80, 92 Cong. 1 sess. (GPO, 1971), pp. 79–80; Memo, Richard P. Nathan to Director, "Social Security Cost of Living Escalator," March 17, 1970 (File BRD/FAB [FY 1970–1971] Income Security: Social Security System, Office of Management and Budget, Washington, D.C.). According to this memorandum, those presidential advisers who supported indexing did so "essentially on political grounds in light of Congressman Johnny Byrnes' strong interest in this principle."

Lyndon Johnson's economic advisers had also recommended against indexing when Republican members of Congress had proposed it during his administration. Johnson's CEA judged it to be bad economics, and his budget director, Charles L. Schultze, feared that Congress would continue to pile ad hoc increases on top of the automatic ones, with the result that much too large a share of the country's resources would be committed to the elderly. Memo, Joseph A. Califano to the President, July 18, 1967 (Box 164, Executive, Legislation/Welfare 6, White House Central File, Lyndon Baines Johnson Library, Austin, Texas).

25. Memo, Wilbur J. Cohen to Marvin Watson, July 18, 1968, in ibid.; Ball, "Policy Issues in Social Security," pp. 6–7; and testimony of the AFL-CIO in *Social Security and Welfare Proposals,* Hearings before the House Committee on Ways and Means, 91 Cong. 1 sess. (GPO, 1969), pt. 4, p. 1179.

To any economist, liberal or conservative, the level earnings assumption was an utterly irrational instrument for making public policy. To the extent that it enabled Congress to enact benefit increases painlessly, by a method that regularly put "easy money" at the disposal of the social security system, it provided an escape from the central policy choices inherent in the program—choices that in an economist's view required a measured calculation of how much of the nation's economic product "ought" to go to social security when the claim of that program was weighed against competing claims. To a liberal economist—that is, one who favored a larger public program to support the incomes of the elderly—it was additionally objectionable in that it had a conservative bias. To the extent that it understated the system's future revenues, it depressed benefits.

As early as 1951 an article criticizing the actuary's use of the level earnings assumption had appeared in the *Quarterly Journal of Economics,* and before that objections had been raised within the SSA from officials who were committed to expanding the program.[26] But these criticisms subsided. SSA officials who favored expansion found that the level earnings assumption was not in practice a serious constraint (rather the reverse), while professional economists on the outside of the SSA did not maintain a careful scrutiny of the program through the 1950s. Then, in the late 1960s, the situation changed again. As the program expanded rapidly, professional economists performing as policy analysts in or near the government began to cast about for ways to rationalize social security policymaking and integrate it with budgeting and fiscal policy. The Executive Office of the President, including both the Council of Economic Advisers and the Bureau of the Budget, was one locus of this effort. Another was the Brookings Institution, which published a critical analysis by Pechman, Aaron, and Taussig in 1968.[27] The latter argued that while a conservative bias might be appropriate in the actuarial estimates of a private insurance system, which was obliged to have enough funds on hand to meet all accrued liabilities, it was in-

26. Charles C. Killingsworth and Gertrude Schroeder, "Long-Range Cost Estimates for Old-Age Insurance," *Quarterly Journal of Economics,* vol. 65 (May 1951), pp. 199–213.

27. Joseph A. Pechman, Henry J. Aaron, and Michael K. Taussig, *Social Security: Perspectives for Reform* (Brookings Institution, 1968), pp. 153–61. See also Nancy H. Teeters, "The Payroll Tax and Social-Security Finance," in Richard A. Musgrave, ed., *Broad-Based Taxes: New Options and Sources* (Johns Hopkins University Press, 1973), pp. 87–112.

appropriate for a public program, which could depend on the government's tax power to get it out of financial trouble. The argument that the assumption protected the system against unexpected deficits (because it did not use the returns from rising wages until those returns were actually available) was unconvincing to them.

Meanwhile, program executives were casting about for ways to finance major expansion at a time when resistance to payroll tax increases was rising and acceptance of general revenue financing had yet to be secured. With a common interest in adopting dynamic earnings assumptions, which in one bold stroke would both rationalize policymaking for the program over the long run and justify an extraordinary benefit increase right away, program executives and professional economists shaped the financial recommendations of the 1969–71 advisory council.

The advisory council recommended that social security cost estimates be based on the assumption that earnings would rise. This was one of a set of financial recommendations—the closing part of the council's report—that were drafted by Commissioner Ball and by the assistant commissioner for program evaluation and planning, Alvin M. David, in the spring of 1971 after the council had ceased to meet.[28] Informally and

28. The council's last meeting was in January 1971. David sent a draft of the recommendations to Kermit Gordon, who was chairman of the council's subcommittee on cost estimates, in March. He wrote:

Here is the financing section of the report of the Advisory Council on Social Security. Bob [Ball] and I hope that you can give us your reactions before we send the draft to the rest of the Council.

We have rewritten the section a number of times . . . we think it's time that you had a chance to comment, and we would much appreciate whatever reactions you can give us.

Bob is anxious to get the report out—partly because people like Wilbur Mills will be asking where it is, and partly because the Council's recommendations on financing would have great interest for the Ways and Means Committee, and should by all means be in the public domain before the Committee goes ahead with its work on social security legislation.

We'll be happy to hear from you—or perhaps I should say we'll be happy to hear from you if your comments are not too devastating. (Alvin M. David to Kermit Gordon, March 14, 1971 [Kermit Gordon papers, folder "Advisory Council on Social Security, May 1969–1971," Box 21, John F. Kennedy Library, Waltham, Mass.]; I am grateful to Molly Gordon for granting permission to use her late husband's papers.)

Upon reading this, Ball commented: "The policy decisions had been made before and what was at issue was how to write up in actual report form something that had been agreed upon. There's nothing unusual about the staff taking on such a task and

confidentially, this recommendation was backed by the staff of the Bureau of the Budget.[29] Publicly, it was backed by a report of a five-member panel of actuaries and economists, consultants to a council subcommittee, which set forth a critique of past practice and found, inevitably, that if dynamic earnings assumptions were used, the system was heavily overfinanced. With dynamic assumptions, the panel projected a balance of $281,899 million in the trust fund in 1985.[30]

Much depended at this point on the more or less fortuitous positioning of key participants. Had Robert Myers not departed as chief actuary in May 1970, revision of the level earnings assumption would have been much more difficult, for Myers was wedded to the technique. Soon after he left, the advisory council set up a subcommittee to examine the reasonableness of the methodology used by the Office of the Actuary in making cost estimates and specifically to recommend whether the level earnings assumption should be retained. The questions addressed to the subcommittee, which Commissioner Ball drafted, constituted the most explicit possible invitation to recommend dynamic assumptions. That this subcommittee was headed by a professional economist, Kermit Gordon, president of the Brookings Institution, was also important. A former member of the Council of Economic Advisers and former budget director in the Kennedy and Johnson administrations, Gordon shared the view of economic analysts generally that the level earnings assumption ought to be revised, and he appointed the consultant panel of three economists and two actuaries who did the technical work for the subcommittee. Two of the members, Otto Eckstein of Harvard and Nancy Teeters of Brookings, were liberal economists who had "discovered" the level earnings assumption in the course of government service and were eager to change it. One was an actuary, Murray Latimer, who had shared in designing the old age insurance program in 1934. Organized labor had suggested his appointment. He too was eager to make the change. The other two panel members, an actuary in private practice

---

clearing it with the chairman of the subcommittee before final submission to all the council members. It was not necessary that they meet again, but it was approved by them." Ball transcript.

29. The Budget Bureau's position is detailed in File BRD/FAB (FY 1970–1971) Income Security: Social Security System, Office of Management and Budget, Washington, D.C.

30. *Reports of the 1971 Advisory Council on Social Security,* H. Doc. 92-80, pp. 90–103.

in Seattle and a conservative economist from the University of Chicago faculty, raised no objections.[31]

The recommendation to use dynamic earnings assumptions received very little attention in the advisory council and stirred no controversy there. One reason is that the technical panel worked hurriedly and reported late; the council held only one meeting after receiving its report. A more fundamental reason is that this issue was subordinate in the minds of council members to the issue of whether to adopt an indexed benefit formula, which had caused intense debate. Led by Charles A. Siegfried of the Metropolitan Life Insurance Company, conservative members of the council objected vehemently to this, paradoxically in opposition to Myers. Once this had been settled and the council had decided to recommend tying benefit increases to rising prices and tying the wage base to rising earnings, the recommendation to change the method of estimating costs followed logically.

Myers had always maintained that he had to use static assumptions because he could not legitimately assume that Congress would raise benefits in the future or guess by how much, and if he could not assume rising benefits, he could not assume rising earnings. If Congress were to stipulate that benefits would rise in proportion to prices and the wage base in proportion to earnings, it would no longer be necessary—indeed, it would be preposterous—to maintain the fictional assumptions that neither benefits nor earnings would rise.[32] Myers's successor, Charles L.

31. Interview with Nancy H. Teeters, May 20, 1977. Documents in the Gordon papers illustrate Ball's active role in managing and staffing the advisory council's work. In mid-March 1970, he wrote to Gordon asking him to serve as chairman of the financial subcommittee, telling him that a formal request from Council Chairman Flemming would follow soon and proposing to meet with Gordon to discuss a charge to the subcommittee "after I have had a chance to work something up." Ten days later, Ball sent a draft and proposed that he and Gordon review it before Ball suggested to Chairman Flemming that it be sent to subcommittee members along with a letter asking them to serve. (Kermit Gordon Papers, Folder, "Social Security Subcommittee on Cost Estimates and Financial Policy," Box 23, John F. Kennedy Library, Waltham, Mass.)

32. In presenting the Nixon administration's indexing proposal to Congress in 1969, Myers took the position that the automatically rising benefits could be financed with an automatically rising wage base. As long as taxable earnings increased at least as fast as consumer prices, the new automatic features would be "self-financing." Other proposed changes he continued to evaluate with the use of the level earnings assumption. This meant that some features of the program would be estimated using dynamic assumptions and others using static asumptions. It was an awkward, untenable position. Neither Byrnes nor Myers foresaw that their initiative in support of indexing would culminate in a revision of the level earnings assumption and,

Trowbridge, who left a job with a private insurance company to join the SSA in 1971, approved of the switch to dynamic assumptions on the condition that it be linked to the adoption of indexed benefits.[33] Siegfried, who was at least as opposed to expansion as Myers and who greatly feared the implications of indexing, nonetheless discounted the significance of actuarial estimating techniques and did not make an issue inside the advisory council of the proposed change to dynamic assumptions.[34]

The change in actuarial assumptions might have been discussed by the Board of Trustees of the Federal Old Age and Survivors Insurance and Disability Insurance Trust Fund, which consists ex officio of the secretary of the treasury, secretary of labor, and secretary of HEW. The board "holds" the trust funds and makes an annual report to Congress on their status. Traditionally, however, these were purely nominal functions, and the board was virtually a fictional entity. It met once a year in perfunctory fashion and heard a report from the social security commissioner. Its own report then was prepared by the SSA actuary. The secretaries of treasury and labor had no independent staff in their

---

as a corollary, an extraordinary benefit increase. Neither, of course, foresaw that Myers would leave office in 1970. Eventually Myers would concede that static assumptions were inconsistent with an indexed formula, but if he had remained in office as chief actuary and accepted the use of the dynamic earnings assumption, he might have mitigated its effects with conservative "corrections" at other points. See Myers's article in the Wall Street Journal, July 28, 1972, in which he argued that social security policymakers seemed oblivious to the "hidden hazard" of declining birthrates. If Myers had been making the actuarial assumptions in 1972, it is unlikely that they would have justified a 20 percent benefit increase.

33. Trowbridge concluded that the advisory council wished to switch to dynamic assumptions even if indexing were not adopted, and he objected strongly to that. For his interpretation of the change in assumptions, see Trowbridge, "Social Security Amendments—1969–72," Transactions of the Society of Actuaries, vol. 25 (March 1974), pp. 642–45.

34. In a brief exchange with Myers before the Society of Actuaries in the fall of 1971, Siegfried suggested that Myers erred in attaching so much significance to the level earnings assumption. "I believe the key decisions have not been and will not be affected in any vital degree by variations in actuarial methods," he said. (Letter, Charles A. Siegfried to author, May 11, 1978, and enclosure.) Siegfried may have been right in discounting the importance of the level earnings assumption. It is not unreasonable to suppose that the system would have been no different had dynamic assumptions always been used, and that Myers exaggerated the utility of static assumptions as a device of fiscal restraint. However, in retrospect there is no way to deny that the change to dynamic assumptions in 1971–72 made possible an exceptionally large benefit increase that otherwise could not have been defended technically.

capacity as board members, knew little about social security policy, and rarely gave evidence of caring. To the extent that Treasury showed any interest, it was confined to the management of government bonds; Treasury's staff man at these meetings was a career official who specialized in investments. At the meeting in 1971 Commissioner Ball described the financial recommendations of the advisory council, including the proposed change to the dynamic earnings assumption. Secretary Richardson of HEW endorsed the council's recommendations, and neither Secretary of the Treasury John B. Connally nor the representative of the secretary of labor raised questions or objections. Their departments had no position, pending completion of staff work. There is no formal record of the board's having approved the new actuarial methodology at this or any other meeting although official publications say such approval was given. The board's annual report, issued late in the spring of 1972, contained two sets of actuarial projections, one based on static assumptions, the other on dynamic assumptions, which it recommended be used if indexing were adopted.[35] It is extremely unlikely that "the board" recognized the significance of the question that had come before it.[36]

35. "Minutes of the Meeting of the Boards of Trustees" (Washington, D.C.: December 15, 1971); and 1972 *Annual Report of the Board of Trustees of the Federal Old-Age and Survivors Insurance and Disability Insurance Trust Funds*, H. Doc. 92-307, 92 Cong. 2 sess. (GPO, 1972).

36. Despite the easy acquiescence of the board at this meeting, officials of the SSA recall that there was opposition inside the administration to the changed financial assumptions of 1972 and that it delayed publication of the trustees' report by two months. The objections came from OMB Director George P. Shultz. They appear not to have been directed against the conversion to dynamic assumptions, which the OMB analysts of social security strongly favored, but rather against another financial change pending at this time—adoption of a policy of "current-cost financing" under which annual revenues would be planned to match annual expenditures while for contingency purposes the trust fund balance would be maintained at a level approximately equal to one year's expenditures. This, too, had formed part of the advisory council recommendations. According to an analysis prepared at the time within HEW, the opposition actually originated with one of Shultz's colleagues, Arthur B. Laffer, who had made two arguments: that current-cost financing would restrict OMB's ability to use trust fund surpluses and deficits as a fiscal policy weapon, and that the trust fund should accumulate large surpluses in order to reduce the volume of public debt instruments in private hands, with the object of stimulating private saving. For Laffer's views on social security, see Arthur B. Laffer and R. David Ranson, "Some Economic Consequences of the U.S. Social Security System," in National Tax Association—Tax Institute of America, 1973 *Proceedings of the Sixty-sixth Annual Conference on Taxation* (Columbus, Ohio: NTA-TIA, 1974), pp. 211–31. The work of Martin Feldstein also argues for a large trust fund ac-

Perhaps the switch to dynamic assumptions would have received more attention inside and outside the government had it been clear just how large the resulting actuarial windfall would be. Not until early in 1972 was it apparent that the change would justify a benefit increase as large as 20 percent. Social security experts understood, though, that a sizable windfall from the change was inevitable, and politically astute experts presumably expected politicians to waste no time in using it. That conservative experts did not put up more resistance is explained both by the fact that the impending adoption of indexing made the actuarial change logical and by the political ambiguity of the change itself. While liberals could welcome the immediate prospect of an actuarial windfall with which benefits could be increased, conservatives could welcome the long-term prospect of a system that would no longer generate windfalls in every election year. The advisory council recommendations were cast in "conservative" terms. The report said that "the discipline inherent in the contributory program would be strengthened" (on the assumption that Congress would be forced to raise taxes whenever it granted increases greater than were required to compensate for increases in the cost of living).[37]

Without itself recommending a 20 percent increase, the advisory council paved the way. Bigger in raw percentages than the 1969 or 1971 increases and more extravagant in its departure from the cost of living increase, the 20 percent increase was also different in kind. The first two were financed in traditional ways—in 1969 out of the actuarial surplus generated by the rise in earnings between 1967 and 1969, in 1971 by a combination of a wage base increase, a future tax rate increase (effective in 1976), and an actuarial surplus generated by rising earnings. The 1972 increase was financed largely by a change in actuarial assumptions, which not only took account, in traditional fashion, of the increased earnings of the immediate past but projected future ones and took advantage of them, too. The wage base was raised, but tax rates (future rates, to be sure, not actual, present rates) were *lowered*.

---

cumulation so as to increase private savings. See, among others, "Toward a Reform of Social Security," *The Public Interest*, vol. 10 (Summer 1975), pp. 75–95; "Facing the Social Security Crisis," *The Public Interest*, vol. 12 (Spring 1977), pp. 88–100; "The Social Security Fund and National Capital Accumulation," in *Funding Pensions: Issues and Implications for Financial Markets* (Federal Reserve Bank of Boston, 1976), pp. 32–64.

37. *Report of the 1971 Advisory Council on Social Security*, H. Doc. 92-80, p. 66.

The Metamorphosis of Wilbur Mills

Politically, the most remarkable thing about this extraordinary benefit increase was that Wilbur Mills sponsored it. Late in February 1972,
he introduced a bill for that purpose in the House.[38] By the actuarial
standards that Mills was accustomed to apply, only a small benefit
increase could be justified; the customary actuarial techniques showed
only a narrow actuarial surplus. From a man who had always stood for
"fiscal soundness" and who moved cautiously when he moved at all, this
sudden, seemingly reckless stroke came as a great surprise.

It cannot be said that Mills did not grasp the implications of what he
was doing. Over the years, Mills had mastered the actuarial principles
of social security. He fully understood the working of the level earnings
assumption at a time when fiscal economists scattered in offices about
the capital city had never heard of it. In 1964, in a speech to Arkansas
constituents, he had explained his opposition to medicare on the curiously technical ground that it was hard to reconcile with the level earnings assumption, a point that must have baffled the Kiwanis Club
meeting to which it was addressed.[39] At Mills's insistence, the actuarial
techniques for hospital insurance assumed dynamic earnings because in
that part of the program they would be the safer, more conservative approach. It is one of the many ironies of 1972 that Mills's insistence on
dynamic assumptions for medicare in 1965 helped pave the way for
abandoning the level earnings assumption in the cash benefit program.
The advisory council was able to argue in 1971 that what was best for
medicare was best also for cash benefits.

One possible explanation for Mills's changed conduct is that his
political aspirations changed. Early in 1972 he announced that he would
be a candidate for the Democratic nomination for the presidency, an
astonishing move by a man who lacked a national political following
but had much power as a veteran chairman of perhaps the most important committee in Congress. It was facetiously asked why he would
want to step down to run for president. Most observers supposed that

38. *Congressional Record* (February 23, 1972), pp. 5269–72.
39. "Remarks of Wilbur D. Mills before the Model Luncheon Meeting of Arkan-
sas-Missouri District Kiwanis Convention," Little Rock, Ark., September 28, 1964, in
Congressional Record (October 3, 1964), pp. 24014–16.

Mills sponsored the social security benefit increase to advance his presidential prospects.[40]

Another interpretation, not wholly inconsistent with the first, is also possible. He may have taken the initiative in the belief that if he did not, President Nixon would. Though cautious and temperamentally inclined to conservatism, Mills was also tactically agile, as his post-1964 leadership of medicare legislation had shown. As a legislative leader, he was adroit at anticipating pressures. Perhaps in 1972 he anticipated a bold initiative by the politician in the White House, who, he may well have supposed, would be irresistibly tempted by an actuarial windfall in social security in a year when his own office was at stake.

The President, however, after an initial display of some uncertainty by his administration officials, advocated a cash benefit increase of only 5 percent, a position he affirmed in late March in a special message to Congress on older Americans.[41] Beyond that, the only liberalizations in social security proposed by the administration in this message were several that were already pending in Congress as part of H.R.1, the administration's comprehensive welfare and social security proposal.

40. Whereas at the time it seemed that a desire for the presidency had changed Mills's behavior, later it seemed possible that the man himself had changed. Mills resigned his chairmanship in 1974 and confessed to having become an alcoholic. He left Congress in 1976. Later, in an interview with a *Washington Post* reporter (January 4, 1978), he said that his heavy drinking began in 1969 and had increased by 1973, and was accompanied by the use of pills to alleviate the pain of a ruptured spinal disc. It is, of course, impossible to know whether or in what way alcohol and painkillers affected Mills's political behavior.

41. "Special Message to the Congress on Older Americans," March 23, 1972, in *Public Papers of the Presidents of the United States: Richard Nixon, 1972* (GPO, 1974), pp. 461–84. The administration's earlier indecision was manifest in hearings before the Finance Committee in late February. Chairman Russell B. Long pressed administration witnesses for assurance that the President was not planning to sponsor an extraordinary increase himself. Senate Democrats obviously suspected him of it. Neither HEW Secretary Elliot Richardson, Budget Director George Shultz, nor Secretary of the Treasury John B. Connally could provide any such assurance. Genuinely undecided as to its own proposal, the Nixon administration appeared to be keeping its options open. Long evoked the politics of the situation:

If not only my party but the Republican Party as well is going to leave me between now and November, I would like to know about it. . . .

I am being told from all sources and that is why I want to get it from as near the horse's mouth as I can that one reason Chairman Mills came out and advocated this is that the President is likely to advocate it any day. If there is going to be a parade, I think I would rather be at the front of the parade rather than the tail end. (*$450 Billion Debt Limit*, Hearing before the Senate Committee on Finance, 92 Cong. 2 sess. [GPO, 1972], pp. 61–62.)

(They included indexing of benefits to the cost of living, increases for widows, widowers, and persons who delayed retirement beyond the age of eligibility, liberalization of the earnings test, and repeal of the requirement that participants in part B of medicare pay a monthly premium, a step that was roughly equivalent to a 4 percent cash benefit increase.) The administration's response to the actuarial windfall resulting from changed assumptions was to recommend that the scheduled future tax rates incorporated in H.R.1 be reduced.[42] That the President stood firm for a cash benefit increase of only 5 percent was a victory for the administration's fiscal conservatives. Within the cabinet committee on the aging, where the special message on older Americans was prepared, representatives of HEW along with Arthur Flemming had argued for greater liberalization, though not even they proposed a cash benefit increase as large as 20 percent.[43] The President's domestic counselor, John D. Ehrlichman, told a journalist that the 20 percent proposal was "a political ploy and cannot be considered seriously."[44]

It is possible that the administration could have averted this extraor-

42. Under existing law in the spring of 1972, the OASDHI tax rate was 5.2 percent each for employer and employee and was scheduled to rise in steps to a maximum of 6.05 percent in 1987. Under H.R.1 as approved by the Ways and Means Committee, it would have risen in larger steps and reached a maximum of 7.4 percent in 1987. Under the administration proposal that followed from the changed financial assumptions, the scheduled step increases in H.R.1 were scaled down so that the rate for 1987 would have been 6.4 percent, which was still higher than in existing law even if lower than in H.R.1. Note that the Nixon administration proposed only future reductions in tax rates, not current ones. The administration proposals were contained in letters to the chairmen of the Ways and Means and Finance committees on May 23, 1972.

43. I have been unable to establish what HEW's precise position was or whether it had one. It is clear that there was considerable sympathy for the 20 percent increase among Secretary Richardson's immediate staff. Early in March, the assistant secretary for planning and evaluation, Laurence E. Lynn, Jr., sent Richardson a memorandum that virtually endorsed Mills's proposal. It cited a substantial increase in social security benefit levels as one of the goals that the department should pursue after welfare reform, embodied in H.R.1, had passed, and strongly implied that it might be a good idea to accept it right away. None of the several sources I interviewed, including Richardson himself, could recall what position the department took, but I infer that it did not argue inside the administration for the 20 percent cash benefit increase if only because the President's immediate advisers in the White House and OMB obviously would accept no such thing. After Congress passed the 20 percent increase, Richardson recommended to the President that he sign it. So, with some reservations, did the OMB.

44. Natalie Davis Spingarn, "Congress Debates Application of Billions in Social Security Funds," *National Journal*, vol. 4 (April 29, 1972), p. 733.

dinary cash benefit increase, which was quadruple its own request, if it had come forward with a more liberal proposal of its own, one that would have spent some portion of the fresh windfall by fattening the package of liberalizations pending in H.R.1 rather than applying it to a reduction of H.R.1's proposed tax rates. A member of the administration later speculated that if it had taken a more liberal position, Ball would have felt obligated to gather support among the Democrats in Congress for something near the administration's position, and Ball, in an interview, agreed that this was so. Both the Republican source and Ball presumed that congressional Democrats would have followed Ball's advice in the matter.

It is also possible that nothing Republican executives might have done in 1972 would have affected the outcome at all. Once the idea of a 20 percent increase was afloat in an election year and endowed with expert justification from the advisory council, partisan political bidding was bound to start. George McGovern, a Democratic senator who would be a candidate for the presidency, proposed a 20 percent increase ten days before Mills did.[45] A week before McGovern proposed it, it was proposed by Frank Church, chairman of the Senate Special Committee on Aging, a committee whose staff has developed into an aggressive internal lobby for the aged on Capitol Hill.[46] This staff often acted in collaboration with the external lobbies of senior citizens, which were themselves becoming more aggressive as the numbers of aged grew and their dependence on government programs increased. It also benefited greatly from the "technical assistance" of civil servants in the SSA, from whom staff members first learned that a 20 percent benefit increase in combination with reduced tax rates could be justified under the new actuarial assumptions. By May, Church and his staff had gathered forty-eight cosponsors for the 20 percent increase, and the *Senior Citizen News* was assiduously publicizing their names.[47]

Congress hastily added the 20 percent increase, along with the indexing provisions, in late June to a bill increasing the ceiling on the national debt. The initiative for this move came in the Senate, whose open procedures made irregular action possible. Significantly, within the Senate it came from Church, not the Finance Committee, which refrained from sponsoring a benefit increase even as pressure mounted to pass the

45. *New York Times,* February 10, 1972.
46. *Congressional Record* (February 7, 1972), pp. 2785–91.
47. Ibid. (May 10, 1972), pp. 16573–74.

Church proposal. The 20 percent increase carried by votes of 82 to 4 in the Senate and 302 to 35 in the House, where Mills as chairman of Ways and Means raised no objection to attaching it to an increase in the debt ceiling.[48] On the floor, senior Republicans in the Ways and Means and Finance committees tried to win support for a 10 percent increase and were beaten 66 to 20 in the Senate and 253 to 83 in the House.[49] Congressional Republicans were badly divided on all of these votes, and in no case did a majority of Republicans vote in support of the administration. Uncharacteristically, the Ways and Means Committee was divided, too. Byrnes and several other senior Republicans on Ways and Means stood firm against the 20 percent increase. The House-Senate conference divided exactly along party lines. The administration seriously considered a veto but decided against it. Noting that the bill would add $3.7 billion to the budget deficit, President Nixon said it failed the test of fiscal responsibility and called on Congress to offset the increase with cuts in other federal programs.

Congress did not treat the big increase in cash benefits as a substitute for other liberalizations. In the fall it enacted the Social Security Amendments of 1972, containing a mixture of liberalizations. Particularly noteworthy was the extension of medicare protection to disabled beneficiaries who had been on the benefit rolls for at least two years; this was not an administration measure. The OASDHI tax rate, which stood at 5.2 percent on a wage base of $7,800 in 1971, rose to 5.85 percent on a wage base of $10,800 in 1973.

Expansion of the Program

The expansion of social security during the Nixon administration is best measured by changes in the wage base and replacement rates. At $13,200 in 1974 (the result of the amendment sponsored by Mills and Church in 1972 and then a further amendment in 1973), the proportion of earnings in covered employment subject to social security taxation approached 86 percent, an increase of about 5 percentage points from the level that had been maintained since the 1950 amendments. While

48. Ibid. (June 30, 1972), pp. 23512, 23738–39. According to a congressional source, Mills did raise an objection in private conversation with Church but when Church replied that if he did not attach the 20 percent increase to the debt ceiling bill some other member of the Senate would, Mills relented.

49. Ibid., pp. 23511, 23738.

this was not as high as the proponents of expansion would have liked, it was a sizable upward step. Replacement rates in 1975 were approximately 67 percent for a married man earning average wages and 92 percent for a married man earning the federal minimum wage—up from 50 percent and 67 percent, respectively, a decade earlier, on the eve of the drive for expansion. Half or more of this increase took place between 1972 and 1973.

Like its predecessors, this third major campaign for expansion of social security succeeded, but it did not precipitate the intense pressure group contest that accompanied both of the earlier expansions or the extensive mobilization of opinion that occurred in connection with medicare. Compared to the earlier expansions, it occurred in a flash. The crucial 20 percent increase came as a lightning stroke in the election-year summer of 1972. The stakes were obscured and debate was discouraged by two persistent traits of social security policymaking—incrementalism and technicality.

To appraise the significance of cash benefit increases it was necessary to know at what point an increment was so big as to constitute a change in kind. Where would a critical threshold between the public and private sectors be crossed? No one could answer with confidence. No one would know until some years after the legislative crossing occurred, and even then causes and effects would in all likelihood remain obscure. In the meantime, the change of a few percentage points in replacement rates or in the proportion of covered earnings represented by the wage base was not the sort of issue around which an intense contest could be sustained—the kind of contest that stems from issues of principle or from vital threats to large corporate or professional interests. If there was an issue of principle here, it had been drained of much of its political potency by being rendered in narrow, technical terms and reduced to an issue of degree.

But the ultimate triumph of the technical approach lay in the application of changed actuarial projections. The 20 percent increase was justified through sheer technical artifice. "The American people will not be fooled," Representative Byrnes said. "If we are going to pay out 20 percent more in benefit dollars, someone will have to pay 20 percent more in tax dollars than they otherwise would have had to pay. It is that simple."[50] But Congress hastened to act without any weighing of

50. *Congressional Record* (June 30, 1972), p. 23733.

costs, benefits, or long-term consequences after having been assured by Mills that the 20 percent increase was "actuarially sound" because derived from the recommendations of a distinguished advisory council and its panel of expert economists and actuaries.

Representative Barber Conable, a conservative Republican on the Ways and Means Committee, chastised Congress for its mindless deference to expertise. To Mills's repeated assurance that the extraordinary benefit increase was sound because experts had pronounced it sound, Conable had a caustic response:

> In effect the chairman says, in recommending this increase on the basis of new dynamic actuarial assumptions, that "all the experts agree." I will not dwell on the question of whether the experts . . . are entitled to our confidence. I say only that we in the Congress are not entitled to the confidence of the American people if we allow ourselves to be stampeded into this vote.[51]

Despite its technicality, social security might have received more attention and debate at this time had policymakers in both the executive and the legislature not been so engrossed in the distinct yet related question of welfare reform. That the program executives' campaign for a higher level of benefits coincided with a heightened concern in the national government about poverty had important consequences. The interest in antipoverty legislation during the Johnson years, which carried over during the Nixon administration into the campaign for the family assistance plan (FAP), encouraged the expansion of the social security program in two ways. It lent momentum to welfare legislation generally, and because social security was the most popular and feasible form of such legislation, it won support when more controversial forms were stymied. There was some disposition in the HEW of Elliot Richardson, as there had been a disposition in the White House of Lyndon Johnson, to support big increases in social security because that was the only place where big increases in social welfare spending could easily be had and hence the only way in which large numbers of persons could be moved above the official poverty line. At the same time, the intense discussion focused on antipoverty politics during the Johnson administration and on FAP during the Nixon administration—which were enticing subjects if only because they were "new"—tended to divert the policymakers' time and attention from the thoroughly familiar and superficially mundane topic of social security. Incremental changes in well-established programs do not attract attention. Neither the press

51. Ibid., p. 23734.

nor pressure groups are drawn to them as they are to measures of "reform" and "innovation" such as FAP was perceived to be, or before it the community action program of the war on poverty. That few pay attention to incremental changes makes it relatively easy for them to be made, with the result that they become, over the long run at least, much more important than the alleged "reforms" by which they are overshadowed on the public agenda at any given moment.

The Disintegration of Policymaking

Much that was characteristic of social security policymaking was evident in the events of 1972, especially the manipulation of technique to avoid politics as conflict and to facilitate politics as the solicitation of votes. Yet in some respects this event was an aberration—a departure from established norms of policymaking—and as such was profoundly disturbing to some leading participants. John Byrnes, who would later say, in an interview with the author, that he was "despondent" at this exceptional turn of events, responded at the time with an exceptional speech to the House:

Mr. Speaker, to appear here as a member of the Committee on Ways and Means, to discuss a matter of this importance with so little information for the members of the committee, of the House, or of the Congress, is something that I thought I would never have to experience in my service in this House.

This is no way to treat vitally important legislation.

Some may call what we are doing here today cute politics. I call it irresponsibility. . . .

At no point has there been a study by the Ways and Means Committee of the new method of financing that has produced the "windfall" that now is going to be used for the 20 percent benefit increase. Not one word of testimony in public or executive session has been received on this subject. This fundamental change in the criteria by which the soundness of the social security trust fund has been measured for one-third of a century is being adopted willy-nilly by the Congress without even a cursory review. . . .

Today we wonder why we hear expressions of disenchantment with the Congress of the United States. I do not think we need wonder any longer when we sit here and conduct our business in this fashion. How can we help but bring about a disrespect for our actions when we treat such serious questions in such a cursory fashion? We are contemplating taking steps that can lead us into very serious problems as far as this system and the many people involved in it are concerned.[52]

52. Ibid., pp. 23732–33.

While social security policy had never been much debated or understood in Congress as a whole, and still less by a larger public, since at least 1950 it had been carefully considered within the small family of official and quasi-official proprietors of the program. They had not always agreed among themselves. Program expansion, health insurance especially, divided them along partisan and ideological lines, and they could reconcile their differences only after prolonged delay, bargaining, and testing of external pressures. On such occasions, they engaged in "outside" coalition building as well as "inside" negotiation. There was nothing hasty about this process. By any standard, the issue of whether to enact hospitalization insurance took a long time to settle.

In particular, the Ways and Means Committee had acted in a measured fashion, calculated to maximize agreement. On medicare, it seemed, Mills had wanted to hold hearings forever. In Ways and Means the sense of trusteeship regarding the program was very strong and a tradition of careful deliberation and of consensual decision was well developed. That the committee remained cohesive in 1967 when the Johnson administration proposed a big benefit increase was one sign of this. Another sign, perhaps even more telling, was the continued cohesion of the committee in 1969, when the Nixon administration asked for a smaller increase than actuarial estimates permitted. Byrnes and the other Republicans in Ways and Means broke with the administration and sided with the committee majority in supporting a 15 percent increase. For Ways and Means Republicans, committee and programmatic norms proved more powerful than partisan ones. (In contrast, Republican members of the Finance Committee backed the administration.)

It was a truly radical departure in 1972 when Mills proposed the 20 percent increase without consulting the committee. He did not pretend to have consulted it, but invoked his personal authority to justify the extraordinary increase. "I would be the last one, frankly, to want to get this program in a position where it was not actuarially sound," he told the House, drawing heavily on his long-established reputation for fiscal caution.[53] The cautious, consensus-building style that had marked Mills's leadership for fourteen years was suddenly cast to the winds. On top of that, at the last moment he concurred in the Senate's decision to

53. Ibid., p. 23731.

attach the 20 percent increase to a bill raising the debt ceiling, a procedural irregularity that he would normally not have countenanced.

In retrospect, Mills's changed behavior as committee chairman was
part of a general upheaval in policymaking for social security and was
in some measure its cause, but it would be implausible to suggest that
a well-established system for policymaking began to break down simply
because its legislative leader was suddenly seized with presidential ambitions. There were too many other symptoms of disintegration. Some
were visible in the legislature, where Mills suffered an extraordinary
defeat on the floor in 1970 regarding the indexing of benefits. Some were
visible in the executive, where the enduring, familiar expertise of Myers
had suddenly been displaced by a panel of outsiders attached to a
council of citizen advisers. Some were visible in the currency enjoyed by
a novel idea—the automatic adjustment of benefit levels to changes in
the cost of living index. That change logically implied a reexamination
of actuarial assumptions, from which, in turn, Mills's action followed.

What was going on was something more than an upsetting change of
personages and personal behavior (Myers's departure, Mills's meta-
morphosis) within a familiar policymaking system. It was, rather, an
adjustment of the system to changing circumstances. The program had
become so large ($39.4 billion out of federal outlays of $231.9 billion
in fiscal 1972) and was expanding so rapidly that "outsiders" (like the
economic analysts in the Budget Bureau and the Brookings Institution)
were looking ever harder for ways to influence it, while conservative
"insiders" (like Byrnes and Myers) were looking for politically acceptable ways to contain and regularize the rate of expansion. At the same
time, liberal "insiders" (like Ball and David) were more than willing to
accept changes if they could be made to serve the goal of expanded
benefits. Indexing and the switch to dynamic assumptions together were
that sort of change.

The expansion of 1972 was a complicated event. On one interpretation, it represented the "old" system of policymaking carried to a perverted, pathological extreme. A significant change in policy, a quantum
increase in benefit levels, was enacted on the authority of a handful of
experts that it was the "sound" thing to do. This could happen the more
easily because Congress had never developed the habit of debate over
social security. It had usually trusted the experts and avoided the hard
questions, and its avoidance of them here reached an absurd extreme.

But the legislation of 1972 may also be viewed as at least potentially a transitional event, marking the breakdown of an old system, in which a small group of program specialists was dominant, and the institution of a new system that would be more accessible to nonspecialists and more comprehensible, and that would be better designed to pose policy choices in a way that would elicit debate.

When Congress enacted the 20 percent benefit increase, it also enacted the automatic procedure governing future increases in benefits and the wage base. Benefits were to rise with prices, and the wage base with earnings; in this way, the program was tied overtly and directly to the performance of the economy. Economic analysts assumed in 1972 that if Congress henceforth wished to deviate from the indexed formula and grant bigger benefit increases than those generated automatically, it would be compelled to raise taxes. In that sense, politics would be injected into the program—the politics of the hard and, ideally, rational choices by which public policy is made.

CHAPTER EIGHTEEN

The Conditions of Controversy: A Summary Analysis

ONE INTERPRETATION of politics and policymaking in American government portrays a spirited contest. One or another actor seeks to achieve something, others whose interests are threatened mobilize in opposition, and both sides gather allies. A struggle ensues. Politics is exciting, accessible, competitive. Virtually any significant move by any actor can be expected to stimulate a variety of others to get into the act.

However, the literature of political analysis also contains images of a very different sort. Another widely accepted interpretation portrays small "subsystems," or "iron triangles," in which leaders of specialized bureaus, specialized congressional committees, and client groups collaborate to make policy for some sphere of government activity in which they have a shared interest. They engage in conflict when outsiders—generalists or members of other specialized subsystems—try to get in on "their" act.[1]

Part 1 portrays such a subsystem for social security, consisting of the leadership of the Social Security Administration, the leadership of the Ways and Means Committee and to a lesser degree of the Finance Committee, social security specialists in organized labor, and leading members of the advisory councils—not exactly a neat triangle, but nonetheless a very limited and stable set of actors with a high degree of autonomy and well-developed doctrines to guide their decisions. Part 2

1. Both of these interpretations may be regarded as "pluralistic" in that they depict a dispersion of power. Elitist interpretations of American politics and policymaking, which argue that the power of a few persons is pervasively dominant, have been rare.

complicates this picture by describing cases of policymaking in which the subsystem (or "system," as I call it here for the sake of simplicity) did not function in this way.

Part 1 argues that program executives typically practiced politics by trying to avert conflict and minimize the cost of action, and that this mode was thoroughly compatible with an institutional milieu in which deference to specialists was the norm. Even in such a system, though, political entrepreneurs always run the risk of stirring things up. They may miscalculate the reaction of others, for it is hard to know where the threshold of indifference lies for each potential political actor, and it may lie in different places at different times. Or these actors may be so committed to achieving their ends that they are willing to accept conflict. They set out knowing that they will provoke sharp reactions but are ready to pay that price for what they want to do.

In response to all three of the issues described in part 3, sharp cleavages developed within one or both of the congressional committees; between organized representatives of business and labor; and between the two major political parties, although divisions never precisely followed party lines. These cleavages persisted until the final votes were cast in Congress: the Senate barely passed disability insurance; the House defeated Byrnes's substitute for medicare by only forty-five votes; many congressional Republicans, though not a majority, followed the administration in preferring a benefit increase only half as large as was enacted in 1972. Dissension replaced consensus even in the inner family of program proprietors, and on each issue they had to bargain with "outsiders," those drawn into the contest who were not program-oriented. These combined processes of inner division and outward expansion increased the complexity of policymaking for the duration of the issue. The rest of this chapter is concerned with what caused conflict to develop and with analyzing responses to it. This book began by asking why there had been so little dispute regarding the social security program, but in retrospect the question needs refining, and one needs to ask how and why the intensity of dispute varied.

A clear pattern emerges when the cases discussed in part 3 are juxtaposed with events described in part 2—conflicts in 1935 over enactment of old age insurance, over the government's proposed sale of individual annuities, and over the Clark amendment, which would have exempted corporate employers with their own pension plans, along with subsequent controversy over the size of the wage base. Boundary issues, which entail enlarging the scope of the public sector, produce much more conflict than distributive issues, which entail the allocation of the costs and benefits of public activity.[2]

Perhaps there is something in American political culture or ideology that accounts for this. People fight over what they believe to be important, and how to divide the public from the private sphere may in general seem more important to Americans than how to distribute the costs and benefits of what is public. Social class, the prime category of distribution, has been less relevant to politics in the United States than in most other Western countries. In discussions of social security, political leaders have avoided talking about it at all. Perhaps politicians have been genuinely unconscious of class divisions and therefore have not constructed a vocabulary with which to discuss them. More likely, they have preferred to treat the subject as taboo, fearing that to talk about such matters would exacerbate latent divisions in society, undermine the popular myths of the social security program, and make their own work of policymaking more difficult. But whereas political rhetoric understated distributive issues in social security, it overstated public-private issues. The merest shadow of a threat to the interests of the private medical profession evoked the specter of "socialized medicine."

Another possibility is that boundary issues were more divisive because they engaged organized interests in a way that distributive issues did not. The groups affected by distribution in social security were so large and amorphous that they were not self-conscious and readily organizable. They were inclusive categories of the population—active workers as distinct from retired workers, high-income taxpayers as distinct from low-income taxpayers, participants in the system as distinct from nonparticipants. Another way of putting it is that because costs and benefits in social security were very widely dispersed, their incidence generated only a low level of conflict even though the stakes, as

2. I would also classify the intense dispute in the late 1930s over the plan of finance as primarily a boundary issue. The essence of the Republican attack was that the accumulation of a large reserve entailed an unwarranted expansion of the public sector. The incidence of taxation was not the issue (see chapter 11). It may be argued that boundary issues if analyzed in depth would turn out to consist largely of distributive elements. The conservative objection to extension of the public sector may plausibly be presumed to arise out of fear that public action will result in redistribution of wealth. I am, however, content at this point to deal only with what is manifest, and the manifest politics of boundary issues is much more intense than the manifest politics of distributive issues.

measured by numbers of persons affected or volume of expenditure, were large. Boundary issues pitted large formal organizations against one another—the Social Security Administration, in alliance with organized labor, against the business federations and the insurance companies, which happened to have little zest for the fight, and against the AMA, which had an enormous zest. Formal organizations, having a sense of purpose and a command of resources, impart vigor and intensity to the political contest, and are likely in turn to mobilize a larger national audience. Organizational politics can stimulate partisan and electoral politics, as happened with medicare and to a much more limited extent with disability insurance.

A third explanation for the relative intensity of boundary politics is that expansion of the public sector typically entailed tax increases, and tax increases automatically elicited resistance. Congress disliked raising taxes, and if new public activity was to be authorized and the taxes to pay for it enacted, Congress had to be pressured. Such pressure generated counterpressure from opposing interest groups, and a political contest would ensue. Distributive measures, which had to do with the incidence—not the increase—of taxes, did not have the same capacity for triggering automatic response.

Finally, from a purely tactical point of view boundary issues were much harder to obscure than distributive issues. Whether or not they were thought to be more important, they were usually more visible, and this made them more contentious. The distributive properties of the program were so thoroughly beclouded by propaganda, implicit political compromises, and impenetrable technicalities that they were practically invulnerable to challenge or dispute. Major enlargements of the program were by comparison much harder to disguise. There were always some sectors of interest and opinion that did not want to cross the threshold of innovation and had to be coaxed or compelled to do it.

For an analysis of social security policymaking, it is less important to ask why boundary questions are relatively divisive than to ask what consequences these divisions had for the way in which policy was made.

In the disability and health insurance cases, conflict produced prolonged agitation and debate, consideration of alternatives other than those favored by program executives, initial adoption of a public assistance program, continued agitation for expansion of the insurance program by program executives and their interest group and partisan allies, recurrent compromise of the program executives' proposals in an effort to reduce opposition, and ultimately adoption of a much compromised bill securing an expanded insurance program but making concessions to opponents either in the form of retrenchments and restrictions (the disability case) or the incorporation of a major feature inconsistent with insurance (part B of medicare). The inner proprietary core retained responsibility for resolving conflicts and writing a satisfactory bill.

The third case of expansion, in which the 20 percent benefit increase was the central event, was very different from the first two, however. Here there was no agitation and debate, virtually no public consideration of other alternatives, the most obvious of which would have been a mixed package of liberalizations or liberalizations combined with a tax cut, and no search for compromise. Participation was extremely narrow. The Ways and Means Committee, as a committee, took no action. Its chairman took the lead, uncharacteristically indifferent to consensus within the committee. In the Senate, it was not the Finance Committee that acted; it was the chairman of the Special Committee on Aging. In this case, the system did not successfully adapt to conflict; it disintegrated.

Whether a government incursion into the private sector elicits a strong response depends very much on who is defending the boundary. It depends, that is, on whether private actors feel threatened by the incursion and have the will or capacity to defend themselves. When the highly politicized medical profession was the defender, as in the disability and health cases, boundary crossings were hard fought, but the doctors had no interest in the big benefit increase of 1972, and if insurance companies or other managers of private investment had a stake, they failed to perceive it and mobilize in response.

Perceptions of private actors, of course, are crucial, and perceptions in 1972 may have been clouded by the nature of the impending change. It developed in a hurry, following release of the advisory council report, and whether a "boundary" was being crossed at all was problematic. After the change in benefit levels was achieved, Robert Ball would see in it and the accompanying switch to indexed benefits a new social security program, but when it was pending, it was not presented as any such thing. The burden was on the opposition to show that a significant incursion into the private sector was occurring, but because the big benefit increase did not add a whole new type of coverage and was in fact an increment to a well-established program, that was hard to do.

Only in retrospect does it seem an increment so sizable in degree as to amount to a change in kind. By contrast, the threshold properties of disability and health insurance were self-evident. Though program executives trimmed their proposals and called them by names calculated to minimize their innovative character, opponents never underestimated the stakes or failed to make a point of them in debate.

The burden on potential opponents in 1972 was much increased—and made impossible, really—by the anomalous fact that the increase was achieved with no increase in tax rates. Here, in the absurd costlessness of it, lies the final and probably most fundamental explanation for the failure of this issue to generate greater contention. The exceptionally large increase of 1969 was costless because the (prior) use of the level earnings assumption, in combination with a booming economy, generated a large actuarial windfall, and the still larger, much more exceptional increase of 1972 was possible because abandoning the level earnings assumption created another, even larger windfall. Though both disability and health insurance turned out to be much more expensive than they were originally estimated to be, neither could be presented as costless. Disability insurance, in theory, was to require an additional tax of only 0.5 percent, and medicare, again in theory, an initial tax of 0.35 percent and an ultimate tax of only 0.8 percent, but even at these modest rates, resistance remained strong, contention vigorous, votes close. It was only when policymakers could pretend, through technical artifice, that the program could be expanded at *no* cost that a prolonged contest could be successfully averted.

It is tempting to interpret the 20 percent benefit increase of 1972 as the extreme operational example of constricted, proprietary policymaking with a built-in bias toward inertial expansion, in view of the extremely narrow participation and the failure to consider alternatives other than program expansion, yet the fact is that some of the leading proprietors were pushed aside in the rush of events, including most of the Ways and Means Committee membership and the whole of the Finance Committee. In the cases of disability and health insurance, the constricted, program-oriented system of policymaking had shown persistence and adaptability, admitting new participants and the consideration of unorthodox (that is, noninsurance) alternatives, and culminating in compromise after long debate, bargaining, and coalition building in which program-oriented actors took the lead. But no such functional adaptation took place in 1972, when policymaking turned precipitous and chaotic. Social security was highly vulnerable to this sort of event, given the long-standing reliance on experts. The arcane technicality of social security gave ordinary men a license to suspend the application of ordinary common sense. However, to attribute this lapse solely to the "system" would overlook the fact that the system disintegrated under the impact of this particular divisive issue.

After a boundary is broken, politics can be expected to subside. The country may pause for a long time at the threshold. It was at the threshold of medicare for ten to twenty years. This is the stage in which political mobilization occurs, but once the threshold is crossed the issue loses much of its mobilizing power. Opposition fades. Perhaps this is because opponents, if ideologically motivated, are demoralized by defeat and either reduce their political activity or look for other, still unbroken boundaries to defend. Or, insofar as they are motivated by interest, it may be because in the course of the political contest they have won protective concessions. At least in the short run, neither disability insurance nor medicare damaged the interests of the medical profession. Extensive concessions were made to protect them. Finally, it may be that the pragmatic spirit of American political culture encourages on all sides a willingness to accept whatever is and to make it "work." This spirit has been abundantly evident in the leadership of the SSA, who hasten after their victories to put representatives of the defeated enemy on advisory committees and to engage them in the preparation of administrative rules.

Whatever the reasons, there is a strong tendency for the constricted pattern of social security policymaking to reassert itself. Conflict subsides, participation contracts, and the incremental enlargement of the program resumes with a small group of official and quasi-official program proprietors again in control. This was emphatically the pattern in disability insurance, much less so in medicare. The difference between them seems to be largely accounted for by differing experience with cost. In disability insurance, the cost was low for a long time, and enlargements could be achieved within the tax rate initially established or with small increases. In medicare, cost immediately exceeded the scheduled tax rate, increased the level and widened the scope of post-enactment politics, and put a brake on inertial expansion.

In the case of the big benefit increase of 1972, the threshold character of the change did not become fully evident until after the change had been enacted and the costliness of it was revealed. In this case, contention arose more in the aftermath than during the threshold crossing. In the aftermath of that change lie the contemporary politics of social security.

To understand the politics of policymaking and to estimate the capacity of the political system for change, it is necessary to be alert to variations over time. To look only at controversial, innovative acts— which analysts tend to do because such events are the most interesting —risks underestimating the dynamism of policymaking. Major innovation, such as the crossing of public-private boundaries entails, comes hard in American politics. It comes after a long wait, and then it comes with many compromises. Analysts who focus on it see classic pressure group politics, in which organized forces are mobilized against organized counterforces, all of which in the end are satisfied to some extent. The result, such analysts generally conclude, is "incremental" (that is, minor) change. But to study the whole process over a long period of time reveals events of another kind: small steps, taken as the result of agreement among an expert, specialized few, to whom others defer. None of these steps by itself is significant enough to cause potential opponents to risk the costs and aggravations of political action; not everyone, after all, can stay mobilized all the time for all possible issues. The steps are mere increments to a statutory foundation on which consensus has already been reached, very likely after a hard-fought conflict in which participants spent much of their energy and political resources. Put together, though, they amount to something important. If analysts would look at the politics of minor increments, they would see in the accretion of them substantial change—even radical change, if not necessarily in the distribution of benefits among social groups, at least in the division of activity between the public and private sectors.

If this portrayal of policymaking is correct, the ebb and flow of tides of opinion or party fortunes is less important than it has sometimes been made to seem. In policymaking for social security, the politics of expansion did not rise and fall with changes of partisan regimes or popular moods. On the initiative of executive leaders of the program in collaboration directly or indirectly with organized labor and liberal Democrats, a major item of expansion was always on the agenda and on its way (if slowly) to becoming law. But the politics of policymaking did not consist exclusively of the resolution of these "leading" issues on the frontiers of program development. Even when new breakthroughs were impending, earlier ones were being consolidated and enlarged upon in consensual fashion. And, whenever a new breakthrough finally did come, it enlarged the base on which future increments could be built. This last point is important because it reiterates the radical potential of incremental changes. One reason that the political system appears to have a very limited potential for change is that it has a limited capacity for managing conflict. It was in recognition of this fact that program executives regulated the agenda of innovation so carefully. They learned from experience not to have more than one major innovation pending at a time. Yet once the threshold of innovation has been crossed and agreement reached on the principle of a new government activity, the possibilities for repeated small enlargements are practically endless. The potential of incremental politics increases as government grows. Whereas the politics of innovation are always difficult, minor increments eventually become extensive and routine.

How much conflict accompanies innovation and how much change may be achieved through incremental acts depends very much on the properties of the particular program for which policy is being made. Disability insurance, health insurance, and the big benefit increase of 1972 all were enacted more easily because they were advanced as additions to an extremely popular program. In social security, the politics of innovation merged indistinguishably with the politics of incrementalism, and both were much affected by the fundamental popularity of the program and by the normally constricted, program-oriented character of the policymaking system.

It is difficult to draw from the complicated cases in part 3 a conclusive judgment on whether the policymaking system or the nature of the program has had the more profound effect on the shape of politics. Both have been important, and they have interacted, each influencing the other and influencing the consideration of particular issues. They also change. Additions to the program have altered its character and increased its cost, and these changes in turn affect the policymaking system. Medicare provides the best illustration. The extreme unpredictability and volatility of costs were disruptive because policymaking had been predicated on the notion that costs could be predicted accurately and would rise slowly. The inapplicability of the level earnings assumption was disruptive, too, and contributed to the severe disruptions of 1972.

Part 4 turns to the contemporary politics of the social security program and takes up the question of how its newly high and sharply rising costs are likely to affect politics and policymaking.

PART FOUR

The Rising Conflict

CHAPTER NINETEEN

The Deficit

THE LEADING ISSUES of social security changed after 1972. The extent to which policymaking may change too under the impact of the change in issues is an open question.

The basic program of cash benefits for the aged had remained noncontroversial for many years. Basic choices about the distribution of costs and benefits were treated as if they were settled for eternity. Within this fixed framework, ad hoc benefit increases were enacted routinely. The politics of the system arose out of proposals for major expansion—disability insurance and then medicare. Finally, after medicare was enacted, a big enlargement of the underlying program began. Always, an item of major expansion dominated the policymakers' agenda, having been placed there on the initiative of the program executives.

After 1972 the leading issue of social security policy was how to finance a growing deficit. Beginning in 1973 official annual reports on the financial condition of the system projected a deficit over the long run (seventy-five years), and, as the 1970s advanced, these long-run projections became steadily more pessimistic. A deficit estimated in 1973 to be 0.32 percent of taxable payroll, or 3 percent of the long-run cost of the system, was estimated in 1977 to be 8.2 percent of taxable payroll.[1] According to these estimates, instead of the scheduled tax rates of 11 to 12 percent in the twenty-first century, rates would have to be 20 percent or more. Beginning in 1975, these same reports also

1. See *1973 Annual Report of the Board of Trustees of the Federal Old-Age and Survivors Insurance and Disability Insurance Trust Funds*, H. Doc. 93-130, 93 Cong. 1 sess. (GPO, 1973), p. 31; and *1977 Annual Report* . . . , H. Doc. 95-150, 95 Cong. 1 sess. (GPO, 1977), p. 2.

predicted a short-term deficit. Social Security Commissioner James B. Cardwell, who succeeded Robert Ball in 1973 (President Nixon having decided to purge his second administration of those high-ranking officials whom he did not trust), testified that expenditures were expected to exceed income in every future year and that the trust funds would be exhausted in the early 1980s unless additional revenue were provided.[2] Events promptly began to confirm the forecasts. Expenditures exceeded income by $1.5 billion in 1975 and $3.2 billion in 1976. As news stories proliferated, anxiety spread over the threatened "bankruptcy" of the system. Former leaders of the program—departed secretaries of HEW and commissioners of social security, led by Wilbur Cohen and Ball—tried to quell the alarm with assurances of the soundness and durability of social security, but there was no escaping the fact that further financing was called for.[3] Whether or not the alarm was justified, the deficit was real.

And unexpected. "I want to make it clear that this legislation is financed on a conservative basis," Wilbur Mills had told the House in 1972, as he argued for the 20 percent benefit increase. "If we enact the 20 percent increase with the tax adjustments that are in my bill . . . I can assure the membership of this House that we will [over the next seventy-five years] take in each year more money than we will be paying out."[4] Shortly before leaving office in 1973, Commissioner Ball assured a Senate committee that the tax rate would be sufficient well into the next century. "I have a lot of confidence in that," he said, adding that there was a considerable margin of safety in the actuarial estimates and that official projections erred, if at all, on the conservative side.[5] Four years later, Congress enacted tax increases that were expected to raise an additional $227 billion in the next decade.

The financial troubles of the system demonstrated the limits of the policymakers' vision. Policymaking for social security had always been conducted as if the policymakers could tell what the future held. The

2. *Financing the Social Security System,* Hearings before the Subcommittee on Social Security of the House Committee on Ways and Means, 94 Cong. 1 sess. (GPO, 1976), pp. 3–38.

3. Edwin L. Dale, Jr., "Ex-Officials Back Pension System," *New York Times,* February 11, 1975.

4. *Congressional Record* (March 6, 1972), p. 6987, and ibid. (June 30, 1972), p. 23731.

5. *Future Directions in Social Security,* Hearings before the Senate Special Committee on Aging, 93 Cong. 1 sess. (GPO, 1973), pt. 1, p. 34.

appearance of a deficit was unsettling not just because it required painful action, but because it forced at least a faint recognition, also painful, that a high degree of uncertainty in policymaking is inescapable.[6]

The Sources of Surprise

Three factors—rapidly rising disability claims, a declining fertility rate, and adverse changes in the economy—account for the sudden, unexpected appearance of a deficit in the program.

A higher-than-expected incidence of disability was not new. As a Ways and Means staff report noted in 1974, chronic deficits had developed in the disability portion of the program in the previous decade. In five years, the estimates of disability insurance costs had almost doubled. The SSA was studying the causes but had come to no conclusion. In the face of continuing adverse experience, the actuaries kept revising their estimates. This more than any other single factor accounted for the long-range deficit reported in 1973, and it contributed to the later, much larger ones.

In 1972, two years after his departure from office as chief actuary, Robert Myers warned of the declining birthrate in a newspaper article.[7] In the next century the ratio of workers to retired persons would be lower than expected. Myers argued that this "hidden hazard" should have been taken into account before the 20 percent benefit increase was enacted. The official failure to use current fertility data made the long-range costs of the system appear artificially low, he said. Two years later, with the use of newly published data from the 1970 census, the actuary's office finally did revise its demographic assumptions, with

6. Congressmen, who had to enact the tax increases, suffered more of this pain than the program executives. Senator Russell B. Long, the Finance Committee chairman, publicly complained that the executive's faulty actuarial estimates in 1972 had proved "disastrous to the actuarial soundness of the Social Security System." (Adam Clymer, "Carter Welfare Bid Is Criticized by Long," New York Times, September 16, 1977.) Robert Ball, on the other hand, when asked by a House committee for an explanation of why things had gone so wrong, found the answer solely in the perverse performance of the economy and the decline of the birthrate. He could recall no major mistakes on the part of policymakers in 1972 or at any other time. Social Security, Hearings before the Subcommittee on Retirement Income and Employment of the House Select Committee on Aging, 94 Cong. 1 sess. (GPO, 1975), pp. 130–31.

7. "Social Security's Hidden Hazards," Wall Street Journal, July 28, 1972.

the result that a very large long-term deficit in the system was projected. The declining birthrate had no effect, however, in the short term.

The third cause of the deficit—changes in the economy—had both short-run and long-run effects. In 1974 the country experienced an anomalous and unexpected surge of inflation combined with high unemployment. Expenditures for social security rose in response to the inflation, while receipts fell below expectations because of the unemployment. The impact on the system was immediate but not merely temporary. Benefit obligations unexpectedly incurred would have to be met far into the future; income unexpectedly lost was lost forever. Partly in response to this new and unprecedented experience, SSA officials revised the economic assumptions on which their financial projections were based. Whereas in 1972 they assumed that average earnings would rise by 5 percent and the consumer price index by 2.75 percent a year, in 1976 they were assuming a rise in average earnings of 5.75 percent and a rise in the CPI of 4 percent.[8] Thus they were assuming only a 1.75 percent annual increase in real earnings, compared to the 1972 assumption of 2.25 percent.

The seriousness of the long-term deficit was of course problematic. Projections had erred in the past; they could err again. Fertility rates, which had unexpectedly fallen, could unexpectedly rise. Inflation could subside, productivity increase. But on paper, at least, the long-run deficit was alarmingly high, and a current deficit had become an undeniable fact. Policymakers had to decide what to do.

The Constraints on Response

Responding to an unexpected deficit in the program was a good deal harder in the 1970s than it would have been ten or twenty years earlier.

Automatic increases. One reason for this was the new benefit formula that tied increases automatically to the cost of living beginning in 1975. Had the traditional practice of irregular, ad hoc adjustments survived, Congress would have had more room for maneuver. Ironically, Congress had made the system depend directly on the performance of the economy just when the economy became erratic.

No safety margins. A second reason for the lack of adaptability in the system was that built-in margins for error had been used up in the

8. *1976 Annual Report* . . . , H. Doc. 94-505, 94 Cong. 2 sess. (GPO, 1976), p. 46.

early 1970s in the course of the big expansion of cash benefits. Again ironically, defenses against error were abandoned just at the time when major error occurred. The level wage assumption had been one such defense. In the past, the (technically unanticipated) returns from rising wages had been available to make adjustments in the system, and adjustments were tailored to the size of the actual gain from earnings and other changes in the system. When dynamic assumptions were adopted this possibility ceased.

Another protection had been the use of a narrow "allowable margin of deficiency." The concept of this margin was introduced in 1958 when the program had a current deficit for the first time. The Ways and Means Committee had promptly raised taxes and declared that "the actuarial status of the system should be improved . . . so that the actuarial insufficiency is reduced to the point where it is virtually eliminated, namely below one-fourth of 1 percent of payroll."[9] This margin, plus an additional 0.05 percent for the disability portion of the program, became the benchmark for fiscal soundness. In 1965, when the long-range estimates began to be made for a seventy-five-year period rather than into perpetuity, the allowable margin was reduced to 0.1 percent at the actuary's recommendations. For a decade, the Ways and Means Committee observed these norms faithfully, and the Finance Committee breached them only once, but in 1970 Ways and Means compromised for the first time and approved a benefit increase that would have left the system with a deficit of 0.12 percent, over the vigorous dissent of the committee's Republican minority.[10] Later the same year, the Finance Committee endorsed a bigger breach, and in the fall of 1973 the committees accepted a deficit of more than 0.5 percent of payroll, five times what had hitherto been thought acceptable.[11]

Finally, room for error was sacrificed by the adoption of current-cost financing in 1972. Congress's practice since the mid-1950s had been to set tax rates so as to produce small annual increases in the social security trust fund and to maintain it at a level significantly exceeding annual expenditures. The excess was very large in the early years of the program, diminished in the 1950s and early 1960s, and began to rise again

9. *Social Security Amendments of 1958*, H. Rept. 2288, 85 Cong. 2 sess. (GPO, 1958), pp. 27–28.

10. *Social Security Act Amendments of 1970*, H. Rept. 91-1096, 91 Cong. 2 sess. (GPO, 1970), p. 78; Republican dissent appears on pp. 142–43.

11. *Staff Data and Materials Relating to Social Security Financing*, prepared by the staff for the Senate Committee on Finance, 95 Cong. 1 sess. (GPO, 1977), p. 45.

with the prosperity of the late 1960s. The 1971 advisory council, which had recommended abandoning the level earnings assumption, also recommended that the financing of the program should be sufficient only to meet current costs and to maintain the trust fund at a level approximately equal to one year's expenditures. This change helped to finance the 20 percent benefit increase of 1972, but contributed further to reducing the cushion for error at a critical time. In an effort to compensate for these sacrifices, the actuary introduced an explicit safety margin of $\frac{3}{8}$ of 1 percent of payroll into the long-range estimates in 1972, but this was swallowed up by the surging deficits of succeeding years.[12]

A mature program. A third reason for the declining room for maneuver was the advancing maturity of the system. In the past, it had been relatively easy to capture new revenues by extending coverage to hitherto uncovered groups of workers (farmers or self-employed professionals, for example). In the 1970s, there were no major uncovered occupational groups except for federal government employees, who had demonstrated over decades the power to resist inclusion in the system, and a sizable minority (about 30 percent) of state and local government employees. To raise the tax rate was one possibility. This had often been done in the past, but it had often been willfully avoided, too, and it had never been easy. Politicians appeared to believe that it got harder as the rate got higher, and in 1973, at 5.85 percent each on employer and employee, the rate was undeniably conspicuous and, for many taxpayers, burdensome. Also, tax increases had been sweetened in the past with simultaneous benefit increases, but when the principal purpose of an increase was to cure a deficit, sweetening could be offered only in relatively small amounts. To lower benefits, on the other hand, was all but inconceivable, judging from the past practice of policy-

12. Except for the social security actuary, who conceived the $\frac{3}{8}$ percent cushion, no one inside the government argued in 1971–72 for preserving a substantial margin for error. Indeed, economists in HEW's Office of the Assistant Secretary for Planning and Evaluation argued that the $\frac{3}{8}$ percent factor should be eliminated. Economic analysts in general were preoccupied at this time with what they saw as the contrived overfinancing of the social security program. As they interpreted it, the level earnings assumption and other such devices were not so much a prudent provision for error as they were devices calculated by program executives to produce automatic surpluses and thereby assure the unchecked future expansion of the program. Almost without exception, economic analysts inside and outside the government keenly favored the switch to dynamic assumptions and current-cost financing, independent of ideology or organizational location. Interview with Charles L. Trowbridge, November 15, 1977; Memo, Assistant Secretary for Planning and Evaluation (Laurence E. Lynn, Jr.) to Chief Actuary, SSA, "Comments on Draft of OASDI Trustees Report," March 23, 1972.

makers, and if it was all but inconceivable in a partially established program, it was utterly inconceivable in a nearly mature one, from which over 30 million persons were benefiting and most of the remaining millions expected to benefit eventually.

In this situation, two different responses of the policymakers might be predicted by extrapolating from the analysis of this book. One line of argument has been that visible cost precipitates political conflict. From this, one would predict a much higher incidence of conflict as a result of the deficit, broadened participation, and examination of a wider-than-usual range of courses of action. Another line of argument has been that the basic pattern of policymaking is incremental enlargement of the program. From this, one would predict that an unexpected deficit would become simply one more occasion for expansion. Reduction of benefits would be automatically rejected and new financing would be improvised, so that past enlargements of the system would be confirmed or new ones advanced. Both types of response are clearly discernible, but on balance the second prevailed over the first.

The Political Response: Widened Debate

The financial troubles of the social security system galvanized policy analysts in both private and public settings. At every hand, models began to be built and assumptions tested. The Brookings Institution, the American Enterprise Institute for Public Policy Research, the Hoover Institution on War, Revolution, and Peace, the Institute for Contemporary Studies, the new Congressional Budget Office, and the Office of the Assistant Secretary for Planning and Evaluation in HEW prepared books, pamphlets, and technical papers.[13] "It's sometimes hard

13. The following list of titles is not exhaustive: Alicia H. Munnell, *The Future of Social Security* (Brookings Institution, 1977); J. W. Van Gorkom, *Social Security—The Long-Term Deficit* (Washington, D.C.: American Enterprise Institute for Public Policy Research, 1976); Robert S. Kaplan, *Financial Crisis in the Social Security System* (American Enterprise Institute for Public Policy Research, 1976); Rita Ricardo Campbell, *Social Security: Promise and Reality* (Stanford, Calif.: Hoover Institution Press, 1977); Michael J. Boskin, ed., *The Crisis in Social Security: Problems and Prospects* (San Francisco: Institute for Contemporary Studies, 1977); Congressional Budget Office, *Financing Social Security: Issues for the Short and Long Term* (CBO, July 1977); Lawrence H. Thompson, "An Analysis of the Factors Currently Determining Benefit-Level Adjustments in the Social Security Retirement Program," Technical Analysis Paper (HEW, Office of the Assistant Secretary for Planning and Evaluation, Office of Income Security Policy, September 1974).

to keep up with everybody," a high official in SSA remarked. "It's like the economists have discovered money."[14] An array of congressional committees was galvanized too. The Joint Economic Committee, a new Select Committee on Aging in the House, and the Senate's Special Committee on Aging held hearings, in addition to those held by the Ways and Means Committee.[15] At the request of a member of Congress, the General Accounting Office issued a report on the financial troubles of the system.[16] More significant, though, was the appearance of new activity and a newly critical attitude among official actors with direct stakes in the program.

The Treasury Department, which had ignored social security policy for nearly thirty years, suddenly was aroused. In the fall of 1973, following the first official announcement of a long-range deficit, the department commissioned an independent actuarial audit of the system by two private consultants. They were asked to examine the assumptions used by the SSA actuary, to construct a computer program that would enable the Treasury Department to make independent estimates of the cost of the system, and to comment on the system's economic effects. Issued in 1974, this report sharply criticized the failure of the SSA actuary's office to use current population projections, questioned the realism of its economic assumptions, and urged a study of the effect of the social security system on private saving.[17] In a newspaper article published shortly before the Ford administration left office, its secretary of the treasury, William E. Simon, wrote that he had been "shocked" to discover the financial condition of the system and urged that the rate

14. Interview with John Snee, September 26, 1977.
15. *Future Directions in Social Security*, Hearings before the Senate Special Committee on Aging, 94 Cong. 1 sess. (GPO, 1975), pts. 9–11; *Social Security*, Hearings before the Subcommittee on Retirement Income and Employment of the House Select Committee on Aging, 94 Cong. 1 sess. (GPO, 1975); *Financing the Social Security System*, Hearings before the Subcommittee on Social Security of the House Committee on Ways and Means, 94 Cong. 1 sess. (GPO, 1975); *President's Social Security Proposals*, Hearings before the Subcommittee on Social Security of the House Committee on Ways and Means, 94 Cong. 2 sess. (GPO, 1976); *The Social Security System*, Hearings before the Joint Economic Committee, 94 Cong. 2 sess. (GPO, 1976).
16. Comptroller General of the United States, *Financial Problems Confront the Federal Old-Age and Survivors Insurance and Disability Insurance* (General Accounting Office, 1975).
17. Robert S. Kaplan and Roman L. Weil, "An Actuarial Audit of the Social Security System" (U.S. Treasury, Office of the Secretary, September 1974).

at which benefits grew be reduced. Otherwise, he warned, the government would not be able to keep its promises.[18]

Even more significant, perhaps, was the appearance of a critical, independent spirit among the official proprietors in Congress. Soon after the appearance of the trustees' report of 1974, which predicted a very large long-term deficit, the Senate Finance Committee created a panel of private actuaries and economists to prepare an independent analysis. Published early in 1975, this report found that the financial condition of the system was indeed serious (and probably worse than the trustees' report had said), that the recently enacted formula for determining benefits responded irrationally to changes in the rate of inflation, and that the official methodology for forecasting costs was inadequate for the system's magnitude and complexity. It recommended that "strong measures be taken to restore the financial health of the OASDI Program," that the benefit formula be rationalized, and that "improved procedures be adopted to reveal the costs, implications and controllability of this program."[19] All of this was notably strong language from an officially sponsored source, and there would be more. The same panel, slightly reconstituted, was soon engaged by the Congressional Research Service to study ways in which the benefit structure might be revised. Just as Congress's willingness to ask this question was remarkable, so was the panel's answer to it.

The Hsiao report, as it was called (after the panel's director, William C. L. Hsiao, an economist and actuary on the faculty of the Harvard School of Public Health), appeared in the summer of 1976. It recommended a revised benefit formula that would eliminate irrational responses to the inflation rate and also eliminate the long-range deficit in the system. It would have done this by an indexing plan that tied benefit increases strictly to increases in the cost of living. The automatic formula enacted in 1972 had also tied benefits to increases in the cost of living, but had done so in a way that overcompensated for them if there was a rapid rate of inflation. The Hsiao formula corrected for this anomaly. It was also designed to produce a system with a stable long-run tax rate, which the Hsiao panel argued was a major advantage. "The panel believes that future generations of workers should not be

18. William E. Simon, "How to Rescue Social Security," *Wall Street Journal,* November 3, 1976.

19. *Report of the Panel on Social Security Financing to the Committee on Finance,* Committee Print, 94 Cong. 1 sess. (GPO, 1975), p. 4.

committed in advance to materially rising tax rates," the report said. Future choices of Congress and of the citizenry regarding the size of the program should be kept open. Whether benefits would fall under this plan depended on the criterion of measurement. Benefits as measured by purchasing power (that is, their relation to consumer prices) would be stabilized, but replacement rates (the relation of the benefit to the pre-retirement wage) would probably fall. Congress, of course, could always enact ad hoc increases whenever it wanted to. The aim of the Hsiao panel was to avoid committing Congress in advance to any increases other than those necessary to keep pace with price increases. "The emphasis of this Panel's proposal is upon congressional control," the report said.[20]

The assertiveness of the Treasury Department along with the adventurism of the Finance Committee and its panel together posed a significant challenge to orthodox patterns of participation and thought in policymaking for social security. Not for years had the official proprietorship been so subject to criticism and challenge from official sources. Putatively independent inquiries such as those by the advisory councils had usually been vulnerable to cooptation, but the independence of the Hsiao panel was written on every page of its report. In arguing that future generations should be able to decide whether they wanted to pay for social security benefit increases, the panel was attacking a fundamental premise of the program: that future generations were, and ought to be, irrevocably committed to whatever promises the present generation might put into law. It is no wonder that Robert Ball called the Hsiao plan a "very dangerous proposal."[21]

To some extent, this new assertiveness and independence may have been a response to changes within the family of official proprietors. Long-dominant figures had departed. Because Myers had left office as chief actuary in 1970, Ball as commissioner in 1973, Mills as chairman of the Ways and Means Committee in 1975, and Byrnes as the ranking Republican in 1973, diverse claims to expertise could more easily be asserted. Changes in structure and procedure in both the executive and the legislature also encouraged wider participation. Mechanisms for including generalists in policymaking had developed considerably inside the executive branch since 1965, principally through the Office of

20. *Report of the Consultant Panel on Social Security to the Congressional Research Service,* prepared for the use of the Senate Committee on Finance and the House Committee on Ways and Means, 94 Cong. 2 sess. (GPO, 1976), pp. 2, 5.

21. *The Social Security System,* Hearings, p. 33.

Planning and Evaluation in HEW and the Executive Office of the President, within which OMB and elements of the White House staff, variously organized in different administrations, competed for a share of affairs. In Congress, committee and conference sessions had been opened to the public, and the Ways and Means Committee, under the instructions of House Democrats, had instituted the use of subcommittees, a practice all but abandoned during Mills's chairmanship. Also, the size of the committee had been increased. And both the Ways and Means and Finance committees added staff assistance on social security. All of these changes caused doors to open on what had long been the closed proprietorship of policymaking for social security. But had it not been for the appearance of the deficit, fewer claimants to participation would have stepped forward.

It remains to ask just what effect this new development had on the course of policy. I argue below that it had little or none. Ultimately, the central fact about the Hsiao report was that it was completely rejected by policymakers. Policy continued to evolve in the expansive pattern of the previous forty years.

The Policy Response: Continued Expansion

Late in 1977 Congress responded to the deficit by increasing taxes and revising the benefit formula. The tax increase applied both to the rate and to the wage base, and in regard to the latter was very large. By deciding to raise the base to $29,700 as of 1981, Congress in effect decided to tax an estimated 91 percent of the earnings of covered workers, thus continuing expansion of the public program as measured by this basic indicator. At 91 percent, the program would approach the standard of 1935 and far exceed the standard of 81 percent that had prevailed for two decades after the 1950 amendments. This change represented one more fulfillment of the program executives' objectives. They had long wanted to tap much more of the taxable payroll, and when a financial deficit developed Robert Ball's first and foremost recommendation was to do just that.[22]

22. Ball, though no longer in office, was no more retired from proprietorship of the program than Wilbur Cohen had been in 1956. He remained in Washington working on a book on social security and was very much on hand to give advice to Democratic officeholders and candidates, who were as much as ever inclined to ask him for it.

In regard to benefits, Congress adopted a formula that tied the benefits of retired persons automatically to increases in prices, as had the formula of 1972, but that tied the benefits promised to active workers automatically to increases in wages. Whether this represented an expansion of the program, a contraction, or simply the correction of a technical flaw, as those who devised the new formula asserted, is a complicated matter. At a minimum it confirmed the expansion of 1972, which Congress in its haste to act had understood very poorly and justified hardly at all in the scant residue of legislative history that it left behind.

The Benefit Formula: Wage Indexing versus Price Indexing

The first issue to be resolved in the policy deliberations of 1974–77—arguably more fundamental than financing—was how to design the benefit formula. It is the volume of benefits promised that determines the amount of taxes needed, although the relation is distinctly reciprocal in social security, inasmuch as benefits are related to wages and an increase in the wage base has the effect of increasing the benefit obligations of the system.[23]

That policymakers should have chosen to revise the benefit formula at all in 1977 requires explanation. A deficit could have been met by raising more revenue. Why tinker with a benefit formula that had only just gone into effect?

The answer to this is that the indexed formula that was enacted in 1972 and began to be applied in 1975 did not work properly in the inflationary conditions of the mid-1970s. Robert Myers, who presented that formula to Congress in 1969, understood perfectly well that it was unsuited to an inflationary economy but discounted the risk. He told the Ways and Means Committee that by providing for automatic adjustment of the wage base as earnings rose, the formula "would very conservatively finance automatic benefit increases, unless we came into a time when there was a run-away inflation." Without explanation, he

23. The Ford administration acknowledged the centrality of benefits by its initial reaction to the deficit, which was to propose that in 1975 the automatic benefit increase be limited to 5 percent without regard to the actual increase in the consumer price index, which was certain to be higher. ("Income Security," *Congressional Quarterly Weekly Report*, vol. 34 [January 24, 1976], p. 134.) For this quixotic proposal the administration did not find a single congressional sponsor. It then turned to consideration of both benefit and tax revisions.

added that "that possibility can be ignored."[24] The flaw, then, is to be attributed not so much to a want of expertise as to an excess of optimism, the expert's characteristic confidence that he can foresee, if not actually engineer, the future course of events. Mills appears to have shared this confidence. Though leery of indexing and unwilling to recommend it to the House, Mills seemed to agree that inflation would be brought under control. "Oh, no. We are not going to let [the] cost of living continue to go up," he told Myers. "We are going to stop it here one of these days. . . . We are already committed to that."[25] The inflation rate that year was 6.1 percent. History showed that it had averaged around 2 percent a year, and that was where Mills expected it to remain. That the inflation rate in 1974 rose to 12.2 percent, twice that of 1969, and that price increases exceeded wage increases, contrary to all recent experience, was a surprise to everyone. No economic experts predicted any such events, but the fact of surprise was particularly incongruous and unwelcome within the world of policymaking for social security, which had proceeded with the faith, or as if with the faith, that there would be no surprises, and which had not in the past been subjected to the tempering discipline of either adverse experience or the power of rival experts.

The flaw in the formula of 1972 lay in the "coupling" of benefit adjustments for active workers with those for retired workers, which could result in overcompensating active workers for the effects of inflation. When retired workers had their benefits raised in proportion to increases in the cost of living, equivalent changes were made in the formula that governed the benefits promised to active workers. But these workers meanwhile were gaining in another way. Their actual wages were rising, in response at least partly to changes in the cost of living. Their future social security benefits, which were related to their wages, rose as their wages rose—and then rose additionally as promised benefits were increased with each 3 percent increase in the consumer price index. The result was that under conditions of severe inflation, active workers in the long run could get absurdly high benefit payments.

There was nothing new in the coupling of cost of living adjustments for active and retired workers. The same practice had been followed in the ad hoc benefit increases of the 1950s and 1960s, and this explains

24. *Social Security and Welfare Proposals*, Hearings before the House Committee on Ways and Means, 91 Cong. 1 sess. (GPO, 1970), pt. 1, p. 204.
25. Ibid., p. 203.

why Myers incorporated it in the indexed formula. To the best of his ability, he was seeking to reproduce past practice. This arrangement had worked well enough—indeed, had tended to produce surpluses for the system, not deficits—as long as wages increased faster than prices, the rate of increase of both remained relatively low, and the relation between the two rates remained fairly stable; but when the velocity of change increased and the relation between wage and price increases became unstable, the formula proved to be erratic. Replacement rates could in time rise or fall precipitously as the rates of price and wage increases varied.[26]

Even before the new formula began to be applied in 1975, it was clear to experts in social security that revision was essential. Under the revised economic assumptions that the actuaries began using in the mid-1970s, besides causing replacement rates to behave erratically, the formula contributed to the large long-range deficit that suddenly appeared in the system. It magnified the adverse effects of the economic changes that were occurring. Accordingly, at one of the first meetings of the 1974–75 advisory council, the SSA staff circulated a proposal for revision. The formula that Congress enacted had its genesis there.

The proposal to the advisory council had been prepared by Charles L. Trowbridge, who succeeded Myers as chief actuary of the SSA but resigned himself in 1973 after only two-and-a-half years. In 1974 he was serving as a consultant to the advisory council.[27] Trowbridge's proposal,

26. In addition to sources already cited, see *Reports of the Quadrennial Advisory Council on Social Security*, H. Doc. 94-75, 94 Cong. 1 sess. (GPO, 1975), chaps. 3 and 7, and app. A; Colin D. Campbell, *Over-Indexed Benefits: The Decoupling Proposals for Social Security* (Washington, D.C.: American Enterprise Institute for Public Policy Research, 1976); Ernest J. Moorhead and Charles L. Trowbridge, "The Unresolved Decoupling Issue," *Transactions of the Society of Actuaries*, vol. 29 (1977); Lawrence H. Thompson, "Toward the Rational Adjustment of Social Security Benefit Levels," *Policy Analysis*, vol. 3 (Fall 1977), pp. 485–508; *Decoupling the Social Security Benefit Structure*, Hearings before the Subcommittee on Social Security of the House Committee on Ways and Means, 94 Cong. 2 sess. (GPO, 1976).

27. An employee of the Bankers Life Company of Des Moines since 1938, Trowbridge in 1970 had sought the job as chief actuary in the expectation that a decade of public service would constitute a satisfying end to his career. Instead he found that he could not tolerate the chaos of Washington, where he was bombarded with demands that he had to meet no matter how arbitrary they seemed or what the motives behind them might be. The "whole atmosphere" drove him "up the wall," he later explained, and he soon went back to the orderly, stable, and comprehensible routines of Bankers Life (interview, November 15, 1977). Trowbridge was a

on which he had begun work while still in office, rested on the assumption that the overriding aim of revision should be the stabilization of replacement rates.[28] This was a debatable matter. Members of the Hsiao panel would later argue that replacement ratios should not be regarded as the only test of the reasonableness of the benefit structure. Another possible test was the maintenance of purchasing power, and still another might be the relation between the value of benefits and the value of taxes paid by the individual and his employer.[29] But within the SSA, the advisory council, and at the top of HEW, replacement rates were established early in the discussions as the touchstone, and this laid the conceptual foundations for the outcome of 1977. Though policymakers had only recently begun to employ the term and it was still not part of the currency of public discussion, replacement rates had suddenly become fundamental.[30]

In order to stabilize replacement rates, Trowbridge and other actuarial and economic consultants to the advisory council devised a new benefit formula that "decoupled" benefit increases for active workers from those for retired workers and indexed the benefits for active workers to the movement of wages rather than prices. One of Trowbridge's principal collaborators was Myers. His expertise, undimmed by exile or by the appearance of error in the system he had done so much to establish, was increasingly in demand as policymakers considered how to cope with their troubles. Myers had originally suggested a

psychological dissident, unlike Myers, who in 1970 had been a political dissident. It took the SSA more than a year to replace Trowbridge, and his successor, A. Haeworth Robertson, likewise distinguished within the profession, appeared to have no more taste for the Washington life than Trowbridge and left office himself in 1978. During congressional consideration of legislation in 1977 he was nowhere in sight, and the congressional committees turned once again to Myers for actuarial advice. After seven years he was filling the vacuum on Capitol Hill that his own departure from office had created. In retrospect, Myers appears as a truly singular figure. No other chief actuary approached him in combining technical talent with a taste for the political milieu.

28. Moorhead and Trowbridge, "The Unresolved Decoupling Issue," pp. 72–74.

29. President's Social Security Proposals, Hearings, pp. 392–94.

30. The concept might have achieved more currency if it had been more useful politically. An economist who worked in HEW in the early 1970s complained of social security program executives that "privately they talked replacement rates but publicly they talked poverty." Lifting the poor "out of poverty" had more appeal than raising anybody's replacement rate. In connection with revising the benefit formula, however, the political utility of replacement rates increased and the concept instantly gained currency.

different approach to revision of the benefit formula for active workers. He would have limited benefit increases to the percentage increase in the consumer price index or to half the percentage increase in average earnings, whichever was smaller, an approach that would have paid less heed to replacement rates, but he acquiesced in the wage-indexing approach as he saw a consensus developing for it and contemplated some of its technical properties.

As agreement took shape among the experts attached to the advisory council, it also took shape among interest groups. This was the nature and function of the advisory councils, which brought different interests together. In social security it was especially important to have support from organized labor, which continued to be the leading private share-holder in the proprietorship of the program. Its representatives on the advisory council were reluctant to endorse the new formula, which they were initially inclined to interpret as a deliberalization. Only when they were convinced that the coupled formula was not necessarily liberaliz-ing, but was above all erratic, and that the substitute would prevent replacement rates from falling—as well as rising—did they acquiesce in revision, and even then they did so grudgingly.[31] Commissioner Cardwell, who was eager to secure prompt enactment of a decoupled formula, appealed for their support. So did Robert Ball, who was mov-ing about behind the scenes to round up backers for the wage-indexed, decoupled formula, of which he heartily approved. (Ball would always have preferred wage indexing to price indexing, but could not have found support for it in 1969–72, when the very concept of indexing was novel.) When the SSA's decoupling proposal went to President Ford in the fall of 1975, it went therefore with the support of the advisory council and of organized labor. To the best of the ability of the social security program's leadership (both the incumbent official leader, Card-well, and the nominally retired but still highly influential Ball), the politics of decoupling was already settled. It had been averted by an-ticipation, which had been the mode in social security for many years.

That the matter did not remain settled and that President Ford was presented with a significantly different alternative to the SSA proposal is one sign that there was a "new" and more vigorous politics of social security after 1972. It was bureaucratic politics. Conflict was develop-ing inside the executive branch as the Treasury Department began to

31. Moorhead and Trowbridge, "The Unresolved Decoupling Issue," p. 76; *Reports of the Quadrennial Advisory Council on Social Security*, H. Doc. 94-75, p. 70.

press for changes in the actuarial estimates to correct what it believed to be an optimistic bias. Together with the Council of Economic Advisers, the Treasury Department argued in the fall of 1975 that when the social security benefit formula was decoupled, benefit levels for future retirees should be tied to the growth in prices rather than wages. This less expansive method was expected to eliminate the long-range deficit in the system, whereas indexing to wages was expected to no more than halve the deficit. For several months in the second half of 1975 an interdepartmental working group considered this and other issues connected with social security finance. The threatened "bankruptcy" of the system was now in the forefront of public attention, and in preparation for presentation of the budget early in 1976 the Ford administration was considering what if any recommendations to make to Congress.

At the end of 1975, the issue of how to index social security benefits reached the President.[32] His domestic council, which had been staffing and coordinating executive discussions of the subject, prepared a long options paper that solicited his decision in that matter as well as short-term issues of social security finance. In the paper, which he may or may not have read (very possibly he depended on oral presentations only), he was told that he could defer action on decoupling, choose to decouple in a way that maintained the current role of social security (SSA's proposal, which had by now received the sponsorship of departmental officials in HEW), or decouple in a way that reduced the future role of social security (the Treasury-CEA proposal). The reductions could vary in degree. The pros and cons of each choice were outlined for him briefly.

In regard to the HEW proposal, which the paper labeled "neutral" decoupling, the President was told that this would prove the least controversial choice among constituent groups and in the Congress. The AFL-CIO and organizations of the elderly had already agreed to it. It would ensure that the benefits of future retirees would keep pace with the nation's standard of living. "You could propose to 'decouple' in this manner now," the President was told, "and come back later after further analysis and consensus building, with a broader proposal to change the structure and role of Social Security over the long-term." The argu-

32. My account of the Ford administration's internal deliberations is drawn from an excellent article by James W. Singer, "Social Security Fund's Problems Take on New Urgency," *National Journal*, vol. 8 (February 14, 1976), pp. 198–204, as well as interviews with several of the participants.

ments against this choice were that it would eliminate only half of the deficit and sacrifice some bargaining power if the President later should decide that he did want to reexamine the role of social security. In support of the price-indexing proposal, the paper said that it would eliminate the entire long-term deficit, allow future tax reductions, and permit people to invest more heavily in private pensions, thereby stimulating capital formation. However, the paper said, such a far-reaching change in the system would prove very controversial politically.[33] The whole thrust of this presentation to the President was that the HEW proposal did not represent a policy change at all, but merely an endorsement of the status quo in social security. The domestic council staff, like HEW, took replacement rates as the touchstone.

The President was told that the secretary of HEW advised prompt endorsement of a neutral decoupling proposal. The domestic council, whose staff was very much in sympathy with the HEW position, concurred in this recommendation (in reality this was the position of the council staff, inasmuch as the council, a cabinet-level group, was moribund). Alan Greenspan, chairman of the CEA, argued that it was premature to ask the President to " 'choose among the few extremes presented in the memo which have not really been worked out in all their ramifications.' "[34] Little or no technical work had been done inside the government on any alternative to the SSA proposal, since no one outside the SSA had the time, data, or technical capacity to prepare a detailed alternative. Miscellaneous advisers on the President's White House staff endorsed either no action or the Treasury-CEA alternative.

Many of the executive staff who were aware of this issue expected the President to postpone action. He could have confined his recommendations to short-term financing and waited for the next election to pass and for the executive branch to study this important issue more carefully, meanwhile keeping his options open—a strategy that politicians are generally presumed to prefer. But President Ford apparently was convinced that it would be irresponsible not to act promptly, since the deficit in the system was causing public anxiety and the 1972 formula, which was one cause of the deficit, was already having adverse unintended effects on the system. Replacement rates and benefit obliga-

33. Memorandum for the President from Jim Cannon, "Social Security Financing," December 17, 1975.
34. Quoted in ibid., p. 15.

tions were creeping up as the coupled formula responded to an inflated economy. And, if the President were to pick any decoupled formula, it is very hard to see how he could have picked one other than that proposed by HEW, which was described to him as "neutral" and "noncontroversial" and blessed with the support of Congress and pertinent interest groups. It is hard to see how at the beginning of a presidential election year he could have favored a choice that he was told would "reduce" the role of social security as against one that would merely "maintain" it.

Except in SSA, whose new commissioner, Cardwell, was very much afraid that political conflict would prevent the passage of any decoupling plan, none of the executive participants was well satisfied with the quality or progress of deliberations on this difficult subject. Even among those of the domestic council staff and in the Office of the Assistant Secretary for Planning and Evaluation in HEW who thought that the Treasury-CEA position was outlandish and politically suicidal ("I couldn't believe that we were having this discussion in this place at this time," a domestic council staff member later said),[35] there was nonetheless a feeling that the issue deserved far more study than it had received. Reflecting this view, a view quite characteristic, of course, of people whose prime function is policy analysis, the options paper that the domestic council presented to the President also recommended a comprehensive study of the social security system. Among those whose proposals had been defeated, there was a feeling that they had as usual lost out in a grossly unequal contest with the program specialists. "When you have SSA against you, it's pretty much hopeless," the Treasury staff man later said.[36] "Social Security is always ahead," the CEA economist observed. "No one else does it full time, and it's very difficult to compete when you have no equipment and no time."[37] Program leaders alone had reason to be well satisfied, having added the President to their growing coalition in support of a decoupled, wage-indexed formula. His budget message in January announced that the administration would propose a new benefit formula that would stabilize replacement rates and reduce the long-range deficit by half.

Such was the sense of dissatisfaction within the administration, however, that it was possible to reopen the issue, an extraordinary occur-

35. Interview with Pat Gwaltney, October 17, 1977.
36. Telephone interview with R. David Ranson, December 16, 1977.
37. Telephone interview with June O'Neill, October 4, 1977.

rence. Presidential decisions, especially those that have been publicly announced, are usually hallowed. In this case the initiative for reconsideration came from OMB's assistant director for economic policy, Rudolph G. Penner, and the excuse for reconsideration was the appearance of the Hsiao panel recommendations, which were presented to the Ways and Means Committee in oral testimony in February 1976 (the published report did not appear for another six months).

After the budget message had been delivered with its promise of decoupling legislation, SSA prepared a bill for that purpose, and within OMB the staff specialists on social security sent the bill to Penner for review. It was "pure wage indexing," he later recalled. "When I saw the legislation and saw Hsiao and saw the enormous magnitude of the cost differences, I went back to the options paper. I saw what they [the proponents of wage indexing] were after and I didn't think they were at all clear."[38] Penner discussed the matter with the deputy director and director of OMB, who had participated in the President's decision, and they agreed that the President had probably not been made aware of the implications of that decision. More interdepartmental meetings were held, another options paper was prepared that was not very different from the first, the President was briefed more fully on the implications of his choice, and he reconfirmed his earlier decision. The whole world already knew that the President had chosen wage indexing because the President had said as much in his budget message, and to back off at this point would cause a great uproar and sacrifice the consensus that had been achieved in support of decoupling. Again, the President's decision was a forgone conclusion.

In the spring, the only new element in the situation had been the appearance of the Hsiao recommendations, which gave concrete and technically defensible form to the price-indexing approach. That the Hsiao recommendations had been solicited by Congress and were the work of competent and experienced technicians (Hsiao had actually been employed in the office of the SSA actuary) gave them some claim to serious consideration, but they still had no political foundation. The options paper that went to the President then did not gloss over this fact.

In Congress, the Hsiao proposal momentarily had some appeal. "You could see their eyes light up, especially on the Republican side," a staff member later said. The Hsiao plan had the advantages that it would

38. Interview with Rudolph G. Penner, October 5, 1977.

cure the long-range deficit and stabilize the purchasing power of social security benefits, but a moment's reflection confirmed that it was politically untenable. Because it would allow replacement rates to fall, it would be interpreted as a reduction in benefits. The opposition from organized labor, from the elderly (even though the current generation of the elderly would not be adversely affected), and from liberals generally would be so intense and widespread that only very conservative congressmen would risk voting for it. "Reducing social security" was simply out of the question. The only overt show of interest in Congress came from a junior Democrat on the Ways and Means Committee, James Jones of Oklahoma, a professional economist who had served on the staff of the Council of Economic Advisers during the Johnson administration and who introduced a bill embodying the Hsiao plan.

That Jones alone was willing to sponsor a price-indexed benefit formula is indicative of the special politics of this issue, which divided political officeholders from economic analysts. Whether inside or outside the government, economic analysts favored the Hsiao plan as a way of keeping future choices open. Their support crossed ideological lines. Similarly, support for wage indexing crossed ideological lines. Neither conservative Republicans in Congress nor the business federations nor the insurance industry rallied behind the Hsiao plan. The argument that Congress should retain discretion over benefits had no appeal to them, for they assumed that discretion would always be used in a highly expansive way. It was, after all, the conservative Republicans' distrust of discretion that had provided the political sponsorship for indexing a few years before. An indexed formula that did not invite expansion (because it was liberal to start with) was probably preferable, in the conservatives' view, to an indexed formula that did invite action by allowing replacement rates to decline. Accordingly, the conservative politicians and interest groups joined the liberals in support of the wage-indexing principle and differed from them only in arguing that replacement rates should be rolled back to levels prevailing earlier, possibly even to the point where they were before the 20 percent benefit increase of 1972. In taking this position, they depended heavily on advice from Robert Myers, who advocated the wage-indexed formula but conceived of the "rollback" as a way of containing expansion.

Because the Hsiao plan was so far from being politically acceptable, it may, if anything, have facilitated adoption of the wage-indexing proposal by turning the latter into a middle-of-the-road solution. The expansionist extreme (assuming that official actuarial assumptions and projections were correct) would have been to preserve the coupled formula, under which replacement rates were expected to rise. The restrictive extreme was the Hsiao proposal, under which replacement rates were projected to fall. The wage-indexed proposal, under which replacement rates were expected to stabilize, became a compromise. Also, the wage-indexed formula had the great advantage of ambiguity. It was both a contraction (because it cut the long-range deficit in half) and an expansion (because, by tying benefits of active workers to wages rather than prices, it enlarged upon what the Nixon administration had announced it was doing with the indexing proposal of 1969–72).[39]

No one had a nicer appreciation of the ambiguity of the new proposal than Robert Ball, who remarked to a congressional committee that "you have this wonderful combination of really improving the system, and also at the same time having a reduction in the cost as compared

39. Political leaders did not perceive the implications of the coupled formula, and the program specialists, who did understand them, took no pains to point them out. *Reports of the 1971 Advisory Council on Social Security,* H. Doc. 92-80, 92 Cong. 1 sess. (GPO, 1971) is the best source of the policymakers' stated intentions in 1972, given the thinness of legislative history. This report put no emphasis on replacement rates, nor did it mention the hypersensitivity of the indexed formula to wage and price changes over the long run. In 1970, after the indexed formula had been presented to Congress, social security analysts in the Budget Bureau perceived the hazard in it and unsuccessfully sought prompt revision. Not that the bureau staff foresaw the extraordinary inflation of 1974, but it did comprehend that the "coupled" formula could have unintended, irrational effects. A bureau staff paper on this subject concluded in 1970 that it was probably too late to revise the administration's proposal to Congress in view of the gathering momentum for enactment, but that corrective legislation should be prepared promptly. In the event, the faulty formula was not enacted until 1972, and planning for revision was delayed until 1973–74. ("Staff Paper on the Implications of Future Changes in Benefit Levels of Social Security," attachment to memo, William H. Robinson to Mr. Schlesinger, April 29, 1970, in OMB File BRD/FAB [FY 1970–1971] Income Security: Social Security System; interview with William H. Robinson, December 1, 1977.) It remains puzzling that policymakers proceeded to adopt a benefit formula recognized in advance to be faulty. The explanation appears to lie in their habitual pragmatism as well as their habitual optimism. They assumed mistakenly that the economy would continue to perform as well as it had in the past, and they also assumed that if trouble did occur, they could fix it. Believing that they were faithfully repeating familiar practice with the formula, they had no incentive to devise new techniques until events forced them to. Finally, the advocates of an automatic formula were not likely to call attention to the technical problems in it if they really wanted to get it enacted, and both Ball and Myers, the arch experts on whom everyone else relied, did want to get it enacted, as did Republican political leaders.

with current estimates. . . . It would be a very good thing to do, and quickly, it seems to me."[40] It was a little like 1972 all over again. Then Congress enacted a major liberalization and simultaneously reduced the long-run tax rates. Five years later it could rectify about half the projected long-range deficit by enacting what was, arguably, a more liberal benefit formula. The highly technical and future-oriented character of policymaking for social security made strange things possible because current actions were evaluated by their hypothetical future effects.

In retrospect, the policymakers' choice of wage indexing rather than price indexing in the decoupled formula appears to be so "natural" as not to require much explanation. It represented stabilization whereas the Hsiao plan represented retrenchment, and retrenchment in social security was politically unthinkable whereas stabilization is inherently noncontroversial. Whatever has been agreed on before can be agreed on again. On this interpretation, the choice of a wage-indexed formula in 1975–77 suggests that there is a tendency in policymaking to continue doing the same things but not necessarily a tendency to do those things on a larger scale.

However, to see wage indexing as simply an endorsement of the status quo or a reincarnation of past practice fails to grasp its full political significance and overlooks the manipulative advantages enjoyed in this contest by the program specialists in public office. That they and allied proponents of wage indexing inside the executive branch chose to describe it as neutral did not make it so, nor did their stress on its stabilizing features mean that it was stabilizing altogether. Their use of symbols obscured the political content of the official proposal. To some extent, the political disadvantages of the Hsiao proposal were not inherent, but were imparted by the symbolic terms with which the dominant policymakers described and interpreted what they were doing.

An innocent outsider, the mythical visitor from another planet, if asked to say which decoupling proposal would maintain the role of social security in the future, would have had a hard time answering in the absence of cues or definitive criteria. Under wage indexing, average replacement rates would be stable but social security taxation and expenditures as a percentage of GNP would rise. Under price indexing, taxation and expenditures as a percentage of GNP would be stable but

40. *Future Directions in Social Security*, Hearings, pt. 11, p. 947.

average replacement rates would fall.[41] The role of social security would in some sense be stabilized in both cases.

What, then, of consistency with past practice or with the policymakers' intentions in 1972? Here, too, the choice of terms by the proponents of wage indexing put the burden of change on their rivals, whose proposal was represented as "reform," "overhaul," and an attempt to "change the system and its fabric."[42] In truth, both proposals could lay a claim to traditional antecedents, but neither had a perfect claim. In the past, stabilization of replacement rates had not been an explicit policy goal, but fluctuation had in practice been confined within a relatively narrow range—25 to 33 percent for high-income individuals, 47 to 55 percent for low-income individuals.[43] In presuming that Congress would make ad hoc adjustments in the future (on top of indexed changes), the Hsiao plan was harking back to the pre-indexed past, not making a revolutionary overhaul, and in proposing that automatic increases be indexed to the cost of living it was proposing to do what most members of Congress very probably thought they were doing when the formula of 1972 was enacted. Congress had not known in 1972 what "replacement rates" it was setting, and to assert now that the rates should be stabilized was no mere technical matter. This was in the profoundest sense a political decision. It shaped the system, just as surely as any rival proposals could be said to shape the system. And it shaped the system in an expansive direction. In affirming that benefits promised to active workers would henceforth rise with wage levels, it stipulated a principle of expansion—a policy, in short—that had never been affirmed before and had only been approximated, never fully realized, in the improvised practices of the 1950s and 1960s.[44]

41. For individuals with the same real income over time, the Hsiao plan would have produced a stable replacement rate and the wage-indexing approach a rising rate. The Hsiao plan meant a decline in replacement rates, and wage indexing meant stabilization of such rates only in regard to average earnings, or the whole distribution of earnings.

42. For example, see the testimony of HEW Secretary David Mathews and of Commissioner Cardwell in *Decoupling the Social Security Benefit Structure,* Hearings, pp. 35, 40, 43.

43. Robert J. Myers, "Summary of the Provisions of the Old-Age, Survivors, and Disability Insurance System, the Hospital Insurance System, and the Supplementary Medical Insurance System" (Temple University, January 1978), p. 24.

44. Whether wage indexing was expansive in relation to the coupled formula then in use is impossible to say, given the erratic properties of that formula. The decoupled, wage-indexed formula was reliably expansive, whereas the coupled formula was unreliably so.

That the proponents of wage indexing easily won assent for their own proposals cannot be attributed simply to the fact that their proposals satisfied the characteristic preference of all policymakers to stay comfortably close to precedents and the characteristic preference of politicians to avoid reducing benefits to their constituents. Nor can it be attributed simply to the nice ambiguity of the SSA proposal, for the Hsiao plan had an equally nice ambiguity. Under the Hsiao plan, after all, benefit amounts were guaranteed to rise; the purchasing power of benefits was guaranteed to remain stable; and nearly the whole of the financial deficit in the system was eliminated. That was a very appealing combination, or could have been if replacement rates had not suddenly emerged as *the* criterion by which benefits were to be judged. By that criterion alone, the Hsiao plan would have reduced benefits, and that was sufficient to disqualify it from serious consideration.

The success of the program's leadership, then, must be attributed in some significant measure to their capacity to define the terms of debate. They supplied more than a proposal for action; they also supplied the language with which perceptions were shaped. With their emphasis on replacement rates, they defined the base from which changes in direction were to be gauged, and in a system where backward steps are inconceivable and the tendency of policymaking is either toward more of the same (inertia) or more of the same plus a bit (incremental change), the capacity to define where one is starting from is of crucial importance. When program executives did this, they spoke with the great advantages of authority and expertise. As interpreters of the properties and intentions embodied in the program, they were virtually immune to challenge. Also, they continued to monopolize initiative even as other participants proliferated. They were still the first to enter the field of action even though the field was now more crowded than it used to be. And, if only by being first they had great influence in defining the point from which discussion should start.

Even in the more competitive milieu that developed after the deficit appeared, program executives continued to retain great advantages, and the history of this period suggests that these advantages will consistently be used in support of expansionist measures. To find otherwise would be surprising, but the point is worth noting because this period provided a test of it. The new commissioner after 1973, though a career civil servant, was not a career program executive. Most recently he had been comptroller of HEW. His specialty was control of expenditures, and this commended him to the Nixon administration as head of the government's biggest "uncontrollable" program. Within the SSA, morale fell when an outsider, a budget man, replaced Ball. Cardwell did not have the missionary spirit that was so marked in the program's founders—the unshakable belief that the program was a wonderful thing and that whatever made it bigger and better was wonderful too. Congressmen also noticed the difference, Cardwell was so passive and reticent by comparison to his predecessor. They were often not sure what he wanted. Yet Cardwell advocated a benefit formula in no way distinguishable from what Ball in his place would have advocated. (In fact, it was what Ball did advocate as a frequent congressional witness in 1975–77 and worked for behind the scenes when the Ford administration was debating what to do.) No commissioner of social security could have advocated less; internal organizational commitments and external political constraints both precluded it, and the commissioner's position was not, in any case, one that a reasonable and responsible man would have found hard to defend on the merits. Wage indexing was used in some other countries, it was not so very different from what had been done in the United States, and it was certainly arguable that future retirees should share in the general increase in the standard of living and be reliably informed by their government of the relation between their social security benefits and their preretirement wage. There were very good reasons for stabilizing replacement rates. Advocates of the price-indexing approach did not deny it. On the merits, there was much to be said on both sides.

This being so, it is noteworthy that deliberations inside the executive branch did not produce for the President's consideration a range of compromises or combinations between the two courses. This was not because the experts were incapable of conceiving any. Technically, indexing was a marvelously complicated matter. Different elements of the formula could be indexed in different ways, and many permutations and outcomes were possible. The very importance of the issue, however, tended both to produce a rendering in gross, highly simplified terms and to polarize the executive participants. Had the issue not been important and divisive, it would not have reached the President, and as it approached him for decision the choice was framed in a highly simplified way, with alternatives drawn in sharply contrasting terms. One reason that the executive contest did not effectively widen choice is that executive decision processes were framed so as to serve a busy generalist, the President, who could not be expected to pause for long over the technical nuances, even if it was in the realm of technical nuance that realistic choices might be identified. Moreover, the appearance of the Treasury-CEA alternative, which most other participants viewed incredulously as a radical measure of reduction, served to unite these other participants and to destroy whatever latent, marginal differences existed among them.[45]

Finally, there is yet one more reason why greater competition and conflict in the mid-1970s had no discernible effect on the expansionary bias of policymaking. Potential opponents of expansion were so conditioned to expect defeat that they anticipated expansion and, in anticipating it, made concessions to it. This was so of the business-oriented interest groups and conservative Republicans in Congress, who endorsed wage indexing partly because they assumed that a less liberal form of indexing could not be relied on to govern the future conduct of Congress. A parallel calculation may also have influenced Cardwell. Because decoupling could be interpreted as deliberalization, Cardwell believed that organized labor might veto it, and this shows how deep an inertial bias is, or at least is perceived to be. In the inflationary conditions that developed after 1972, no responsible person defended the coupled formula. Expert opinion was unanimous that it must be revised, so erratic were its potential future effects. Yet Cardwell, as the executive responsible for the social security program, could not safely presume that Congress would revise it if the perception spread that revision meant deliberalization. Hence he became extremely anxious to devise a decoupled formula that could win support from organized labor and be passed by Congress with a minimum of debate and delay.

In the event, Congress enacted the new decoupled formula late in 1977, along with new measures to raise revenue. In the meantime the administration of Jimmy Carter had taken office, but it made no substantial change in the Ford administration's recommendation regarding the decoupling procedure. Carter, who received advice on social security from Robert Ball during his campaign, had pledged not to reduce replacement rates. However, in a concession to conservative pressure,

45. Some of the participants outside of HEW thought they detected signs of disagreement between SSA and HEW's Office of the Assistant Secretary for Planning and Evaluation in the early stages of deliberation. The latter seemed willing to consider a wider range of alternatives, including possible variants of price indexing, but if there was a difference between them it quickly disappeared when HEW confronted the Treasury Department.

Congress included a rollback of 5 to 10 percentage points in the replacement rates that had been reached under the coupled formula. Over the long run, the replacement rate for retirement at the age of sixty-five for a low-income earner would be stabilized at around 54 percent; for a worker of average income, at around 42 percent; and for a high-income earner, at around 26 percent. These were approximately the levels that obtained in the mid-1970s, shortly after the 1972 amendments were enacted.[46]

Financing

It remained to raise the taxes. The Ford administration had proposed in 1976 to raise the payroll tax rate, but Congress took no action. The Carter administration's proposal, presented to Congress in 1977, was more novel. It would have taxed employers on all wages and salaries, removing the ceiling on taxable wages in regard to their share of the tax whereas for employees it would have raised the ceiling only slightly. Taxes, then, would no longer be levied equally on employees and employers. Revenues for the system would have been greatly increased without anything like a comparable increase in benefit obligations. Second, the Carter administration proposed to introduce general revenues whenever unemployment passed 6 percent. The Treasury would transfer general funds in an amount equal to the difference between what payroll tax revenues would have been at 6 percent unemployment

46. When decoupling was enacted, recipients of old age insurance were protected against a sudden reduction in promised benefits. The benefit levels effective in 1979 will continue to apply in a five-year period (1979–83) during which the transition to a decoupled system will occur. (*Summary of the Conference Agreement on H.R. 9346: The Social Security Amendments of 1977,* House Committee on Ways and Means, Committee Print 95-61 [GPO, 1977], p. 3.) However, the transitional guarantees were not applied to recipients of disability or survivors insurance, with the result that persons newly disabled after December 31, 1978, or newly entitled to survivors benefits as the result of a worker's death, will get benefits very much lower than comparable persons who became eligible late in 1978. For example, the replacement rate for a worker of average income newly disabled in 1978 was approximately 59 percent, whereas for the same worker in 1979 it would be 42 percent. (Robert J. Myers, "Summary of the Provisions of the Old-Age, Survivors, and Disability Insurance System," p. 27.) This was a rare instance of benefit reduction. It was politically possible both because the highly technical nature of social security legislation obscured the meaning of change and because the victims of the reduction—the soon-to-be-disabled or soon-to-die and their immediate survivors—were unorganized, far fewer than prospective retirees, and far less certain of the likelihood of becoming eligible since disability and death are much less predictable than retirement.

and the payroll tax revenues actually collected. Made retroactive to 1975, this would have yielded an estimated $14 billion for the program by 1982. It would ostensibly have been a temporary measure, but no one pretended that it was not likely to become permanent. No new increases in the payroll tax rate were proposed until 1985.

The divergence between the Ford and Carter tax proposals illustrates the effect that a change in party regimes can have on executive policies for social security. Carter had pledged in his campaign not to increase the payroll tax, which liberals had long criticized as regressive and which was of course growing more unpopular as it got higher. His pledge meant that the new Democratic administration had to meet the deficit by enlarging the wage base or drawing on general revenues. It decided not to raise the wage base for employees because this would have raised old age benefits for the relatively well-to-do. Instead it chose an enlarged wage base for employers in combination with the use of general revenues, in sharp contrast to the Ford proposals. Substantive differences aside, though, policy deliberations inside the Carter administration resembled those of its Republican predecessor in that HEW's proposal won the President's approval after an unequal contest with rival suggestions.[47]

The HEW proposal was prepared by the Office of the Assistant Secretary for Planning and Evaluation and the SSA. Within the administration, objections came from Secretary of Commerce Juanita M. Kreps, who argued that the heavy additional tax burden on employer payrolls would increase inflation and unemployment, besides departing from the long-accepted principle of equal tax liability for employers and employees. Charles L. Schultze, chairman of the Council of Economic Advisers, argued that most of the increase in employer payroll costs would be pushed forward into prices, which, when combined with other inflationary pressures, would have a serious adverse effect on the economy. Both Kreps and Schultze argued for much heavier reliance on general revenues, Schultze for introducing them via the medicare program, Kreps for introducing them directly and explicitly in the basic program of cash benefits until they financed a third of the cost.

47. For the account of deliberations inside the Carter administration, I have relied on James W. Singer, "Carter Is Trying to Make Social Security More Secure," *National Journal*, vol. 9 (June 11, 1977), pp. 893–95, but supplemented this excellent report from confidential sources.

These arguments surfaced only very shortly before the President made his decision. There was much less interdepartmental preparation for the presidential decision than there had been in the Ford administration, and the preparation was more chaotic. Carter was confronted with no fewer than five memoranda—one each from HEW, his economic policy group, his domestic council, Robert Ball, and OMB. A sixth, from the Council of Economic Advisers, arrived after he had made his choice. (Not the least remarkable aspect of this process is that Ball's position was being solicited as if he were an agency of the executive branch.) The alternatives in opposition to HEW's recommendation had developed so quickly and had received so little staff work that they were never seriously in the running. The President's staff believed that the real choice was between endorsing the HEW proposal or postponing action, which was analogous to the choice that was presented to President Ford. Carter, like Ford, concluded that action was imperative (issues are not likely to reach the President at all unless the pressure for action is intense), and, also like Ford, he chose the HEW proposal, which his domestic council staff had endorsed. After his decision was made on the basis of briefing papers, he reviewed it in a meeting with the interested officials and also Ball, all of whom had a chance to argue their positions. Carter reconfirmed his initial choice.

Congress received the Carter proposal skeptically and dealt with it harshly. It raised the wage base for both employers and employees, preserving parity between the two; raised the payroll tax rate; and rejected any use of general revenues. Congress favored the customary and familiar. It preferred to add incrementally to existing tax elements, especially the wage base, rather than break precedents and reach for new revenue sources. The development of policy was inertial as usual, but the politics of dealing with a deficit was distinctive for its divisiveness. Republicans in the House developed their own proposal, which would have raised payroll tax rates beginning in 1982; transferred revenues from the medicare fund, thereby raising the prospect of introducing general revenues in that portion of the program; raised the age of eligibility for social security beneficiaries beginning in 1990; eliminated the earnings test beginning in 1982; covered federal government employees; and reduced replacement rates to the levels of 1972. The Democratic bill, with its mammoth increase in taxes, passed after a sharp debate. The vote was 56 to 21 in the Senate and 189 to 163 in the House. In the House, a rule making action possible carried by only 3 votes.

Social Security Prevails

President Carter signed the bill in late December. The same day, his administration announced plans for a large cut in taxes on individual incomes and corporate profits in order to stimulate the economy and help fight inflation. This action was designed in part to offset the adverse effects of the social security tax increase. When juxtaposed, the two actions would have the effect of transferring funds from other public programs to social security or of increasing the national debt. In the implicit competition between social security and other government programs for a share of public resources, social security had won. And, within the program, the tension between the demand for benefits and resistance to taxation had been resolved in favor of more taxes. This had been a painful choice for Congress, however. "There are not going to be any more easy votes on social security," Ways and Means Committee Chairman Al Ullman told the House as the final debate began.[48] This was a candid if elliptical acknowledgment that the favorable political conditions of an immature program had come to an end and that no more technical sleights of hand could be performed to obscure that fact, such as had made possible the 20 percent benefit increase of 1972.

48. *Congressional Record*, daily ed., December 15, 1977, p. H12973.

CHAPTER TWENTY

Keeping Society's Options Open

POLICY CHOICES for social security can be summed up in two maxims: a little bit more is always a good thing; anything less is inconceivable. There is always forward movement along a familiar, if not actually predestined, path. Sometimes there are delays, as with the enactment of disability and health insurance. Sometimes there are temporary deviations, as with the enactment of public assistance programs for the needy disabled and ill. Eventually, though, the insurance program advances and displaces any alternative. Expenditures and tax rates rise steadily and, under the statute, are planned to rise still more in the future. The product of the incremental, inertial process is a mammoth program approaching nearly $100 billion a year in volume of expenditure and apparently immune to the least reduction even if decreasingly immune to criticism. The result of the many steps, each small in itself yet in practice irreversible, is a massive shift of resources to the public sector.

It may be argued that this program is what Americans have because it is what the majority wants. In a democracy, there is some presumption in favor of whatever policy exists: presumably it was arrived at by legitimate, majoritarian processes after an open debate. Yet to suppose this is to take too much on faith. One has to judge the reality of democracy, which is inevitably very complicated, rather than trust the theory of it. And when they have looked at the realities, students of social security in recent years have often been disturbed. "I must admit," Representative William A. Steiger of the Ways and Means Committee remarked in 1975, "I had no comprehension as to the fact that by and large the Congress—and, I would judge administrations of whatever political party—have not watched carefully this system with [its] immense [effect on] the American political, social, economic characteristics."[1] Similarly, a member of the advisory council of 1974–75 confessed to the Ways and Means Committee that newcomers to the council had been surprised at what they had learned about social security and had been "appalled at the fact that the public is so grossly misinformed."[2]

The quality and extent of the public's understanding are difficult to judge in the absence of more data, but I believe that critics such as these are right to be disturbed. The nature of the program in the short run has been such as to disguise the true cost of it, the true relation between costs and benefits, and the true principles by which benefits and costs have been distributed. The nature of policymaking did little to correct, but instead reinforced, a complacent, poorly informed acceptance of the program—participation was so narrowly confined; expert, proprietary dominance was so complete; debate was so limited; the technicality was so intimidating; the propaganda was so appealing; and the forward steps each seemed so small. Except when important public-private boundaries were unmistakably about to be crossed, conflict was muted and narrowly contained. Other courses of action than orthodox, incremental measures of expansion received little attention. In this respect, the quality of recent decisions is hardly more reassuring than that of early ones. By the 1970s the program had grown so large that the social and economic stakes were manifest and critical expertise was beginning to develop and be institutionalized outside the SSA, but in the whole history of the program it would be hard to find an important decision taken more precipitously and with less careful legislative consideration than the big benefit increase in combination with a faulty benefit formula in 1972. And when President Ford had to confront the aftermath in 1975–76, a staff system designed in theory to widen his options presented him with virtually no options at all except to do nothing to a system already in trouble or to approve what the SSA was proposing.

It may seem late to ask how options may be widened. It *is* late. A large program is in place, benefits have been indexed so that they depend automatically on the future performance of the economy, and trillions of dollars in promises have been made to future recipients, the

1. *Financing the Social Security System*, Hearings before the Subcommittee on Social Security of the House Committee on Ways and Means, 94 Cong. 1 sess. (GPO, 1975), p. 428.

2. J. W. Van Gorkom in ibid., p. 109.

reward for their willingness to pay taxes now to support today's retirees. On the other hand, the system will not be static. There will be pressure to remove perceived or real inequities, such as the eternally unpopular retirement test and discriminatory treatment of married women who work. There will continue to be issues over how the program is to be financed, for a rising wage base and rising tax rate are certain to cause discontent. Universal coverage, which apparently has become a goal of the legislature, will not be achieved easily. So one can expect a stream of continuing demands on the system to necessitate continuing choices regarding its characteristics.

Broad changes in the society and the economy may also imply a need for adaptation of the system. Demographic projections show that the ratio of retirees to workers will turn sharply upward late in the first quarter of the next century as the babies of the postwar boom reach old age. The economic burden of social security will be much heavier for working generations of the mid-twenty-first century than for the present generation. How will the system adapt? Can it be expected to adapt at all, or is it a juggernaut hopelessly out of control? Social security, the columnist George Will has written, "is so woven into the nation's life that its difficulties jeopardize almost everything but itself. . . . Unquestionably, Social Security's basic commitments will be met. The problem is the effect that this will have on the economy that makes Social Security—and everything else—possible."[3] Suppose that future generations do not want to bear the social security burden that predecessor generations have committed them to. Will benefits be reduced? What will the social, economic, and political consequences be if they are? Or if they are not?

These are the important questions regarding future policymaking for social security, and there are no present answers to them, but their import suggests a need to consider how, whether, or in what degree society's options regarding social security may be kept open. It is true that the history and analysis presented here must be read as supporting Will's point. Far more to the point, so do the acts and understandings of politicians, who in their candid moments acknowledge that the social security benefits incorporated in law are sacrosanct. Reduction is simply unthinkable, no matter what the method of financing or the inflationary

3. *Washington Post*, May 22, 1977.

effects might be: "We have the capacity under the Constitution, the Congress does, to coin money, as well as to regulate the value thereof," an iconoclastic but astute senator remarked in hearings on social security in 1976. "And therefore we have the power to provide that money. And we are going to do it. It may not be worth anything when the recipient gets it, but he is going to get his benefits paid." The social security commissioner agreed.[4] Before tackling the question of whether or how choice may be preserved, it is desirable to consider more carefully why the preservation of choice matters.

The Need for Choice

A political theorist would take it as axiomatic that choice in some sense is crucial to maintenance of a democratic regime. Coercion is legitimate in a democracy only when it is based on consent, and for consent to be meaningful choices must be posed and publicly examined. An economic analyst would argue that comparison of alternative courses is the essence of rational action. If society wishes to be guided by an ideal of rationality, it must try to choose in a systematic way. A social analyst might say that to preserve itself and function well by various criteria, a society must be able to change, and to change requires a capacity for choice. Choice, then, is an important instrumental value, a crucial component of freedom and rationality in the conduct of public affairs and a means of social adaptation.

Few would quarrel with brief and abstract assertions of this sort, but few would deny that as an abstract value the preservation of choice conflicts with other values, and that as a practical matter it is unavoidably restricted in innumerable ways. If "choice" means the maximization of popular choice, it is clear that democracy in the United States has not been constructed on that principle at all. Popular choice is in general limited to the choice of governing officials, who have the right to make decisions regarding policies. The nation is governed by its elected representatives, and many kinds of institutional constraints are imposed on their choices and on their right to decide. To arrive at

4. *The Social Security System*, Hearings before the Joint Economic Committee, 94 Cong. 2 sess. (GPO, 1977), p. 28.

choices, there must be alternatives, and maximization of choice may therefore imply institutional arrangements for the formulation of conflicting alternatives. But as a practical matter, political institutions are not ordered to maximize conflict and debate, and Americans probably could not govern themselves if they were. In Congress, power gravitates to committees that have perfected techniques of consensual decisionmaking and to leaders who are skilled at construction of coalitions rather than at partisan debate. Large areas of government action, including the conduct of foreign policy, the management of monetary policy, and those areas under the jurisdiction of independent regulatory commissions, have been insulated from partisan politics and, by implication, from the overt conflict associated with it. This is done because unconstrained debate is considered harmful, but limits on debate also limit choice. Deciding how to institutionalize the making of choices rather than simply asserting in the abstract the importance of freedom to choose raises difficulties. What kinds of choices must be posed, how often, to whom, and in what form, are matters much open to discussion, and answers may vary from one area of government activity to another.

The executive leaders of social security have believed their program to be a special case that merits insulation from partisan politics and standard processes of budget preparation, which are leading mechanisms of choice. In a quintessential statement of the leadership's attitude toward the relation between social security and the political system, Robert Ball wrote that "just about every American has a major stake in protecting the long-term commitments of the social security program from fluctuations in politics and policy. The administration of social security by a separate government corporation or instrumentality and the separation of social security financial transactions from other government income and expenditures would strengthen public confidence in the security of the long-run commitments of the program and in the freedom of the administrative operations from short-run political influence. It would give emphasis to the fact that in this program the government is acting as trustee for those who have built up rights under the system."[5] This view of government as merely a convenient and essentially passive overseer (a "trustee") of funds offered up by a willing public has been the prevailing orthodoxy among the program's

5. *Congressional Record* (March 28, 1974), p. 8866.

executive leadership and their private allies in organized labor.[6] The executive leaders have sought to foreclose the options of future generations by committing them irrevocably to a program that promises benefits by right as well as those particular benefits that have been incorporated in an ever-expanding law. In that sense, they designed social security to be uncontrollable.

Empirically, it is impossible to accept the proposition that the government has been merely a trustee in regard to social security, a detached agent through which the public is enabled to help itself. The government officials who have headed the program have been tireless, ingenious advocates of its expansion, constantly engaged in an effort to influence public policy. Were it not for their own deep involvement in processes that are indubitably political (in the sense that the competing values intrinsic to policy choice are at stake), it would be much easier to credit their public assertions that the management of social security ought to be apolitical. It would be much easier to credit the argument that this is not a government program if officials of the government had not been prime movers in its growth.

The normative issue raised by this claim to antonomy is not whether social security should be "political." The government's largest domestic program is inescapably political. Policy choices made for social security are important choices for the society. To make them is to exercise power and distribute things of value—and that is politics. The question is not whether there will be politics in this process, but what sort of politics it will be. Should it be a politics dominated by program specialists and characterized by incremental enlargements of the program, or should it be a more open politics that risks a higher level of conflict than has ordinarily prevailed and policy outcomes that are hard to predict? A

6. See, for example, the remarks of labor's Nelson Cruikshank to the Senate Special Committee on Aging in 1975:

> People look on this system as if it were essentially a Government program, in the same way that the Government is the builder of bridges or the dredger of canals, which are Government programs.
> Well, in a certain technical and narrow sense it may be, but in the essence of the program it is not.
> It is a program where people are engaged in a vast self-help program, where they use the mechanics of government to participate in this cooperative self-help undertaking of meeting their need. Social security is just as much that kind of program as, say, the old friendly societies were. (*Future Directions in Social Security,* Hearing before the Senate Special Committee on Aging, 94 Cong. 1 sess. [GPO, 1975], pt. 11, p. 939.)

more open politics would not necessarily put a brake on expansion. In the past, the congressional proprietors of social security, especially the leadership of the Ways and Means Committee, feared that open politics would produce uncontrollable pressures for benefit increases. The closed rule and the norm of fiscal soundness, which were the procedural expressions of program-oriented policymaking, were bulwarks against demagoguery. In reducing conflict and confining participation, they also thwarted the impulse of elected politicians to act irresponsibly, for short-term electoral advantage. Elected politicians in the legislature have been very concerned to minimize the risks of policy choice, and they therefore endorsed a gradually growing program and put in law a tax rate rising steeply over the long term rather than reveal something like true costs to current taxpayers.

To plead for a politics of social security more sensitive to differences of interest and opinion and more informed by debate is not to argue for any particular outcome. The argument rests on the belief that democratic politics, however ordered, is more than just a way of making choices; ideally, it is a way of keeping choices open. Viewed in this light, it is important that there be "enough" politics, and constricted participation and limited conflict in an extraordinarily important public program become a cause for concern. In the absence of a vigorous and competitive politics, there is no assurance that a wide range of alternatives has been considered, and there are grounds for questioning the quality of the general consent to what government is doing.

My own conclusion is that there has not been "enough" politics in social security. How much conflict and agitation are desirable and how prolonged the consideration of conflicting proposals should be depends very much on the consequences of the government activity for individuals, society, the economy, the relations among social classes, and so forth. That the gross features and relative burdens of the leading government programs should be open to debate, and therefore vulnerable to fluctuations in politics and policy, would seem essential to any realistic theory of democracy. Nor should any public program have an absolute and unconditional claim on any particular proportion or amount of public resources, and none has, or ought to have, an absolute immunity to change as economic and social conditions may create the need for change. Politics should open and reopen possibilities for change, not foreclose them.

How, then, might the politics of social security be arranged so as to highlight choices? Assuming that preserving choice is of value, what does this imply for current actions?

I believe that it implies preserving the visibility of costs by continued reliance on an earmarked tax and adherence to a policy of self-support: revenues for the system should balance expenditures, and the public should be made aware of how large the tax burden is. In this way, policymakers, the elected politicians in Congress in particular, are compelled to weigh demands for benefits against resistance to higher taxes. The system is structured so as to focus such competing pressures upon them and force them to make a choice.

As costs rise, this arrangement might constrain them, yet it is well to remember that such an arrangement has been in effect for forty years and has proved thoroughly compatible with steady, incremental growth. The official claim that this particular financing technique imposed restraint has always been dubious inasmuch as the immature program embodied artificially low tax rates. Even now, tax rates are artificially low, although high by past standards. If projections are correct, they will be much higher in the future. The point is not that visibility will contain their rise, only that it will tend to make policymakers confront hard choices about the size of the program by generating conflicting pressures that they must reconcile. Today it would be gross hypocrisy for officeholders to abandon this arrangement as the program matures and the rates begin to be seriously burdensome, after they have proclaimed for years that self-support through an earmarked tax was the essence of fiscal discipline.[7]

It may be argued that there are better ways to compel choices. Rather than juxtapose social security costs against social security bene-

7. It is remarkable that even when faced with a presidential proposal for the use of general revenues, the congressional committees reaffirmed their traditional position in 1977, and did so in response to their leaders' belief that to rely on general revenues would be fiscally irresponsible. The Finance Committee chairman, Russell Long, remarked in hearings that "when you talk about financing social security out of general revenues, I think that is very misleading. We do not have any general revenues to finance it with. . . . It bothers me with the Federal funds fairly badly in deficit to start financing this program with printing press money as well. That is why it seems to me, just by way of responsibility, we should try to muster the courage to vote whatever taxes are needed to fund this program before we offer Senators and House members the easy way out in saying, we will just increase the debt limit, tell the Federal Reserve to print more money down there." *Social Security Financing Proposals*, Hearings before the Subcommittee on Social Security of the Senate Committee on Finance, 95 Cong. 1 sess. (GPO, 1977), pp. 21, 23.

fits in a financially autonomous system, it would be possible to press for greater integration of social security into the budget, and hence into the process by which expenditures for different activities of the federal government at least in theory are juxtaposed in competition with one another. Had social security been structured this way from the start and financed by general revenues, the preceding history would be very different. There would surely have been a higher level of conflict; very probably a different sort of program, giving benefits to more of the aged sooner; and a more realistic juxtaposition of costs and benefits than was possible in a gradually maturing program. Whether this would have produced a bigger or smaller program no one can know.[8] To introduce general revenues and bring social security more deeply and directly into the budget process might seem the logical way to generate conflict and compel choice today. However, at this stage of the program's evolution direct competition between social security and other programs is bound to be grossly unequal, its claims are so compelling both in doctrine and politics. If general revenues were introduced, very likely they would be committed to the program automatically and uncontrollably, as some fixed proportion (presumably a third) of total expenditures, and there would be no occasion for debate over how much ought to be spent.[9] My guess—and it is only a guess, as are all prescriptions about government policy or organization—is that juxtaposing costs and benefits *within* the social security system will highlight choice more effectively than would juxtaposing social security with other programs in an integrated, comprehensive budget.[10]

In considering how social security should be financed, there are, of course, other values and goals than fostering explicit choices, which is my central concern here. Those who argue for the use of general rev-

8. My supposition is that in the short run there would have been a bigger program and in the long run a smaller one.

9. The Carter administration's proposal of 1977, which would have tied the introduction of general revenues to the rate of unemployment, called for bypassing the appropriations process. General revenues would have been transferred automatically to the social security trust fund. *Social Security Financing Proposals,* Hearings, p. 24.

10. My argument does not apply, however, to proposals to separate medicare from the rest of the program and finance it wholly with general revenues. The logic of that proposed change is very compelling because of the lack of a direct relation between wages and taxes on the one hand and benefits on the other. See the recommendation in *Reports of the Quadrennial Advisory Council on Social Security,* H. Doc. 94-75, 94 Cong. 1 sess. (GPO, 1975), pp. 55–56.

enues usually do so on the ground either that income and profits taxation is less inflationary than payroll taxation (because it is less likely to be passed through by corporations into product prices) or that it is fairer, because more progressive. Contrary to my argument, some analysts also argue that general revenues would nurture debate as among competing claims on government expenditure.

My argument that taxes should be highly visible (that is, earmarked) and sufficient to support the program does not necessarily imply reliance on payroll taxes; portions of the individual or corporate income and profits taxes could just as easily be earmarked for social security. Realistically, though, to favor an earmarked tax and a self-supporting program is tantamount to favoring perpetuation of the traditional method of payroll tax financing. For a debate on the merits of that tax, the reader will have to look to the economic literature on social security. It is enough here to say that I am satisfied that the payroll tax is defensible in a system that relates benefits to wages, and that my argument for its continued use on another ground—that it will create pressures for choice—need not be undermined by the contention that the payroll tax is unjust.[11]

Competition and Generalist Supervision

Despite having argued above for the continued financial autonomy of social security, I do not in general reject the commonplace assumption that control of any government program is improved by direct competition with other programs under generalist supervision. In respect to organization if not financing, greater integration of social security with other functions of the government should continue to be sought, generalist supervision by the President's staff should be strengthened, and the capacity of potential bureaucratic rivals, especially the Treasury Department, to advance alternatives to those of the SSA should be improved, even if efforts in the past decade to increase generalist participation and provide "semi-detached" expertise from

11. Economists now seem to be uncertain about the inflationary effects of the payroll tax. But that argument against using it is relatively new, an outgrowth of the recent preoccupation with controlling inflation. See George L. Perry, "Stabilization Policy and Inflation," in Henry Owen and Charles L. Schultze, eds., *Setting National Priorities: The Next Ten Years* (Brookings Institution, 1976), p. 314.

within the executive branch do not appear to have significantly changed policymaking. More executive officials outside of the SSA have become involved, but at so late a stage and with such limited resources as to have had little effect. The potential importance of this development may, however, be inferred from the fact that partisans of the system would like to reverse it by reestablishing the original organizational autonomy of the social security system. In 1974 Senator Frank Church, chairman of the Special Committee on Aging, introduced a bill that would have separated the SSA from HEW and created a three-member governing board appointed by the President to administer it. It would also have separated the financial transactions of the social security trust funds from the operations of the unified budget and prohibited the mailing of announcements with social security checks that made any reference to a public official—a measure intended to prevent presidents from claiming partisan credit for benefit increases.[12]

While I believe that this bill ought not to pass and that more organizational competition for the SSA within the executive branch and more generalist supervision, informed by a detached expertise, are desirable, it would be easy to overestimate the impact of organizational changes. Prescriptions for the improvement of policymaking are very likely to be addressed to organization and process, since these are relatively susceptible to manipulation. There is a tendency to disregard forces that operate more or less independently of organizational structures, including the force of ideas. The proposal for restoring the original autonomy of the SSA is significant not for the organizational and procedural changes it would make (it is not likely to pass anyway), but for the philosophical

12. The proximate inspiration for this was President Nixon's attempt to claim credit for the 20 percent increase of 1972 by including a self-serving notice in checks mailed to social security beneficiaries after the increase and before the 1972 election. Robert Ball was so incensed at this that he threatened to resign as social security commissioner, and Republican officials in HEW altered the style and format of the proposed notice so as to make it conform to precedents. Nixon was not the first president to cause such a notice to be sent, but he would have been uniquely flamboyant about it. His White House aides proposed to color the notice red, white, and blue and to decorate it with the President's picture and seal. Also, the fact that he had not supported the 20 percent increase made his effort to claim credit for it seem hypocritical as well as partisan and self-serving. Democrats in Congress protested vehemently, and Church immediately introduced a resolution that would have prohibited any notice of an increase in social security payments from referring to any candidate for elective office. This prohibition was later incorporated in a bill, and still later in the more extensive bill to reestablish the independence of the SSA. See Elliot Richardson, *The Creative Balance* (Holt, Rinehart, and Winston, 1976), p. 90.

premise on which it rests: that social security is not a government program legitimately subject to competition from other government programs, but an inviolable trust the statutory terms of which the government may not abridge without violating its obligations as a trustee.

The conclusions in this chapter are based on a very different set of premises: that social security is a government program, as its coercive character demonstrates; that for the coercion embodied in it to be legitimate, mechanisms for consent and renewal of consent must be provided; and that competition with other government programs is an indispensable condition of consent. To suppose that government is a "trustee" for this program but has some other role (that of political decisionmaker?) for other programs ignores the realities of policymaking for social security. It also ignores the realities of the program. If social security were simply a program in which people "got back what they paid for," the view of government as a passive instrument, a holder of funds in trust, would be more credible. But social security is something very different from that. It redistributes income. Active workers are obliged to pay taxes to provide a level of income stipulated by law for retired and disabled workers and their dependents and the surviving dependents of deceased workers. Society does this because, through the medium of government, society has decided that it is a socially desirable thing to do. And, in deciding how much of it to do, society needs to weigh social security against other socially desirable things.

It may be argued that the purposes of social security give it a claim to special status, and that support of social security beneficiaries at some specified level is more important than the purposes of other government programs. Without question, important values are served by social security and by insulating the mature program from fluctuations in politics and policy. A public pension system should be predictable and reliable. People need to know what the order of magnitude of their publicly financed old age benefits will be; their private investment decisions, as well as their psychological well-being, to some extent depend on this knowledge. Nor would anyone deny that it would be undesirable for Congress to make new decisions each year about what age groups will be eligible the following year or how much they will be paid, depending on whether the federal budget happened to be in balance that year. To provide the elderly with a sense of security is a very important value, as the name of this nation's old age support program suggests. But it is not an absolute value, and the only way to judge

its importance in a democratic polity such as the United States is for it
to compete with other values through political processes.

Policymaking for the Future

A more open politics in social security carries with it the prospect of
heightened tension between workers and nonworkers and of expedient
actions by elected politicians who historically have been constrained by
the closed proprietorship of social security. It carries too the possibility
of future debate over the level of benefits and the distribution of benefits. Is it likely, then, to result in reduction of benefits, and if so would
that violate a "social compact" between generations or a solemn obligation of the government?

Time is a particularly important dimension of analysis in social
security. The program depends on the willingness of each working generation to support nonworkers of its own time. The program does not
assume that this willingness is altruistic, but implicitly embodies the
promise that when today's workers retire they will be supported in
return for having made tax payments while working. But what happens
if tomorrow's workers believe that the burden of social security alone
or in combination with other government programs is insupportable?
Can they reduce it by reducing social security? It is hard to argue that
they have no right to do so—at their own risk, of course. Even if today's
citizens have the moral right to make decisions for future generations
of taxpayers (a highly questionable assumption), they lack the fore-
knowledge of economic and social conditions that is required to judge
what they would do themselves under tomorrow's changed conditions.

In theory, the promise contained in social security is not irrevocable.
Congress explicitly reserves the right to amend or alter any section of
the law. In fact, the obstacles to reduction of benefits are enormous.
Against the inertia of an established public institution and the power of
veto groups (retired persons and organized labor, in this case), attempts
at reduction are all but guaranteed to fail. The fate of the proposal of
Ways and Means Republicans in 1977 to raise the age of eligibility by
steps in the distant future is a good illustration. On the face of it, this
idea deserved serious consideration. It would have reduced the high
projected costs of the future program; it would have imposed no disadvantage on anyone for a long time, and then only with full warning;

and it was consistent with the spreading view that work and productivity in later life are good for the elderly as well as society (hence the recent interest of Congress in bills that would prohibit mandatory retirement from private employment before age seventy). However, it attracted no support outside or inside the Republican party, one of whose senators was quick to brand it "harebrained," and it was strongly opposed by Robert Ball, who argued that private employers must adapt to society's need for more productivity among the aged but was unwilling to grant the need for adaptations of the social security system if they were in any respect deliberalizing.[13] At first glance it might be thought costless for today's politicians to enact reductions in benefits for the distant future, just as it is costless for them to enact distant increases in taxes, but the politics of social security does not work that way, for reasons that are instantly apparent. Distant reductions in benefits fall on current taxpayers, that group whose acquiescence is most needed to sustain the current system. Irrationally, perhaps, but no less surely, they are also opposed by current beneficiaries, who feel threatened by them.

Obstacles to reduction derive also from the doctrines and practices of social security policymaking, which program executives, to the best of their ability, have designed to establish the sanctity of benefit promises, protect social security against competition from other programs, and give it a special, preferred status should competition occur. The doctrine of benefits as a right, earned through work and taxpaying, is one such protection, of course.[14] Others are found in the long-standing financial autonomy of the program, attempted maintenance of organizational autonomy, the recently enacted practice of indexing benefits to price and wage changes, and the orientation of legislative decisions

---

13. The angry Republican senator was Bob Packwood of Oregon. (*Washington Post*, September 11, 1977.) Ball's position is stated in his book on social security, *Social Security: Today and Tomorrow* (Columbia University Press, 1978), p. 472.

14. The practical effects of this doctrine are illustrated by the reaction of a House Appropriations Committee member to the Carter administration's proposal in 1977 to limit the size of benefits for college students under the social security program. Representative William H. Natcher protested that change "seems to run contrary to the whole concept of an earned insurance benefit." He added that private insurance carriers could not do any such thing and demanded to know why the administration thought it "acceptable for Social Security to change the benefits after the wage earner has paid his premium." *Departments of Labor and Health, Education, and Welfare Appropriations for 1978*, Hearings before a Subcommittee of the House Committee on Appropriations, 95 Cong. 1 sess. (GPO, 1977), pt. 6, p. 253.

to a distant future. The future orientation of policymaking has been manifest in long-range actuarial projections, in the rising schedule of tax rates embodied in the law, and in the accompanying claims of long-run actuarial balance. By presuming to foresee the future, policymakers justified their right to prescribe for it. By acting as if to bind future generations, they probably helped to bind them in fact.[15]

If the inertia of established institutions and the power of veto groups did not by themselves make benefit reductions extremely unlikely, I would be reluctant to urge changes in policymaking doctrines and procedures that would make them more likely. But I see little prospect of social harm from treating social security as a government program like other government programs, legitimately subject to competition from them, nor do I see a reason why reduction of social security benefits should not be removed from the realm of the unthinkable and brought within the realm of legitimate political debate, where it would fall into the very large category of things that it is fair to talk about but probably not feasible to do.

Whatever political analysts may prescribe or executive leaders of the program strive for, more conflict over social security is on the way—is, indeed, already here. One reason for this is that the program is changing. It has become much more costly, both in the absolute tax rate and in the ratio of costs to benefits for individual participants. A worker who entered the system in 1937 and paid the maximum tax for the next thirty years would have paid a total of only $2,673.60 if he

15. The future orientation has the appearance of fiscal responsibility. It is normally accounted a sign of prudence to take the long run into account. That the future orientation has actually worked to discipline the growth of the system may be doubted, however. While in principle policymakers operated on a long time horizon, in practice they operated on a very short one. They made frequent ad hoc changes in the system in response to immediate pressures and opportunities, on the basis of calculations of the willingness of current taxpayers to pay for current benefits. That they simultaneously announced higher rates for future taxpayers is at best a qualified form of prudence. Furthermore, the future orientation, seemingly so responsible, sometimes had the perverse effect of making possible immediate benefit increases on the basis of hypothetical future increases in revenues or reductions in cost. This was the case in 1972, when hypothesized future increases in earnings were used to finance a 20 percent increase in benefits with no increase in taxes. In a more complicated and ambiguous way, it was the case in 1977, when a liberalized benefit formula was justified on the ground that by correcting a technical flaw in the existing formula it would substantially reduce hypothesized long-run deficits in the system. There are no cases, however, in which a hypothesized long-run deficit resulted in a current decrease in benefits.

retired at the end of 1967. He would have paid for a very small fraction of his benefits. But the worker who entered in 1968 and pays at the maximum rate will have paid $27,511.24 after only twenty years, assuming that scheduled increases in the tax rate and wage base are not changed. The huge windfalls that went to participants in the early years will come to an end, and some high-income workers may pay for more than the cost of their own benefits. Congress today is committed to paying social security benefits to a very large and rising proportion of the population, in amounts that depend on economic events (the movement of prices and wages) over which it has no direct control. It must raise the taxes to pay for these benefits from a shrinking proportion of the population, with no prospect of windfall gains. Sources of revenue other than tax increases have dried up or been deliberately sacrificed. The payroll tax rate (6.13 percent each on employee and employer as of 1979), has attained a level characteristic of a relatively mature program and is scheduled to go higher (by steps, to 7.65 percent) even if no further benefit increases are enacted.

A second reason for the rising conflict is that the economic and social context of policymaking is changing. Economic growth, with which expansion of government activity could be financed, has slowed, and popular resistance to government expansion appears to be rising. The Carter administration's budget for fiscal 1980, responding to these circumstances and to an unacceptably high rate of inflation, was relatively austere, and included $600 million in cuts in social security. Predictably, the coalition of program proprietors responded that cuts were illegitimate; the Carter administration, Nelson Cruikshank charged, failed to understand "the very nature" of social security.[16] Congressional leaders immediately rejected most of the cuts as unrealistic, except that the Ways and Means Committee proceeded to hold hearings on ways to cut the cost of disability insurance, a portion of the program that appears to be much more vulnerable politically than old age insurance.

In these uncertain circumstances, the institutionalization of the incremental mode through the technique of an automatic benefit formula has particular importance. It will be recalled that fiscal conservatives in public office urged adoption of such a formula in the hope that it would discipline expansion. They assumed that ad hoc congressional action

16. Spencer Rich, "Carter Aide Hits Proposed Slash in Social Security," *Washington Post*, February 8, 1979.

POLICYMAKING FOR SOCIAL SECURITY

based on current calculations of political costs and benefits would continue to fuel the expansionary thrust. It is intellectually interesting, even if idle, to wonder whether this would have been so. It hinges on the highly problematic question of whether there is a level of taxation at which pressures against added taxes would begin to outweigh pressures for added benefits.

Growth of the system through the 1950s and 1960s depended crucially on the politicians' calculations that incremental additions were advantageous, but the context was highly favorable to expansion. If the method of ad hoc adjustments had survived, politicians might have changed behavior in the very different context that has been developing since the mid-1970s.

The pattern of ad hoc incremental expansion may still continue, even with an automatic formula in place and even in the presence of heightened resistance to expansion, but if so it is likely to be attended by much higher levels of conflict than were characteristic of the past and by the introduction of general revenues to obscure the costs, a change that is always possible even if Congress rejected it in 1977. As it is, the use of an automatic, technical device, wage indexing, assures that some degree of expansion (assuming benefit increases in excess of cost of living increases to be "expansive") will occur independently of political calculations.

Partly in response to heightened contention over the program, but also because of changes in organization, leadership, and staffing in Congress and the executive branch, the highly program-oriented mode of policymaking portrayed in part 1 of this book has been modified. A greater variety of participants is involved, long-established doctrines have been challenged and long-standing procedures revised. The policymaking system and the program are both changing and, as always, interacting with each other as well as with the society to determine the nature of social security politics. During much of the history of social security they interacted in a way that dampened contention. In the late 1970s, they are interacting in a way that will admit more of it, and I think that is, on balance, a good thing.

Chronology

Legislation

1935: The Social Security Act (P.L. 271, Seventy-fourth Congress) passed, following the recommendations of the Committee on Economic Security and of President Franklin D. Roosevelt. It established a system of federal old age benefits covering workers in commerce and industry. Benefits were to be based on cumulative wages and to be payable beginning in 1942 to qualified persons aged sixty-five and over. A payroll tax of 1 percent each on employers and employees, payable on a wage base of $3,000, was to be imposed as of January 1, 1937, and was scheduled to rise in steps to 3 percent by 1949. Congress rejected both the Clark amendment, which would have exempted employers with private pension plans, and a provision for sale of voluntary annuities by the government.

1939: The Social Security Act Amendments of 1939 (P.L. 379, Seventy-sixth Congress) passed, following the recommendations of the 1937–39 advisory council and of President Roosevelt. It authorized supplemental benefits for dependents of retired workers and for surviving dependents in case of death. The starting date for monthly benefits was advanced to 1940, and benefits were based on average monthly wages rather than on cumulative wages. A tax rate increase to 1.5 percent, which was scheduled to take place in 1940, was postponed to 1943.

1942: The Revenue Act of 1942 (P.L. 753, Seventy-seventh Congress) deferred the tax rate increase until 1944.

1943: House Joint Resolution 171 (Seventy-eighth Congress) postponed the tax rate increase until March 1, 1944.

1944: The Revenue Act of 1943 (P.L. 235, Seventy-eighth Congress), passed on February 25, 1944, continued the tax rate at 1 percent until 1945 and included the Murray amendment authorizing the use of general revenues to make up any financial deficit in social security.

1945: The Revenue Act of 1945 (P.L. 214, Seventy-ninth Congress) deferred the tax rate increase until 1947.

1946: The Social Security Act Amendments of 1946 (P.L. 719, Seventy-ninth Congress) deferred the tax rate increase until 1948.

1947: The Social Security Amendments of 1947 (P.L. 379, Eightieth Congress) deferred the tax rate increase until 1950.

1948: Congress passed a bill to exclude "certain vendors of newspapers or magazines" from the Social Security Act. President Truman vetoed the bill, and Congress overrode the veto (P.L. 492, Eightieth Congress). Congress also passed a joint resolution to prevent the executive from issuing new regulations defining the terms "employ," "employer," and "employee" under the Social Security Act. President Truman vetoed the resolution, and Congress overrode the veto: "The issue involved in the proposed regulations is whether the scope of social security coverage should be determined by the Congress or by other branches of the Government" (H. Rept. 1319, 80 Cong. 2 sess.).

1950: The Social Security Act Amendments of 1950 (P.L. 734, Eighty-first Congress) passed, following the report of the 1947–48 advisory council, recommendations by President Truman, and prolonged consideration by Congress. Eligibility standards were liberalized. The amendments extended compulsory coverage to the nonfarm self-employed, except for certain professional groups (principally doctors, lawyers, and engineers), and to regularly employed domestic and farm workers. They authorized optional coverage for employees of state and local governments and nonprofit organizations and revised the definitions of "employment" and "employee." Benefits were increased by 77 percent, and the wage base was to be raised to $3,600 in 1951. The tax rate was allowed to rise to 1½ percent in 1950. Authorization to use general revenues was repealed, contrary to the recommendation of both the administration and the advisory council. Director O. C. Pogge of the Bureau of Old Age and Survivors Insurance said of these amendments: "A tremendous advance in the long journey toward a universal, sound, and adequate means of providing security for all Americans through a method consistent with our system of individual incentives and free enterprise" (Director's Bulletin 169 to all bureau employees, July 27, 1950).

1952: The Social Security Act Amendments of 1952 (P.L. 590, Eighty-second Congress) passed. Benefits were increased by 12.5 percent.

1954: The Social Security Amendments of 1954 (P.L. 761, Eighty-third Congress) passed, following the recommendations of President Eisenhower. Compulsory coverage was extended to self-employed farmers, categories of farmworkers not covered by the 1950 amendments, and miscellaneous self-employed professional groups (architects, funeral directors, accountants). Voluntary coverage was extended to ministers and members of religious orders. With these amendments coverage was almost universal except for federal government employees. The wage base was to be raised to $4,200 in 1955, and benefits were increased by 13 percent. Provisions were made for a "disability freeze" to protect workers from loss or impairment of benefit rights during periods of total disability. Congress permitted the tax rate to rise to 2 percent, under a schedule enacted in 1950, and in the 1954 amendments increased tax rates for the distant future (1970s).

1956: The Social Security Amendments of 1956 (P.L. 880, Eighty-fourth Congress) passed. Disability insurance benefits were added, payable at the age of fifty. Women were permitted to retire at the age of sixty-two with actuarially reduced benefits. Coverage was extended to lawyers, dentists, veterinarians, and optometrists. The tax rate was increased by 0.25 percent to finance disability benefits. The wage base remained unchanged.

1958: The Social Security Amendments of 1958 (P.L. 85-840) increased benefits by 7 percent and raised the wage base to $4,800. Benefits were added for dependents of disability insurance beneficiaries, and the eligibility standard for disability insurance was liberalized. The tax rate was increased to 2.5 percent for 1959.

1960: The Social Security Amendments of 1960 (P.L. 86-778) eliminated the age limitation of fifty for monthly disability benefits.

1961: The Social Security Amendments of 1961 (P.L. 87-64) permitted men to retire at the age of sixty-two with reduced benefits and made miscellaneous liberalizations, such as an increase in widows' benefits. The tax rate was increased to 3.125 percent for 1962.

1965: The Social Security Amendments of 1965 (P.L. 89-97) passed. After years of debate health insurance for the aged became law. Benefits were increased by 7 percent. The tax rate was increased to 4.2 percent and the wage base to $6,600 for 1966. Miscellaneous liberalizations were enacted, and coverage was extended to doctors.

1966: The Tax Adjustment Act of 1966 (P.L. 89-368) passed, containing the Prouty amendment that automatically provided a flat monthly benefit at the age of seventy-two.

1968: The Social Security Amendments of 1967 (P.L. 90-248) increased benefits by 13 percent, raised the wage base to $7,800, and made many miscellaneous liberalizations. The tax rate, under the schedule enacted in 1965, was 4.4 percent.

1969: The Social Security Amendments of 1969 (title 10 of P.L. 91-172, the Tax Reform Act of 1969) increased benefits by 15 percent. The tax rate, under a schedule enacted in 1967, was 4.8 percent.

1971: A 10 percent benefit increase was included in an act to increase the public debt limit (P.L. 92-5). The wage base was raised to $9,000. The tax rate, under a schedule enacted in 1969, was 5.2 percent.

1972: A 20 percent benefit increase and the automatic adjustment of benefits and the wage base were included in an act to increase the public debt limit (P.L. 92-336), passed in July. Automatic adjustments were to begin in January 1975. The benefit increase was made possible by a change in the method of making actuarial assumptions. The wage base was raised to $10,800 for 1973. The Social Security Amendments of 1972 (P.L. 92-603), passed in October, contained many liberalizations, such as increased benefits for widows and widowers, an increase in earnings permitted to beneficiaries, and a reduction in the waiting period for disability benefits. The tax rate for 1973 was raised to 5.85 percent.

1973: Public Law 93-66, passed in July, increased benefits by 5.9 percent as of 1974, but this legislation was superseded by Public Law 93-233, passed in December, which provided for a 7 percent benefit increase for March–May 1974 and a 4 percent additional increase for June 1974. Automatic adjustments were rescheduled to begin in June 1975. The wage base for 1974 was raised to $13,200.

1974–78: By automatic adjustment, the wage base was raised to $14,100 in 1975, $15,300 in 1976, $16,500 in 1977, and $17,700 in 1978.

1977: The Social Security Amendments of 1977 (P.L. 95-216) were passed to meet an unexpected deficit. The tax rate increase already scheduled for 1978—to 6.05 percent—was not changed, but an increase to 6.13 percent in 1979 was scheduled, along with higher tax rates for subsequent years. Wage base increases in excess of expected automatic adjustments were scheduled: $22,900 for 1979, $25,900 for 1980, and $29,700 for 1981. The formula for automatic adjustments was revised to control erratic effects of the 1972 formula.

Administration

1935: A three-member Social Security Board was created to perform duties imposed by the Social Security Act and to study and make recommendations as to the "most effective methods of providing economic security through social insurance." The board was responsible for old age insurance, unemployment compensation, and public assistance.

1939: The President's Reorganization Plan No. 1 created the Federal Security Agency and located the Social Security Board within it, along with the Public Health Service, the Office of Education, and other formerly independent agencies.

1946: The President's Reorganization Plan No. 2 abolished the Social Security Board and transferred its functions to the federal security administrator, who was to perform them himself or designate officers to perform them "under his direction and control." The administrator in turn created the Social Security Administration to carry on the functions of the Social Security Board and created a commissioner for social security to head it.

1949: The President's Reorganization Plan No. 2 transferred unemployment compensation from the Federal Security Administration to the Department of Labor.

1953: The President's Reorganization Plan No. 1 abolished the Federal Security Agency and transferred its functions and powers to the Department of Health, Education, and Welfare. The commissioner for social security was replaced by a commissioner of social security, to be appointed by the president with the advice and consent of the Senate and to perform "such functions concerning social security and public welfare as the Secretary may prescribe."

1963: A reorganization order of the secretary of health, education, and welfare removed public assistance functions from the Social Security Administration and placed them in a newly created Welfare Administration.

1974: The Social Security Administration became responsible for administration of the Supplemental Security Income program, created by the Social Security Amendments of 1972, which set federal standards of income support for the needy aged, blind, and disabled.

Principal Executive Officials

Chairman of the Social Security Board

John G. Winant, 1935–37
Arthur J. Altmeyer, 1937–46

Federal Security Agency Administrator

Paul V. McNutt, 1939–45
Watson B. Miller, 1945–47
Oscar R. Ewing, 1947–53
Oveta Culp Hobby, 1953

Secretary of Health, Education, and Welfare

Oveta Culp Hobby, 1953–55
Marion B. Folsom, 1955–58
Arthur S. Flemming, 1958–61
Abraham Ribicoff, 1961–62
Anthony J. Celebrezze, 1962–65
John W. Gardner, 1965–68
Wilbur J. Cohen, 1968–69
Robert H. Finch, 1969–70
Elliot L. Richardson, 1970–73
Caspar W. Weinberger, 1973–75
David Mathews, 1975–77
Joseph A. Califano, Jr., 1977–

Commissioner of Social Security

Arthur J. Altmeyer, 1946–53
John W. Tramburg, 1953–54
Charles I. Schottland, 1954–58
William L. Mitchell, 1959–62
Robert M. Ball, 1962–73
James B. Cardwell, 1973–77
Stanford G. Ross, 1978–

Index

Aaron, Henry J., 164n, 228n, 258, 261, 351
Ackley, Gardner, 343
Actuarial procedures, 55–58, 174; importance in policymaking, 277–78; and indexing, 355. *See also* Dynamic earnings assumption; Level earnings assumption
Actuarial Society of America, 163, 176, 181, 355n
Actuaries, 163, 171; functions, 172–73; within SSA, 173–82. *See also* Myers, Robert J.; Trowbridge, Charles L.; Williamson, W. Rulon
Adams, Carolyn Teich, 10n
Administration of social security program: executives for, 18–20, 25; flexibility in, 21–22; personnel for, 27–30
Administrative budget, 169
Advisory councils, 78; accomplishments, 94–95; action on disability insurance, 105, 107, 140, 297, 298; appointment, 91–95; benefit study, 99; composition, 95–96, 102; and dynamic assumptions, 350, 352–57; functions, 100–01, 396; and health insurance, 103–04; indoctrination of outsiders, 105–06; on medicare, 140; payroll tax recommendations, 239–40; policy-making, 89–90, 109; relations with SSA, 96, 99–100, 105; staff, 96–97; and trust fund, 91, 234–36, 386
AFL. *See* American Federation of Labor
AFL-CIO. *See* American Federation of Labor–Congress of Industrial Organizations
Aged: bases for organization among, 269–70; and neutral decoupling,

397; pressure for social security expansion from, 197–98, 343; social security bias toward, 258–59. *See also* Townsend plan
Agricultural workers, social security coverage, 49, 263, 264, 267
ALC. *See* American Life Convention
Alger, Bruce, 45
Allen, Jodie, 166
Altmeyer, Arthur J., 11n, 17, 18, 55, 64n, 88n, 98n, 103, 104, 111n, 122, 123, 125n, 144, 155, 159n, 167n, 218n; on actuarial effectiveness, 174; and advisory council, 90, 101, 106–07; and AFL, 114, 197; on benefits, 22–23; on congressional reactions to flat pensions, 221; on congressional tax levying, 215–16; on coverage, 264; and disability insurance, 296; on earnings test, 226; on financing, 249–50; and health insurance, 317–18; on pay-roll tax rate, 237–38, 240; personnel policy, 28, 29n; on popularity of social security program, 198; on President Roosevelt's proposals, 229–30; response to social security critics, 168; on SSA administrators, 19–20; on Wagner-Murray-Dingell bill, 84; on Wilbur Cohen, 53
AME. *See* Average monthly earnings
American Association of Retired Persons, 270
American Economic Association, 163
American Enterprise Institute for Public Policy Research, 387
American Federation of Labor (AFL): and blanketing in proposal, 153, 155; and general revenue financing, 243; and payroll tax, 230–31; and social

435

436

INDEX

insurance, 111–12, 196, 197; social security department, 115; and social security legislation, 119; sponsorship of Eliot bill, 112; and unemployment insurance, 259; on union-negotiated pension plans, 120–21; and Wagner-Murray-Dingell bill, 243. *See also* American Federation of Labor–Congress of Industrial Organizations

American Federation of Labor–Congress of Industrial Organizations (AFL-CIO), 65; advancement of social insurance, 116; and advisory councils, 93–94, 106n, 110; collaboration with SSA, 74–75, 76–77, 117, 125–28, 130–31; federation, 121, 125; and health insurance, 73, 75, 197; and neutral decoupling, 397, 407; and President Johnson's proposals, 130; and social security cost estimates, 58. *See also* Organized labor

American Hospital Association, 324

American Life Convention (ALC), 138, 139, 143

American Life Insurance Association, 138, 181

American Medical Association, 118, 132; and disability insurance, 296–97, 300–01, 302, 303, 307, 312; and government reinsurance, 135; opposition to health insurance, 96, 133n, 141, 157n, 316, 318, 325, 329, 331, 337

American Public Welfare Association (APWA), 124, 125, 274

Armstrong, Barbara N., 103

Association of Life Insurance Presidents, 136

Average monthly earnings (AME), 256n

Baker, Howard, Sr., 154

Ball, Robert M., 5, 6, 11, 18, 19, 64n, 65, 67–68, 76, 77, 123, 125n, 138n, 150, 170n, 201n, 306, 349, 350n, 352, 361; on actuarial procedures, 267, 277–78; and advisory councils, 97, 98, 100, 101, 104n, 106, 107; on benefit increases, 277, 344; criticism of Hsiao plan, 390; and deficit, 383, 391; and Eisenhower administration, 78–79; expertise, 33; and health insurance, 319, 320, 325n; on HEW secretaries, 72; on inequities in benefits, 261,

262; and Nixon administration, 62, 179–81; opposition to raising eligibility age, 425; on pay-as-you-go system, 240; on relations of political and social security systems, 23, 253, 416; on social security priorities, 339–40, 341–42; on SSA administrators, 20; on soundness of social security system, 382; on wage base, 284, 340; wage-indexed formula, 402–03

Baroody, William J., 153n

Benefit-cost ratio, social security, 266–70, 426–27. *See also* Distributive bias

Benefits, social security, 3, 6; adequacy versus equity in, 213–16; advisory council study of, 99; blanketing in, 150–53, 216, 274; coupled formula for, 393; decoupling of, 395–99; expediting payment of, 272–73; expenditures for, 274; by flat payments, 218, 221–22, 256, 289; formula changes, 1950–65, 275; increases in, 46, 47, 50, 63, 274–80, 342–43, 346, 358–59, 362–64; level wage assumption for, 349, 350–51, 353, 385, 386; politics and, 346, 373–75, 425–26; progressivity, 255, 256, 263, 291; student, 169n; wage-based, 256–57, 271, 278–87, 290, 340, 362–63; women's, 260–62. *See also* Distributive bias; Indexing; Replacement rates

Bernstein, Merton C., 342n

Bixby, Lenore E., 262n

Blanketing in proposal, 150–53, 216. *See also* Coverage

BOASI. *See* Bureau of Old Age and Survivors Insurance

Boskin, Michael J., 4n, 6n, 164n, 387n

Bowen, William G., 4n

Bradley, John P., 186n

Brewster, Agnes W., 334n

Brittain, John A., 228n, 269n

Bronson, Dorrance C., 173, 256

Brookings Institution, 162, 351, 367, 387

Brown, J. Douglas, 55, 170, 258, 259n; and advisory councils, 100–01, 102–03, 108, 234; on congressional tax avoidance, 49; on expediting benefit payments, 272–73; on wage base, 283, 285

Brown, Lawrence D., 337n

Budget, 169. *See also* Bureau of the Budget

Buley, R. Carlyle, 137n